Reminiscences of My Life

Emmanuel Abraham, Addis Ababa, March 2009

Emmanuel Abraham is one of the leading Ethiopian personalities of the twentieth century. Born in 1913 in Boji, western Ethiopia, he attended school in his birthplace and in Addis Ababa. He began his career as a teacher and headmaster in eastern Ethiopia and entered public service in February 1939 at the Ethiopian Legation in London. Emperor Haile Sellassie I later appointed him to various diplomatic posts in London, New Delhi, Rome, and high level government positions in Addis Ababa, including among others Chief of Political Affairs in H.I.M.'s Private Cabinet; Minister of Posts, Telegraphs and Telephones; Minister of Communications; and finally, Minister of Mines. In 1974, the military junta which overthrew the imperial government detained him along with other former officials but he was freed after nine months.

In 1963, Emmanuel Abraham was elected President of the Ethiopian Evangelical Church Mekane Yesus and led the church for the next 22 years. Emmanuel Abraham, 97, survives his wife, Elleni Alemayehu, who passed away in 2002. They have four children and three grandchildren. He lives in Addis Ababa.

Reminiscences of My Life

Emmanuel Abraham

The Red Sea Press, Inc.
Publishers & Distributors of Third World Books

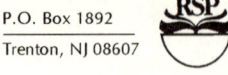

P.O. Box 1892   P.O. Box 48
Trenton, NJ 08607   Asmara, ERITREA

Copyright © 2011 by Emmanuel Abraham
First Printing 2011

All rights reserved. No part of this publication may be reproduced, stored in a retrieval system or transmitted in any form or by any means electronic, mechanical, photocopying, recording or otherwise without the prior written permission of the publisher.

Cover photo: The author at age 23 in London, 1936
Book design: Guenet Abraham

Library of Congress Cataloging-in-Publication Data

Emmanuel Abraham, 1913-
  Reminiscences of my life / Emmanuel Abraham. -- [Rev. and updated, 1st American ed.]
      p. cm.
  Includes bibliographical references and index.
  ISBN 1-56902-325-5 (hardcover) -- ISBN 1-56902-326-3 (pbk.)
  1. Emmanuel Abraham, 1913- 2. Ethiopia--Officials and employees--Biography. 3. Evangelical Church Mekane Yesus--History. 4. Haile Selassie I, Emperor of Ethiopia, 1892-1975. 5. Ethiopia--Politics and government--1889-1974. I. Title.
DT387.92.E46A3 2010
284.1092--dc22
[B]
                      2009048092

**In Loving Memory of
My Life Companion, Elleni Alemayehu,
and My Parents**

Contents

Note on Ethiopian Names *xii*
Abbreviations *xii*
Glossary *xiii*
Foreword *xv*
Introduction *xvii*

Section One: In Government Service
1. Boji: At Home with My Parents, 1913-1925   *3*
2. At School in Addis Ababa, 1925-1931   *8*
3. Asbe Tafari: Headmaster of School, 1931-1935   *17*
4. London: Secretary of Legation, 1935-1939   *21*
5. London: 'Secretary for Government Affairs,' 1939-1943   *34*
6. Addis Ababa: Director General, 1943-1947   *51*
7. New Delhi: Minister Plenipotentiary, 1949-1952   *60*
8. Rome: Ambassador Plenipotentiary, 1952-1955   *82*
9. London: Ambassador Plenipotentiary, 1955-1959   *119*
10. Addis Ababa: Chief of Political Affairs in His Majesty's Private Cabinet, 1959-1961   *167*
11. Addis Ababa: Minister of Posts, Telegraphs and Telephones, 1961-1966   *187*

VIII *Reminiscences of My Life*

12. Addis Ababa: Minister of Communications, 1966-1969 *197*
13. Addis Ababa: Minister of Mines, 1969-1974 *210*
14. Addis Ababa: In Detention, 1974-1975 *227*

15. **Section Two: In the Service of the Church**
    1 Introduction *259*
    2 Membership of the Mekane Yesus Church and my Service in the Lutheran World Federation *260*
    3 Establishment of the Mekane Yesus Church *262*
    4 Achievements in the First Four Years *262*
    5 Establishment of Radio Voice of the Gospel *264*
    6 My Election to be President of the Church *266*
    7 Why are non-clerical Persons elected to be Leaders of the Church? *266*
    8 Why was it necessary to establish another Church besides the Orthodox Church? *268*
    9 The Functions of the President and the Duties of the General Secretary *269*
    10 The Construction of the Central Office and Youth Hostel *270*
    11 Frequency of the Executive Committee Meetings *273*
    12 The Establishment of a Pension Fund *273*
    13 Second Registration of the Church *273*
    14 Signing of the Agreement on Integration Policy *276*
    15 The Call of the Norwegian Missionary Society *285*
    16 The Merger of the Kambata Church *288*
    17 Proclamation of the Gospel and Human Development *290*
    18 A Book on the Origins of the Mekane Yesus Church *295*
    19 Membership in the International Christian Organizations *296*
    20 Bethel Church Integrated into Mekane Yesus Church *296*
    21 The State of the Synods *301*
        1. The Western Wollega Synod (The Western Synod) *301*
        2. Sidamo and Gamo-Gofa Synod (South Ethiopia Synod) *304*
        3. The Dissolution of the North Ethiopia Synod *307*
        4. The Establishment of the Addis Ababa Synod *310*
        5. The Strengthening of the Central Synod *312*

22 **Development Work of the Mekane Yesus Church** *319*
   1. The Bako Project *319*
   2. Wondo Gennet Agricultural and Trade School *323*
   3. Wuchale and Selekleka Agricultural Schools *323*
   4. Dabena Trade School *324*
   5. Nejo and Chalia Trade Schools *324*
   6. Arba Minch Hostel and Vocational School *324*
   7. Henna Rural Development Pilot Project *327*
   8. Didessa Dimtu and Dilla Settlement Programmes *329*
23 **Confiscation of the Church's Central Office Building** *330*
24 **Appendices** *332*
   1. The First All-Africa Lutheran Conference *332*
   2. The Second All-Africa Lutheran Conference *338*
   3. The Third All-Africa Lutheran Conference *346*
   4. On Caring for Creation *356*

"The author would like to express deep gratitude to the Swedish Evangelical Mission (SEM), Uppsala and Ruth E. Abraham (Addis Ababa) for sponsoring the publication of this second edition (and first paperback edition) of *Reminiscences of My Life*; and to Rev. Dr. Ezra Gebremedhin and Gennet Awalom for their efforts in securing the generous financial support provided by the SEM. The author also thanks Kassahun Checole of the Red Sea Press (RSP) for readily undertaking publication of this new edition, Naomi Desta, Ezekiel Gebissa, and Damola Ifaturoti (RSP) for their substantive contributions to the production of this book, and also Guenet Abraham for the book design and typography."

Note on Ethiopian Names

Ethiopians, whether Christian or Muslim, do not have family surnames. As a result, the common practice, which is followed here is to either write their names in full (i.e. the individual's name followed by his/her father's first name) or to use only the first names. This is also how Ethiopian names appear in the index; by their first names, followed by his/her father's first name.

Abbreviations

ADC	Aide-de-camp
ALM	American Lutheran Mission
CMCR	Committee of Mutual Christian Responsibility
EECMY	Ethiopian Evangelical Church Mekane Yesus
ETBURC	Ethiopian Building and Road Construction Company
GHM	German Hermannsburg Mission
H.I.M.	His Imperial Majesty
IBTE	Imperial Board of Telecommunications of Ethiopia
LWF	Lutheran World Federation
NATO	North Atlantic Treaty Organization
NLM	Norwegian Lutheran Mission
NMS	Norwegian Missionary Society
PAC	Provisional Administrative Committee
RVOG	Radio Voice of the Gospel
SEM	Swedish Evangelical Mission
UN	United Nations
UNDP	United Nations Development Programme
US	United States
USA	United States of America
USSR	Union of Soviet Socialist Republics

Glossary*

abba - "father;" a title of a church official.
abiot - "protest," revolution.
addé - "mother," corrupt form of adday in Tigrinya.
aleqa - "chief;" a title bestowed on church literati.
amba - "flat topped hill;" a fortification.
ato - "sir," now used as the Amharic equivalent of 'Mr.'
azazh - "commander," an honorific title during the imperial period.
balambaras - "commander of a fortification," military title equivalent to lieutenant.
bejrond - treasurer, formerly Minister of Finance and Customs.
besa - derived from peso, a coin now out of use.
birr - "silver," Ethiopian currency.
bitwoded - "beloved;" a title of nobility.
blatta - "youth;" an intellectual of legal and religious traditions; later, a court official in charge of maintaining palace protocol.
blattengeta - "lord of the youth," master of wisdom or intellectual who is supposed to teach the young princes; later, title bestowed on learned men appointed as court officials serving as administrator of the palaces.
cahen - "priest," minister.
dejazmach (dejach, abbreviated form) - "commander of the gate;" a military title equivalent to general.
derg - "committee," name of the regime that ruled Ethiopia from 1974-91.
dulet - a special Ethiopian dish of tripe, tenderloin and liver of lamb.
falashas - name of Ethiopian Jews, also known as Beta Israel.
fitaurari (fit., abbreviated form) - "leader of the vanguard;" a military title equivalent to colonel.
gabbar - "serf," landless farmers in southern Ethiopia.
gasha - land measurement unit equal to about 40 hectares.
ge'ez (Ethiopic) - language, now used in church liturgy.

injera - fermented flat bread made from "teff;" a staple of Ethiopian food, injera is eaten with 'wott.'
kegnazmach - "commander of the right;" a military title equivalent to major.
kentiba - mayor.
kik wott - split yellow peas or other beans cooked in a red pepper or turmeric sauce.
lij - "child, son;" a title of the sons of the nobility.
mesqel - "cross;" a festival commemorating the finding of the true cross.
nebure-id - "the laying-on of hands," indicating the holder's role in ordaining and anointing others; title of the spiritual and temporal ruler of Axum, considered equivalent to Ras.
neftegnoch - "gun bearer;" northern soldiers settled in southern Ethiopia with rights over and labor of the locals.
qalicha - derived from the Oromo qalu, ritual leader of their traditional religion.
qebele - city precinct.
qes - a priestly title.
ras - "head;" a high military title, equivalent to field marshal.
ras bitwoded - "beloved-head;" a title bestowed on high nobility.
teff - a domestic cereal and staple crop used in making "injera."
tej - mead, local fermented wine made with honey.
timqet - the festival of Epiphany.
tsehafé-tizaz - "scribe of orders;" a title conferred on a royal private secretary.
weizazir - princes and princesses (during Gonder era).
woizero - "lady," now used as the Amharic equivalent of 'Mrs.'
wott - a traditional meat-based or vegetarian stew cooked with red pepper and/or other spices.
zéma - "melody," musical sound or arrangement.

* Word in quotation marks denotes literal meaning of the Amharic word.

Foreword

Fourteen years have elapsed since this volume of my reminiscences was published (1995). I have just completed 96 years of life on earth. The Lord God has been gracious to me in spite of the fact that I have saved very little for old age; and that little was lost during the revolution that overwhelmed the land with nationalization.

I lost my very dear life companion, Elleni Alemayehu in 2002 after more than half a century of married life. I am deeply thankful that she gave me four children. We had placed great emphasis on education for them and they were very successful in that field. All of them completed the university courses of their choice and delighted our hearts. They are now my great assets. Their filial love and generosity have been a source of joy.

My grandchildren, Naomi, Thomas and Daniel have also graduated from universities in the United States. Thomas has since married.

The Church I had served for many years, the Ethiopian Evangelical Church Mekane Yesus is flourishing. The membership has shown tremendous growth, five million believers this year. It was just under one million when I retired in 1985. It is the Lord's doing; blessed be His most Holy Name.

Emmanuel Abraham
Addis Ababa, March 2009

Introduction

I have tried to record in the following pages what I consider to be the main reminiscences of my life. It is now more than 80 years since I started this earthly pilgrimage. Ever since I left my parents' home at the age of 12, many have been the persons who gave me a helping hand in my journey through life, going up and down hills and crossing plains; and the individuals who tried to hinder my progress and cause me harm were not a few.

But as the Apostle Paul wrote, "We know that all things work together for good to those who love God, who are called according to His purpose." As I love God and believe that I am called according to His purpose, I have proved the truth of the Apostle's words through all I have experienced in the course of my life. I trust this will be clear to the readers of these pages.

I began to write these reminiscences in April 1985 on completion of my service in the Mekane Yesus Church. I was impelled to undertake the task due to the strong desire I had had to testify that my faith in Christ all through my life, the abundant blessings I had received and the deliverances from many trials and predicaments that attended me, were solely due to the grace of my Creator and Saviour and the guidance of His Holy Spirit.

On completion of the Amharic draft, my daughters and some friends urged me to render it into English. Even though I had misgivings that I might not have the ability and the strength to complete the task owing to advanced age, I started writing in September 1990 and was able to complete it in March 1993, just before my 80th birthday.

"Who is like the Lord our God, the One who sits enthroned on high, who stoops down to look on the heavens and the earth? He raises the poor from the dust, and lifts the needy from the ash heap; He seats them with princes, with the princes of their people" (Psalm 113:5-8).

Emmanuel Abraham
Addis Ababa, March 1993

In Government Service

The author leaving Quirinal Palace after presenting Credentials to the President of Italy, Rome, June 1952.

ONE

Boji:
At Home With My Parents
1913 - 1925

I was born on March 17, 1913, in Wollega Province, Ghimbi district, Boji sub-district, Babbo area, in a place called Benti Adere (Adere Crest), to my father Abraham Tato and my mother Qanatu Malimo, in the home of my grandfather, Malimo Gama. Just before my birth, my parents had left the Allé Ambalto area, near Ghimbi, where they had been living, and moved to Boji Karkaro where the governor of Boji, Fitaurari Dibaba Bakare was in residence. They had to leave Allé Ambalto because the official of the area tried to impose a levy on my father. It was said that the population had to pay the levy to defray the expenses incurred for the reception accorded to Lij Iyasu, the Heir to the Throne, who had passed through Ghimbi district in November 1912 in the course of his visit to South Western Ethiopia. My father was unwilling to pay the levy because he had been directly employed by Fit. Dibaba and so considered it improper for the local official to impose it on him. He therefore went to present the matter to the Governor at Boji Karkaro who remitted the levy and gave him a house and an allowance so that he could be near him. In the meantime, my mother who was expecting a child went to Babbo to stay with her parents, and I was born in the home of my grandparents on Adere Crest.

I was not my parents' first child. Two girls and a boy had been born to them, but had died in infancy. When I was born they were very apprehensive that I might pass away in the same manner and were deeply engaged in prayer to the Creator. I learned from my father that after I was born he heard a voice in a dream that said he should call me Emmanuel (God is with us) and that Borou Siba should be my godfather. Just before my christening, he visited Ato Borou at Siban, ten hours' walk from Boji, and requested him to be my sponsor. Ato Borou readily agreed and came to Boji when I was baptized at Boji Mariam Church. At the christening the priest asked my father what my name should be, and demurred when he was told that my name was to be Emmanuel, and said it was not a usual name, I should be called Wolde Emmanuel. My father rejoined that the priest could name me as he wished but that for him my name was Emmanuel.

In addition to the voice he had heard in a dream, my father had determined that I should be called Emmanuel, because he and my mother had earnestly hoped that the Lord would hear their prayers and spare me from being lost as soon as I was born like their previous children. (My maternal grandmother, Safi Hirpa, called me Abdisa which means 'His Promise').

The gracious Lord heard their prayers and I was not only spared from the hazards and ailments of infancy, but grew up to live here on earth for 80 years (in 1993). Glory and praise be to His omnipotent Name!

The story as to how my father heard the Gospel and believed in Christ is as follows. In 1898, when he was about 14 years old, a native of Hamasen (Eritrea) called Pastor Gebre Statios Zemikael and his wife, Woizero Gumesh Wolde Mikael, accompanied by a native of Gudru (Wollega), called Ato Daniel Lulu and his Eritrean wife, Woizero Tiru Gebre, were sent to Wollega by the leaders of the Swedish Evangelical Mission (SEM). The Mission was established in Eritrea, to carry the Gospel to and teach the Oromo people who had not heard the Gospel up to that time. They met Fit. Dibaba, Governor of Boji and explained their mission to him. Dibaba took the matter to Dejazmach Kumsa Moroda (also called Gebre Egziabher), Governor of Naqamté, Wollega, and obtained his consent to employ Gebre Statios as a secretary and to allow him and his companions to preach the Gospel and open a school.

Although my father had been orphaned at an early age, he had the good fortune of being taken to Gebre Statios by Danki Tufa, Justice for Dibaba at Boji, together with his sons and relatives. The boys heard the Gospel and learned to read and write in the Oromo language. My father believed in Christ and was baptized; his Christian name was Abraham. (His original name was Soresso which means 'wealthy').

In April 1905, Gebre Statios died suddenly in a conflagration. As Ato Daniel had also died of illness earlier, the leaders of the SEM in Asmara sent an Evangelist, Ato Gebre Yesus Tesfai, to replace the deceased and carry on the preaching of the Gospel and the educational work initiated by them.

Ato Gebre Yesus Tesfai had to go back to Eritrea in 1911, and my father and six other young men determined to accompany him to see the place from where the Gospel had come and to meet the people who sent the Evangelists. They travelled to Asmara on foot for about four months and met the Swedish missionaries as well as the Ethiopian Evangelical Christians. They stayed with them for almost one year and returned to Wollega in 1912, just before the rainy season. Almost a year after my father returned from Eritrea, my parents left Ambalto and moved to Boji Karkaro just before my birth. As Ato Gebre Yesus Tesfai had continued to teach at Boji, he admitted me to his school when I was about five and taught me to read and write. The main reader at the school in those days was a Bible story book consisting of 52 stories each from the Old Testament and 52 from the New Testament with numerous illustrations. The book was available in both Oromo and Amharic and it was thus possible for me to read the stories in both languages. I had to read the stories every day under my father's strict supervision until I was eight years old. And, although I could not understand their deep significance at that time, the stories were imprinted on my mind. As I grew in stature and understanding, the meaning was gradually made clear to my mind, until by God's grace, I was enabled to come to the knowledge and faith of my Lord Jesus Christ. I must say though that in those days I strongly resented the compulsion imposed on me by my father and hated reading my story books. As I was fond of playing beyond measure, I used to be attracted to the boys who were playing near our house. So much so that, to make sure I was reading, my father had to compel me daily to read aloud under the eaves of our house while he worked inside.

This had an unexpected effect. Although I could not speak Amharic, I was able to read it as easily as I could read Oromo. And when I came to school in Addis Ababa at 12, I could follow the lessons that were given and within one year, speak and write Amharic on the same footing as Amharic-speaking children. As my tongue and mouth were practised in pronouncing Amharic words, my Amharic teacher used to wonder and tell me that I must be an Amhara. But I used to assure him that I was one hundred percent Oromo. (In later years, some persons argued and wagered on several occasions on this point and came to me to help them decide the matter)!

After 1918, Fit. Dibaba was so old that he had to leave Boji Karkaro and return to Naqamté and, as many people who lived at Boji because of him also departed, the village looked deserted. The widow of Pastor Gebre Statios, Woizero Gumesh, and her children left for Addis Ababa soon after. Seeing that the number of his friends had dwindled, my father moved in 1922 to Boji Choqorsa, an hour's walk away, to live with his boyhood companion, Ato Samuel Danki. I lived there until 1925 when I went to school in Naqamté.

In those days, Boji Choqorsa was administered by two nephews of Dejazmach Gebre Egziabher, Fit. Benti Mosisa and Kegnazmach (later Fitaurari) Galata Gobana. My uncle, Sima Tato, had earlier gone from Boji to Naqamté and was in the employ of Fit. Benti and Fit. Makonnen Gebre Egziabher. Fit. Benti favoured my uncle so much that he made him his best man when he married his second wife. As a consequence, he got to know my father and, when he went to Boji Choqorsa as governor, heard of my schooling and that I was a boy of ten. He asked my father to allow me to stay in his household and teach his wives to read. My father acceded to the request and I went to live with the Governor's family for about a year (in 1923), teaching his two wives as well as Galata's wife to read Amharic. Being eager to learn, they were able to read in a short time, and they were fond of me. I even used to enter their bed chambers and run errands for them. Since adults were not allowed to enter the inner enclosure of the residence, I had to pour 'holy water' on the heads of the ladies at the time of 'Timqet.'

My father always regretted that he could not continue his education as he was married and had to work hard to maintain the family. He therefore determined from the time of my birth that I should not miss the opportunity to be educated. For this reason, he caused me to start learning when I was hardly five years old and compelled me to appreciate the value of education through his daily supervision. I liked to go to my grandparents' home at Babbo and my mother used to take me there periodically. After I had been there for a week or ten days, however, my father would go and bring me home. My grandmother Safi loved me dearly and I was exceedingly fond of her. So I used to cling to her and cry so as not to return home. But my father would be unmoved with his vision in view and I had to go back. Although he consented that I should stay at Fit. Benti's for a short time to teach his wives, his set aim that I should be sent to Addis Ababa to study at the school of the SEM was ever before him. He explained this to Fit. Benti and took me back home in 1924.

My father's firm decision was confirmed by an incident. Two years earlier, in 1922, he and his boyhood companions whom he called his friends, Ato Samuel Danki and Ato Borou Siba had decided to take their sons to Addis Ababa and put them in the newly opened Swedish Mission School. At the time of departure, Ato Samuel, taking advantage of my father's absence from home, left me behind and set off with his own son and a relative's son to meet Ato Borou in Siban from where they travelled to Addis Ababa with their youngsters. My father was deeply chagrined and became more determined than ever to send me to school in Addis Ababa. So, in the early months of 1924, he asked my cousin, Ayana Desso, who was going to the Capital as a trader, to take me along with him. We proceeded to Naqamté and I stopped at the home of my uncle, Sima Tato.

Dejazmach Gebre Egziahbher had died in 1923, and the Ethiopian government had decided to replace him by his son Lij Habte Mariam. As the Heir to the Throne, H.H. Ras Tafari was due to travel on his first visit to Europe in April 1924, Habte Mariam received an urgent summons to go to Addis Ababa to be appointed governor. Ayana who was anxious to escape bandits wanted to join the retinue of Lij Habte Mariam which had to travel with all speed, and judging that I could not keep pace, left me at my uncle's house. I lived in Naqamté for about six months. As Ato Samuel happened to be returning to Boji, he was asked to take me along with him. The month was September (1924). The mud in the Didessa valley, over which the feet of so many animals had passed, was drying and had many protruding points which hurt my bare feet as I tried to walk over them and made me cry. Ato Samuel who was on muleback was irate and made a remark to me as bitter as aloes: "You big head! Did you set out to be equal with the likes of Oljirra? Go and earn your living as a deacon!" Oljirra was the son whom he took to Addis Ababa in 1922 when he left me behind.

We spent the night near the Didessa river and the next day I somehow crossed the hot valley and arrived at Worra Gada Dissi, near Ghimbi. Ato Samuel left me there at the home of my uncle's in-laws and my father came and took me home. I had a mosquito bite the night I slept by the Didessa river and within a short time of my arriving home I developed a severe bout of malarial fever. My temperature was so high that I was unconscious for three weeks. My parents were deeply grieved because they thought I was going to die. I became conscious again however and was on the way to recovery when a boil developed in my left armpit. I suffered greatly from this. When the boil matured, my father who was expert at such things opened it and I was quite well again in a few weeks. The effort made for me in 1924 to go to school in Addis Ababa was thus thwarted. But my father who never said die kept pondering how he could get me to school.

TWO

At School in Addis Ababa
1925 - 1931

In the Autumn of 1924, a friend of my father's and Ato Samuel's brother, Ato Terfa Danki went from Boji Choqorsa to Naqamté to marry Fit. Qena'a Borcha's daughter, Woizero Likyellesh. He asked my father to accompany him and they went and brought the bride home. Another friend of Ato Terfa's had been asked to be his best man, but could not get to the wedding in time. So my father replaced him and gave the bride every help possible on the way home in the tradition of best men. From that time on Woziero Likyellesh and my father became close friends.

Before his death in August 1923, Dejach Gebre Egziabher had opened a school in Naqamté near his residence where instruction was given in Amharic and French. Dejach Habte Mariam and his deputy, Fit. Qena'a, had decided that instruction should also be given in English and Ato Terfa, who was a student of the Swedish Missionary, Dr. Karl Cederquist, was appointed to be the teacher. So, at the end of his honeymoon, Ato Terfa prepared to move to Naqamté. My father thought this was a good chance and told me to request Ato Terfa to take me to school with him. I applied to him in my then indifferent Amharic and he consented to take me along. I followed him to Naqamté, stayed in his house and began to attend the Governor's school. I began to learn some English and had been at the school for six months when suddenly I met with a stroke of good fortune no one had foreseen.

His Highness Ras Tafari Makonnen had opened on April 25, 1925, a modern school, named 'Tafari Makonnen School.' His aim was that, besides the boys who lived in Addis Ababa, young people from all parts of Ethiopia should come and be given the benefit of modern education together. He therefore ordered a number of provincial governors to select and send school age youngsters to Addis Ababa. Dejach Habte Mariam was also instructed to send boys from Wollega and 23 boys were chosen from among those studying Amharic, French and English. His notables also presented their sons and the sons of their relatives and dependents. Preparations were made for them to depart for Addis Ababa in September 1925, after 'Mesqel.'

A few days before their departure, a woman whose son had been selected to go to Addis Ababa went to the governor's residence early one morning and shouted an appeal. The governor called her to his presence and asked her the reason. She replied that she had heard that he was sending her son to a foreign country and, since he was her only son, she was apprehensive he would die there. (In those days people in Wollega considered Shoa a foreign country). Although her husband had died, the governor knew why the boy had been chosen to go to school, and he tried to convince her it would be better if he were to go. She insisted however that he should not go lest he would die there. He was disappointed but accepted her request. He was ill at ease because he had informed the Heir to the Throne that he would send 23 boys and they were on the point of departure.

Ato Terfa, who had gone to the governor's residence that morning, heard the story and went to the governor's Chief Secretary to tell him that I was learning with the boys who had been selected and that my name should therefore replace that of the boy who was left behind. Not knowing me and perhaps having some other boy in mind, the Chief Secretary would not accept Ato Terfa's suggestion. Ato Terfa then approached Fit. Qena'a and explained the matter to him. Fit. Qena'a then and there called the Chief Secretary and peremptorily ordered him to include my name in the list. My name was then included and I thus obtained an unexpected chance of going to school in Addis Ababa. True, it was unexpected by me and by my teacher but, as I look back on all that has happened in the course of my life, I believe it was the set purpose of my God and I praise Him with all my heart.

When Ato Terfa returned home for lunch that day, I was offering him water to wash his hands when he said in Oromo, "You are going to Shoa." Woizero Likyellesh asked him what that meant and he told her the above-mentioned story. When the day arrived for the boys to proceed to Shoa, they set out under the care of Fit. Kidane Mariam (Abba Gurmu), Fit. Qena'a's brother. Mules were provided to one or two boys each by those parents who could afford to do so. But several boys, including myself, had to walk. Ato Terfa gave me a Birr's (thaler's) worth of piastres for the journey. We were travelling at a slow pace and as my companions allowed me to ride their mules occasionally, I arrived in Addis Ababa without much fatigue about the middle of October, and we camped in Dejach Gebre Egziabher's compound in Gulele.

Fit. Kidane Mariam was Dejach Habte Mariam's agent in Addis Ababa in those days. So he went to the Heir Apparent's palace and announced the arrival of the 'Wollega boys.' The date was set for our appearance before His Highness and the Fitaurari had new clothes made for all of us. We were taken to the Palace in the afternoon of October 19. We were lined up in three groups according to the language we had begun to learn. We were identified with ribbons, green for French, yellow for English, and red for Amharic. The Prince then arrived surrounded by a crowd of retainers and we did obeisance. Fit. Kidane Mariam read an address after which His Highness made the following remarks: "Do not be concerned because you have left your home district or because you are separated from your relatives; We shall make every effort to look after you as mother and father." Although for many of us the knowledge of Amharic was rather limited at that time, there were several among us who knew the language well and the remarks were properly explained to us. We returned to our camp happy. We went to Tafari Makonnen School the following day and were received as boarders by Dr. Worqneh C. Martin, the Administrator.

The school was started in April 1925, but boarders had not yet been admitted. The boys from Wollega had thus the privilege of being the first boarders. Boys from Addis Ababa and the provinces were shortly afterwards received as boarders. At first all the meals were prepared and sent to us from the Heir Apparent's palace. Sweets which we called 'sugar' and cakes used to be sent regularly to the 'Wollega boys' by order of His Highness. As the number of the boarders grew, buildings were put up and workers employed for the preparation of food, and our meals were cooked in the school compound. Even then, on Thursday of every week 'Our Lady Woizero Menen' (later Her Majesty the Empress) used to bring us specially cooked food and honey water. She would sit at the head of one of the tables and watch while we ate. The Prince would drop in and move from table to table talking to some of the boys and encouraging us. In this way, both the Prince and the Princess took care of us like father and mother, and we pursued our studies in comfort with a sense of well-being.

Educationally, the Tafari Makonnen School was divided into two sections, French and English. Amharic tuition was given in both sections. On the grounds that it was the language studied by the Heir Apparent, two-thirds of the student body chose to learn French. Quite a number of the boys who came from Wollega however took up English. Those studying French used to wonder why and asked us what use it would be to us. When after the Second World War, English became more predominant than French around the world as in Ethiopia, my old school mates expressed regret that they did not study English. The main reason why we from Wollega were inclined to learn English was not only because our parents and the people of Wollega in general knew nothing about France and its language, but also because our neighbour the Sudan, which was under British administration, was called 'the land of the English' and many people used to visit the border to trade. English was therefore known to the people of Wollega.

Since we were strangers to Addis Ababa as well as to the Amharic language, our first school year (1925-26) was rather difficult for many of us. I remember I was sixteenth in the first form that year out of a class of about thirty. But as I became familiar with everything in the succeeding years, I became top in my class in the last three years and was awarded many prize books. I was given a thaler-sized medallion by the Empress Zauditu in 1929, and another by the Emperor Haile Sellassie in 1930 cast in their images as special prizes. 1930 was the year of His Imperial Majesty's Coronation and I was awarded, as a special prize at the end of the 1930-31 school year, a pocket watch on which the Emperor's monogram (HSI) was inscribed in Amharic letters. Moreover, I grew both physically and intellectually.

I was pursuing my studies with diligence and contentment in these circumstances when some of my companions from Wollega and myself came to face an unexpected difficulty at the end of the second school year (1927) after our arrival at the Tafari Makonnen School. Due to the young age of Dejach Habte Mariam, Fit. Qena'a had been assisting him as his right hand man in administering his district ever since he was appointed governor in 1924. Qena'a was a forceful administrator and appeared to exercise more authority than his peers. His fellow-notables and especially those who were blood relatives of the Dejazmach were jealous and intrigued to make the two men to fall out with each other. Qena'a came to Addis Ababa and started a lawsuit against his adversaries. Because of his quarrel, the governor decided to stop the annual payment of school fees amounting to 90 Birr for each student which he used to pay for the boys sent to the school through the intermediary of Fit. Qena'a. Seven boys were affected and therefore expelled when the school was closed for the holidays in July 1927. I was one of them.

Fit. Qena'a was in Addis Ababa at the time and most of us spent the rainy season in his home. As it appeared that all hope of our continuing our studies was lost, we were greatly distressed. We were so eager to get back to school, however, that we frequently went to the Heir Apparent's Palace to appeal to him. He ordered first Lij Fiqré Yayehirad and later Blattengeta Herouy to be our intermediaries and ask Dejach Habte Mariam the reason for non-payment of the fees. We importuned Blattengeta by continually going to his house in Gulele at 5 o'clock in the morning, walking barefoot on biting frosty footpaths. He telephoned several times to Naqamté and spoke to the governor who told him he would not pay the fees because we belonged to his enemy (meaning Fit. Qena'a). We became desperate on hearing this.

While we thus agonized over our situation, the school holiday came to an end and the day for the opening of the school, October 11, 1927, arrived. On that day, about five of us were sitting under some eucalyptus trees adjacent to the Muslim cemetery in Gulele and chatting after lunch at Fit. Qena'a's about the opening of the school, when it occurred to me that H.H. the Heir Apparent was wont to visit the school on opening day, and I suggested to my companions that we should go and make a final appeal to him to allow us to return to the school. They agreed and, calling the other boys who were living elsewhere, we went to the school and saw that the buildings were in a very good condition, having been renovated and the classrooms freshly painted. Many boys and their parents were there awaiting the arrival of His Highness. We mixed with them and requested a friend, Lij Tesfa Yayehirad, who used to come from the Palace to learn some French, to explain our predicament to the Prince. The Heir Apparent came and toured the school compound, inspecting everything. When he stopped somewhere, we stood in front and began to cry. He asked us what was the matter and Lij Tesfa approached him and explained our concern.

The Administrator of the school, Azazh Worqneh Ishetu (Dr. C. Martin), had been sent that year on an official mission to the Government of the United States of America and had asked his wife to act for him in school matters. The Heir Apparent turned to Woizero Qetsela-Worq Tullu and told her to take us back as boarders and he would pay the fees for us. We bowed low and returned to Gulele with great joy to tell Fit. Qena'a. We went back to school the next day like the boys who had been on holiday and did not miss a single day's lessons! I praise my God that through the generosity of His Highness, I could return to school as a boarder, lest my schooling be interrupted and I become a permanent drop-out. After this, I continued my studies without any worry for four more years, until the end of the 1930-31 school year.

I lived at the Tafari Makonnen School for six years and spent the last two years in the sixth form. I had completed the school programme set for six years in five years and since my teachers said they could do no more for me, I spent most of the sixth year reading various books from the library. I also attended class with my companions to follow what they were learning. Seeing that I had completed the set curriculum, my teachers recommended to the then Minister of Education that I should be sent abroad to continue my studies. Since he withheld approval, the period of formal education ended for me in 1931.

The Minister of Education was an official who was not kindly disposed to students whether they studied in the country or abroad. He therefore created a sense of hatred in the hearts of many a young man. The main reason for this ill-use of the students became apparent after the aggression of the Fascist Government of Italy in 1935. Since Mussolini was determined to appropriate Ethiopia for settlement by Italian nationals, he was apprehensive lest too many young Ethiopians should be educated to become leaders for our people in resisting his policy. He therefore suborned the Education Minister to do all in his power to hamper the development of Ethiopia's educational programme. The world knows that, after they overran our country, the Italians hunted down and exterminated the majority of our educated young men in accordance with Mussolini's set purpose.

Accordingly, on the day following the closing of the Tafari Makonnen School for the holidays in July 1931, without warning, without a single thaler for food and travel, and in the height of the rainy season, the Minister expelled me from the school; a youth to whom on speech day H.M. the Emperor had awarded, besides 17 prize books, a special prize of a pocket watch on which his monogram had been inscribed. About thirty other young men, who had been studying for several years like me, suffered the same fate that day.

Aware that I had no relatives or friends to go to in the City, I had very seldom left the school. But since we had to leave the school that very day by order of the Minister, four of my companions and I went to Fit. Deressa Amenti (later Blatta), the only person of note from Wollega known to us, and solicited his assistance. He was concerned about our predicament and received us temporarily.

Most of my school mates who were sent out of the school went to the Grand Palace in a procession and appealed to the Emperor who was very displeased and summoned the Minister to the palace. He feigned illness. (It was often told in those days that whenever he was called to the Palace due to something wrong he had done, the Minister would have a recrudescence of his ailment). The secretary of the school was then called to the palace and ordered to take a list of the students and let them return to school. They were immediately taken back. I was not present when the students appeared before the Emperor, but my best friend, Aseffa Haile Sellassie, saw to it that my name was included in the list. He came to me the next day to tell me the good news and asked me to go back with him. I told him I had no desire ever to return to that school again. Aseffa was an extremely intelligent young man who had like me completed the educational programme of the school and been prevented from going abroad for further studies. He likewise had spent the previous year reading books he could find. He pleaded with me to return to school so that we could continue our reading. I told him that I had realized from what had happened to us that ours was a government that educated young people and then threw them to the wolves. I thereupon gave my considered view that, since in any case there was nothing there for me to learn, I would not go back to Tafari Makonnen School whatever happened to me. Aseffa actually wept and we parted for good. A year later he was appointed director of a school in Dire Dawa and died there soon after. I understood he had tuberculosis and the climate was not congenial. I believe the untimely death of Aseffa Haile Sellassie was a great loss to our country.

As Blatta Deressa had no spare rooms, he let us sleep in his sitting room for three nights and gave us food. Then he sent word to tell us, that due to living conditions in Addis Ababa, he could no longer keep us and we should find somewhere else to stay. My school mates somehow found temporary shelter and went away. I was at a loss where to turn when there came a message for me from Woizero Gumesh who had heard of my predicament. She sent her son, Kibre-Ab Gabre Sellassie, who was my childhood friend and school mate. This was the message: "Are you not my child even though I did not give you birth? Did I not breast-feed you? Why is it you do not come to me when you are in difficulty? Come to me now with Kibre-Ab."

I have indicated in Part 1 of these *Reminiscences* that Woizero Gumesh was the wife of Pastor Gebre Statios, the first evangelist sent from Asmara to Boji in 1898 to preach the Gospel to the Oromo people. She was known in Wollega as 'Mother Gumesh' and was a keen evangelist herself. She taught school at Boji Karkaro with Ato Daniel Lulu and his wife, Woizero Tiru Gebre. Moreover, she gathered a number of young women, instructed them in the Gospel and taught them domestic science as practised in Northern Ethiopia. My father took my mother to her before they were married and she was instructed in the Faith. She believed in the Lord Jesus Christ and was sponsored by Woizero Gumesh at her christening. She also learned to read in the Oromo language. My parents went to live at Boji Karkaro just before I was born and they became neighbours. Woizero Gumesh had given birth to a son, Zaga-Ab, from her second husband about the time I was born. So when my mother went to market or somewhere else, both of us infants were breast-fed by Woizero Gumesh, and when she was away from home my mother breast-fed us. We thus lived like one family. I should recall here Addé Nassisé Liban, a companion of my mother's, who likewise used to breast-feed me. Nassisé had given birth to a son called Gamachu about the time Zaga-Ab and I were born. All three mothers breast-fed the three infants whenever necessary.

Since I was averse to going out of school when I was in Addis Ababa, I did not visit her during that period, except with my father whenever he came from Wollega to see me. As a result, I did not make bold to go to her when I was chased away from school. As soon as I received the message, I collected my clothes and books and went with Kibre-Ab to her house in the neighbourhood of the Armenian Church. I spent the rainy season there. She moved later to a place opposite the Bethsaida Hospital and was given a room by her son-in-law who worked in the hospital. I stayed there with her until October 31, 1931.

In addition to what is stated above, I had a special reason why I did not wish to go back to the Tafari Makonnen School. It arose from a letter written to me by my father on March 22, 1931. He wrote among other things: "I had intended to come but I had fallen seriously ill with boils on my hand for three months; I am somewhat better now. Why don't you find work in your native district, if possible? Have you not acquired enough knowledge? I am racked with illness; levies are ever increasing; conditions in the countryside are not what they used to be. I cannot till the land any more. Your mother does the harvesting in addition to housework. Many of our cattle have been decimated by disease. We are otherwise well!" I was quite upset when I read this letter. I felt it was time for me to leave school, look for a job and support my parents. So after I decided not to return to the Tafari Makonnen School and began to stay with Woizero Gumesh, I decided to go to the Ministry of Education and solicit the Minister to give me a job. I presented an application to him, enclosing my father's letter, and entreated him to give me some work in the Naqamté or Goré areas, or wherever possible, so that I could serve my country and help my parents with what little knowledge I had acquired. I further told him I was anxious lest my ailing father should have gone down to the grave in sorrow because I had done nothing for him. Perhaps to humour me, the Minister took me to his house one day and gave me lunch. He then told me to stay with him to keep my request before him. Since my wish was to get a job quickly, earn some money and help my parents, and not to live in his house as a hanger-on, I pressed him to give me a job. The job I had in mind was to teach in one of the schools being opened in those days in various parts of the country. The Minister spoke one day in a firm voice that I should exercise patience since he did not carry jobs in his pocket. I concluded from this that I had no hope of ever obtaining work in the Ministry of Education and should therefore stop irking the Minister any more.

After this, I wandered from office to office carrying applications, in the hope of finding work in one of the government departments. There could be found not a single department that cared to look at my application and give me a reply. Then I wrote applications in English and went day in day out from legation to legation and from consulate to consulate. But none of them deigned to give me a job, in spite of the fact that, considering the state of education in those days and my age (I was 18), persons were not lacking who admired the English of my application.

Convinced that there was no hope for me to obtain work in Addis Ababa, I decided to send an application to Azazh Worqneh Ishetu, the former administrator of our school and then Governor of Chercher district in Harar Province. I had to send the application through the mail but I lacked money to buy a stamp. I was worrying how to get it when Paulos, Qes Badima's son, came to see me one day. He also had left school and was likewise trying to find a job. I told him what I was planning to do. After a discussion we agreed that I should write an application in English to Azazh Worqneh for both of us and that he should ask his father to give him a 'besa' for a stamp. Paulos came back a few days later with the coin, and as the application was ready we posted it.

Azazh Worqneh was concerned that his former students were in a bad way and decided to take Paulos and me to Asbe Tafari and give us work. It happened that Lij Kifle Dadi (later Dejazmach) who was then Trade Commissioner for Chercher district, was then proceeding to Addis Ababa and the Governor charged him to bring the two young men with him. Lij Kifle did not know where we lived in the City and therefore asked his younger brother, Aklilu Dadi (later Captain), who was our school mate, to look for us. Paulos could not be found because Ras Hailu Tekle Haimanot had sent him to Beirut for further education before a response to our application had arrived. A short time before Lij Kifle came from Chercher, Aklilu and I had happened to meet and have a chat in front of the house where I lived, near the back entrance to Bethsaida Hospital. He did not come into the house. Not knowing the house, and believing I would come out if he called my name, he went where we had met and repeatedly shouted out, "Emmanuel." I was reclining on my bed and reading at the time and got out to see who was calling and met Aklilu. He told me he had to shout out since he was not sure as to where I lived and thought I would come out when I heard him calling. He then said his brother had arrived from Asbe Tafari with the instruction that he should take back with him Paulos and Emmanuel, and had asked him to find where we were. I was pleased and asked him where he was staying. He said he was at 'Sebara Babur' in the Gulele Quarter and we immediately went to Lij Kifle. (Lij Kifle was one of the young men who used to attend the Tafari Makonnen School by order of the Heir Apparent. We were thus acquainted). He told me that Azazh Worqneh had received our application and asked him to take us to Asbe Tafari. After I told him that Paulos had gone to Beirut, he said he would stay in Addis Ababa for some time but I should get ready so that I could go with someone who was proceeding to Chercher earlier. He then gave me ten Birr to buy some clothing. I returned home with great joy and told the good news to Mother Gumesh. I purchased a shirt and a pair of trousers and spent a few days awaiting the day of my departure. On October 31, 1931, I travelled by train with Ato Metaferia Wudé, Commissioner of Works for Chercher district. We arrived at Asbe Tafari in the evening of November 1 and I spent the night in Ato Metaferia's house.

THREE

Asbe Tafari: Headmaster of School
1931 - 1935

Early on November 2, Ato Metaferia Wudé took me to the residence of the District Governor, H.E. Azazh Worqneh, and introduced me to him. He welcomed me and said that he intended to let me stay with him to help in secretarial work. The occasion was the first anniversary of the Coronation of H.I.M. Haile Sellassie I. The reception hall looked festive with the Emperor's photograph and several national flags unfurled around the hall, awaiting the arrival of the district officials, the office workers and a number of the residents of the town. Bottles of drinks and glasses had been made ready to celebrate the occasion. Towards the middle of the forenoon, the district director, the department heads, the secretaries and others entered the hall, bowed to the governor and stood around the hall. The governor returned their greetings and caused some of them to sit while the others remained standing. Drinks were passed around and the governor made a speech in commemoration of the coronation anniversary. He wished good health and long life to H.I.M. and then proceeded to make remarks concerning a matter he had been pondering over for some time - education. He made it quite clear that while the rest of the world had far advanced in education and technology, the

Ethiopian people had lagged far behind, that this was a matter for sadness and preoccupation, that the number of schools in the country was minimal, that there was no place to learn in Asbe Tafari, and that therefore he intended to open a school in the town. But since there was no fund in the treasury allocated for this purpose, he urged the officials, the parents and others there assembled to make contributions to this worthy objective so that a school could be started quickly. He then announced he would contribute 500 Birr. Those in the hall also indicated the amounts they could contribute and a list was made. Over 2,000 Birr was collected and placed in the treasury.

After the anniversary celebration, the governor caused four rooms to be built adjacent to his residence, with wood plastered with mud and mixed with stubble. They were covered with corrugated iron sheets and had earth floors. He had carpenters who came from Addis Ababa make desks and benches as well as blackboards. A white soft limestone was found and served as chalk. Things necessary for school works were thus made ready and the governor decided that the school be opened on November 30, 1931. He invited a number of government employees and townspeople to bring their children in the afternoon, and 18 boys were brought. The governor announced that school work was being started and that I was to be the leader and teacher. He then gave advice both to the parents and the children, and told them classes would begin the following day.

The boys were assembled on December 1 and I began to teach them. There were a few who had begun the Amharic alphabet. I had to write the letters on the blackboard and teach them to read. Many of the boys were diligent and it did not take them long to master the alphabet. There being no textbooks, it was not easy to teach them to read. Nevertheless, I wrote words on the blackboard and taught them until the term was over in January 1932. The governor saw the difficulty of teaching without books, that the number of the boys was increasing and that therefore it was becoming impossible to instruct them all in one room. He therefore consented to my going to Addis Ababa to purchase reading books, exercise books and pencils, as well as employ someone from among my former schoolmates to help in teaching. I bought what was needed, employed Ato Betre-Tsidk Kassa, a native of Gojam, and returned to Asbe Tafari quickly. A little later, Ato Kibre-Ab Gabre Sellassie was employed as a teacher. As we had classrooms, I retained the boys who came first and divided the others between the two teachers. We then proceeded in earnest with the business of teaching. As soon as the boys could read and were able to understand what they read, they began to appreciate the value of schooling and were assiduous in their study. Their parents, observing that they had learned to read and listening to the stories they read to them or told them orally, and seeing they could do sums as well, were gratified and gave them every encouragement.

The 1931-32 school year thus came to a close and, when the school was closed early in July for the holidays, officials were assembled at the governor's residence, a report was read and the top boys were given prizes by the governor. He also gave advice to the boys and their parents. Seeing that the youngsters were developing mentally during the second school year, I made my class begin to learn English. This was no easy matter due to lack of books. I therefore made a list of the textbooks for beginners which I had used at the Tafari Makonnen School and presented it to the governor to order them straight from England.

He readily took the list and sent it to the publishers with a covering letter asking them to send the books directly to Asbe Tafari. In addition, exercise books, ink, pens, pencils, slates and slate pencils as well as paper were ordered from London in substantial quantities. The governor paid for them all from his bank account in London. I observed that it was from his own money and he never asked for reimbursement. In this way, the school was run without a hitch and free from the bureaucratic red tape of the Ministry of Education. As we had no contact whatever with that Ministry, it is doubtful whether it even knew that the Asbe Tafari School existed.

Due to the ever increasing number of school boys, it became imperative that more teachers be employed and seven more teachers were added in the course of the second and third school years. Speech days were held in the governor's residence at the end of the second and third years; the headmaster presented reports on the progress of the school and prizes were distributed to the top students. Ato Betre-Tsidk, who had profound knowledge of both Amharic and Ethiopic (Ge'ez) wrote songs and plays which he made the boys rehearse. These were presented annually before the governor and many people; they aroused patriotism and evoked the pleasure of the governor, the parents and the other spectators.

In addition to the usual school subjects, instruction was given in weaving and carpentry as well as in physical exercise. The students also played soccer, and competitions were held with members of the armed forces. The older boys were taken for a week's camping at Easter two years running to Qunni, Bedessa and Hirna. They enjoyed the outing because they learned something about nature and did some scouting. They made bonfires and spent the evenings singing and playing. We took cooks with us to the camps with provisions and encountered no difficulty in this respect.

Many boys in the countryside, who saw the schoolboys and heard the songs, pressed their parents to send them to school in Asbe Tafari. This brought about a considerable increase in the number of pupils and more classrooms had to be added. As a number of the boys from the countryside had nowhere to stay in town and nothing to pay, the governor had a house constructed to accommodate them as boarders. I therefore had additional duties to employ domestic staff to prepare meals for the boarders, to supervise the dormitory and look after the boys, and see to the careful accounting of school funds. This over and above the supervision of weaving and carpentry shops. We also held evening classes for government employees and other adults interested in acquiring more knowledge.

Because of my young age (I was under 23), and being entirely devoted to the work, I felt no fatigue. There was nothing in my long years (42) of service that gave me more pleasure than my work at the Asbe Tafari School. To observe the young people grow in mind as well as in body was sheer delight. My main purpose was to pass on to them all the knowledge I had gained at Tafari Makonnen School and then let them go wherever they could obtain higher education. As this was also the intention of my fellow teachers, they shared their knowledge with their students without stint.

After I had discharged in this spirit my duties as teacher and administrator at the Asbe Tafari School for three and a half years, a piece of good fortune which I had never expected came my way in April, 1935. It was a chance to go abroad and acquire more knowledge; a chance denied me by the highest official in the Ethiopian Ministry of Education on two occasions.

There is one thing I should mention here the recollection of which still gives me immense pleasure. Although several of the young men in my class had to sacrifice their lives for love of country during the Italian war of aggression, many survived the Fascist massacres and were able, at a time when shortage of personnel was most acute after the liberation, to hold in course of time positions of responsibility in the government as ambassadors, generals, colonels, secretaries, section heads, teachers and in other capacities. Many of the pupils in the other forms also gave appreciable service in clerical, accounting, administrative and teaching positions in Harar Province, especially in Chercher district.

FOUR

London: Secretary of Legation
1935 - 1939

With the determination of avenging the humiliation it suffered at Adwa 40 years earlier and the declared aim of making Ethiopia its colonial dependency, Fascist Italy under the leadership of Benito Mussolini began in 1935 to disturb the peace of the Ethiopian government, not only by sending to Eritrea and Somalia large troops and a vast quantity of military equipment but also by provoking incidents inside Ethiopia on any pretext. Italy had placed so called commercial agents in some parts of Ethiopia and posted through the Catholic Consolata Mission, so-called missionaries in Addis Ababa, and Western and Southern Ethiopia under the pretext of preaching the Gospel. Their main objective was to spy out the country and draw maps. Worse still, they suborned high government officials, provincial governors, district notables and local leaders, and tried to convince them of Italian civilization and might. They did their utmost to induce them to betray their country and their sovereign, and to be instrumental for the destruction of not only Ethiopia's freedom but of its very existence.

As the time drew for its invasion of Ethiopia, Italy picked up quarrels with the government in Harar, Gojam and Begemder Provinces, culminating in the provocation of the incident, known in history as the 'Wal-Wal Incident,' when its troops moved into Ethiopia for about 100 km, attacked our military post there, killed a number of our troops and occupied the post. The Ethiopian government was alarmed and brought to the notice of the League of Nations in Geneva, Switzerland the injury it had suffered at the hands of Italy, and asked for justice. The League was the organization set up after the First World War to keep peace and security, and to guarantee the independence of both great and small nations. It spent a long time discussing the issue and, in spite of the fact that it knew very well which party was the aggressor, it chose to betray Ethiopia and appease Italy, since the great powers of the day were fearful that Mussolini might side with Hitler to provoke a European war. This was a fact the world had to take note of with sorrow. The activity of the Italian government was such that the Emperor and the Ethiopian government were seized with apprehension and, in addition to doing all they could to obtain military equipment and alert the people, they realized that it was most important to do their utmost in the diplomatic sphere. To this end it was decided to select some trustworthy persons and send them to Europe.

Azazh Worqneh, the governor of Chercher, happened to go up to Addis Ababa after the 'Wal-Wal Incident.' The Emperor summoned him one day and consulted with him about the threatening attitude of Fascist Italy and about his fear that it might invade Ethiopia. Recalling that in those days the number of Ethiopians who could stand up to Europeans and argue with them was negligible, he told Azazh Worqneh of his desire to send him to Britain as his Envoy Extraordinary and Minister Plenipotentiary. Azazh Worqneh reminded the Emperor that his training was in medicine and not in diplomacy and that he was therefore afraid the task might prove to be too much for him. His Majesty then said that he was an Englishman in every respect except his ethnic origin and pressed him to go to London for him. Seeing that the Emperor felt he would be of use to him, he accepted the assignment.

In 1868, when the British Expedition came to Ethiopia to fight the Emperor Theodore, he took his own life and Amba Maqdela was fired. People on the Amba panicked and ran away. A British officer (Col. Chamberlain) found a three-year old waif on the Amba and carried him away to India. The colonel died not long after and his fellow officer, a Col. Martin, sponsored the child and educated him. He also had him christened after which he was known as Charles Martin. It came to be known upon his return to Ethiopia that he belonged to a family descended from the royal stock known as 'Weizazir' who lived in Gonder city in the vicinity of Adebabai Yesus Church; and his name was Worqneh Ishetu.

In 1935, Ethiopia's diplomatic service had not been organized on modern lines and trained personnel were non-existent. Moreover, the amount of money spent for the purpose was extremely limited. When a minister plenipotentiary or a consul was sent abroad therefore, he was allowed to take along with him someone of his choice to assist him as secretary. No sooner was it known that Azazh Worqneh was going abroad than some young men went and pleaded with him to take them to London. He turned them away however by telling them that he had already selected a young man for this purpose.

I was pressing on with my educational work, not knowing what had been decided in Addis Ababa concerning his future work as well as mine, when I received a letter from Azazh Worqneh dated May 3, 1935. The letter read as follows: "As I am going to England on duty, I have considered taking you with me as a student to help me in secretarial work without pay. Let me know if you wish to go." I was so elated with the offer that, in replying to him on May 10, I thanked him very sincerely that he had so kindly thought of taking me with him without my even thinking of it, so that I could visit the country and learn some more with a view to obtaining more experience for my future work and said: "I assure Your Excellency that, given food and clothes, I am ready to follow you wherever you go and assist you with whatever small capacity I possess without expecting any remuneration!"

As indicated in Part 3 above, when I arrived at Asbe Tafari, he allowed me to stay in his house and help in secretarial work. I slept at his residence and, at lunch and dinner, a small table was laid for me so that I could partake of whatever he ate. Since he often wrote letters abroad after dinner, he used to dictate them to me in English and show me how to type. I thus learned the art of writing letters and typing. I used to translate into Amharic the annual reports he wrote in English on the progress of the work in Chercher district for submission to the Emperor. Moreover, the Amharic secretary, Ato Hailu Kabtih-Yimer and I used to read to him after dinner the petitions which the public presented to him daily. We then set down his directives on the petitions for him to initial. They were sent every morning to the District Office to be distributed to the officials and to the petitioners. Even though a school was opened a month after I arrived at Asbe Tafari and I was appointed teacher and administrator, I continued my duties as secretary, and my salary was twenty Birr a month to begin with. Periodically, I was given increments of five or ten Birr so that it amounted to forty Birr after three years. It was adequate for the time and it helped me satisfy the desire which impelled me to look for a job, so that I could help support my parents. Until my departure for Britain, I remitted at intervals money and clothing to my parents, to my sister and brother, and to relatives who lived in Naqamté. I was able to meet my father twice in Addis Ababa. My brother who had ear trouble was brought to Addis Ababa for treatment and was then placed in school. However, the schools were closed not long after due to the Italian invasion and he was unable to learn anything.

After I had lived in the governor's residence for about two years, I indicated my desire to go and live with the other unmarried young men who had been called from Addis Ababa like me for employment. The governor told me that it would be better for me to stay on with him. But I insisted I should join them and he consented. I moved to the house given to the young men for habitation and which adjoined the school. As there were quite a number of us, we called it 'Ten Boys' House.' Nevertheless, since I often had to perform my secretarial duties in the evenings, I continued to have dinner with the governor.

After working for over three years under the instructive guidance of Azazh Worqneh, I acquired experience in educational and office work. The fact that I had to correct the students' homework daily contributed a great deal to the habit of working with care and patience. Being himself meticulous in writing, it appeared that he was concerned that I should acquire the habit. I had a feeling, even before there was any thought of our going to Britain, that he had observed I was taking with pleasure and following with care the instruction he gave me. I believe this was one of the reasons he made a point of my not parting from him when he went to another place. The fact that, on arrival in London, I had to do all kinds of work, use only English, meet, talk and correspond with many people sharpened my mind and developed my knowledge as well as increased my desire and persistence to learn, all added up to give him confidence in my letter-writing skills and in my work generally. As a result, two years after we arrived in London, he would direct to me to draft and type the letters he intended to sign. I would execute them with all the care at my command and present them. He would murmur, "Brought it, my boy," and often sign without reading them. Although I was gratified that a man who was so careful in the choice of words as in correct spelling placed such confidence in me, I felt the responsibility and made every effort to try and write as elegantly as he did. This became such a firm habit that in later years it was my lodestar in everything I did, both in the government and the church. I used to exercise great care in all I reduced to writing.

I wish the reader of these *Reminiscences* to know that all Azazh Worqneh Ishetu (Dr. Charles Martin) taught me and all the good things he did for me have impelled me to cherish his memory with gratitude. They have been a torchlight that led me on my way in the course of the many years I had the privilege of serving my country and people. I shall treasure all the days of my life the support and assistance he afforded me and a large number of fellow Ethiopians, irrespective of their place of birth in this country, and the fine example he set of the true Ethiopian.

After the above-mentioned exchange of letters with Azazh Worqneh concerning my travel to England, I handed over the leadership of the school to Ato Betre-Tsidq Kassa, my deputy, and went up to Addis Ababa in the course of May 1935. I stayed with him in Shola House, Yeka Quarter, and had my passport issued by the Foreign Ministry. My students wept bitterly when I took leave of them. I was also in tears. As the day approached for us to leave for London, I proceeded to Asbe Tafari and arrived there on June 19 to have the school accounts audited. On the following day, Lij Seifu Mikael, deputy governor of the district, appointed two auditors for the purpose and the expenditures were audited on the same day. The income was audited on June 21. The auditors reported to Lij Seifu on June 22 that I was free. He initialled the report and gave it to me as my discharge. As Azazh Worqneh was leaving Addis Ababa by train that day, I said farewell to my friends and left for Miesso Station at 4 p.m. I arrived at the station after an hour and the train came not much later. I took leave of my friends and boarded the train for Dire Dawa. The train arrived in Dire Dawa late in the evening and we proceeded to Bololakos Hotel for the night. I was told that all the beds had been occupied and I joined two camp chairs together and slept on the veranda.

Azazh Worqneh brought with him his four little children (Yohannes, Samuel (Charlie), Leah and Dawit), accompanied by their Black American nanny, Miss Ida Bastian. Abate Bogale, a grandson of his sister, and Beyenech, a cook, also came with him.

On June 23, we got on the train at 6:30 a.m. and travelled to Jibuti arriving at 5 p.m. We stopped at the Continental Hotel. It was the hot season in Jibuti and the heat was overpowering for us who had just come from the highlands. The perspiration was running down our faces like drops of water. There I also slept on the veranda. The French liner, 'Dartagnan,' arrived early on June 24 and we went on board at 5 p.m. I dropped my national dress on that day and began to wear Western clothes. The children and I travelled second class.

We arrived at Suez on June 28 and entered the Canal. On June 29 we arrived at Port Said and were told that the ship would stop there until 4 p.m. I went to town to visit the Ethiopian Consul, Lij Yilma Wolde Gebriel, to whom I handed letters, sent from Addis Ababa. We then went to the liner together. After a chat with the Minister, he went back to town at 4 o'clock. The liner entered the Mediterranean to continue its voyage and we felt cooler temperatures. It took four days to cross the sea and we arrived at Marseilles harbour early on July 4. We immediately disembarked, had our baggage put on the train and started for Paris at 11:30 a.m., arriving in that City at 5 p.m. We took a taxi to the Hotel de la Gare du Nord and spent the night there. On July 5, I accompanied the Minister to the Ethiopian Legation where he met the Minister, Bejrond Tekle Hawariat. We had our baggage placed on the train in the evening and proceeded to Calais. We went on board a steamer there and, crossing the English Channel overnight, arrived at Dover in England. We then travelled by train and arrived in London on Friday, July 6, 1935.

Until Azazh Worqneh's appointment, Bejrond Tekle Hawariat was concurrently Ethiopian Minister to Britain with residence in Paris. He was also Ethiopia's representative to the League of Nations whose head office was in Geneva.

There was a Legation office in London and Ato Efrem Tewolde Medhen (later Blattengeta) lived there as consul and secretary. He welcomed us at Victoria Station and conducted us to N° 13 Elm Park Gardens in South Kensington. After a few days, the Minister went to the Foreign Office to visit the officials and fix the date for the presentation of his Credentials to King George V. He then went to Buckingham Palace and presented his Letters of Credence.

The dispute between Ethiopia and Italy was getting worse at the time and Ato Efrem was transferred to Paris to assist Bejrond Tekle Hawariat in the debate that was going on in Geneva. He therefore turned over to me the Legation office soon after our arrival and departed. Although I had become acquainted in some measure with office work at Asbe Tafari, the type of work I encountered in London was rather strange to me and I was somewhat at a loss for a short while. But because Azazh Worqneh's counsel always attended me and the English I had learned at the Tafari Makonnen School was my main stay, I became familiar with the work and the people in a short time and got on with my duties with diligence. So much so that within a few months I began to speak, write and work as one who had lived in the country for a number of years.

As the house in Elm Park Gardens was built as a dwelling place and not as offices, it was neither suitable nor adequate for office work. But, since the funds available for diplomatic service were moderate and Ato Efrem was living alone, and since there was not much activity until the arrival of the new Minister, and Bejrond Tekle Hawariat stayed at the hotel during his infrequent visits to London, the house could do for that time. After the arrival of Azazh Worqneh, however, the presence of a resident Minister and the resulting rise in importance of the legation's status as well as the size of his family rendered the house inadequate. Moreover, the area was off the central part of the City, which made it inconvenient for people who were beginning to visit the legation in increasing numbers. Due to all this, the Minister rented a sizable house in the Knightsbridge district, Kensington road, called N° 8 Princess Gate. We moved into it around Christmas 1935. He soon after bought a nearby house, N° 5 Princess Gate, where we lived for about two years. It had then to be sold.

In October 1935, Fascist Italy began its invasion of Ethiopia with the intention of taking it over by armed might. This brought an unprecedented volume of work on our Legation. News about the invasion was printed daily in the newspapers and broadcast over the radio. So many British people who felt Ethiopia was grossly wronged and journalists, who were hunting for news, including those from abroad, swamped us with letters and continually telephoned for information. Many also came to the Legation to express their sense of outrage. Since there was no other worker in the office and since due to his age (he was 70) and status, the Minister was not able to receive all who came, the responsibility fell on me.

In addition to receiving visitors and answering telephone calls, I had to type and mail up to 50 letters a day. Fortunately, many of the letters were similar and brief. As English people considered it important that prompt replies were given to their letters, I tried hard so that replies to letters were not delayed. Over and above all this, it was my duty to attend to the internal administration of the Legation, to supervise the purchase of provisions and the work of the domestic staff as well as to see to the comfort of the Minister and the children.

Aware that the work was becoming too much for one person and that it was necessary to get someone to help, the Minister employed Tesfaye (Reginald) Zaphiro who had an Ethiopian mother and a Greek father to help me. He was a little younger than myself. Although he was useful in answering telephone calls and receiving visitors, he had no experience in office work and was not hardworking. That meant that my burden was not much lighter. A little later on, he was sent to New York because American Blacks who were so sympathetic to the Ethiopian cause had requested the Minister to send them someone to speak on Ethiopia at their meetings. A young Jamaican woman called Una Marson was then employed to help me in the office. She was well educated and experienced in office work, and I was glad to obtain her assistance. After a few months, however, she left saying she wished to return to her country. I was thus left alone with the whole burden of the work. Tesfaye returned to the Legation, but as he could not settle down to do office work, he went elsewhere. I was again left alone, but the great affliction my country was suffering weighed so much on my mind that I used to stay in the office and work from early morning to 11 p.m., my youthfulness and perfect health helping me along.

Azazh Worqneh was extremely sad that the armed conflict was getting so intense and that the Italians were pushing into the interior of the country, and he often used to raise his voice on the radio and write to the press to arouse the peoples and governments of the world. In spite of the fact that many British people expressed unequivocally their sympathy with Ethiopia and pressed their government to take steps to halt Mussolini's aggression, the British and French governments, which were most influential in the League of Nations, were determined to betray Ethiopia because they were so intent on appeasing and coaxing Mussolini not to disturb their peace by uniting with Hitler against them. The situation in our country was thus becoming more and more desperate.

After the Ethiopian armed forces and people were slaughtered and dispersed from October 1935 to April 1936 in Northern, Southern and Eastern Ethiopia, struggling not only against Mussolini's armies but also against his bombs, tanks, fire throwers and poison gas, the troops led by the Emperor fought with admirable courage at Maichew and were defeated. The Emperor, the remnant of his retinue and the members of the army that escaped the bombs and the poison gas, retreated towards Addis Ababa. The enemy pursued them by aircraft and massacred many people and animals with bombs and poison gas. The Emperor and his retinue travelled through Lasta with much difficulty and returned to Addis Ababa on April 30.

The Emperor's plan on arrival in Addis Ababa was to proceed to Western Ethiopia and set up an administration at Goré which was thought to be more suited for defence against the enemy. With this in view, a council of the high government officials was called and, after two or three meetings, it became apparent that most of the councillors had voted that it would be better if His Majesty were to proceed to Europe and appeal for justice and assistance for Ethiopia on the international arena. Arrangements were then made for him to leave by train for Jibuti and thence go to the Holy Land by boat, Europe being his eventual destination. The Emperor boarded the train for Jibuti during the night of May 2, accompanied by his family and a number of high officials and ladies. Since the British government had previously been requested and consented to transport the Empress and the children to Jerusalem, a cruiser, 'HMS Enterprise,' was waiting at Jibuti. When news that the Emperor and retinue had arrived at Jibuti safely and gone on board the cruiser was flashed around the world, it was so unexpected and sudden that those of us who were abroad found it difficult to believe. Nevertheless, the cruiser arrived at the port of Haifa in a few days and they disembarked there.

The Emperor travelled to Jerusalem on May 8 and the following day called Azazh Worqneh on the telephone personally to inform him of the reason for his leaving Ethiopia and to instruct him to make his statement known to the world. The Minister was hard of hearing and was unable to take the message, so he asked me to take it. I translated the statement into English at once and transmitted it to the news agencies. It was immediately broadcast over the radio and published in the newspapers. I still remember vividly the crowd of people that besieged the Legation that day and the following days seeking more information. Things calmed down after a few days and we had some relief from pressure.

The Emperor's plan was to go to Geneva by way of Britain and present his appeal to the League of Nations. After a stay of about four weeks in Jerusalem, he travelled to Gibraltar in a British cruiser and thence to England in a commercial liner. He arrived in London on June 3, 1936. Although the British government had to allow the Emperor to visit Britain and to take him in its ships, knowing very well the feeling of sympathy and friendship the British people had for him and the Ethiopian people, it denied him the official welcome due to a head of state when he left the ship or when he arrived in London, since it had already decided to hand over Ethiopia to Italy and had supported it all along. However, many Londoners gave him a warm reception at the railway station and at our Legation. Many used to surround his car and greet him in a respectful and friendly manner whenever they saw him going about in the City.

A millionaire, named Sir Ely Kadoorie, who lived in Shanghai, China, had a well-appointed house, N° 6 Princess Gate, and the Minister telegraphed him to allow the Emperor to stay in it for a short time. He readily agreed. So the Emperor moved straight into it when he arrived in London. This proved to be very convenient for our work.

After the Battle of Maichew, the Italians pushed on and occupied Dessie, and the Commander-in-Chief, Badoglio, entered Addis Ababa on May 5, 1936. Mussolini announced on May 9, that the occupation of Ethiopia by the Italian armed forces marked the founding of the second Roman Empire and blustered with extreme arrogance that no power on earth would change it.

After a stay of four weeks in London, the Emperor went to Geneva and delivered his famous speech to the League of Nations Assembly. It was rated as historic and admired all over the world. He then returned to London. In spite of the fact that his Geneva speech was greatly admired however, the Emperor's effort produced no result since the great powers of the period (Britain and France) had made up their minds to betray Ethiopia to Italy and had arrived at an understanding with the Italian Fascist government to that intent. They were also strongly opposed to any assistance being given to Ethiopia. Nevertheless, there was no time during his sojourn of four years in Britain when the Emperor ceased to remind the world of the wrong and treachery perpetrated on our country and to ask for justice.

The occupation of Addis Ababa and Mussolini's proclamation that Ethiopia had been annexed to Italy opened a new phase for the struggle against Italy. Many officials and military officers, who were in Addis Ababa and did not go into exile with Haile Sellassie I, were determined not to submit to Italy and went out to the countryside to engage the Italian troops in guerrilla warfare. In a short while, patriots sprung up, not only around Addis Ababa and in Shoa, but notably in Gojam and Gonder, and continued their struggle until the Italians were defeated and driven out of Ethiopia in 1941. We used periodically to receive reports of their activities, through various channels, which I translated into English and gave to the news agencies for publication in the newspapers. These clearly showed that, though Italy had overran Ethiopia, the people were not subdued, and, though the Emperor did not go to Geneva whenever the League Assembly was convened, he sent his representative to keep on pleading for justice. All this prevented the European and other governments from forgetting Ethiopia's plight.

However, since the new British Prime Minister, Neville Chamberlain was bent on executing the policy initiated by the previous Prime Minister, Stanley Baldwin, and the Foreign Secretary, Samuel Hoare, to sacrifice Ethiopia and to persuade Mussolini not to upset the peace of Europe in league with Hitler, he made an agreement with him in April, 1938, that the British government recognized that Ethiopia was an Italian dependency and that the King of Italy was the Emperor of Ethiopia, and on other matters. He publicly announced the fact of British recognition in November, 1938. Consequently, the Foreign Office informed the Minister, Azazh Worqneh, of the termination of his mission as Envoy Extraordinary and Minister Plenipotentiary to the British Court. This circumstance grieved the Ethiopians greatly. The Emperor had placed his trust not only in the League of Nations but also in the British government and people, to whom he had gone as friends. But that government had become the leader of the other governments in violating the Covenant of the League of Nations, particularly the principle of 'collective security' which was the mainstay of weak peoples, and treacherously sacrificed Ethiopia to a stronger and aggressive power, thus showing, in no uncertain terms, that there is no justice for the weak in this world. In spite of this, it appeared that there was not a single Ethiopian who believed that Ethiopian independence was irretrievably lost.

Believing in a God who nullifies human decisions and gives justice to the oppressed, we were determined to work harder than ever before to keep the world informed of the guerrilla warfare that our patriots were waging and to speak at a number of meetings so that the British people and others did not forget Ethiopia. Even though they realized they were unable to change the policy of their government, many of the people longed to hear about the situation in Ethiopia, and I often went around to enlighten them. And the Minister, in addition to writing in the newspapers continuously, sometimes spoke at meetings. He also used to appeal periodically for financial aid for Ethiopia, and people who were sympathetic but not so rich used to send us as much as they could afford. Those who were rich, believing that their government's policy of betrayal was motivated by the desire to protect their well-being and to try to prevent a European war, far from sending us contributions, appeared not even to want to hear about Ethiopia's difficulties. Their desire in line with their governments was to sacrifice such weak nations as China, Ethiopia, Albania and Czechoslovakia to the powerful and aggressive powers of the day, Japan, Italy and Germany, so that peace could be ensured for themselves and to enjoy the riches they had amassed by plundering weak peoples. Intensely jealous of the colonial possessions and enormous wealth of the great powers, especially of Britain and France, the latter were determined to have a share in the colonies and the accumulated wealth. Their desire was therefore in vain. We and those like us who were robbed of their countries and their liberty, however, saw clearly that a mighty conflict was in the making and that the peace they so earnestly desired was an illusion and that their fabulous wealth would be consumed by war. We therefore expected in faith and in hope the restoration of the freedom of our countries.

During that disastrous period from 1936, when the Ethiopian government fell and the Emperor went into exile, to 1938, when the Legation in London was officially closed, no funds could be expected from Ethiopia to run the Legation.

Azazh Worqneh had therefore to use the money contributed through his appeal to the public (Dr. Martin's Fund) to defray the expenses of the Legation, and to help the exiles from time to time. Since the building which housed the Legation, N° 5 Princess Gate, was bought with the money thus contributed, and since funds were running low and the time was approaching for the closing down of the Legation, the Minister sold the house. In January 1938, he rented a smaller house, N° 43 Gloucester Square, in the Bayswater district, where we lived for over a year. Even though the British government informed us the following November that it no longer recognized our government and our sovereign, we continued to call our rented house 'the Ethiopian Legation' and proceeded with our work. The public, not considering Ethiopia lost, did not interrupt its contacts with us; and the British government showed no sign of opposition. We also continued to correspond with the Foreign Office when necessary.

As soon as he arrived in London, the Emperor had announced that his Legation in London was the central office for all dealings with his government. The Legation thus remained the only office of the Ethiopian government until he left England in June, 1940. Whoever desired to meet His Majesty telephoned, wrote or came to our office. The Emperor (who lived outside London) sometimes spent the night and received visitors in his Legation.

After living in this manner until April 1939 at N° 43 Gloucester Square, Azazh Worqneh informed the Emperor that he desired to go to India as he had found the cost of living to be too high for him with four small children and asked to be relieved. The Emperor gave him leave to go and he took a house in Kensington until his departure for India.

The Emperor, seeing that this would entail the closing down of the Legation office, caused one floor of a small house, 120 Inverness Terrace, consisting of three rooms to be rented in Bayswater. The largest of the three rooms was to serve as office and the other two rooms as bedrooms for the two secretaries who worked there.

Ato Wolde Giorgis Wolde Yohannes (later Tsehafé-Tizaz) had acted as the Emperor's secretary ever since he accompanied His Majesty to London. He had an office in the Legation and now moved to the newly rented house. His main task was to send replies to letters written to the Emperor by Ethiopians who had been exiled to various countries. He also performed other secretarial duties in Amharic. Since I had been doing whatever had to be done in English in the name of the Legation, it became necessary to find someone to continue the work.

Azazh Worqneh asked me to go with him when he decided to go to India. I told him I did not wish to go to India because I felt I would only be a burden to him and there was nothing useful for me to do in India. Believing that if I went to school in Britain it would help me to acquire more knowledge and get a job, I had requested him to give me 120 Pounds to go to school for two years, but he was not willing to do that. An English friend of Ethiopia who knew that I did not want to go to India had asked me whether I was interested in continuing my previous work and I had told her that if Azazh Worqneh refused to give me some money for school, I would not be averse to continuing the work while awaiting the development of events. The lady was apparently looking for an English secretary for His Majesty and she acquainted him with my view.

I had earlier confided my longing to go to school to an English friend, Mr. Douglas O'Hanlon (later Anglican clergyman) whose acquaintance I had made at Asbe Tafari when he worked there as a missionary and whom I used to visit on and off at his parents' house outside London. He and another English friend had apparently told his parents, who were active Christians and well-to-do, of my desire and his mother, Mrs. Agnes O'Hanlon, had decided to help me and, corresponding with the director of 'Faith Mission Training Home,' a religious institution in Edinburgh, had obtained admittance for me. She then informed me she would pay the fees for me for one year.

In the meantime, the Emperor had decided to ask me to help with what had to be done in English in the new office. He therefore summoned me to Brown's Hotel, Mayfair, one day in February 1939, when he happened to be in London, and asked me whether I would be willing to help him by moving to the newly rented office with Ato Wolde Giorgis when Azazh Worqneh would have left for India, so that there would be no interruption in the work I had been doing at the Legation. He then said, having no wealth he could not make me rich, but he would give me enough money to live on.

It weighed heavily on me to refuse to help him in his difficulty and not knowing the fate of Ethiopia and her people was to change for the better in June 1940, when Mussolini would declare war on Britain and France, I threw away in his presence my chance to go to school with the help of my English friend's mother and told him that, since he thought my service would be of use to him, I was willing to continue doing my former duties and that I would be content with having food and somewhere to live. I then bowed and retired.

I was given seven Pounds a month at that time for food and sundries. It was later increased to eight Pounds. This was obtained from a fund, known as the 'Emperor's Fund' or 'Ethiopia Fund,' which the 'Abyssinia Association' established to aid Ethiopia in its difficulty, solicited from the British public to relieve Ethiopians. This monthly allowance was intended to cover expenses for food, laundry and some minor needs.

Most supplies were brought to Britain from overseas and since German submarines, bent on trying to starve the people, were hunting and sinking British merchant ships in all the oceans, a system of rationing was strictly enforced on all items of food and clothing. Everyone had to use ration coupons to buy food and clothes. The system restricted those who had plenty of money from buying too much and enabled those who like me had very little money to buy enough to keep them alive. I used to buy from the shops what was allowed and prepared my breakfast and supper on the gas ring in my bedroom. I had lunch at the public eating places for two or three shillings. I lived alone thus for nearly three years from the time the Emperor departed for the Sudan until I left London to return to my country.

In April 1939, taking the archives with me, I moved to Inverness Terrace to live with Ato Wolde Giorgis and resume my work. Azazh Worqneh allowed me to take my bedroom furniture. He also gave me a writing table and a chair. This marked the end of my dream to go to school in Britain and the beginning of my term of service to the Sovereign. Nevertheless, I have come to the realization that I could not have acquired from any college or university the knowledge and experience I obtained in the office of the Ethiopian Legation in London during that period of distress and stress, working for eight years in a highly responsible position. For 35 years, from the day in February 1939 when, accepting the Emperor's behest, I became a regular public servant, until February 1974, when he dismissed his cabinet ministers, I had been a loyal assistant to him and served my country and the Sovereign in not less than ten government positions successively, making use of the experience and know-how I had acquired at that time. For this I am deeply thankful to my God.

As soon as Ato Wolde Giorgis and I began to live in Inverness Terrace, we employed a woman to come daily to cook lunch and clean the rooms for us. We ourselves prepared our breakfast and supper alternately. After living in this way for five months, we moved to Sussex, to the south of London, in September 1939, with His Majesty's consent, to live in the home of Mrs. Muriel Shelley-Hudd, a friend of Ethiopia. We continued to work in Inverness Terrace, however, and commuted to London.

This was at a time when Hitler, having defeated France, was attacking Britain by air in preparation for his planned invasion. So it was compulsory to blackout the towns and villages at night. In addition to the tedium of commuting in this condition and in winter, some incidents in the house upset my mind. I therefore informed His Majesty of this and he consented to our returning to town. In April 1940, we moved to the house of a friend of Ethiopia, N° 2 Rosary Gardens in South Kensington and rented a large room for the office and two bedrooms. In June 1940, Ato Wolde Giorgis left to accompany the Emperor to the Sudan. I lived there discharging my duties until April 1943, when I departed to return to my country.

FIVE

London: 'Secretary for Government Affairs' 1939 - 1943

I have indicated in Part 2 above how I had gone to the Tafari Makonnen School in 1925 to pursue modern education and had been dismissed after two years for not having someone to pay the fees for me, and how, through the generosity of H.H. Ras Tafari Makonnen (later H.I.M. Haile Sellassie I), I had soon after returned to the school to study for four more years. Although I could never forget this, His Majesty could not be expected to remember it. Due to force of circumstances, during the period of his exile in Britain, his Legation in which I acted as secretary became his office in exile. I was struggling alone to do the work in the office of the Legation which was growing more and more onerous due to the war. I had a feeling that Blattengeta Herouy who, for lack of room, was constantly sitting in my office, was discussing my work with the Emperor and that His Majesty had also been watching. For instance, not long after he arrived in London, he sent me by Prince Makonnen, a pocket watch on which his monogram was inscribed, of the type he awarded me in 1931 at the Tafari Makonnen School to mark the end of the school year. There was also another instance; he was sitting in the Legation drawing room one day when someone wanted to talk to him on the telephone. He went to my office to answer the call and after he put the receiver down, he turned to me and said: "Herouy tells me that you are assiduous in your work and that you love the Bible." He then uttered a word of encouragement, produced a pocket English New Testament from his pocket, wrote the following words: '1937. To Emmanuel Abraham: H.S.I., Emperor' and gave it to me. Moreover, he had heard that I was going around speaking about Ethiopia's ancient history and her plight. One incident made him realize this more fully and stamped it on his mind in a way he could not forget. It was some remarks I had made on Ethiopia at the annual meeting on June 1, 1937, of the 'United Society for Christian Literature.' His Majesty had been invited to the meeting and accepted the invitation. I had been asked to speak at the meeting but, explaining that I was only a minor functionary, I had declined to speak on Ethiopia in the Emperor's presence without his consent. The organizers of the meeting acquainted His Majesty of this and requested him to allow me to speak at the meeting. They informed me a little later on that his approval had been obtained. I then carefully prepared and memorized a speech to last about 15 minutes.

The Emperor was at the Legation on the day of the meeting and, accompanied by Sirak and me, he proceeded by taxi to Victoria Hotel where the meeting was to be held. The Chairman of the meeting, Lord Lothian, welcomed him respectfully with some other persons and invited him to sit on his right. Sirak and I sat opposite to them. As it was early morning, breakfast was served and then people who came from various areas, mainly those engaged in missionary work in the Far East and Africa, presented their reports successively. When my turn came, I rose and thanked them for asking me to speak at the meeting about my suffering country and the work of the Gospel. I told them that the Gospel of Christ was most needful for my country and then proceeded to remind them that Ethiopia was a country to which Christianity had been introduced in the early centuries; that we had learned from our history that before Ethiopia had accepted the Christian Faith it had worshipped the true God of Israel; that the Gospel had been preached and the Ethiopian Church properly organized in the 4th century A.D. through Frumentius who was also called Abba Selama, Revealer of Light; that about a century later the Church had been strengthened with the arrival of the 'Nine Saints' who had come from abroad and who had translated the Scriptures into Ethiopic (Ge'ez), the language spoken by the people in those days; that although Ethiopic had become a dead language in the Middle Ages, the Christian people of Ethiopia had held firm in their faith in Christ in spite of the great difficulties and acute hardships it had endured at the hands of the Muslims and pagans; that in the 19th Century Protestant missionaries had begun to visit Ethiopia and, although they concentrated on the Falashas in preaching the Gospel, that they had made great efforts for the Bible to be made available in Amharic, the modern language and disseminated among the people; and that the Amharic version of the Scriptures had been the means for the salvation of many souls; and that because this version had not been acceptable to the Ethiopian Church, H.I.M. Haile Sellassie I had the Bible translated by Ethiopian scholars into Amharic, printed at his own printing press in Ethiopic and Amharic for distribution to the churches and monasteries. I then thanked the Christian Society for having 100,000 copies of Amharic readers for beginners printed at its own expense for distribution to our forces. I concluded my remarks by soliciting their prayers that the God of Love deliver the Ethiopian people from the spiritual and physical suffering that was afflicting them and that He open the door for the spread of God's Word in Ethiopia.

At the end of the meeting, after Lord Lothian had accompanied him to the lift and taken leave of him, His Majesty turned to me and expressed his pleasure by saying, "You have made Us proud today." After the Italians had been expelled from our country, Ethiopia regained her liberty and the Emperor sat on his throne once again, I had to stay on in London on duty and the Emperor wrote to me in his own hand on June 12, 1941, recalling my remarks on that occasion, and said, "Although I had occasion to know you when we were together in England and though I am not forgetful of the speech you made at the meeting of the friends of Ethiopia when we separated with pride and not embarrassment at hearing one of my countrymen speak on equal footing with other people, the lucid reports you have sent me since I returned to my country have enabled me not only to know you more but also to get both benefit and pleasure out of them. It has therefore become necessary to reveal this to you and to thank you. We are telling you this since We feel it will adversely affect your future work if you are not aware of the estimation We have for you. For the future: Every person who does not know how to take advantage of his opportunities is a loser and not a beneficiary. You should take the utmost care that your character which is in the process of favourable development should not be crippled through unconcern or self-satisfaction."

After I returned to my country, trusting these encouraging words of the Emperor and believing that he would not allow me to come to grief, I served him unstintingly with all the ability at my command in spite of the fact that I had constantly to encounter various trials and foes during the long period of my service in the government. That my confidence was not misplaced will be seen here and there in this document.

In the same way as they betrayed Ethiopia and Albania to Mussolini, the British and French governments in September 1938 sacrificed Czechoslovakia to Hitler at Munich. Due to the intense propaganda the British government was spreading, the British people were exceedingly apprehensive and fearful, and believed that the treachery of its government would truly ensure its peace. When Prime Minister Chamberlain returned from Munich therefore a huge crowd went out to welcome him and assembled in the square in front of Buckingham Palace. He appeared with the King on the balcony of the Palace and declared; "I have brought peace for our time," and the crowd cheered him with delight. I was standing in the crowd listening and watching. I still wonder whether that head of government came to the realization that he was deceiving himself and his people only when Hitler began to invade Poland a year later when he announced over the radio that Britain and Germany were at war! The blind leaders of the great powers who thought nothing of betraying any weak nation, be it African, Asian or European, in order to appease and humour the dictators not to start a war, had to witness a war the like of which had never before been seen and heard in world history, and which brought on them inestimable loss of human life and material destruction. Although the British and French peoples succeeded, after many years of terrible struggle and with the help of America and the Soviet Union, to weaken and defeat their enemy, the war had also weakened and impoverished them to such an extent that their former might and renown have escaped them for good.

Believing that with the start of the Second World War in Europe the fate of the world's peoples would not be the same after the war and that the oppressed peoples would not remain oppressed, we continued to tell those who desired to know as well as those who had no wish to know that our patriots had been stepping up their guerrilla warfare in Ethiopia, that our people had never been subdued by the enemy but that it was ever continuing its struggle. Nine months after the start of the war, in June 1940, we heard the good news we had been expecting with fervent hope. And that was that Mussolini had allied himself with Hitler and declared war on Britain and France on June 10.

It would not be an exaggeration to say that it was considered by every Ethiopian as the day of his/her country's liberation. The great efforts made by the leaders of Britain and France to wean Mussolini away from Hitler by sacrificing weak peoples were frustrated. The British government was compelled to declare that the Fascist government of Italy had become its enemy, and it became one of its tasks to strive to deliver Ethiopia from Mussolini's clutches. There ensued a lot of bloodshed and material destruction. We returned thanks to our Creator, believing that the time was approaching when our country would regain her age-old independence.

As soon as he heard Mussolini's declaration of war, the Emperor Haile Sellassie who lived with his family in the city of Bath, in the west of England, waiting for that day, went to London and, while staying at Paddington Hotel, wrote a letter to Mr. Winston Churchill (later Sir), the new Prime Minister. He stated in the letter that since the Fascist government of Italy, siding with Britain's enemy, had declared that it was the enemy of the British people, he wished to request the assistance of the British government to return to his country as one of the

Allies to fight the common enemy and struggle for the restoration of Ethiopia's independence, and that he be provided with arms and the necessary supplies.

After he stayed in London for about a week awaiting a reply, Mr. Churchill sent him a non-committal letter. Afraid lest time might be wasted in discussion and something unexpected might happen, His Majesty requested Mr. Churchill forcefully to help him to return to his country and join his people. Churchill consented and ordered that the Emperor proceed to the Sudan and that the necessary military preparations be made for him there; and he placed an aircraft at his disposal to fly to the Sudan.

He thus left for the Sudan in secret on June 24, 1940, accompanied by his second son, Prince Makonnen, Ato Lorenzo Taezaz (later Blattengeta), Ato Wolde Giorgis Wolde Yohannes (later Tsehafé-Tizaz) and Mr. George Steer, correspondent of 'The Times' newspaper. He directed me before he left to stay on in London and discharge the functions of a secretary and assist his family.

This was given me in writing and, though my desire was to return to my country and share his fate, I could not refuse his behest to remain in Britain and help him as much as I could from that side. He introduced me to a British army officer as intermediary for communication. This is in part what His Majesty wrote to me concerning my duties on June 19, 1940, as he was preparing to return to Ethiopia: "As the time appointed by God's will for Us to return to Our country and struggle against our enemy has arrived, you are directed to stay at the office in Rosary Gardens and act as secretary for the affairs of Our government. Since the Empress and the Crown Prince will remain here with the family for the time being, you are entrusted to consult with them and assist them in any way you can whenever either of them informs you of what is needful for the family."

Knowing that the Emperor Haile Sellassie would not sit idle after Mussolini had gone to war against Britain and France and wishing to meet and talk to him, British and foreign newsmen began to hunt for him everywhere. After they were assured that he was not at home in Bath, they pestered me by coming or telephoning to know where His Majesty was. I had put them off for a few days, saying he was on holiday and that I could not reveal where he was, when the British government announced that he had returned to Africa and arrived at Wadi Halfa, on the Egyptian-Sudanese border. The matter had been held in such strict secrecy that even the administrators of the Sudan did not know that he was on his way there until he arrived in Alexandria. They were resentful but could not oppose the order from higher authority. So, claiming they had to prepare an accommodation for him, they kept him at Wadi Halfa for a week and made him travel to Khartoum by train. When he arrived there, he was made to stay outside town at a place called 'Sherif Hussain's House.' They told him that no military preparations had been undertaken since his presence there was so sudden, and that he had therefore to wait until preparations were made. He had consequently to stay in Khartoum from the first week in July until January 20, 1941. Since he had gone out fully aware that it was a matter of life and death, he endured with equanimity and patience the vexations and difficulties he had to encounter. He repeatedly urged the British government to expedite the preparations so that he could return to his country and rejoin his people. At the same time, he continued his correspondence with the Ethiopian patriots. He came to an understanding with the British to send some persons to Ethiopia to encourage the patriots and the people, to ascertain and report on the state of guerrilla warfare the patriots were waging and the situation of the Italians. A team was therefore sent through Gojam under the joint leadership of Azazh Kebede (later Dejazmach) and Colonel Daniel Sandford (later Brigadier). The two men worked strenuously until the Emperor entered Ethiopia, touring Gojam to study the situation, and Azazh Kebede reconciling the patriot leaders who had fallen out with one another and coordinating their efforts, forwarding the Emperor's messages and proclamations to the patriot leaders, announcing his imminent arrival, and receiving and transmitting the reports he had received from them.

In the course of the six and a half months that he had to stay in Khartoum, the Emperor met General Wavell, Commander-in-Chief of the British armed forces in the Middle East and Africa, as well as Mr. Anthony Eden (later Sir), who was then Secretary of State for War. He impressed on them strongly that it was in the interests of both Ethiopia and Britain to enable him urgently to return to his country. They assured him they would expedite the preparations, and thus the day came for him to enter Ethiopia. He flew to Omedla, on the Ethiopian-Sudanese border, and crossing the frontier hoisted the Ethiopian flag on January 20, 1941. Accompanied by a battalion of Ethiopian refugees who had been trained in Khartoum and a battalion of Sudanese troops with a few British officers, he travelled to Mount Belaya by truck and sometimes on horseback. The famous war hero, Colonel Orde Wingate (later Major General) was appointed to command the troops that escorted him. The country between Omedla and Belaya being an arid wilderness, it was extremely difficult to cross it. On arriving on the plateau after strenuous effort, the patriots welcomed the Emperor and, defeating the enemy troops he encountered on his way, he entered Debre Marqos on April 6. The British forces occupied Addis Ababa on the same day after beating the Italians in South Eastern Ethiopia.

After the Emperor's departure for Africa, the Second World War raged in Europe and I made it my main task to continually send him reports with my views on the military and political activities in Britain and around the world. I read about events in the newspapers, listened over the radio and discussed them with some friends. I sent him through the Foreign Office long reports related to happenings in every country for three years, until I handed over the work to the new Minister, Blatta Ayele Gabre. His Majesty sent me replies and instructions through the same channel. There were occasional delays in the delivery of some dispatches since they were opened by the British who were trying to know their contents, but none were lost. I had reason to know that one cause for the delay was that they had no one in London at that time that could read and properly translate the documents for them.

Drafting the long reports and writing them out again in the form they were to be sent to His Majesty, there being no Amharic typewriter, weakened my right hand and the horrifying bombs that continuously fell on London day and night for nine months wearied me. So, at the invitation of Christian friends, I travelled to Glasgow by night train in July, 1941, for a few days rest at Kilcreggan. When I woke from sleep on the train, I found my right hand and arm paralysed but felt no pain. I was given electric massage in Glasgow with the help of my friends and I had it continued in London. My tired nerves were gradually reactivated and I could in time move both my hand and arm, and eventually use them again for writing. The effect of the paralysis is still with me, however, and I feel continual tingles in my right hand and arm; a reminder of my life in London.

Since I could not write with my right hand for three months, I had to learn to write with my left hand and thus continue to send my reports to His Majesty. The dispatches contain matters too detailed to include in these reminiscences. But as they have been arranged in chronological order, I trust they will be read one day in conjunction with this document and the Emperor's letters and memorandums.

When I was in London, one of my duties was to solicit the British government to allow the Ethiopians in Britain to return to Africa and eventually to Ethiopia, and to see them off. It was thus made possible for the following persons successively to proceed to the Sudan and to Ethiopia in August 1940, H.H. Crown Prince Asfa Wossen, Major Abye Abebe, Ato Tafarra Worq Kidane Wold, Abba Hanna Jima and Lij Asfaw Kebede; in October 1940, Lij Asrate Kassa and Lij Sirak Herouy; in June 1942, Her Majesty Empress Menen and Princess Tsehai Haile Sellassie with attendants. The Princess Tenagne Worq and her children lived in Bath with a few other Ethiopians.

Moreover, as Ato Aklilou Habte Wold, former Ethiopian Chargé d'Affaires, and a few former government officials and students had informed me that they had fled Paris after the defeat of the French government and the occupation of the city, I requested the friends of Ethiopia to send them financial assistance to enable them to escape to Spain and Portugal, and the British government to help them return to their country. They all returned to Ethiopia in due course.

After seeing off the majority of Ethiopians who were in England I lived all alone in London until it was my turn to go back home. Except for two occasions when I went out of town for a rest, I shared the lot of the people of London and was an eye and ear witness of the horror of bombs that rained not only on the City but also on all of Britain. I watched with admiration the hard life endured by the citizens of London and the discipline and indomitable spirit of the British.

For my part, I placed my whole being in the hands of my Creator and continued my task of preparing detailed reports for the Emperor on the war situation and the havoc inflicted on the City. While the buildings around the house in which I lived were blasted by bombs and many lives were lost, not even a windowpane of my room was broken. I experienced in the situation in which I found myself at that time the truth of the words of the Psalmist which he wrote in Psalm 91:7, "A thousand may fall at your side, ten thousand at your right hand, but it will not come near you." I regained my native land without any mishap or illness; I had the privilege after that of serving my country and people for over 40 years in the Government and the Church; I got married and had four children; I rejoiced to see my grandchildren. What sacrifice can I offer my Creator except praise for all the grace and loving-kindness He vouchsafed me?!

The Emperor arrived in the heartland with much difficulty and defeating the forces of the enemy from Western Gojam to Addis Ababa through the efforts of the patriots and with British help, entered his Capital on May 5, 1941. The inhabitants of Addis Ababa who had been longing to see him, the patriots who had spent the five years of occupation struggling against the enemy in Shoa under the leadership of Ras Abebe Aregai and others, together with the British Commanding General and troops, welcomed him with great joy and respect. The enemy forces in the various districts were defeated and made to surrender, and Ethiopian territory was freed from the ruthless invader. The Ethiopian people were overjoyed once again to find in its midst the Emperor, symbol of its freedom and honour. Ethiopia thus became the first of the victims of brutal aggression to regain its liberty.

In other parts of the world, especially in Europe and North Africa as well as in East Asia, the war was being prosecuted viciously. On this pretext, the British military officers who were in our country, considering Ethiopia not as an ally that had regained its freedom but as occupied enemy territory, set up a provisional military administration and tried to run the country as they wished. The Emperor, insisting that his country was an ally and not occupied enemy territory, rejected the attempt of the British authorities and, five days after his return to Addis Ababa, appointed cabinet ministers by proclamation. Considerable difficulty was experienced however since there were no funds.

Although he considered it essential to acquaint the British government of the oppressive activities of the British military officers in Addis Ababa, the Emperor's difficulties were worsened by the fact that all the means of communication were in the hands of the officers. In the event, he was able to send me, by courtesy of a friend, a memorandum written on August 20, 1941, giving details of the difficulties he had encountered. I translated the bulk of the memorandum into

English as soon as I received it and sent it through a friend to Mr. Eden, the Foreign Secretary. I also prepared a shorter memorandum based on the original and distributed copies to friends of Ethiopia who could make their voices heard. I sent a copy to the Archbishop of Canterbury and requested his assistance. I heard soon after that Mr. Eden had been distressed on reading the document, that he had presented it to the war cabinet where it had been discussed, that a cabinet committee had been formed to look into it, and that Mr. Churchill had sent a telegram to His Majesty. Our friends, who deplored the arbitrary actions of the military officers, took up the matter with the government, asking questions privately and in Parliament, and doing all they could to get the problem solved with justice. The Archbishop of Canterbury informed me that he had written to Mr. Eden at some length, putting before him the main points I had brought to his notice and assured me that Mr. Eden had given and was giving careful consideration to the points I mentioned, and that he (Mr. Eden) hoped that, after the inevitable period of military administration was definitely over, it would be possible to transfer the entire responsibility for administration to the Emperor.

The arrival of the Emperor's memorandum in London made it possible for the matter to be taken out of the hands of the British military officers in Ethiopia and elsewhere in Africa and to be considered on the level of cabinet ministers. It also gave occasion openly to make known the government's political position as regards Ethiopia. His Majesty the King of England, speaking in Parliament on November 12, 1941, said: "I welcome the restoration to his Throne of His Majesty the Emperor of Ethiopia. Thus the first country which fell victim to aggression has been the first to be liberated and re-established."

These words of the King indicated the policy the British government had decided to adopt, viz. that it had accepted the fact that His Majesty the Emperor had reoccupied his Throne and that Ethiopia, the first victim of aggression, had become the first to be freed. After the British government made this declaration to the world by the mouth of its King, the plot set afoot by some British authorities in Africa to make Ethiopia a protectorate fell to the ground, and it became evident that the departure of the British from Ethiopia would be determined only by the war situation.

The officials in the Foreign and War Offices who were masterminding the plot, seeing that the matter had been directly presented to Mr. Eden, that a number of questions had been asked in Parliament and that the cabinet had taken it in hand, were so disappointed that it had been taken out of their hands that Colonel Mackereth, who was in charge of Ethiopian affairs in the Foreign Office, asked me to go and see him. As soon as we met, he asked, "Why did you spread this news around? The British government was not pleased with it." I retorted, "You were mistaken if you had helped the Emperor to return to his country with a view to making Ethiopia your protectorate. It would be good if you realized that it is useless to expect the Ethiopian people to get rid of the domination of one European power to fall under the rule of another European power." He assumed a serious attitude and said that I should not forget it was wartime and that there was such a thing as detention. I replied equally seriously that they could do what they wished, but that I could not be silent while a supposedly friendly government was oppressing my people. I then took leave of him.

Since that official knew that placing me under detention at that time would be heard in next to no time and would expose, not only the military officers in Ethiopia but also the British government, his threat was only meant to express his anger and try to frighten me. It was obvious to us both that it could not be put into effect. An agreement was signed in Addis Ababa after some months and Col. Mackereth invited me to visit him at the Foreign Office. He met me with a smile and congratulated me. I thanked him and, after a brief conversation, we separated with diplomatic smiles!

In this connection, I wish to pay tribute to the memory of one distinguished British citizen, Miss E. Sylvia Pankhurst, whom I remember with admiration and appreciation. Miss Pankhurst championed Ethiopia's cause at a time when virtually the whole world considered its independence irretrievably lost. She pointedly launched her newspaper, 'New Times and Ethiopia News,' on May 9, 1936, the very day Mussolini proclaimed his vaunted Roman Empire. She defended our cause with determination and devotion, placing the plight of our people before the British public and others with cogency. She documented the epic struggle of the Ethiopian patriots and the atrocities inflicted on our defenceless people by the heartless and cowardly invader armed with the most modern weapons of war. Miss Pankhurst rejoiced to witness the liberation of Ethiopia and after the war lived in Addis Ababa until her death in September 1960. She was buried with great honour in Holy Trinity Cathedral.

After the King's remarks in November (1941) concerning the Emperor and Ethiopia had heralded its decision to recognize the independence of Ethiopia, the British government, desiring to reach an agreement with His Majesty, conducted negotiations in Addis Ababa for two months and Mr. Eden announced in the House of Commons on February 3 that a two-year agreement had been signed on January 31, 1942. Under the terms of this agreement, the British government fully recognized the independence of Ethiopia and the prerogatives of the Emperor, and the two governments agreed to exchange diplomatic representatives. It being wartime, a military convention was signed together with the agreement. The British armed forces were given the right to move about freely in Ethiopia due to the war situation. It was made clear that Ethiopia would not be required to pay for the assistance it received during the war. They agreed that the British government would provisionally run the railway, the radio, the telegraph, and telephone services at its own expense. To enable Ethiopia to re-establish its administration, the British government undertook to provide the Ethiopian government with 2.5 million Pounds for the first year and 2 million Pounds for the second year. Moreover, the British government agreed to train freely on modern lines the Ethiopian armed forces. Thus, the Emperor and his assistants found it convenient to set up the framework of the country's administration on a more sound basis before the end of the World War. The Emperor telegraphed President Roosevelt to allow Ethiopia to join the United Nations (UN) and the President informed him in October 1942 that he had accepted the request with pleasure.

With the conclusion of the agreement, I realized that the period I was required to stay in London and 'act as secretary for the affairs of Our government' was at an end, and my longing for my country growing ever more intense, I reminded His Majesty in a memorandum dated March 10, 1942, that it was almost seven years since I had left Ethiopia; that the English climate was debilitating my constitution; that, owing to the change in the situation in Ethiopia, I no longer knew what I was expected to do; and that, due to the difficulty of communication, it was hard to obtain news from Ethiopia. I therefore requested him to send his duly appointed diplomatic representative and allow me to return to my country without delay. He informed me that the new Minister would be sent to London as soon as practicable. Blatta Ayele Gabre was appointed and sent. I was happy when he arrived in London on August 30. Ato Tekle Rorro and Ato Abebe Retta were designated secretaries.

In response to my request to allow me to return to my country, His Majesty wrote me in his own hand on June 12 as follows: "As We wrote you by last mail, you should have returned to your country to meet your relatives and renew your life as soon as the Minister We have appointed to London arrived there. We have not overlooked the fact that you went abroad before Our exile and lived there for many years. In spite of Our awareness of all this, We are also mindful of the fact that the Minister and the others being new for the work, it will be a matter of remorse for Us as well as for you as long as you live, if all that is designed to yield good results goes wrong and becomes fruitless. We have therefore determined that you remain there for the time being, help the others as much as you can to re-establish the work and come back to your country. Let your accustomed participation in Our difficulties consider this as justified." In a letter he wrote me on September 11, 1942, the Emperor said: "You will remain with the Minister for about three months after his arrival. We have provided for you an adequate monthly salary so that you do not suffer administratively while there." (The salary I was paid after the Minister reached London was 125 Pounds a month)!

In a letter I wrote him on September 21 I stated as follows: "I tender my deep thanks for graciously permitting me to return to my country after remaining in London and helping the new officials re-establish the office. It is proper for me to stay here until the Minister and the new Secretary are acquainted with the country and the work. It will weigh heavily on me to leave my countrymen in the lurch, especially those who have been charged with weighty matters of the government and the people and who are strangers in this country in many respects. I shall not have a clear conscience and enjoy the rest and happiness I long for if I leave them and return to Ethiopia under the circumstances. I shall therefore remain here for the time being in accordance with Your Majesty's wish. The weariness I feel of life in this country is due to my physical condition and not my spiritual state. I trust in the gracious Lord to give me the necessary strength as hitherto. I am very grateful for the adequate salary You have ordered for me while I remain here."

I then proceeded with my duty of re-establishing the Legation and assisting the newcomers. As His Majesty had ordered me to look for a building suitable for a legation before the Minister arrived, I looked around and learned that the house in Knightsbridge, N° 6 Princess Gate, which was next to our former Legation and in which the Emperor had stayed when he went into exile, was for rent and fully furnished. I had been negotiating with the persons who wished to rent it and I showed it to the Minister upon his arrival. He thought we should take it on a provisional basis and we rented it for six months beginning on September 25, with the option to extend the rent if desired.

The Minister met the Foreign Secretary, Mr. Eden, on September 15 and presented his Credentials to King George VI on September 17. He then started his diplomatic functions by making courtesy calls on foreign Ambassadors and Ministers. As he often desired that I accompany him on these visits, I went along with him. I took him to some places of interest, such as the art galleries, Madame Tussaud's, and the department stores to introduce him to the City. His knowledge of English was limited, so it was necessary that either Ato Tekle Rorro or I accompany him whenever he went out.

My main task being to familiarize the Secretaries with office work, I used to show them by action how to draft diplomatic notes, answer telephone calls, and receive and see off visitors. It was found that they would need more time to get practised in all this which meant that I had to stay on longer than I had expected. And since they preferred to watch me do things rather than try them themselves, I was hard put to accomplish my task.

Moreover, there appeared an unexpected problem to prevent the two Secretaries from working together harmoniously. In their letters of appointment to work in the Legation, it was stated that Ato Tekle Rorro be First Secretary and Ato Abebe Retta Second Secretary and Counsellor (adviser). It would appear that Ato Abebe Retta was designated Counsellor because, having lived in Britain for a number of years, it was thought he could help the Minister and the First Secretary with advice. In diplomacy, however, the word Counsellor has a special connotation. When a functionary is called Counsellor of Embassy or Legation it means that he is senior in grade to all other secretaries and able to deputize for the Ambassador or Minister. It is therefore not possible for a functionary to be both Second Secretary and Counsellor at the same time. In the circumstances, the two men were seized with a sense of rivalry and clashed with each other daily. It became my lot to try to reconcile them with each other every time they quarrelled, and the Minister was at a loss to find a solution up to the time I left. I heard later that the higher authorities appreciated the problem and transferred Ato Tekle Rorro elsewhere. Ato Abebe Retta was caused to remain there.

Due to this and other reasons, it was not possible for me to return home after three months as determined by the Emperor. Since the Minister pressed me hard to remain longer and as, due to the war, it was not easy to get a berth at will on board ship, I decided to stay for six months and asked the Minister that in the meantime he request the British government to book a berth for me. They made me wait for six more weeks and I therefore remained with the Minister for seven and a half months. As soon as the Foreign Office notified me that a berth had been booked for me, I travelled to Liverpool by train on April 13, 1943, and went on board ship in the course of the following morning. Lady Winifred Barton, wife of the former British Minister to Ethiopia, Sir Sidney Barton, and a medical doctor called Dr. Young boarded the same ship to go to Ethiopia. The ship joined a convoy protected by warships and began its voyage to Africa on April 15. It was originally a cargo boat but had been partly converted after the start of the war to accommodate about a hundred persons, with a dining saloon and a lounge. It thus carried both people and cargo.

When we arrived opposite Gibraltar, about 50 vessels proceeding to North Africa separated from us. And in West Africa, as soon as we arrived off Sierra Leone, the rest of the ships left us. We headed alone for South Africa and after a week arrived in Walvis Bay, a port in South West Africa (now Namibia). As soon as we arrived there, Lady Barton, wishing to gain Addis Ababa quickly, started to cross South Africa to Durban and set off with Dr. Young by train. She pressed me not to be separated from them; but I chose to continue my voyage because I had no desire to leave to chance the baggage I had taken with me. Besides, since I could not escape the various discriminatory laws enacted by the South African government to oppress black people, I felt the result would only be to upset and embarrass her. The pair boarded the train for Durban on May 17 and the vessel I was in left Walvis Bay on May 19 and arrived at Cape Town at noon on May 24. We had heard that the part of the ocean between the two ports was then very dangerous, and that several ships had been sunk by German submarines. Mercifully, our vessel went through safely.

As soon as I arrived in Cape Town, I began to inquire for a vessel that would sail to Aden; and as there was no hotel for Africans, I wondered where I would stay until I found a ship. I had made the acquaintance on board ship of an Anglican cleric, the Rev. Francis Scott, who was extremely affected by the cruelty perpetrated on the black race in South Africa and which we used to discuss often while on board. He was apprehensive that I could not obtain an accommodation and asked me as we were preparing to disembark if I knew where to stop. I told him that, not knowing anybody in that city, I did not know where to go. As soon as we disembarked, he said he would not leave me until I had found somewhere to stay and took quite some time going with me from place to place. He finally telephoned to a Mission called 'Society of St. John the Evangelist' and asked whether there was a room for me. They told him they would welcome me gladly and he took me there and introduced me to the Head of the Mission. He was an elderly man who had lived in South Africa for many years and had a thorough knowledge of the country's politics. He told me many things during the four days I remained there. Since he had been following Ethiopia's plight, he expressed his pleasure that the Emperor had returned to his country and that Ethiopia had regained its freedom.

On arrival in Cape Town, I went to the Transport Office, told them where I intended to go and informed them that before I left London I had been told by the Foreign Office that a telegram would be sent to them to assist me. The man in charge received me well and told me to give him a phone call the next day. When I called he told me to go to the Union Castle Company's office which had been given instructions. I proceeded there at once and paid the fare for a passage to Aden. I was told to return to the vessel in which I had come as it was continuing its voyage to the East. I had my baggage taken to the ship and went on board on May 28.

On the day following our departure from Cape Town, we learned that two ships sailing with us were sunk by submarine and that only four persons were rescued. We arrived at Port Elizabeth on May 30 and had to stop over for five days until the cargo was unloaded and loaded with other cargo. The voyage was continued on June 5 and the vessel arrived the next day at East London where we stayed for a week. We proceeded to Durban on June 13 where we arrived on the following day. As the port was jammed with ships, we had to wait outside for three days. The vessel docked on June 18 and unloaded its cargo. We went ashore to stretch our legs. Since an African like me was not allowed to rest on a bench in the parks, let alone enter a café bar, I could find nowhere to sit even for a short time in any of the towns we stopped at. One read on all the park benches the warning: 'For Europeans Only.' We stayed in Durban until June 22.

About a hundred women and children, mostly Greeks, came on board at Durban. They had fled to South Africa two years earlier when it was feared that the Axis Forces would invade Egypt and now desired to return there. The daughter of the former Shah of Iran, Reza Shah Pahlavi, Princess Ashraf, also came on board with two attendants. When the Western powers and the Soviet Union asked the Shah to consent to the use of his country and to intern the Germans who were in Iran, he insisted that his government was neutral and refused to accede to their request. Thereupon, they invaded Iran and he had to abdicate, leave his throne to his son, Mohammed Reza Pahlavi, and go into exile in South Africa. Princess Ashraf was returning from a visit to her parents. One of the attendants was a diplomat (Etesham), and the ship's officers asked me to let him sleep in my cabin. I readily agreed and we had opportunity to discuss a number of things until we arrived at Mombassa. Our views were so similar on many matters that we had become friends when he disembarked a week later.

The vessel stopped at Mombassa harbour for ten days and proceeded to Aden on July 11. As it was feared there would be danger of submarine attacks between Mombassa and Aden, all the male passengers were asked to stand sentry, and every man kept watch for three hours in 24. Fortunately, the ship arrived at Aden on July 17 without mishap. I disembarked on July 18 and went to a hotel. I visited the governor's office the following day and requested assistance to cross over to Jibuti. A booking was made for me on a small vessel and I went on board towards evening on July 22 arriving at Jibuti the next day before noon. I visited the town officials on July 24 and requested their good offices to obtain a booking on the train. I boarded the train with their help on July 27 and was welcomed at Dire Dawa railway station at 6 p.m. by Ato Makonnen Gebre Heywot, the governor of the town, who informed me that he had been commanded by His Majesty to receive me and give me accommodation. He also told me that the Emperor had arrived in Harar the same day. On the following day, Ato Makonnen placed a car at my disposal by order of the Emperor, and I went up to Harar in the afternoon where I was happy to meet His Majesty and members of the Imperial Family.

I returned to Dire Dawa on July 29 for the night, and took the train for Addis Ababa early next day where I arrived on July 31. Tsehafé-Tizaz Wolde Giorgis and Ato Tafarra Worq were at the station to welcome me and took me to the Imperial Hotel. I praised the Lord with all my heart for His gracious protection from every trial and danger and for enabling me to regain my country and people after eight years and one month. For one week, many friends who had heard of my arrival came to the hotel to bid me welcome, and I visited several in their homes. The Emperor returned from Harar on August 6 and we had several long conversations on the following days.

His Majesty told me he would give me no work until my return from a visit to my mother; that he would give orders to provide me with everything I needed to travel to Wollega; and, aware that it would be practically impossible for me to find somewhere to live in Addis Ababa, he told me early in August that he would see to it that a house was found for me. To keep me busy in the meantime, he ordered me to translate from English into Amharic a book on etiquette, (i.e. on rules for polite behaviour in good society).

A small lorry driven by a palace chauffeur, full of supplies and a sleeping kit was placed at my disposal and I was given 500 Birr. I set off on September 15, 1943 for Boji Choqorsa where my parents lived. I spent the night at Ambo and, travelling all day the next day, I stopped at Sibu Siré for the night and arrived at Naqamté on September 17. The then Governor General of Wollega, Col. Abye Abebe (later Lt. Gen.) was in Addis Ababa and directed that I stay in his residence at Naqamté. I spent a few days there meeting relatives and friends. It being the rainy season, I saw that the track was not suitable for wheeled traffic beyond Naqamté and bought a mule. Leaving the chauffeur and the lorry behind, I borrowed a packhorse from the local military commander (Col. Waqjira Serda), and continued my journey on September 21. I arrived at Boji Choqorsa at 3 p.m. on September 25, and my parents and relatives welcomed me with great joy. My other relatives and friends who had heard of my home-coming came from far and near to meet me and congratulate my parents until the day I started to return to Addis Ababa. I left Boji for Addis Ababa on October 7 and arrived at Naqamté on October 12. I spent four days there and continued my journey on October 17 arriving in Addis Ababa on October 20. I went to the Palace on the following day to pay my respects and report my return. I continued the translation of the book in the office I had been given in the Palace.

Since I returned from London to Addis Ababa two years after the enemy had been expelled and as all the dwelling houses built by the Italians had been occupied, it was no easy matter to get a house. As a result, I had to stay in the hotel for 15 months. By command of His Majesty, Abba Hanna spent several months looking for a house for me. He found a house occupied by an officer, near Mesfin Harar street (Gojam road). The officer was given another house and the Emperor summoned me one day to tell me that, since I liked quiet, a suitable house had been found for me and Abba Hanna would show it to me. He took me to see it the next day and, sure enough, I liked it as it was off the main street. I reported this to His Majesty and requested him to order the construction of domestic quarters. This was soon done and I was relieved of the tedium of hotel life by moving in October, 1944, to the house I was given.

As I indicated in Part 1 above, the Eritrean Qes Gebre Statios and his wife as well as the Oromo Ato Daniel Lulu and his wife had been sent by the Missionaries of the SEM in Asmara to carry the Gospel of Salvation to Boji in Wollega. As a result, my father and mother had heard the Gospel while still young and had believed and were baptized. My parents had a strong desire that I should follow in their footsteps, believe in Christ and get an education. Therefore, as soon as I was able to read while still very young, I was made to read daily and repeatedly, both in Oromo and Amharic, under the direction of my teacher, Ato Gebre Yesus Tesfai, and the strict supervision of my father, the Bible Story readers of the period, printed in Asmara in both languages. It was beyond my mental capacity at that time to understand all the stories I read, but they were impressed on my mind and spirit. I did not have the opportunity to go to a Mission school and obtain the Evangelical education that my father had desired and strove for, but the meaning of the Bible stories gradually became clearer to me as my mind developed with instruction at the Tafari Makonnen School. I read regularly the Oromo Bible which was in the library and this led to the steady growth of my faith in the Lord Jesus and my love for Him. And as I caused my pupils at the Asbe Tafari School to read the Bible Story readers, the stories became much clearer to me as I tried to explain them to the class. Moreover, the presence of some English Missionaries (Bible Churchmen's Missionary Society) at Asbe Tafari made it possible for me to meet with them in prayer on Sundays and to take turns to speak on a text of Scripture.

After I went to London, I resorted to Westminster Chapel, the Congregational Church, on Sundays to attend Divine service, and on Friday evenings I went to the Bible studies given in the same Church by Dr. George Campbell Morgan, the famous Bible exegete. I got to know a group of fervently Evangelical British Christians and used to attend their conferences at Honour Oak in South East London. I also went twice to their 'Conference and Rest Centre' at Kilcreggan in Scotland to spend some time with them for physical rest and spiritual refreshment.

On my return to Ethiopia in July 1943, after almost eight years in Britain, grown in faith and stronger in my spiritual life by God's grace, I joined the congregation known as the Addis Ababa Mekane Yesus and led by the pastor, Qes Badima Yalew, and Ato Emmanuel Gabre Sellassie (later Dr.). It had been started in Addis Ababa by the Swedish Missionaries. After the Swedes were expelled by the Fascist invaders, a Waldensian cleric was put in charge of the congregation. On the expulsion of the Italians in their turn, the leadership of the congregation passed to Ethiopians. The leaders gave me their 'right hands of fellowship' and I soon became one of the elders, eventually being elected president of the congregation on several occasions. I was president in 1949 when I was sent to India, and I laid the foundation stone of the new Church building before my departure. On returning home after ten years of diplomatic service, I resumed my membership of the congregation and continued to serve in it. The story will follow later in these *Reminiscences*.

SIX

Addis Ababa: Director General
1943 - 1947

On November 8, 1943, the Emperor summoned me to his office and, in the presence of Tsehafé-Tizaz Wolde Giorgis, spoke about the service I had rendered and thanked me. He then proceeded to tell me that he wished that I should work as Director General in the Ministry of Foreign Affairs. I bowed and left his presence. I had heard that upon my return from Britain, some friends of Ethiopia who had been observing what I had done in London had written to the Emperor to indicate that they thought it would be good if he assigned me to work in the Ministry of Foreign Affairs. It appeared that he was also inclined that way. Although due to his exile in Britain he was in a position to know me during the four years he lived there and, as he revealed to me after his return to Ethiopia, I had the privilege of being better known to him from the reports I used to send him, many of his counsellors did not know me and had no occasion to read my reports. So they regarded me as a stranger suddenly arrived on the scene. Even though the few persons who were in exile with the Emperor knew both me and my work, they were averse to my being too near the Sovereign. And since I had no relatives or supporters in Court circles, priority was given to the man who had relatives and supporters and he was therefore appointed Vice Minister of Foreign Affairs around the middle of October.

It was my judgment that the Emperor was advised to tell me of this appointment himself in the belief that I would not refuse his direct command. (It must be stated here that this procedure had been practised on me several times in the course of the period of my service in the government). Just to indicate that I was not happy with the appointment, I continued the translation of the book in my palace office for ten days and went to the Foreign Ministry and asked the Vice Minister to give me an office. Ato Aklilou showed me a room in which there was neither table nor chair. I told him to request the Emperor to order that a table and a chair be provided. He did that and a table with a chair with one arm broken was supplied on loan! On November 22, I began the administrative work assigned to the Director General. I cleared the correspondence that had accumulated for various reasons and, while answering daily correspondence and discharging other routine office work, completed the translation of the book on etiquette and presented it to His Majesty. It was printed in 1945.

I was admitted to Ras Desta Hospital on December 24 to have a nasal operation to get rid of a growth in both nostrils occasioned by the polluted London air during my long stay in England. A hasty Italian doctor overdid the operation and removed the whole membrane. As it cannot be replaced to enable the dust breathed in with the air to be easily removed, this has become a lifelong nuisance.

In the course of the following months, I had no business to take me before the Emperor and I usually appeared before him just to pay my respects. I took one day some letters which had arrived by diplomatic bag, and the Emperor said, "You are not the Amanuel We formerly knew; We had hoped you would help Us with the work." - I rejoined, "Since You have given me a superior, I am doing all that he assigns to me. I have nothing to bring me before Your Majesty." - He said, "No, you have become slack." - I replied, "My superior can testify that I am not slack; I carry out all the work he gives me to do as much as I am able." I then bowed and withdrew. My remarks were meant to convey the idea that he would not have placed someone over me if he had desired that I should serve him directly and that therefore I had no wish to bypass my superior. I had the impression that the point was well taken.

Within a week of this conversation, I was summoned to the Palace on May 17 and led to a place where several people were waiting to be given appointments. When it was my turn, I was called and told by the Tsehafé-Tizaz that it was His Imperial Majesty's good pleasure and command that I be appointed Director General of Education and Fine Arts, and we paid our respects to the Emperor and returned to our various homes. After a few days, I went to see the Emperor on some matters and he said, "An important task has been given you." - I replied, "Yes, Your Majesty, I am already feeling it's weight;" and we parted smiling.

In course of time, I heard from an unimpeachable source that when the Emperor told his assembled counsellors that he had intended to appoint me to the Ministry of Education, some demurred and one of them said, "Where do we know him?" His Majesty was not amused with the remark and retorted, "Where were you? We know him if you don't." (He was alluding to the time when I was with him in Britain. That gentleman was nowhere there). But the consensus being that I should not be named Vice Minister at once but tested as Director General, the Emperor said, "It is immaterial to him whether he is called Vice Minister or not, but since we have assumed the position of Minister, no one will be placed over him; and he is capable to administer the teachers and the students." The matter was then closed.

As I was starting my new assignment, the following statement was published in 'Addis Zemen' newspaper on May 20, 1944, to introduce me to the public: "An Important Appointment: Ato Amanuel Abraham has been appointed Director General of the Ministry of Education and Fine Arts. Ato Amanuel Abraham is a native of Wollega. He was educated and acquired much knowledge at the Tafari Makonnen School. He later went to England on duty and lived there serving his country loyally. He remained there after the liberation of our country and, on his return, was appointed Director General of Foreign Affairs. He has now been appointed Director General of the Ministry of Education and Fine Arts."

On the Emperor's return from exile, the person chosen to be Minister of Education was one of those considered young at that time. Though he did not lack education his character left much to be desired. As a result, he was a target of much complaint and considered to be unworthy to be a minister. Consequently, it was decided in council that no person was to be appointed to the office of minister until his performance and his character had been tested. This led to the creation of a lesser title called Vice Minister, and it became imperative that all those responsible for the positions the former chief officials (grandees) could not fill should be called Vice Ministers. Thus, the persons appointed to head the Ministries of Foreign Affairs, Finance, Public Works and Public Health had to work as Vice Ministers for a considerable number of years. But, since it was the judgment of the counsellors that the title of Vice Minister was too much for me, I was restricted to that of Director General in spite of the fact that I had replaced both the former Minister and the Director General of Education. This caused me no harm however but opened the door widely for my work during the period I was in the Ministry of Education. I was free from attending the Council of Ministers; I went to the Council only once or twice a year to present the budget of the Ministry which was sent to the Council after my Minister (The Emperor) had scrutinized and approved it. Within a few months of my transfer to the Ministry, I was given the salary of a Vice Minister (800 Birr) through His Majesty's considerate initiative. (A Vice Minister was enraged at this and urged several Directors General to remonstrate with His Majesty. The response was a reprimand).

During my three-year tenure of the Ministry of Education, the budget was increased many times over. It was 800,000 Birr when I moved to the Ministry in 1944. It was doubled in 1945. It was increased to 7 million Birr in 1946, and to 10 million Birr in 1947. When I presented a 10 million Birr budget, the Ministers tried to compel me to reduce it to 7 million Birr as in the previous year. I brought my predicament to His Majesty's attention. Since he had been following the expansion of the work closely, the Emperor directed me to write to Bitwoded Makonnen Endalkachew (Prime Minister) as follows: "His Imperial Majesty has commanded me not to reduce the budget by one cent." Accordingly, I wrote him the order and sent a copy to the Ministry of Finance. The budget had to be passed at 10 million Birr. On seeing this, one of those who had expressed opposition to my being named Vice Minister showed his jealousy and anger by remarking, "How is it that he, a Director General, is granted so much when to us, the Ministers, only one or two million Birr is allotted?" When this complaint reached the ears of the Emperor, the response was, "One should work as he does."

It will not be an exaggeration to state that the authority I wielded in connection with my work in those three years was not less, but was even greater, than any Minister's. This was quite evident from the activities and from the considerable number of schools that were built. The Emperor who was my Minister never placed any obstacle before me. On the contrary, he urged me on and gave me or caused to be given me whatever I requested as necessary for the work whenever I made a request.

For my part, having come early in life to the belief that education was the prime remedy for the development of the Ethiopian people and having begun life as a teacher, even though I was then no longer able to teach in the classroom, I was very happy to have had the good fortune of helping thousands of pupils and a sizable number of teachers, of building schools and dormitories, and of providing various kinds of school supplies. And I was diligent in my work.

Many youngsters from Addis Ababa and the countryside used to stand day by day at the gate of the Ministry and outside my house to plead with me to admit them to school since they were orphans or because their parents could not afford to pay school fees. Some even tried to fall under my car as soon as they saw me, exclaiming, "Teach us or kill us." I admitted many hundred as free boarders. Recalling that I obtained admission to school with strenuous effort and tears, I personally used to collect from the street two or three boys at a time and place them in school. I have witnessed with joy that many of the youngsters pursued their studies to the end and became graduates and self-supporting. They were moreover able to render service to the succeeding generation as medical practitioners, teachers and professors, bank executives, lawyers and judges, military and police officers and administrators.

I was pressing on with the execution of this most important task when, ten months after my transfer to the Ministry of Education, invitations were sent to the members of the UN by the four great powers, (USA, Britain, USSR and China) to attend a conference to write the Charter of the UN. Ethiopia being a member, the Emperor selected a seven-member delegation and, deciding I should be a member, summoned me to tell me that, even though the educational work was important, he desired to follow in as much detail as possible the preparation of the Charter and, as he had found my previous reports to be useful, he wished me to go to San Francisco, where it was intended to write the Charter, and send him detailed reports on the proceedings. I left for America on March 30, 1945 with the other members of the delegation.

It is a long-standing practice, when a high official is absent from his office for a limited period, to charge another high official to look after his department in an acting capacity. Accordingly, the Vice Minister of Finance was directed to run the Ministry of Education until my return. Having completed my assignment, I came back after four months. While all the other acting heads relinquished to the incumbents the posts they had been holding, the Vice Minister of Finance conceived the notion that he had been appointed to the Ministry of Education and was not acting head and, since he was a Vice Minister while Amanuel was a Director General, he was his superior. When he realized that his claim was unacceptable to me and that His Majesty frowned on it, he stopped going to the Ministry of Education and, calling the Chief Secretary to the Ministry of Finance, proceeded to give him orders. He also went around to the Addis Ababa schools and gave in person directives to the headmasters and the employees. But the directives and orders had to come to me for execution and I countermanded them. He concluded that his pretensions could not last and gave up after about six months. Nevertheless, he never stopped trying to hamper my work in the Ministry of Education and in the other departments in which I served until both of us left government service in 1974. Even though his opposition, not motivated by the national interest but impelled by personal feelings did no damage to my work, it brought on me a sense of sadness.

In addition to the increase in the number of schools in and around Addis

Ababa, many more were built from Dessie to Goré, to Dangila, to Bonga, to Chencha and to Negelle in Borena. The schools started by the government and the people soon after the enemy was expelled (e.g. in Tigrai and in Wollega) were extended. Young people flocked to the schools in large numbers. My companion during the frequent visits to the provinces was the English architect, Mr. Selby Clewer. He was most helpful in the execution of the school building programme.

Although I was happy that modern education was fast spreading, I was apprehensive that tuition in Ethiopian history as well as religious and cultural instruction was practically non-existent. As a result, the youth who frequented the schools were being brought up strangers to the religious traditions of Ethiopia. I therefore wrote once or twice to the Archbishop of the Ethiopian Orthodox Church and the Prime Minister urging them to designate trustworthy persons to give them instruction. But it appeared that they were more intent on spreading tales about me on every occasion than give thought to this serious matter, and they did nothing before I left the Ministry. Who will ever be able to assess the harm brought about by this indifference?

The more modern education took root and spread, the more fear and anxiety disturbed the hearts of the chief officials (grandees) and the authorities of the day. Because of this, slanders and rumours were put about within a year of my transfer to the Ministry of Education. On the pretence that they were concerned for the welfare of the country, several persons presented complaints to the Emperor orally and in writing. Since he was following my activities closely, the Emperor gave appropriate replies to all their complaints. Nonplussed, they resorted to a stratagem. They spread a report in 1947, which said, "Amanuel educates only Gallas." They got together and went to the Emperor to accuse me of this. In reality, they were indirectly accusing His Majesty since he was the Minister of Education. While their aim was to halt the spread of education, it was an intrigue to get me discredited and dismissed on the ostensible grounds that large numbers of Gallas were going to school and to make the so-called Amharas feel neglected and offended.

The Emperor realized this and was vexed. He therefore went one day, without my knowledge, to a school which had the largest number of students and directed the headmaster to make a list of the pupils in ethnic groups and present it to him. He did that and out of a total of 991 pupils, 701 said they were Amharas. The rest came from the various ethnic groups. The Emperor showed me this and, after telling me why he had asked for it, commanded me to get him in ethnic groups a list of all the pupils in the Addis Ababa schools. I presented a complete list in a few days. In April, 1947, 4,795 students attended the Addis Ababa schools. Of those, 3,055 said they were Amharas and the remaining 1,740 were from the other ethnic groups. Of these, 583 said they were Gallas. On the basis of this, it was obvious that the great majority of the students of that period were not Gallas but Amharas.

The Emperor who had been angered by the tale that was set about ordered that the list be printed in the newspapers. It appeared to me that there was no point in having it publicized and that it was not suited to his government's policy. I therefore expressed the view that it should not be published. He said it was a command and I gave the list to the official who was in charge of the Ministry of Information telling him that it was His Majesty's command that it be printed in the newspapers. On hearing this, my accusers were alarmed and, realizing that it could be dangerous if it were widely known that it was the Amharas rather than the Gallas who were being educated in large numbers, prostrated themselves before the Emperor and implored him not to allow the list to be published. The Emperor reprimanded them severely and reversed the order. The list was never published.

Even though they were covered with shame due to their malice, my slanderers persisted in getting me out of the Ministry of Education. Changing their tactics, they went to the most highly placed persons who had great influence on the Emperor, persuaded and caused them apprehension that education was spreading too fast and endangering both the State and the Church and should be slowed up (my being non-Orthodox was one of the main reasons for accusation). They then got them to plead with His Majesty to remove me from the Ministry of Education. The Emperor was under such strong pressure that he reluctantly consented to my being replaced by another person, it being a political necessity to humour many people rather than one individual.

On June 6, 1947, I was summoned to the Palace together with people who were to be appointed to office, and the Minister of the Pen gave me before witnesses the following message from His Majesty the Emperor: "We are exceedingly pleased with your work; wait until we give you another important work." Almost two years had to elapse while I awaited the work!!

During the period I was in the Ministry of Education, my relatives and friends used to urge me from time to time to get married. They gave me names of young girls in Addis Ababa and the countryside who had some education. At the suggestion of my relatives, I was drawn at first to a young woman whose age I estimated to be about 20. Her parents were Eritreans but she was born and brought up in Addis Ababa. Apart from the fact that she had a pleasing appearance, I was impelled to approach her because her parents were Evangelical Christians which led me to believe that our faith would be similar and lead to a lasting married life. I had also understood that she had attended the Mission and Empress Menen Schools.

Considering all this, I wrote her a letter early in 1945 and sent it by a friend. I visited her several times at her parents' home with their permission and asked her if she would agree to be my life partner. Before anything tangible could be achieved, however, I had to go to the USA in March 1945 to attend the UN Conference on International Organization which was to write the Charter of the UN. On my return home after four months, I learned that she had been engaged to marry some other person. As a result, my first attempt at matrimony was aborted.

Persuaded by my relatives and friends, I decided to have a second try at marriage and, in the Autumn of 1945, sent a proposal to a girl whose parents were living in Naqamté, Wollega, while she was attending school in Addis Ababa. She indicated that she was willing to marry me. Wishing to find out whether her parents would give their consent, I requested two of my friends to travel to Naqamté, explain the matter and ask them to give their approval. They neither approved nor disapproved but said they would consult with their relatives. My friends were disappointed and told me on return that they did not feel it would be successful. As soon as she knew her parents' intentions, the young woman sent word to say that she was still willing to marry me, even if they did not consent. Judging that marriage without the approval of parents and relatives was bound to be attended with ill-feeling and would not last, I informed her that I could not marry her. Thus ended my second try to enter married life.

One of my friends who had been to Wollega took the matter of finding me a young woman to marry seriously. He obtained information about a girl called Elleni Alemayehu whose parents were from Gonder and Gojam. She was born in Addis Ababa on December 25, 1926 and brought up in Naqamté, trained in traditional housecraft, and she was then attending the Empress Menen School. He went to the house where she lived on a pretext early in May 1946, and watched her at work. He was pleased with her personality and deftness and concluded she would suit me. He then advised me to watch her and meet her by appointment. I took his advice and watched her from a distance while she walked to school. We then met at a friend's house and I proposed to her. Having been acquainted with the matter beforehand, she consented without hesitation. We then met from time to time, got to know more of each other, and were engaged in July, 1946. A marriage contract was signed on January 5 in the presence of the Elders of the Addis Ababa Mekane Yesus Church, and the wedding took place on January 12, 1947.

Our God blessed our marriage and we had two daughters, Ruth and Sarah, and two sons, Amenti and Dawit. Our union was thus cemented and our married life rendered a success. Our children grew up, became assiduous in their studies and graduated from University. We are exceedingly happy that they have thus become self-sufficient and are able to serve their country and community. Moreover, we rejoice to have been enabled to see our grandchildren.

In the summer of 1947, while considering the membership of the delegation that was to be sent to the second UN General Assembly, the Emperor decided to send me to New York as one of the delegates, and directed me to send him, as usual, detailed reports on the deliberations of the Assembly. The delegation left on September 11 and arrived in New York on the 16th. In addition to being assigned to sit on one of the UN committees, I sent successive reports to His Majesty.

My wife was feeling unwell after the birth of our eldest child, Ruth. But, in duty bound, I had to depart and leave them on their own. Since I had no regular work, the Ministry of Education had been instructed to pay my salary and to give me the monthly petrol allowance. Accordingly, I drew my salary from the Ministry until the end of Nehasé (August). Believing this would be continued and having no savings, I could not give much to my wife. She had to be admitted to hospital after I left for America and asked the new Director General of the Ministry of Education to give her petrol. He refused. He also declined to give her my salary for Meskerem (September). As a result, my wife who was ill in childbed and my infant daughter Ruth were left to starve. The Emperor was displeased when he heard they were in distress and asked the Director General why this happened. He reported that my salary was not included in the Ministry's budget and therefore he could give them nothing. His Majesty then summoned the Chief Treasurer and ordered him to pay my salary every month from the Contingency Fund. Thus, I drew my salary from the Treasury until I was given regular work.

SEVEN

New Delhi: Minister Plenipotentiary 1949 - 1952

After I left the Ministry of Education in 1947, I became one of those waiting for an appointment ('sitting at the king's gate') in accordance with the custom of the land. I had to go to the Palace about twice a week to do obeisance to His Majesty. Having discharged this duty, I would stop for a short time to chat with some of the people standing around and return home to read and perform whatever needed to be done for the day. Months succeeded weeks while I waited to be given work. I thought after some time, rather than just restrict myself to reading; I should translate a book from English into Amharic as a reminder of the months I spent without work. Aware that Ethiopia was beginning to have diplomatic relations with some governments at that time and knowing that the persons who were being sent for this purpose were strangers to diplomatic practice, I thought it would be useful if I translated a book entitled, 'Diplomacy,' written by the British politician and diplomatist, Sir Harold Nicolson. One day, when I was at the Palace to pay my respects, the Emperor called me to his presence and asked what I was doing. I replied I was waiting for an appointment. He smiled and agreed that was the case; he then inquired whether I was not fond of reading.

I said that had become my main occupation and I had started to translate a small book on diplomacy. He smiled and said he wished to see what I had translated. I presented it to him the following day. He called me after a few days and told me that he was pleased to read the chapters I had given him and that he would order someone with a good handwriting to copy the script for me, and forthwith ordered one of the clerks from the Ministry of the Pen to do the job. I would give him a chapter as soon as I had translated it and he would copy it beautifully and return it to me. I would then present it to His Majesty who read it and gave it back to me. As soon as I completed the translation, I gave him the whole book and requested him to have it printed. He accepted the idea and had it published after a long delay, in 1964.

Even though I continued to draw my salary and retained the service car which I had used in the Ministry of Education, I was depressed in spirit due to the fact that many months had passed and my hope to be given a job was long delayed. Towards the end of the second year, I happened to talk to His Majesty when I went to pay my respects and I said that, since I was used to working, my spirit was getting low, would he give me some work? He said it was he who had sustained loss and I should exercise patience.

From flying rumours which used to come my way from time to time, I understood that whenever the Emperor mentioned a job which he thought would be suitable for me, his counsellors would advance reasons to oppose it. Their complaint against me was that I was aloof and unsociable. But their main purpose was to strive to prevent me from being appointed to any Ministry and to keep me outside their council. It was rumoured at one time that I was going to be Vice Minister of the Ministry of Health. It was just a rumour. Hoping to get me removed from Addis Ababa, counsel was given that I should go to the USSR as a diplomatic representative. Recalling that my right hand had been disabled in England, the Emperor cut the suggestion short by saying he would not send me to Russia to become a paralytic. It would appear that a recommendation followed that I should be sent to China since it was beginning to be reckoned as one of the great powers, and it was therefore necessary to have relations with Chiang Kai-shek's government. Their hope was dashed because it was becoming evident that Mao Zedong would overthrow Chiang's government and set up a communist regime. They were thus appointing and dismissing me behind the scenes when, towards the end of my second year of unemployment, it was mooted, since India had regained its independence, it was time to establish diplomatic relations with its government. When the question came up as to whom to send, the various counsellors presented lists of their friends and protégés. The Emperor however determined that I should be sent and on March 11, 1949, I was summoned to the Palace and told by the Minister of the Pen, in the presence of two other Ministers, that I had been appointed His Imperial Majesty's Envoy Extraordinary and Minister Plenipotentiary to India.

After a few days, the Emperor called me to his office and told me that he was pleased with my patience. I saw clearly then that one reason why I was made to sit idle all that time was because it was desired to make it a time of temptation for me! Obviously, there were people who had been hopefully waiting for me to say something offensive or do something wrong out of desperation. There were also false friends who came to my house and ate with me so as to spy my way of living. I realized that the Emperor deigned to reveal his pleasure with my patience because my slanderers could find no grounds to accuse me.

May the Name of the Lord my God be praised for ever who delivered me from their snare!

On May 13, 1949 two months after I had been ordered to go to India, I boarded an Ethiopian Airlines 'plane for New Delhi with my wife and two infants, Ruth and Sarah who was born on October 9, 1948. We arrived in Bombay in the evening of the following day. We stayed in Bombay until May 19 waiting for the person who had been appointed First Secretary. Since he did not arrive, we left on that day by an Air India airliner and arrived at the New Delhi airport at noon. We were welcomed by the Chief of Protocol of the Indian Foreign Ministry and Sardar Sant Singh, who was the leader of the Indian Goodwill Mission to Ethiopia and was later the first Envoy Extraordinary and Minister Plenipotentiary to Ethiopia. We were conducted to the Imperial Hotel. It was very difficult in those days to get a residence in New Delhi and all the Diplomatic Corps had to queue for houses. We had therefore to stay at the hotel for almost two years. As it was the hot season, we felt the heat as if we were standing by a furnace. It was oppressive for us who had just arrived from the Ethiopian highlands.

On May 24, I visited Pandit Jawaharlal Nehru, Prime Minister and Foreign Minister of India, and gave him a copy of my Credentials as well as His Majesty's greetings. I later ascertained the date for the presentation of my Letters of Credence to the Governor General, Mr. Chakravarti Rajagopalachari, and was informed that it would be on May 30. The Chief of Protocol came at noon that day and conducted me in a government car, and I presented my Credentials to the Governor General in the great hall of Government House. He then led me to his office and after chatting for a quarter of an hour we went to the reception hall where members of his family and invited guests were gathered; I was introduced to them. My wife had arrived earlier and made their acquaintance. We then moved to the dining room and lunch was served. We took leave after lunch and returned to the hotel. In the late afternoon of June 7, I placed a wreath on the site (Rajghat) where Mahatma Ghandi was cremated.

After the presentation of my Letters of Credence, I visited a few Indian Ministers by appointment arranged by the Chief of Protocol. I wrote to the diplomatic representatives in New Delhi that I had presented my Credentials and then visited them successively. Ato Wolde Endeshaw, who had been designated First Secretary, was working in our Cairo Legation and I had been told that he would proceed straight to India. But since he was delayed more than I had expected, I was left without an assistant for several weeks. It was wearisome, with the heat, to act as secretary and minister, drafting and typing letters meant for the Indian Foreign Ministry and the Diplomatic Corps, answering telephone calls and receiving visitors. At diplomatic receptions, I was at a loss what to answer when asked whether I had no secretaries. I had to point out all this repeatedly to the Emperor and the Foreign Ministry before the Secretary was sent!

At the time when I was designated to go to India as a diplomatic representative, there was a lot of discussion about the South African government's desire to expel the Indians who had gone to South Africa many years previously for various reasons and multiplied there. Being non-Whites, they were found to be unsuitable for the racist policy of its government. The government of India strongly opposed this move and periodically presented the matter to the UN for debate. The Emperor and the Ethiopian government who had been following the case over a period, were considering at a high level whether it would be conducive to Ethiopia's lasting benefit or not if a section of the Indians to be deported from South Africa were to be allowed to settle in some part of Ethiopia with a view to helping the development of the country by contributing their wealth and their knowledge, and by mingling their blood with that of the Ethiopians. Seeing that I was going to India, it would appear that it occurred to them that they should know what I had to say on the matter. The Emperor summoned me one day and directed me to present my views. Believing that settling Indians in Ethiopia could be compared to contracting a chronic ulcer which succeeding generations of Ethiopians could not get rid of easily, I submitted to His Majesty on March 18, 1949, a memorandum opposing the idea and detailing the reasons. I feel the memorandum should figure in these *Reminiscences* in full and it reads as follows:

"It is widely reported that the white South African government desires to expel people of Indian descent, who had settled in South Africa more than a century ago for reasons of work and trade and who have increased in number, because as non-whites they are found not to be suited to its policy. The United Nations Organization ever since its inception has been debating the matter at its General Assembly at the instance of the government of India. It is expected that it will again be raised when the General Assembly reconvenes at the beginning of next month. The South African government however maintains that this is an internal matter and not for the United Nations. It has even hinted that if the United Nations presses the matter too much, it may leave the Organization. It appears that, seen from any angle, this is a very difficult problem.

"In response to the question as to whether it would be in Ethiopia's lasting interest, in the event the white South African government were to succeed in putting its policy into effect and the Indians were to be deported, for Your Majesty's government to allow a section of these Indians to come to Ethiopia and help in its development by contributing their wealth and knowledge and by mingling their blood with Ethiopian blood, I submit my humble opinion to Your Majesty as follows. History records that many of the Indians, especially those living in Northern and North Western India, are more akin to Europeans than to any other people, in spite of the fact that the Indian people is composed of many ethnic groups with various shades of colour, black being the most conspicuous and nearest to the complexion of the Ethiopian people. These are the Indo-Europeans which include all Europeans, Persians and North Indians. Moreover, the South African Indians who are to come to Ethiopia and settle among us are the type who have lived on African soil for over a century and who have seemingly developed an inner feeling that all Africans are to be despised like the African people among whom they have lived and who are treated even worse than themselves and have the least standard of knowledge. There is no doubt that the injury and death recently inflicted on Indians in Durban, though obviously instigated by the Europeans, was motivated by the African sense of being despised by the Indians and was meant to be a revenge. It may be argued in reply to this that, although Ethiopians are Africans they cannot be placed on the same level as the pagans who live in South and East Africa and that the Indians also cannot lump us together with them. This may be true, but in the final analysis a person or a people can only command respect and consideration when seen by other persons or peoples to possess knowledge, technical know-how and power. One wonders what the percentage of Ethiopians would be who can be given this estimation. In respect of trade, Indians control as middlemen the economies of the various countries from South Africa, through East Africa, to Addis Ababa so that the less educated and unfortunate African, who is unable to compete with them, hates them passionately. The South African government oppresses the Indians found in its territory by virtue of its power and authority. It would seem to me that the ruling classes in East Africa would likewise oppress Indians living within their borders when they attain the status and power now enjoyed by South Africa. This would be similar to what has been and is still being meted out to Jews all over the world.

"The United States of America was able to assimilate the various ethnic groups that went there from Europe and other countries from time to time, and impose its culture and language upon them because it is a government whose foundation is immovable and which is developed and self-sufficient. Given its natural fertility and resources, Ethiopia is able to accommodate three or four times more people than its present inhabitants. And if education were widespread and its people able to appreciate who they are, the status in which they find themselves and work with one mind, it could be for its size the equal of such relatively rich countries as Argentina, Mexico and Turkey, and earn the respect and goodwill of the governments of the world. The question then arises whether in these circumstances the arrival of Indians in Ethiopia would help it attain this position or not. In my humble opinion, it will be of no help considering the present situation of Ethiopia and India. The following are the main reasons:

"a) Difference of race and continent, as indicated above; b) Difference in religion and outlook; c) Since the modern resurrection of India has created a new hope in the heart of the Indian race and brought to mind India's ancient history, they are encouraged to strive for a higher state of development in modern civilization, if not in the religious sphere, and therefore consider it a disgrace to change their nationality; d) As has been seen even in Ethiopia to some extent and in the East African countries on a large scale, Indians have not been seen to be considerate in economic matters to the countries and peoples among whom they live. They have lived a miserly life and carried away to their native land the wealth and the property they have acquired; their men do not marry the women of their adopted country, nor do their women marry the men.

"I shall analyse these four points a little further. a) Indians have been racially varied from antiquity. There are people among them who have the fairest and darkest complexions. It is said that those who live in Kashmir in the north are as fair as the Swedes; and those who live in the south have skins hardly less dark than that of the blackest Africans. If the government of Britain had not welded them together and ruled them with a strong arm for about a century and a half, India would perhaps be divided, not in two nations, as was done two years ago, but into twenty. And an Indian who moves from one part of India to another part would be considered a stranger since he differs in language, custom, often in religion, and in the social status called caste. In the same way as British rule, a sense of oppression and the spread of education have made India one people, the English language has enabled and still enables Indians to understand one another. It has been evident that Indians who live scattered in a number of countries are careful not to mix in marriage, custom and religion with the peoples among which they live. For instance, many Indians have lived for many years in neighbouring countries, like Burma, Ceylon and Malaya, but they have not mixed with the inhabitants of those countries. The problem was not so evident when those countries were ruled like India by Britain. But, since Burma and Ceylon have regained their independence, a difficult situation has emerged. I understand that, during the past two years, the government of Burma has expressed the desire to expropriate from the Indians land that they have long held and restore it to the Burmese people. For its part, the government of India is strongly contending that this should not be done, and the two governments are trying to find a basis for agreement.

"Similarly, many Indians have lived in Ceylon for many generations, but now that Ceylon is independent it has obliged the Indians either to become citizens of Ceylon or go back to India. Many of them, being landowners and wealthy and being aware that they cannot find a better life in India, have become Ceylonese citizens. It is my view however that they have done this to overcome the current difficulties and not with the intention of abandoning their country of which they are proud and their ancient history.

"In these circumstances, would Indians who are not able to be assimilated with the peoples of Burma and Ceylon to whom they are similar by race, custom and religion, if they were to come over to Africa and live in Ethiopia, renounce their race, custom, citizenship and religion, mix with the Ethiopian people and become genuine citizens of Ethiopia? I doubt it.

"b) It seems to me that the Indian and Ethiopian peoples are far apart in religion and outlook. Both being Eastern peoples, it may be possible to say that they are strong in spiritual matters. The spirituality of the Indian people however, though it may appear erroneous in our Christian eyes, is so deep that I fear the Ethiopian people have neither the desire nor the ability to understand it in the present circumstances. And since, rightly or wrongly, the Indians have their own special views, I do not think they would easily embrace Christianity.

"This being the case and in view of the serious apprehension caused by the Muslim religion which is with us it would be extremely risky for our Christian faith and ultimately for our unity if the more subtle Hindu religion were to take root in our midst. And it will be most dangerous for Ethiopia's entity and integrity, if the majority of the Indians who are to settle here happen to be Muslims from the faction which is more knowledgeable than their Ethiopian brothers in the faith and which was instrumental in partitioning India itself.

"c) The fact that India has been able, with epic struggle, to establish a government led by its nationals, after it had lost its statehood for almost two centuries and ruled by foreigners with an iron hand, has been a matter of great joy and pride for the Indian race. It has also become a source of great satisfaction and hope for the whole black race. Under these circumstances, it seems to me that however stressed, the Indians will be reluctant to accept an invitation to forsake their country and nation and come over to help Ethiopia by changing their nationality, contributing their wealth and knowledge and blending their blood with ours. In my view, the Indians will be happy to come and live in Ethiopia in large numbers if they are allowed to live here without changing their nationality and religion and without mingling their blood, and if they are permitted to go back to their native land and return to Ethiopia at will. This way of living however will neither benefit the Ethiopian people and government nor enhance Ethiopia's prestige. On the contrary, it is to be feared that, if the educational level of the Ethiopians proves to be inferior to that of the Indians coming here, they will humiliate and impoverish us by dominating our economic life and hiring the labour of our people cheaply. This situation will hardly be any better than the lot planned for us by Italy.

"d) Since, as indicated above, a larger proportion of the resources left over by the Europeans in South Africa as well as in East Africa are in the hands of the Indians, the native Africans are in a state of dire poverty. They would not be averse from slaughtering and despoiling the Indians if they had a convenient opportunity. I hear that it is easier for an African to have a grudge against an Indian than against a European. The reason being that he is in constant touch with the Indian merchant and petty trader in everything that affects his daily life. The African buys from the Indian essentials from a needle to the clothes he wears. Moreover, any office work not done by a European and anything that needs a modicum of knowledge is performed by the Indian. For his part, the Indian despises the African, and this cannot be conducive to mutual love.

"This being the case in other parts of Africa, what will the Indians do if they are granted the rights of an Ethiopian in this country? Since the Ethiopians are conducting the government, they may be restrained for the time being from becoming dominant in the government offices. But as they will be citizens and will have the rights and freedoms of citizens, the opportunity for appointment to office and other privileges will of necessity be open to them after a while. I do not think we shall be able to compete with them in our present condition. It is my view that the white South Africans wish to expel them precisely because they are afraid of their competition. If they are a cause for so much apprehension in South Africa where all the whites go to school, how much more apprehension should they cause in Ethiopia where only three youngsters out of a thousand attend school?

"Your Majesty, my detailed views indicated above seem to be based on fear. But my fear is not that the Ethiopian will be inferior to any foreigner if he is given equal rights and an equal education. Because knowledge and skills are seen to be paramount in this age more than anything else, the Ethiopian people, thanks to Your Majesty's foresight, have begun to master modern knowledge and skills. Nevertheless, if even five thousand foreigners with advanced modern knowledge were allowed to settle in our country, I doubt whether there would be found five thousand Ethiopians able to compete with them and do what they could do. It would therefore be necessary that this mentally immature people should be protected from harm and the State from instability, in the same way as commerce and industry are protected by tariff. It is necessary, nevertheless, in my humble opinion to be careful that this protection is not merely negative. By this is meant that the people should not only be protected from external danger in a short-sighted manner, but that it should be equipped as soon as possible with a weapon that will enable it to stand on its own and compete with others. That weapon is, as was realized by Your Majesty many years ago, the spread of education and knowledge among Your people. Only that will enable Ethiopia to be a truly free nation and government in all respects and to command the esteem and respect of its peers. It is therefore my fervent hope that the good foundation for the expansion of education which Your Majesty has laid will be further extended and developed so that the Ethiopian people will attain equality with the other nations with all possible speed."

The South African government did not carry out its plan to expel the Indians from its country. And on March 18, 1950, the Emperor wrote me as follows on the matter of settling Indians in Ethiopia: "The memorandum you wrote when we were thinking of allowing Indians to enter our country in large numbers and increase our population has been considered and, seeing that your views are good, it has been decided to postpone the entry here of many Indians."

Nevertheless, on March 30, 1951, almost two years after I went to India, the Emperor wrote me as follows: "We are raising with you for a second time about the Indians in Africa because it has been suggested, through the intermediary of Prince Ali Khan, that a select number of Muslim Indians enter Ethiopia, and not only the Muslims but the followers of Hinduism who are willing to engage in farming and livestock raising should also come and settle in Ethiopia and be granted Ethiopian nationality after a limited period. You are to pursue the matter unofficially with the Indian authorities and ascertain their views because we are considering receiving a few select Indians."

I sent His Majesty a memorandum on April 17, 1951 in which I referred to the memorandum I had presented to him before my departure for India and reported what I had observed in the course of my sojourn in India for about two years, namely, that the Indians who lived in the neighbouring countries, rather than being a means of friendship and mutual benefit between India and its neighbours, had become a cause of friction in their relations. The memorandum is as follows:

"Your Majesty, I have received Your Majesty's instructions dated March 30 that I should discuss with the Indian authorities about a suggestion, presented through the intermediary of Prince Ali Khan, that a select number of Muslim Indians in Africa enter Ethiopia and that not only the Muslims but a select number of Hindus who are willing to engage in farming and livestock raising also go and settle in Ethiopia, and that they be granted Ethiopian nationality after a limited period had passed. I hope to present soon the views of the authorities to Your Majesty. But before I do this I would like to know whether Ethiopia will only receive the Indians who are in Africa or whether Indians wishing to go from India are equally welcome.

"Since I had presented to Your Majesty a memorandum dated March 18, 1949, detailing as much as I could, my opinion that a great deal of harm could ensue if in the present condition of Ethiopia many Indians were to settle in our country,

I shall not repeat it here. But, I may make bold to report to Your Majesty on this occasion that, from reading over the memorandum I wrote in Addis Ababa over two years ago and from my residence in this country since, I have come to realize more than ever before that, not only the Indians living in South Africa but those in neighbouring Asian countries, such as Ceylon, Burma and Malaya have been unwilling to be assimilated into the peoples among which they live and have therefore brought a great deal of problems on the government of India and the neighbouring governments, and that their presence in those countries appears to poison their good relations rather than serve as a source of friendship and mutual benefit.

"For instance, there are a million Indians in Ceylon the ancestors of many of whom settled there several generations ago. Since Ceylon regained its independence, its government has enacted in its constitution that all Indians living in the country had to accept Ceylonese citizenship, that if they were unwilling to do that, they had to be deprived of the rights of nationals, and that no more Indians were to be allowed to immigrate to Ceylon in large numbers. A few of the Indians have accepted Ceylonese nationality in compliance with the measures set out in the constitution, but the majority did not wish to renounce their Indian nationality and at the same time have desired to continue to benefit from their stay in Ceylon.

"Although the Indian leaders have urged them to accept the nationality of the country in which they live, the people do not appear to have complied. The Indian and Ceylonese governments are therefore at a loss at what to do. Still they are endeavouring to save their friendly relations from deteriorating and periodically affirm the difficult nature of the problem. While not acute as yet, it is obvious to all that there are similar problems in Burma and Malaya. It is reported that there are about 600,000 Indian nationals in Burma.

"The law passed by the Malan government in South Africa against Africans and all people of colour, under the guise of racial difference, is extremely distressing, but that government has used the stratagem because the governing party has been white for several centuries and has ruled the blacks as it saw fit. If the matter is considered in depth, however, it will be found that the main reason why the South African government is determined to oppress and humiliate the non-white sections of humanity within its borders is to prevent them from gaining parity with the whites. Similarly, even though it is said that the United States is ill-using and oppressing the blacks due to racial differences, the real reason why the two sides are at odds with each other is because the whites do not wish to relinquish their dominant position and because they fear they may not be able to hire black labour cheaply if the blacks achieve equality, and they feel their living standard may depreciate in consequence. The real reason why the government of Ceylon, which is not white, is determined to deny the rights of the citizen and expel from its territory those Indians who refuse to accept its nationality is because it fears their competition and realizes that, if non-national Indians increase in number, they will be a danger not only to its economic life but also to its political independence.

"This state of affairs which is apparently a struggle between white and black is one and the same with the struggle which was widespread before the theory and practice of socialism were widely diffused and which produced the French and Russian revolutions which are landmarks of history. It is a struggle man has engaged in ever since he was created, viz. to assert his economic and political freedom and to be safe from the oppression of the mighty.

"In these circumstances, it is my belief that, if the Imperial government carries out what is now under consideration, it will be leaving a legacy of serious conflict and an obstacle to succeeding generations of Ethiopians. It will also become a source of ill-feeling, as seen in India's neighbouring countries, with the government of India which it is hoped will be a friend and an ally in times of difficulty. I beg Your Majesty to believe that I am writing thus only to express my sentiments as an Ethiopian and my duty as a subject, and not in any way from lack of deference or from a feeling of animosity to Indians. It will be beneficial to keep in mind that the Indians, whom the South African government is now striving to expel from its territory or to deny the status of human beings, were taken to Africa by the authorities of that country who were appointed at different times before Malan and who short-sightedly concerned themselves only with temporary benefits and did not consider the consequences that might ensue."

In the event, I was very happy that the matter of settling Indians in Ethiopia was not raised after I submitted this memorandum to the Emperor and that I returned to my native land without discussing it with the Indian authorities. Believing that these two memorandums helped to save our country from serious economic and political blunder, I offer praise to the Most High God.

It has given me no pleasure to note that the words I recorded in April 1951 had been justified by the time I began to write these *Reminiscences* in April 1985, and to watch a section of the Indian people, the Tamils, whose forebears had settled in Ceylon several generations previously, take up arms against Ceylon (now Sri Lanka) and shed the blood of its people, seeking to establish its own government on Sri Lankan soil.

In view of this, I trust that the gratitude of succeeding generations of Ethiopians will be due to the Emperor when it comes to be known that His Majesty, taking heed of my warning, had decided not to allow Indians to settle in Ethiopia in large numbers as was mooted at that time.

During my tour of duty in India, I presented many reports to the Emperor on the internal administration of India, on its political, economic and social problems as well as on the situations in countries neighbouring India, and on the friendly or hostile relations between them and India. In addition, I was ordered twice to attend the UN General Assembly in New York (1949 and 1950) and to visit Tehran and Jakarta on diplomatic missions. I hope that the reports and the letters I received from His Majesty will someday be read together with these *Reminiscences*.

As it had been planned that attempts should be made, when the UN General Assembly met in New York in September, 1949 to obtain the necessary votes on Ethiopia's demand for the return of Eritrea to Ethiopia, the Emperor sent me two letters addressed to the Governor General of India and to the Emperor (Shah) of Iran with instructions to present the letters and explain the position of the Imperial government in line with the instructions. Accordingly, I went to Government House on September 1, 1949 to deliver the Emperor's letter to the Governor General, to explain the matter in detail and to request that the Government of India should not withdraw its support. The Governor General remarked that he saw no reason why India should withdraw its support, but advised that I should discuss the matter with the Secretary General of the Foreign Ministry. I therefore visited the Secretary General on September 5 and told him that I had placed the matter before the Governor General with the hope that India would continue in its stand that Italy should not return to Africa and that he had told me to meet with and remind him of this and answer any questions. The Secretary General said the fundamental principle on which India stood when the question was raised at the General Assembly was that the former Italian colonies should obtain independence and that if it was found that they were not ready for independence they should be administered under the strict supervision of the UN. He then added that India's position had not changed, and since India knew what it meant to be oppressed by a foreign power, it did not wish any people to be administered by a foreign government. I stated that Ethiopia's position was identical but added that the Eritrean case was different and that it was well-known that, when two years previously the representatives of the four Great Powers were sent to ascertain the views of the peoples of the former Italian colonies, the majority of the Eritrean population had opted to be reunited with Ethiopia; and since historically, racially and culturally it is related to Ethiopia and could not be viable economically, the welfare of the Eritrean people could only be assured if it rejoined the Ethiopian people. I then assured him that the Ethiopian government was soliciting the support of the government of India only due to this fact and not from any desire for territorial expansion. The Secretary General affirmed before we parted that India had no wish that the fundamental principle on which it stood should be shaken, but that they would determine their stand as soon as the leader of their delegation had reported on the views of the various governments.

After this, I left for Iran to deliver the Emperor's letter and photograph to the Shah and urge the government of Iran to continue to lend its support for us at the UN. I arrived in Tehran on September 11, 1949. Next day, I went to the Iranian Foreign Ministry, met the Minister and gave him a copy of the Emperor's letter. We had a discussion about the ancient histories and relations of our two countries and I explained that the main reason for my visit to Tehran was to inform them of the views of the Emperor and government of Ethiopia on Eritrea and to request that the Iranian government continue to give us its support. The Minister told me that he would request an audience for me with the Shah and accompany me. I thanked him and returned to the hotel. I was informed that the Shah would receive me in audience on September 15 at 10:30 a.m. and went to the Palace with the Minister. I delivered my message and thanked His Majesty for the support his government afforded us on the Eritrean question at the UN General Assembly. I then stated that the main purpose of my mission to His Majesty was to solicit their continued support when the Assembly met later that month. Even if there was nothing the Shah told me concerning the object of my mission, the Foreign Minister informed me that he would give instructions to the Iranian delegation before they left for New York on the basis of my letter to him, elaborating the purpose of my visit which he had asked me to write. He also told me he would cause reporters to see me as he would like that my visit to their country should be publicized in the newspapers, and he added he would be glad if I explained that our friendship was from antiquity and clarified the purpose of my visit. I felt gratified to think that this was an indication that the Shah and his government had determined to maintain their previous stand to support Ethiopia.

Since the Minister of the Pen had written on August 18 to inform me that I had been ordered to go to Lake Success as a delegate to the UN General Assembly, I boarded an aircraft on September 16 to get to New York as quickly as possible. I spent the night in Beirut and arrived in Cairo the following day; but I had to stop there for three days waiting for an aircraft. I got on board an airliner on September 20 and arrived in New York the next day.

The committee work assigned to me was to attend to items presented to the Trusteeship Committee, also called the Fourth Committee. The items considered by the Committee that year concerned the territories in Africa and the Pacific which were formerly German and Japanese colonies but were administered by Britain, the USA, Belgium, Australia and New Zealand under UN supervision. The committee's function was to urge that those territories were given adequate education and other necessary things as soon as possible to enable them to be independent. The committee discharged this task by sending representatives annually to study the situation and then give what it considered to be useful advice to the administering powers. In addition, the Committee had to examine, as set out in the Charter, the reports submitted by the administering governments on the stages reached by the territories in the economic, social and educational fields, and to indicate how the peoples living in those territories could be more benefited.

During the discussions on these matters, I supported the delegates of the governments who were striving for the rights of weak peoples in what I believed to be in their best interests. On one item, however, I could be of no assistance, and that was on the territory called South West Africa (now Namibia) which was administered by the South African government. This territory had been taken away from Germany after the First World War and given by the League of Nations to South Africa to administer as a Mandate. Since the League became defunct, the UN, after the Second World War, determined that the former territories be administered under trusteeship and entered into agreements with the administering governments. Most of the governments complied and made agreements with the UN. The South African government, however, was unwilling to comply, refused to present reports on the mandated territory and declared its intention to incorporate it into its own country. Many governments were therefore denouncing the South African government for its intransigent attitude and demanding that it sign the trusteeship agreement. All the while, I was unable to sit on the Committee because the South African government was one of those elected that year to find out the wishes of the Eritrean population, and it was feared that, if we joined the other governments in criticizing it for its intransigence, it might turn upon us and damage our cause. I stayed in New York for almost three months in this way and left by air on December 7, returning to New Delhi on December 12, 1949.

After a brief interval, a telegram arrived from the Foreign Ministry on December 25 that I should proceed to Batavia (Jakarta) to attend as the Emperor's representative the inauguration ceremony of the Indonesian Republic due to take place on December 27. Realizing that the date of the ceremony was very near and that I had to leave the same day, I made inquires of the earliest flights and set out to obtain Dutch and Thai visas. As it was a Sunday as well as Christmas Day, it was not an easy task to track down the diplomatic officials. Nevertheless, the Dutch Ambassador was kind enough to find the personnel and get me a visa. He also informed the authorities in Batavia the date of my arrival there. The Thai Minister also helped me to obtain a visa for his country. As regards the flights, I learned that there was an aircraft flying to Calcutta that night and that a Dutch aircraft was passing via Calcutta on the morning of December 26. I booked seats on both and began my flight at 11 p.m. on December 25. I arrived in Calcutta at 7 a.m. (Dec. 26). I forthwith caught the Dutch 'plane which touched down at Bangkok after a straight flight of six hours. As it had been decided that both the passengers and the crew should have a rest, we were taken to a hotel by bus. After some rest, a guide was given us and we visited the city. We stayed at the hotel until 3 a.m. and, resuming our flight, arrived in Singapore after four hours. We continued our flight after an hour and arrived at Batavia airport at 12:30 p.m. after a flight of two hours. The adviser of the Indonesian Foreign Ministry (an Indonesian) welcomed me and conducted me to the Hotel Des Indes. He then informed me that an escort and a car had been placed at my disposal and that the ceremony would start at 5 p.m. that afternoon. I was glad I arrived in time.

I received an invitation to be present at 5 p.m. at the ceremony of handing over power to the Indonesian Republic by the government of the Netherlands and went to the Palace at 4:30 p.m. At 5 p.m. sharp, the Dutch Chief Representative and the Indonesian Deputy Prime Minister and Defence Minister entered the Hall and all present stood up. The Dutch Queen's Representative made a speech of goodwill. The Deputy Prime Minister spoke reciprocating his goodwill and both signed the instrument of transfer of power. During the same hour, Queen Juliana of the Netherlands was transferring the instrument of power in Amsterdam to Dr. Hatta, the Indonesian Prime Minister. As soon as the signing ceremony was over, the Queen's voice was heard in the Hall over the radio. At the end of the Queen's speech, all in the Hall went out and stood in the square in front of the Palace. The Dutch flag on the Palace was lowered and the Indonesian flag was raised in its place. The Queen's Representative then proceeded to the airport to return straight to the Netherlands. The various government representatives and the other persons present congratulated the Deputy Prime Minister by handshakes and returned to their various places.

December 28 was the day on which Dr. Soekarno, President of the Republic of Indonesia, was returning from Jog Jakarta to the Capital, Batavia. Large crowds of the city's residents assembled at the airport, in the streets and in the Palace grounds awaiting his arrival. The representatives of the foreign governments had been invited to the Palace to welcome the President and they went from 11 a.m. onwards to await his arrival on the Palace verandah. When the President arrived at 12 noon, the people surrounded and welcomed him with shouts and applause. He gave a radio address to the nation as soon as he entered the Palace, calling on the people to be strong in work, in struggle and in protecting the unity of the country. He then went into a room where the foreign representatives greeted him one by one and returned to their places.

It had been announced that the President would receive the foreign representatives at 8 p.m. in the evening. I wrote a letter expressing the good wishes of the Emperor, of his government and of the Ethiopian people and presented it to the President when I went to the Palace. We had a conversation in the course of which he asked me several questions about Ethiopia. I then presented my best wishes again and took leave of him. I left by air at 11 a.m. on December 30 and arrived in Calcutta in the course of the night. I returned to New Delhi by another aircraft.

As the time approached for my wife to be delivered of a child and since our hotel life was not suitable for someone in childbed, and especially since she was unwell due to the Delhi heat of the previous year, I was apprehensive lest something untoward might happen to her during childbirth in the following hot season. She therefore went back to Ethiopia in March to give birth and stay at home for a while. A son was born on April 20, 1950 and we named him Amenti.

I was busy with my diplomatic activities after my return from Indonesia when a telegram arrived on July 29 from the Foreign Ministry stating that I had to go to Lake Success, New York, as soon as I received it. Lake Success was the place in New York City which was then used as the temporary headquarters by the Secretariat and General Assembly of the UN. Even though it was the Emperor's wish that I should attend the Assembly regularly, I always felt depressed because the leader of the delegation who was the then Foreign Minister was not happy about it and at times did things designed to offend me. I therefore thought it was proper to acquaint His Majesty with the fact that I was finding it too onerous to go to the General Assembly and sit around for three months at a time, and sent him a memorandum dated August 1 which read thus in part:

"1. When we meet in New York coming from various places, the leader of the delegation assigns us to one or two committees. But since no one tells us what we are supposed to do and how we should go about it, we are embarrassed every time we sit on the committee in the name of Ethiopia. Weeks and months pass without us opening our mouths and expressing our views for fear we might act contrary to the policy of our government, and the business is dealt with by others.

"2. Although the Eritrean question has been swaying the whole Ethiopian race ever since it was presented to the General Assembly of the United Nations, we the Ethiopians who are Your delegates to the Assembly know nothing about the matter except what we read in the newspapers and what we hear read like any other person by one of us before the Assembly. This depresses our spirit greatly.

"3. In spite of the fact that the daily allowance granted each delegate while he stays in New York is adequate enough, he is placed under stress by having to sign for the food he consumes and by being given very little by way of pocket money. I therefore make bold to make a humble plea to Your Majesty that Your delegates may be given the allowances due to them while in New York and at least be spared worrying about money."

The Emperor replied to my memorandum on August 15 as follows: "We have received your letter concerning your instructions to go to Lake Success and the difficulties you face there. It is helpful that you have brought it to Our notice and written so candidly. It would appear that there should be no difficulty in discharging your duties properly in the committees to which you are assigned if upon arrival in New York you would get together and consult on matters with which you are not familiar, and be briefed by Our Foreign Minister on the policy of Our government. If an additional delegate is required and you may have to go in September, you will send us details of the difficulties you may have to encounter then as well as the previous ones, we shall consider them and whatever is necessary will be done. As regards your pocket money, you are aware that we are not in a position to emulate the other governments due to our financial difficulties. On the matter of sharing what has been granted, you can consult together as indicated above."

Seeing that I had reported clearly that consultation had not been possible, I was mystified by His Majesty's reply. I was under the impression, however, that my memorandum had been effective at least concerning our allowance because when I was in New York at the next General Assembly, each delegate was given what was said to be his daily allowance instead of just being asked to sign for what he had consumed. However, this did not improve but worsened the Foreign Minister's feelings for me. As an indication of this, he called me one morning towards the end of the first half of the Assembly sessions to tell me that he had a mind to assign someone else to my committee and asked me to be his assistant. I felt he did that thinking he was slighting me and told him that it was his right to place anyone he pleased on the committee, but that I would not be anybody's assistant. I then affirmed that if he insisted, I would send a telegram to the Emperor and return to India. We did not meet or talk after this, except once or twice, until the end of the Assembly sessions when we returned to our respective places.

A second telegram arrived from the Foreign Ministry on September 1 that I had to go to the UN General Assembly. I stayed in New York from September 15 to December 7, 1950 and returned to New Delhi. The General Assembly decided on December 2 that Eritrea be federated with Ethiopia. Even though it was not done to the full satisfaction of the Emperor and the Ethiopian government, I thought it was gratifying enough and sent a letter on December 4 to congratulate His Majesty before I left New York. I expressed my views as follows: "Although it is evident that the inclusion of Eritrea with Ethiopia is a joyful occasion, it is no secret that it is also a time of trial and testing. It is certain that the governments of the world will, more than ever before, follow the workings of Your government closely. But it is my fervent prayer that the Lord God, who in former years had given You the strength, the patience and the wisdom to deliver Your people from many tribulations and woes, and from the jaws of death and lead it a considerable way on the path of enlightenment, will grant You divine wisdom and endurance to enable You to bear the additional heavy burden You have now to shoulder."

His Majesty replied by a letter dated December 26 and said: "We have received the letter you wrote concerning the inclusion of Eritrea with Ethiopia. Apart from your good wishes, what you have reminded Us of the past and for the future is helpful and your views are useful. As regards the United Nations, We consider the democratic process to be of enduring benefit and there will be no reason for distancing ourselves from mutual assistance. You have heard that we have declared Our assistance in the Korean War. When you state of your share in the rejoicing about Eritrea, We are not oblivious of the fact that the endeavours of Our servants in this matter has been contributory in enabling Us to bring it about."

On my return to New Delhi, I sent a memorandum to the Emperor on January 1, 1951 reminding him of what I had written earlier concerning the difficulties encountered by the delegates in New York and concentrating on my own difficulties. I wrote thus in part: "I deeply regret to make bold to bring to Your Majesty's notice that my presence at the Assembly had hardly helped to advance Your Majesty's business, and that it had not benefited Your servant but caused me heartache and stress of spirit. It can hardly be said that Your delegates have given any assistance except watch, like any other observer, the activities of the delegates of other governments. The reason is that, when we arrived in New York from wherever we had been, we had no notion as to what we should or should not do, there being no spirit of comradeship among us, called 'team work' by the English...The Assembly adjourned without our meeting even once in the course of the three months we were there. Far from helping in the solution of the problems of other countries, we knew nothing about our own problems; and since it would appear that it was not desired that some of us should know them, our lot has been depression and humiliation...If it is not possible or convenient for Ethiopia to present many matters to the world Assembly in its present condition, it will not be necessary to send many delegates to sit on the various committees, and seemingly no one will blame it. It seems to me that it is sufficient to send four or five persons to New York in order to meet our obligations as a member nation. It would be of help in several ways if about two of those sent annually had never attended the General Assembly. I take the liberty to place all this before Your Majesty because, excepting the San Francisco Conference, this is the third time that I have been sent to New York as one of Your delegates and, from my observation year after year of the work of Your delegates, my conscience has not been at ease, wondering whether we have discharged our duty to Your Majesty and our country, even though we may have derived personal gain. I beg Your Majesty's forgiveness if I have stated anything from ignorance.

"I believe Your Majesty has been sending me to the Assembly of the United Nations in the expectation that I might be of assistance to You in Your efforts for the benefit of Your country, Ethiopia, and in order that I might develop my knowledge and experience in following the activities of the United Nations and in time render better service to Your Majesty and my country. However, on the basis of what I had presented in my memorandum of last July and what

I have tried to state above, and because some of Your delegates with whom I was supposed to work have attempted to keep from me matters on which we were expected to cooperate and have tried to give me offence on some minor matters, and also because one of them has gone to the extent of affronting me in full assembly, I have come to the conclusion that I have not been able to be of use to Your Majesty in the task I was sent to perform. That we are guilty of deception in giving the impression of service from afar has disturbed my conscience and killed my joy. I therefore humbly request Your Majesty to relieve me in Your wisdom from attending that Assembly."

His Majesty on January 11 wrote as follows in reply to my memorandum: "We have read your personal memorandum on matters for which you had been sent to the United Nations Organization. We were very surprised that there was misunderstanding between you in the detailed performance of the work. We are pleased however that you have stated so frankly the truth as well as your views on matters with which you were entrusted. It is a testimony to your sentiments as an Ethiopian and Our servant. In any case we shall discuss it when you come after you have had your medical treatment."

We had no discussion on the matter when I returned to Ethiopia in mid-September 1951. And even if we had a discussion, the ideas and views I had advanced in my memorandums were so clear that, for my part, I could have added nothing. I had not heard whether the Emperor raised the matter with the Foreign Minister, but I was glad that he accepted my plea and that my travels to the UN were discontinued for good.

As stated in Part 5 of these *Reminiscences*, drafting and copying by hand long reports during the period of my sojourn in London and the hail of bombs on the City for many months had such a debilitating effect on my constitution that, at the invitation of Christian friends to go to Scotland and rest for two weeks, I travelled to Glasgow, by night train. On waking from sleep, I found my right arm and hand paralysed. I began at once to have electric massage, with the help of my friends. I continued the treatment on my return to London and was eventually able to use them again.

Nevertheless, I had a constant tingling effect, and my hand and fingers swelled whenever I wrote with them for a long time. Since I was writing long reports to His Majesty while in India, the pain increased. I learned on inquiry that there was a noted surgeon in Bombay and I went to consult him in January, 1951. He advised an operation on my right shoulder across the collarbone. He operated and found a short extra artery which pressed on the main artery carrying blood to the hand and the fingers. A muscle pressed in turn on the extra artery. He removed both and I left hospital as soon as the operation healed. I stayed at the hotel until the surgeon discharged me when I returned to New Delhi. My hand and fingers no longer swelled in writing but there is a constant tingling from my finger tips to the right side of my spinal column. It extends to my right toes in cold weather. I often wake up at night due to numbness and pins and pricks in my right arm and side. I had several times had medical examinations abroad, but the doctors were not able to find out the cause of pain. The pain has been with me ever since 1951 and I feel certain it will stay with me to the end of my days. Even though this is the state of my right hand, I am very glad that it does not interfere with my main occupation, writing, and I praise my God for that!

I have indicated above that it was very difficult in those days to obtain a residence in New Delhi. The diplomatic representatives had to wait in a queue as it were for a long time. After staying in a hotel for two years waiting for my turn, the government showed me a house in 1951 which I thought was adequate for our legation and rented it. The building was renovated and it took three months to get the house ready and office furniture made. I moved our residence and office to the house and after a brief stay there went to Kashmir with my family and the Secretary, to escape the heat of New Delhi. We stayed in a Srinagar hotel for about three months.

My wife was unable to get used to the Indian climate and was losing weight, and as the time was approaching for her to give birth to our fourth child, she went back to Ethiopia for a rest. I accompanied her as far as Karachi and she returned home in mid-July. I received instructions in August to return to my country with my family and I arrived in Addis Ababa with my children on September 15, 1951. This marked the end of my mission to India.

When I arrived in Addis Ababa, relatives and friends came to our house to bid us welcome home as was the custom. I was at the Palace in late afternoon to pay my respects to the Emperor when there came a man who had known me from my boyhood days and who was then working in the Ministry of the Pen. He was visiting me under the guise of a friend welcoming me home. He left information with my wife which it was not easy to say whether it was meant to be good news or bad. The news was that we were not to remain here long and that in fact we were to be sent to Cairo! She told him that it was all right since she had heard that the Egyptian heat was not worse than the Indian. When I returned home she said that an appointment was ready for me. It transpired that the high official who sent that gentleman to break this news to me was under acute apprehension due to the fact that whenever he was reprimanded my name was mentioned as a possible substitute for him. He must have also heard of the misunderstanding in New York between the Foreign Minister and myself. (It should be noted here that the Foreign Minister had been his protégé since 1943). It was evident to me that they had been making strenuous efforts to see that I did not live in my own country.

The Emperor summoned me to his office early in October and gave me a book to translate, entitled, 'The Government of Britain' by Wilfred Harrison. A copyist with a good handwriting (Ato Tibebe Sellassie Kassahun) was assigned from the Ministry of Education to copy each chapter as I completed translating it. I finished the translation in five months and presented the last chapter on February 28, 1952.

My wife gave birth to our second son on October 24, 1951, and we named him Dawit. I was distressed because my wife became seriously ill after the child was born. By God's grace, she recovered and left hospital after three months. I was also greatly concerned because the infant had a harelip and a cleft palate. His upper lip was slit up to the nose on the right side so that he could not suckle his mother's breast or be bottle-fed. Twelve days after he was born, Dr. Anderson of the Empress Zauditu Memorial Hospital made a preliminary operation to mend the lip so that he could be bottle-fed. I found that the cleft palate could not be treated in Ethiopia for lack of a plastic surgeon. I requested Dr. Anderson to make inquiries for an experienced surgeon and he was able to ascertain that there lived in Paris a famous plastic surgeon (Dr. Jacques Récamier) in Paris. He corresponded with him and the surgeon advised that if it were desired that the child's defect should have to be made good properly, he would have to be taken to Paris by February (1952) for treatment before his bones were set. Having no means, I submitted a petition to the Emperor on January 31 requesting leave and 10,000 Birr as part grant and part loan, to be repaid from my salary, so that I could take my child to Paris with his mother, since I had completed the translation of the book. There was no response to my request, I presented two reminders to His Majesty in the course of February to make it possible for me to overcome, before I started on my new duties, the difficulty I faced in connection with the child. As months passed without any reaction, I resigned myself to waiting until I went abroad when I could have the child treated.

During the months I spent in Addis Ababa translating the book, the truth of the information given to my wife on the day I returned from India began to be apparent. While accepting the recommendation that I should be sent to Cairo, the Emperor made it to be known that he wished to raise me to the rank of ambassador. He would not budge from his decision in spite of the efforts of his advisers that it should not take effect. An unexpected event came to light in the meantime. King Farouk of Egypt announced that since the Sudan was Egyptian territory, he was its king and that any government sending a diplomatic representative to Cairo should address him as 'King of Egypt and The Sudan,' or else he would not receive the envoy. In the event, there was no government willing to accept King Farouk's demand; neither was the Ethiopian government ready to accede to it. Consequently, the governments which had no ambassadors or ministers in Cairo at that time continued their activities by assigning 'Chargé d'Affaires.' Even though my appointment to Egypt was confirmed because the Ethiopian Minister had left Cairo earlier, the question arose as to how I should be designated. The Emperor and his advisers had differing views on this. The latter contended that I should go as Chargé d'Affaires, but His Majesty insisted that even if I were to be called Chargé d'Affaires temporarily, he had promoted me to the rank of ambassador. They argued that it was not international practice for an ambassador to be termed a Chargé d'Affaires and presented the opinion of their legal adviser to support their contention. But, seeing that the Emperor persisted in his views, they recommended that he himself tell me of the appointment. So he summoned me one day to his office privately and, after informing me that he had been pleased with the service I had rendered while I was in Britain and in India, told me that from that day on he had given me the rank of ambassador and that he had decided to send me to serve in Egypt. He proceeded to tell me that King Farouk had declared that he would receive no Credentials unless he was addressed as 'King of Egypt and The Sudan' and that Ethiopia did not wish to accept his demand. He had therefore determined that for the time being I should serve as Chargé d'Affaires in Cairo. I affirmed that since my aim was to serve, I was ready to go and serve in whatever capacity His Majesty desired. I then bowed and retired.

Sometime later, the Vice Minister of the Foreign Ministry asked me to see him and when we met in his office he said that since I had been instructed to go to Cairo, I should leave without delay and that a document would be given me as Chargé d'Affaires. I retorted I should inform him, if he had not heard it already, that His Majesty had promoted me to the rank of ambassador and that he was aware that I had been Minister Plenipotentiary. I added he should surely know that the status of a Chargé d'Affaires was below these two. They should therefore give me a letter instructing the Secretary (Ato Petros Sahlou) to hand over the legation to me and let the Egyptians find out who Emmanuel Abraham was. I then warned him that if he gave me a letter as Chargé d'Affaires, I would tear it to pieces and throw it on his desk. He wrote me a letter on February 24 as 'His Imperial Majesty's Envoy Extraordinary and Minister Plenipotentiary,' and informed me that everything was ready for my travel and I should leave for Cairo with dispatch. But, since the desire of the advisers for me and the Emperor's decision could not be reconciled, my departure for Egypt hung fire. As if to make them wonder, the Foreign Ministry was ordered that my salary remain at the rate I had been paid in India. I was therefore paid the salary granted to an ambassador or a minister abroad until I left for Rome. I understood this aroused a good deal of jealousy and complaint on the part of the ministers who had been abroad like me.

EIGHT

Rome: Ambassador Plenipotentiary 1952 - 1955

Due to the state of affairs mentioned in Part 7 above, I remained in Addis Ababa for three more months waiting to know what my next assignment was to be. It had been decided sometime before that diplomatic relations, interrupted because of the invasion of Ethiopia by Fascist Italy, should be re-established and the new Italian government had agreed to it. They had therefore proceeded to exchange diplomatic representatives and the then Vice Minister of the Foreign Ministry, Ato Zaudé Gebre Heywot (later Bitwoded), had been appointed Ethiopian Ambassador in January, 1952. But some high ranking officials who were not pleased with this and who wished that some relative or friend be appointed instead contrived something with which to accuse him as a result of which he was deprived of the post. Thereupon, a number of people presented petitions to the Emperor to secure an appointment to the position. A man who excessively boasted of his brother's authority and influence was going about declaring openly that it had been decided that he should be sent to Rome. Seeing that Ato Zaudé was not to be sent, the Emperor ordered the officials who usually gave him advice on such matters to present names of persons they thought would be suitable for the post, and each adviser submitted his list of names. He looked through the lists and, not finding anyone he considered suitable and my name not being on any of the lists, said "We have selected Amanuel and he is to be told of it." In line with the saying to the effect that one word from the monarch is decisive, there was nothing else to do but to comply with the command. So I was summoned to the Palace in the course of the morning of June 4 and the Minister of the Pen informed me, in the presence of the Prime Minister and the Minister of Defence, that His Imperial Majesty had been graciously pleased to appoint me Ambassador Extraordinary and Plenipotentiary in Rome. (It was said at the time that Ato Zaudé was not going due to illness; diplomatic illness)!

As soon as the ceremony of appointment was over, I went to the Emperor's office with the other appointees 'to kiss hand.' On seeing me, His Majesty called out, "Amanuel, Come" and, when I approached him, said in a low voice, "You had better leave quickly." I said, "All right. It is nine months since my luggage was packed," bowed and retired.

I saw clearly by the way the Emperor spoke that the people around him were not happy with his choice, and more especially the brother of the man above mentioned was chagrined that the post he desired for his brother was denied him. He was so embittered that, even after I went to Rome, he could not get over it and spoke in a derogatory manner about me to someone who had gone from Rome and had visited him. The man told me when he returned to Rome that he had been surprised by the remarks and had wondered what I had done to him. This appeared to me to be an apt illustration of the Amharic dictum, 'Striking the pack-saddle for fear of the donkey,' for I knew of no harm I had done to anyone, and I went to Rome by command of the Sovereign. It had not occurred to me to approach the Emperor to send me to Rome when so many people were presenting petitions earnestly desiring to get the post. (I wish to affirm here that in the course of my long period of service in the Ethiopian government, 35 years, there was no instance when I requested His Majesty to give me this or that appointment). I heard on returning home at the end of my mission that the disappointed brother of the high official had been blustering that he would kill me, as if I was his father's murderer! It so happened that, before my return from Rome, the man's brother was stripped of his high office (April 1955), and he himself fell on evil days, suffering hardship for several years. This appeared to be a confirmation of the truth rhymed by a songstress to the effect that one hardly retained to the end the worldly glory one initially enjoyed!

On June 14, ten days after I was instructed to go to Rome, I set out by air at 12 noon with my family and Ato Kebede Abebe, Second Secretary of the Embassy. We arrived in Cairo at sunset and immediately caught an American aircraft and, continuing our flight, arrived at Rome airport at 3 a.m. on June 15. Officials of the Italian Foreign Ministry received us and conducted us to the Grand Hotel.

I visited the Foreign Ministry on June 16 and met the Chief of Protocol, the Secretary General, and the Director General for Political Affairs. In accordance with diplomatic practice, I should have met the Foreign Minister and given him a copy of my Letters of Credence when he should have informed me the date on which the President should have received me for the presentation of my Credentials. However, since the Prime Minister, Signor de Gasperi, was concurrently Foreign Minister and since he had constantly to be present in Parliament, it was said that he was pressed for time. It was therefore suggested that I should present the Credentials to the President first and later be received by the Foreign Minister. Consequently, I proceeded to the Quirinal Palace at 9 a.m. on June 19 and presented His Imperial Majesty's Letters to President Einaudi. On the same day, at 7 p.m. in the evening, I went to the Foreign Ministry and met Prime Minister and Foreign Minister de Gasperi.

After the presentation of the Credentials to the President of Italy and my acquaintance with the officials of the Foreign Ministry, I spent several weeks visiting and getting acquainted with members of the Diplomatic Corps in the country. Before long, the director of the Roman daily, 'Giornale d'Italia,' asked me to give him an interview in connection with the relations between Rome and Addis Ababa. I accepted his request and he came to the hotel and presented some questions on which I expressed my views. The interview was printed in his newspaper on June 28. From the questions he presented, the ones I thought important were: relations between Ethiopia and Italy and the return of Eritrea to Ethiopia. First of all, he asked which of the matters between Ethiopia and Italy I thought had to be given priority. I told him it was the resolution of the questions decided on in the Peace Treaty. But he stated in his newspaper that he wanted to make light of the questions stipulated in the Peace Treaty. He asked my view on the return of Eritrea to Ethiopia and I told him that it was natural that this should happen and reminded him that Eritrea was an ancient province of Ethiopia. He rejoined that it appeared that Eritrea was more developed than Ethiopia. I asked whether in Italy there would perhaps not be differences in development between the provinces, and whether the same condition did not obtain in France and other countries. I mentioned this in a report I wrote to the Emperor on July 4 and enclosed a cutting of the newspaper.

It happened that a person I could not identify had sent with dispatch a copy of the newspaper to the Foreign Ministry before my report arrived in Addis Ababa, and I received a telegram demanding the reason why I stated to the newspaper that Eritrea was more developed than Ethiopia. The Emperor was also led to be disappointed and on receipt of my report wrote on July 11 as follows, "One thing which extremely disappointed Us in the interview was that when he said Eritrea appeared to be more developed than Ethiopia, you replied that in Italy also one province was more developed than another province. You should know that when a journalist obtains this from you it could indirectly be interpreted in another way. It cannot therefore be said that you gave a good reply unless you convince Us otherwise." From what I heard later on, it had been recommended that I should be recalled at once. But it would appear that my return was postponed pending an explanation from me as indicated in His Majesty's letter. It seemed to me that those who had disliked my going to Rome in the first place thought they had found a good reason to thwart my mission to Italy and had been active to secure my recall. They were not successful!

In a report I wrote to the Emperor on July 15, I expressed deep regret that I caused disappointment while I was striving to please and explained what my view was when I spoke on Eritrea. I wrote, "If it had been possible to read the interview from beginning to end and if what was said about Eritrea had not been taken out of context and given a different interpretation when it was presented, it seems to me that perhaps such disappointment would have been avoided. On reading the interview straight, one could perhaps get the impression that while the journalist was striving to consider Eritrea as equal to Ethiopia, I was equally striving to consider Eritrea as only an Ethiopian province not equal to Ethiopia. The reason why I wondered whether in Italy one province was not more developed than another province was to reiterate my statement that Eritrea had been an Ethiopian province, and that as in Italy one province was more developed than another province, so Eritrea which was again to be an Ethiopian province might be more developed than another Ethiopian province but not than the whole of Ethiopia." Other evidence which I enclosed with the report is found among the documents I had sent from Rome.

On reading the report, the Emperor wrote on July 25 that I had to send a full translation of the article which had appeared in the newspaper after the interview and said, "We enclose for your information what had been written here to explain the matter to Us, and if you conscientiously spoke to him in accordance with your explanation, it is possible to take your word." Even though the identity of the persons who wrote what they called 'a short memorandum' was not revealed to me, I noted they had picked up four points from the interview which they criticized. These were firstly, on economy and culture; second, on opening up Ethiopia to Italy; third, on the federation of Eritrea with Ethiopia; fourth, the matter referred to above, as to whether Ethiopia and Eritrea were equals or not. Having explained fully my view to His Majesty in my earlier reports, I considered it futile to contend with concealed people throwing arrows of criticism at me. So, I had the whole article translated into Amharic and sent it to the Emperor on August 8 with a short letter in which I wrote, "As concerns the memorandum criticizing my remarks and making it appear contradictory to the views of Your Majesty's government, I restrict myself to reminding Your Majesty that when I had to come here, realizing that I had been away from Ethiopia for several years and not being able to follow events in detail, I had requested that detailed instructions be given me in writing concerning the Imperial government's relations with Italy in general and its policy with respect to Eritrea. Your Majesty gave the orders and I repeatedly reminded the head of the department concerned to give me the instructions, but not a single word was given me. If the persons who are now so hasty to find fault with Your servant had been equally hasty to give me the directives I had repeatedly asked for, they would perhaps have had no occasion to distort and misinterpret my remarks to create a sense of disappointment in Your Majesty's mind."

The Emperor wrote on August 15, "We have received what you sent as evidence in Amharic on the interview you gave to the Italian newspapers. We have passed to the Foreign Ministry what the newspapers had published as received from you and the evidence for comparison with what they had found. For your part, it is as We have already written you." No one raised the matter after this. It was obvious that the plot they had hatched had failed, namely, to make the Emperor realize that his choice of me to be sent to Italy was a mistake, and to cause him to harden his heart against me. I gave thanks to my God for delivering me from this unexpected danger and got on with the object of my mission to Italy.

During my sojourn in Rome for three whole years, I continually sent the Emperor, so far as I could follow them, reports on Ethiopian-Italian relations, on Italy's internal affairs and on relations between European governments in general. In addition, I sent two long reports to His Majesty explaining reasons, as far as could be followed from Rome, for the revolution which took place in Egypt in July, 1952, on the initiative of young military officers.

On that occasion, the king and most of the government ministers were in Alexandria due to the hot season. The sections of the Egyptian armed forces and the air force in that city had joined hands with those in Cairo. At dawn on July 23, under the leadership of Major General Naguib, the young officers had had the palace, the government departments, the radio station, the telegraph offices and the main squares surrounded by troops, dismissed the Prime Minister and caused General Naguib to select another person to head the government. In the course of the night of July 22, they had arrested the senior military officers who were at a meeting.

On July 26, the king's two residences in Alexandria were surrounded by troops and the king was given an ultimatum to relinquish the throne in favour of his infant son and leave Egypt the same day. The king, realizing that he had no one to come to his rescue, issued a decree that he had abdicated in favour of his son and boarded a ship to go into exile with his family. Naguib and two officers accompanied King Farouk to the vessel and, when the ship began its voyage, caused a final royal farewell to be given him with a 21-gun salute.

The fact that security was assured in Egypt, except for a few people who were killed in Alexandria when this historic change took place, appeared to indicate not only the precautions taken by the officers but also the extent to which the people had been disenchanted with the king. Looking into the reasons why King Farouk had no supporters when he was so suddenly deprived of his prerogatives and expelled from a land where he was born and reigned for 16 years, I tried to assess what had been said against him for years before July 23 and since and submitted the reports to the Emperor, a summary of which is as follows.

Farouk was 16 years old and was in training at Sandhurst Military Academy in England when his father King Fuad died. He returned to Egypt soon after and became king as Farouk I. The Egyptian people had respect for Fuad and they loved Farouk as his only son and reposed great hopes in him. They also entertained the expectation that a period of progress would be inaugurated in Egypt. The young monarch appeared at first that he would justify the confidence placed in him. As he grew older and gradually took over power, however, he began to evince characteristics not previously seen in him. As he matured physically, he seemed to be unable to contain his passions. He was made to marry but did not seem to honour the sanctity of marriage nor give heed to the weight of responsibility kingship entailed. He made use of any pretty woman he set his eyes on, whether she was married or not, to assuage his passion; and when the husbands of the women appeared to oppose him, he went to the extent of getting them murdered, as if the atrocious treatment done to them was not enough. Apart from his passion for women, he had been poisoned by the love of money. He made it his main occupation to amass riches by fair means or foul and send them out of the country. He squandered large sums on gambling and similar games.

The reason why King Farouk fell out with the Egyptian armed forces which used to adore him and were loyal to him, and why he had to endure the humiliation of being stripped of his crown and expelled from the country was found to be as follows. The war which Egypt and the other Arab governments made on the Jews to prevent the re-establishment of Israel and its government four years before the king was dethroned (1948) can be said to mark the genesis of the affair. Before that war, the leaders of Egypt were in the habit of boasting and spreading the view that Egypt was the leader of the Arab nation and that King Farouk should be named caliph and supreme leader of all Muslims. It was they who urged the other governments to wage war on the Jews. However, the Egyptian army, which previous to that had not experienced war for many years, was no match for the Jews who were struggling for their existence, their faith and to deliver their children from exile and give them a homeland. The Egyptian leaders whose eyes were blinded by false pride and by a feeling of self-importance and who had convinced their people to believe all that, were made to realize their true worth by the war. The Egyptian army returned home defeated, and the Jews brought about the re-establishment of the State of Israel in the Holy Land of which they had dreamt and for which they had longed for many long years.

Although the war with Israel marked the beginning of the disaffection, the reason for the contention between King Farouk and the armed forces was that the weapons of war given to the troops during the fighting was unsuitable for modern warfare, obsolescence and useless, and that when the Egyptian forces tried to use them against the enemies of their country, they blew up in their faces, killing or wounding them. This enraged the armed forces. At the end of the war, General Naguib and the young officers demanded that the government institute an investigation as to how obsolete war weapons, dangerous to the life of the troops were bought. They also presented a petition to the king. An order was therefore given for an investigation to be made. It transpired that not only the War Ministry but the senior military officers were also involved. It was moreover revealed that the advisers around the throne and the king himself were affected. As a result, it was sought to delay the matter by subterfuge. The young officers were much aggrieved at this. They were all the more aggrieved since they had hoped that the king, as commander-in-chief, having witnessed the humiliation endured by the armed forces, would have made every effort for the investigation to be finalized; but he was found to be one of the culprits who shielded them. This alienated them from the king and obliterated the respect they had had for him.

As a result, the young officers stole the hearts of the troops by doing things which demonstrated that it was impossible to put faith in the senior officers and by telling them about the wrongs done to the armed forces as well as the other failings of the government. They were determined to remove from office not only the high officers of the armed forces but also all the officials in the government departments and the political parties, especially those who were notorious for taking bribes and whose names had been known for placing their own interests before those of the country. In this they pleased the people very much. And when the king who was said to delight in such sordid deeds was banished, all those who lived under his wings were exposed, and there was no escape for them.

Since the king who succeeded Farouk was an infant, three men were appointed to act as regents with the prerogatives granted to the king by the constitution. Naguib and his companions then proceeded to reduce the holdings of those who had held large estates for distribution to landless peasants. They also saw to it that the wealth of their country which was accumulated in a few hands should not be squandered but apportioned to that section of the people which was extremely destitute.

After discussing the above-mentioned matters at length, I presented my views thus in part, "I venture to point out to Your Majesty that in the humble opinion of Your servant, a people that has rejected and forsaken the ideals and culture of its ancestors and has not replaced them with the essentials of modern culture but is half-baked, and that is not fortunate in its leaders will have the same fate.

"We Christians believe and know in some measure that our Christian faith is superior to any other, and that it is able to raise the human person to a very high level both materially and spiritually. As a result, when we see someone of another faith at fault, we are at times prone to fall into the temptation of thinking, if not actually saying, 'what is to be expected from a person following such a faith!' Without assuming the attitude of the Pharisee and trying to raise the so-called Christian peoples to a higher plane than the Egyptian people, it seems to me that the modern people of Egypt, and especially that section which has had a smattering of modern education and which in consequence has assumed the leadership of the common people, have abandoned the faith of their forefathers and have not fully grasped modern ideals and knowledge. They are like a man who goes out on a boat without oars."

In reply to the reports His Majesty wrote on September 23, 1952, "We have noted what you wrote about the situation in Egypt. It is a good idea to follow up this matter. You will likewise write Us about the situation in the country where you are."

September 11, 1952 was a day of great rejoicing in Ethiopia as it was the day on which Eritrea was federated with Ethiopia. However, the Italians were unable to hide their sorrow, and they showed their chagrin and hatred on that day, especially those who were guided by the spirit of Fascism. Even though there was nothing the government could be said to have revealed openly, the Italian President was conspicuous by his silence while the leaders of other nations congratulated His Majesty. This was an indication of their inability to overcome their disappointment. I had brought this to the notice of the Emperor and he wrote on October 31, "When we were in Eritrea, except for a few, the difference between their words and their inner thoughts could be read on their faces. As it is necessary to pursue this matter with diligence, what you think and report from time to time is not to be overlooked."

In accordance with the peace treaty signed with Italy in Paris in February, 1947, by the powers that joined forces to fight Nazi Germany and Fascist Italy during the Second World War, Italy had been obligated to pay 25 million Dollars to Ethiopia as war reparations. With a view to reaching an agreement as to how payment should be effected, the Ethiopian government, at the invitation of the Italian government, had sent a five-man delegation to Rome in the middle of October, 1952 led by Ato Yilma Deressa, the then Minister of Commerce and Industry. The Italians, who were not able to conceal their unhappiness and hatred when Eritrea was federated with Ethiopia in September, vented their feelings of anger in the newspaper, 'Giornale d'Italia,' when the Ethiopian delegation appeared in Rome to demand compensation. Thinking nothing of the unspeakable wrong they had done to the Ethiopian people, they gave details of the amount of money they had spent and the work they had done with the desire of making Ethiopia their own. The newspaper wrote, "Apart from not asking the price of all the good things we had given them due to our pride as decent people, it is surprising that people who were eating missionaries when we went to their country sixty years ago and to whom we had taught to eat delicious pasta when we left their country have come to demand compensation for all these good deeds."

Observing this in Rome, I wrote thus to the Emperor on November 4, enclosing a full translation of the newspaper article, "It seems to me that the main reason why the ire of the Italians was aroused and their spirit wounded by Ethiopia's demand for reparations was that they saw in this that the country on which they had set their hearts for expansion appeared to have escaped them for all time and that the people whom they had planned to make 'hewers of wood and drawers of water' have eluded their trap, and with resilience, reasserted convincingly their ownership of the land of their ancestors. Moreover, they have lately suffered a relapse of mental agony which had lasted for ten years and a feeling of despair because of the inclusion of Eritrea into Ethiopia; Eritrea which they had originally snatched to make it a springboard for the conquest of Ethiopia and which they have already used for the purpose. When the Italians who had been smarting under the spectacle of Eritrea's return to its place, of the Emperor of Ethiopia's presence among the Eritrean population for the first time in many years, and of the enthusiastic welcome they accorded to Your Majesty, saw the arrival soon after of the Ethiopian war reparations commission in Rome, the wound which had been festering in the hearts of many burst open and the impetuous temperament of the Italians could not endure and contain it. I make bold to submit to Your Majesty my belief that similar vexing incidents are bound to recur from time to time until all Italians are convinced without a shadow of doubt that Your Ethiopian people cannot be violated and that, even though he may protest about it, no Italian will ever entertain any thought for the well-being of the Ethiopian people. What is disappointing about the Italian attitude is that they do not appear to have a desire to understand the words of the Wise Man that there is a time for everything."

In a letter he wrote on November 7, the Emperor said in part, "We are surprised to note what the Italian newspapers have written and what the senators have said on our demand for payment of compensation. On the other hand, it is not so surprising since, as you have stated in detail in your letter, they cannot help being angered and are incapable to forget the uprooting of what they had conspired and started to do against Ethiopia for so many years. The fact that they forget that time changes everything in the world alerts and impels us to work harder. We have been informed also of the difficulty encountered in what you are working on with Ato Yilma and the others. It is your proper duty to write in such detail on this matter and arouse the conscience. Since every Ethiopian must work diligently so that our present well-being may not be followed by disaster, you will write Us, as much as you are able, everything in detail, and at the same time give Us the benefit of your views."

As stated in Part 7 of this narrative, I was greatly concerned about my son Dawit, who was born on October 24, 1951, had a natural defect on his upper lip and palate, and that I had hoped to take him abroad for treatment by a specialist but was unsuccessful. I had a good opportunity to have the child treated after I went to Italy. I requested and obtained permission of the Emperor to take him to Paris. I took him with his mother on December 27, 1952 and the surgeon operated on Dawit's palate on December 29. We stayed three weeks in Paris until the palate was healed and the surgeon was satisfied that the operation was successful. We were thankful that the child's palate was as normal as any person's after the operation. His nose and upper lip were successfully rectified the following year by another surgeon in Rome.

After trying for three months to have serious negotiations with the Italian authorities and arrive at an agreement on the war reparations, the Ethiopian delegation realized that the Italian government had no mind to reach an agreement, and returned to Addis Ababa late in January, 1953. The Emperor inquired in a letter he wrote on February 12 whether I had heard of any change of mind on their part since the return of Ato Yilma and his colleagues to Addis Ababa.

Thinking that the question should not be left dormant, I went to the Italian Foreign Ministry on March 2 and had a long talk with the Director General for Political Affairs, Minister del Balzo, about the relations between our two countries, and especially about the war reparations. The minister said he thought I was finding my task there to be a difficult one. I replied that it was inevitable that relations which had been interrupted for so long should initially be difficult, all the more so when, additionally, men who had been sent there with a view to removing the last obstacle between the two governments and pursuing mutual relations in a friendly spirit, had to stay in Rome for three months without achieving anything. He said they regretted that the delegates had to go back without the matter for which they had come being settled successfully, but since Ambassador Tacoli (the Italian Ambassador in Addis Ababa) had returned to Addis Ababa with fresh and better instructions, they hoped a better atmosphere would be created which would lead to an agreement. I said the fact that the question of Italian property was mixed with the question of reparations had upset the whole thing, and that even then our delegation had presented once or twice written proposals to serve as a basis for discussion; that they had to stay in Rome for three months without any tangible response had disappointed my government. After a long exchange of views on these lines, he remarked that, after his return to Rome, Ambassador Tacoli had worked hard to straighten up the matter with the authorities concerned and with the Prime Minister. He had taken improved instructions with him to Addis Ababa to enable him to have discussions with the Ethiopian government, and that his hope was that a way to an agreement would be found at an early date. I stated that was also my hope and, having agreed to meet from time to time, we separated.

I wrote on March 3 a detailed report to the Emperor on this conversation together with the discussion I had had with Ambassador Tacoli, who had come to see me before going back to Addis Ababa and the reply I had given him. I then expressed the hope that it would help the better to weigh up the matter and conduct negotiations with goodwill and understanding.

In a reply he sent me on March 17, the Emperor wrote in part, "Reading the account of the discussion you had at the Italian Foreign Ministry with the Director General, Minister del Balzo, We were pleased to note that all you have said was well and properly expressed. It has been proved that, even though truth embitters and is unwelcome for a time, it is bound to prevail in the end. No impartial judge who considers your words as against his can deny that they are a truthful statement of value. The Italian Ambassador has not presented anything to Us, since his return, on the discussions about the reparations for which our delegates had gone to Rome. You are therefore to acquaint the Italian authorities and the ambassadors of other governments at opportune times that under the cover of friendliness they have not abandoned their grudge. It seems to Us that we have done a number of good things for them to induce true and close friendship, but We have not found them to be appreciative and desirous of cooperation and a close relationship. Even though the question of reparations may be stalled, what sign have they shown of considering to restore, let alone restoring, the monuments and works of art they had removed from our country? It is necessary that they realize this is not a good attitude."

I went on March 28 to the Italian Foreign Ministry and met Minister del Balzo for a second time. The reason for my visit was to inquire what the Italian Ambassador had done about the talks on the war reparations since he went back to Addis Ababa, and why they had not restored the works of art and the monuments they had removed from Ethiopia. I also wished to remind them that the longer those matters were protracted the more they would hinder the process of a closer relationship and cooperation. The Minister informed me that Ambassador Tacoli had met the Ethiopian authorities and presented a plan as a first step; that the plan was that the Italian government would pay the Ethiopian government in advance a part of the amount fixed for reparations on the basis of conditions to be presented with the payment. He went on to say that, the matter being mainly economic, he did not know the details and suggested that I discuss it with Minister Scaduto Mendola, Director General for Economic Affairs.

I agreed and proceeded to tell him that it appeared that nothing had been done since I arrived in Rome with regard to the restoration of the works of art and monuments removed by the Fascists from Ethiopia, that this could be an obstacle to the relations between the two governments, and urged him that they be restored to us with dispatch. The Minister said that Minister Yilma Deressa, before his return to Ethiopia, had written them a letter on the matter, and agreed that the early restoration of the articles would help clear the atmosphere between our two countries and should be attended to quickly. He added before we parted that he would make inquires and let me know.

On March 30, I met Minister Scaduto Mendola and asked him to enlighten me on the state of the question of the reparations. He told me that Ambassador Tacoli had been given a proposal to be presented to the Ethiopian government before his return to Ethiopia; that the main point of the proposal was that the Italian government pay the Ethiopian government a portion of the amount fixed for reparations and that the Ambassador had been given the discretion to present the proposal at a time he considered opportune. I told him that I had heard there was nothing the Ambassador had presented on the question of war reparations to my government up to the middle of March, and that was why I had visited him. He said that as the Foreign Minister was not in the country, Tacoli had asked that someone be designated with whom he could start to negotiate. He had not presented the proposal because he had not been informed with whom to talk. I told him that Minister del Balzo had told me earlier that the Ambassador had met the Minister of the Pen and the Acting Foreign Minister, and that this was perhaps the answer to his query as to who to talk to. He then said that it seemed to him that it would be better if the matter were to proceed without too much hurry or too much delay. I retorted that the matter had been dragged out long enough, and that it would be to the benefit of our relations if it were to be speeded up. We separated on this note.

I sent the Emperor on March 31, a detailed report of the conversations I had with the two men. I also wrote that it had been planned to hold general elections for parliament after a month or two and expressed my views as follows: "The Italian government, pursuing its usual duplicity, is misleading the people. The fact that the Ethiopian delegation had stayed in Rome for such a long time and gone empty-handed had suited its propaganda and made it appear a defender of the people. This has evidently given it pleasure in that it has silenced its political opponents at least for the time being. It now seems to wish to cajole us by making noises that it will pay the reparations as soon as the elections are over and it is securely back in power. It would also appear that it wants to tell us that it will duly pay us but only after we have served its propaganda, and we had better not be in too much hurry. In doing this, however, it seems to be overlooking the fact that hope deferred can make the heart of the other party sick and exhaust feelings of friendship."

The Emperor wrote in part on April 17 in reply to the report, "Since his return, Ambassador Tacoli has met the Acting Foreign Minister and Ato Yilma, and told them that his government had instructed him to discuss the difficulties encountered by the two commissions which were appointed in connection with the war reparations, before they met again. He has not indicated as yet what solution he would present to the difficult arguments advanced by the Italian commission; neither has he revealed the conditions Italy will require before a part of the reparations is paid. We have noted the remark of the Italian Foreign Ministry official that it would be better not to proceed too fast with the matter and your comment. We have assumed that the talks the Ambassador was said to pursue are meant only for them to gain more time. For our part, we are considering how the matter could be brought to an early conclusion by eliciting their agreement or refusal. We shall inform you of the progress of the talks in due course."

This being the situation with respect to the question of war reparations, another controversial matter came to light in Rome. It is the practice for an ambassador or a minister to use the occasion of one of his country's national holidays to give a reception to the authorities of the country in which he sojourns, to the Diplomatic Corps and other persons. Following this practice, I chose May 5, of the two national holidays sanctioned to be celebrated abroad, rather than July 23 as suitable for a reception, seeing the nature of the weather in Rome during the summer months. I informed the Italian Foreign Ministry accordingly. The Ministry was not pleased about it and asked us to hold our reception on another day, since it would revive feelings of the old enmity and make them unhappy if we held our reception in Rome on that day. As I had explained why May 5 was to be preferred and obtained the approval of our Foreign Ministry, Ato Mallas Andom, First Secretary of the Embassy, went to the Foreign Ministry and tried to explain to the Deputy Chief of Protocol that we could not alter in Rome a national day which was decreed many years previously and gave examples to show that nowhere else had opposition been shown to the celebration of such a national day. As the official insisted on not agreeing to the national day being celebrated in Rome, Ato Mallas told him that it was not a matter of asking them for permission to give the reception but only of following diplomatic practice and asking for the names of their officials we should invite to the reception. The official did not wish to give him the names of the officials but, as it was necessary that I discuss the matter with the Chief of Protocol, they would ask for an appointment by telephone.

I met the Chief of Protocol, Ambassador Scammaca, on April 24 and we had an open and hard discussion with due regard to diplomatic courtesy. The substance of the discussion was as follows: Ambassador Scammaca said I was aware they had caused their Ambassador to attend the reception with his staff the previous year when the national day was celebrated in Addis Ababa. But a reception given in Rome on that day would hurt the feelings of many Italians who had lost their sons and militate against good relations which had just begun to improve. I had written to them that there were two national days from which to choose; they should be happy if, instead of the one indicated, I were to hold the reception on the occasion of His Imperial Majesty's birthday in July when they would send a telegram to His Majesty.

I replied that I was very surprised that they had raised the matter in the first place. The national day had been established twelve years earlier (1941) by Imperial decree to commemorate the restoration of Ethiopia's liberty and it would be in existence as long as Ethiopia endured. He might moreover recall that a few days earlier the Israeli government had celebrated its Independence Day. He might also remember the bitter struggle Israel had with the British to win its independence. Nevertheless, when the Israeli Ambassador celebrated the national day in London, the British government was far from being displeased about it, and the British Broadcasting Corporation had throughout the day spread widely how the occasion was celebrated in Israel. America had its independence from Britain after a bitter war. Yet when American Independence Day was observed in London every year many British officials and ordinary citizens were seen joyfully to take part in the celebrations. Did not many of the states in the world win or regain their independence in the same way? After hard struggle? Did the states that had opposed them in the past show rancour on their national days? I then proceeded to tell him that their attitude was meant to violate Ethiopia's right to free nationhood. There was another reason why I had chosen to hold a reception on that day; I had arrived in that country the year before during the summer and, when I had wanted to visit and make acquaintance with my colleagues, many of them had left Rome, it being the holiday season. Several months had therefore to pass before I could meet them. Since April was the reception season and I had been invited to many of them, it was my duty to reciprocate before they dispersed. I could not invite them to my reception in July when many of them would have been away from Rome, and I had found our May national day to be well suited for the purpose.

Observing the seriousness of my remarks and what I had said about their violation of Ethiopia's sovereignty, the Ambassador changed the tone of his argument and said what he had meant was that, because it was impossible for their officials to attend my reception, I should give it on another day so that they could all be present. They were not able to prevent me from holding the reception and he would beg me to believe that it was not a matter of opposing our right to freedom of action. I told him what we had wanted from the start was for them to give us a list of the officials we should invite to our reception and that I had tried to convince him that it was not suitable for us to change the date of our reception.

The Ambassador reiterated that holding a reception on May 5 would upset and hurt the feelings of many of their people, and it would be dangerous for the authorities when published in the newspapers. He then expressed the wish that we would give the reception in July when they would attend it without any apprehension; they did not wish that date which was a reminder of that deplorable conflict should be revived but that feelings of friendship between our two countries should continue to develop.

I retorted that what they actually desired was that we should forget what had happened 12 years earlier so as not to displease them. He might not follow as I did what the Italian newspapers printed about Ethiopia, so I would give him an example. The anniversary of the battle of Adwa had occurred the previous March, and some of their newspapers had then written that they should never forget Adwa and their heroes who had fallen at Adwa. What did he think it meant? Did it not mean that they had to avenge themselves some day? How could they ask us to forget what happened 12 years previously when they had not forgotten what took place 57 years before? What their newspapers had printed and what they were now asking reflected the attitude they had shown in 1935. After a long discussion on these lines, the Ambassador said again that he would inform me regretfully that they could not attend the reception. I told him that I also regretted it much, but since he was telling me they were not coming, I would not invite them.

I sent on April 27 a detailed report of the discussion to the Emperor and wrote at the end of the report, "As I have observed from time to time since I arrived in Italy and have reported to Your Majesty as the opportunity arose, the so-called democratic government of Italy appears hardly to be any better in what concerns Ethiopia than the former Fascist government. There has been nothing however that could be said the authorities had uttered in this regard, even if they had shown feelings of enmity and contempt for the Ethiopian people and government through some newspapers under the guise of freedom of the press. Now they have been compelled to reveal their inner feelings on Ethiopia in clear terms on account of the celebration of the May 5 National Day. They had dared to try to suppress the observance of this day in order to obliterate the memory of the unnumbered Ethiopians who had sacrificed their lives in faith and hope for the arrival of this day, and so that the people which had recovered its age-old independence with terrible struggle should not express its joy and thanksgiving to its Creator. All this to save the Italians whose sons had died in Ethiopia from being upset and their spirits disturbed, and so that the Fascists might not be angered, who had boasted that Ethiopia was forever theirs but had been driven out by divine justice. They have said that their desire was that the national day should not be observed in Rome, but they have thus shown, in no uncertain terms, that they would not hesitate, had they had the power, to prevent its observance in Ethiopia as well and thus obliterate the commemoration of the day. I make bold to humbly express the view that this is a useful object lesson for the entire Ethiopian race."

In a letter he wrote on May 19, His Majesty said, "We have noted what you wrote concerning the declining by the Italians to be present at the reception on the May 5 National Day. We are pleased that all your remarks on the matter were to the point."

Preparations were made to hold the reception on May 5 and I sent invitations to my diplomatic colleagues and a number of private Italians. All the invitation cards were sent by hand for fear they might perhaps be intercepted if sent by post. The diplomatists and quite a few Italians came to the Embassy and participated in our reception.

On receipt of my above-mentioned report, the behaviour of the Italians aroused the ire of the Emperor and he sent it to the Council of Ministers with an order to the cabinet to take steps. From what I heard later, some of the ministers were enraged and some said the Italians should be expelled from Ethiopia. In the end, as it happened that the Italian national day was being observed on June 2, instructions were given that no-one of the authorities or government officials should go to the Italian Embassy on that day, except the Chief of Protocol. The Italian Ambassador and the Italians in Addis Ababa were shocked and were very sad at seeing this. The Ambassador and his staff were dismayed and lodged complaints. On the other hand, the Ethiopian authorities saw to it that the Italian residents of the Capital were informed of their government's arrogance and attitude of contempt, and that threats be uttered. As a result panic reigned among them and they flocked to their Ambassador to criticize their government and express fear that the Ethiopian government might expel them from the country; and many addressed their complaints directly to the Italian government. For my part, I was present at their national day observance in Rome on June 2, in accordance with diplomatic practice.

On May 8, I went to the Italian Foreign Ministry and had a talk with the Director General for Economic Affairs, Minister Scaduto Mendola, about the works of art removed from Ethiopia. I remarked in the course of the talk that I had not observed even one instance of the objects removed by the Italian authorities during the invasion being sent back to Ethiopia. He told me that some objects had been sent. I replied that as I was preparing to travel to Italy the previous year, I had heard that some objects had arrived in Addis Ababa, but that nothing had been sent since. He said that the matter had been included in the economic clause according to the peace treaty, and it would be good if my government would raise the matter with their Ambassador and give him a list of the objects when they discussed the reparations. I told him I did not think that the question of war reparations was linked with the question of restoration of the works of art in the peace treaty; a proof of that was that they had sent back some of the objects a year before negotiations were begun on the war reparations. He replied that he was somewhere else when the objects were sent by another department and, from what he had heard, the objects sent were all that could be found in Rome at the time. I rejoined that the said objects were mostly private things; that it was known many other things had been removed to that country and that it was not realistic to ask my government for a list of them. I had nevertheless heard that the Emperor's whole library had been removed and that many ancient objects had also been taken away from the art museum; it was also known that coronets and other objects had been removed from the churches, and above all the Aksum obelisk was standing in the middle of Rome for all to see. Why not send back these until the objects were gathered together? Their indifference was a cause for surprise to my government.

When I mentioned the Aksum obelisk, he produced a copy of the Paris Peace Treaty and read Article 75 under which Italy was obligated to restore plundered property. The article stipulated that Italy had undertaken to restore all property known to be in its hands. I told him that it could not be said that the Ethiopian government had willingly given the monument to the Italian government; why not then send it back until the other things were found? And why not restore the other objects that were found? This would spare the feelings of my government and might be considered as a gesture of goodwill. It could destroy the sense of mutual trust if they appeared to be unconcerned about the matter. I concluded by asking whether the addition of the question of restoring plundered property would not make matters worse when it was known that the question of war reparations was difficult enough. He said that theoretically it was a matter to be settled together with the question of war reparations, but it was also clear, as I had indicated, that the restoration of the objects could be a means of showing goodwill. He would therefore do all he could that something was done about it. He then made a note about the Emperor's library and about the objects removed from the museum and other places. I noticed that he did not include the Aksum monument and told him again that its early restoration was expected. He stared at the floor for about one minute but could not bring himself to utter one word. To me his silence was proof enough that the Italian government, far from restoring the monument to us, had not even given it a thought.

I sent the Emperor on May 9 a full account of the discussion I had with the official and wrote concerning the Aksum monument, "I request Your Majesty's instructions about this work of art which was undeniably taken by force." In a letter dated May 19, the Emperor wrote, "We have designated Ato Yilma Deressa and Ato Menbere Yayehirad to negotiate on the matter. Your statement about the Aksum monument has afforded us special pleasure. You will be informed of the progress of the matter in due course." However, no result could be obtained from the negotiations for several months, since the Italian government had chosen to delay the matter as long as possible to suit its internal politics.

By that time, the Italian people had become disenchanted with the de Gasperi government which had been in power for seven years and, as the period of its mandate was drawing to a close, the leaders and members of the political parties spent two months going around the country to persuade the people to elect them. Parliamentary elections were held on June 7 and 8, 1953. De Gasperi and his associates were apprehensive because the Christian Democracy Party, the leading party in the government, had obtained fewer members than before and the opposition parties had grown stronger. And since the three smaller parties which had been supporting de Gasperi had also suffered loss in the elections and become weaker, it was apparent that they no longer wished to support his party. This was seen as compromising the stability of Italy's administration.

On July 3, the President of Italy summoned de Gasperi and instructed him to form a government. Realizing that the state of his own party and the hesitation of the three parties which had supported him would not permit him to form a stable government, de Gasperi requested the President to give the responsibility to another person, but the President pressed him strongly to try it himself. He accepted the mandate on the understanding that he would try to form a government until July 7 and then present his firm decision. After consultation with the various party leaders, he reported that he was unable to form a stable government with a firm base and advised the President to give the mandate to another person. The President however insisted that de Gasperi try to form a new government in view of the internal and international situation. He spent one week in discussion with his colleagues about the new programme of the government and the ministers to be appointed. He then informed the President on July 14 that he was ready to form a new government and presented a list of the ministers. Seeing that no member of the other parties had joined the government, the impression was given that the policy of the de Gasperi government would not be changed, especially with respect to Foreign Affairs, Finance and fiscal matters. De Gasperi retained the Foreign Ministry. Vanoni and Pella were made to continue in their former posts as ministers of Finance and the Budget and Treasury respectively.

In a report I sent to the Emperor on July 20, I wrote about Pella as follows: "As it is said that Signor Pella, above all the other ministers was opposed to payment being made when Your Majesty's delegates came to negotiate about the war reparations and since he has influence on de Gasperi, it is difficult to believe that the attitude of the new de Gasperi government will be any better as concerns Ethiopia than that of the former government as long as he holds the key to the Treasury and insists on not paying their debt."

The new de Gasperi government appeared before Parliament on July 21 when he presented his government's programme in detail and asked for a vote of confidence. Parliament debated it for about a week but he found no support except from his own party, and when a vote was taken the number of his opponents was found to be larger than that of his supporters. Realizing his defeat, he returned the mandate to the President and resigned. Italy faced a political crisis, the like of which had not been seen since the appointment of Mussolini 31 years earlier. The dissension between the political parties appeared to cause apprehension for Italy's democratic administration and life, and it was feared it might again fall under a dictatorship.

On August 2, the President summoned Attilio Piccioni, who was de Gasperi's Deputy Prime Minister, and asked him to form a government. After working hard to have discussions with the leaders of the various parties, Piccioni could get no supporters, and on August 12, informed the President that he could not fulfil the task assigned to him. The following day, the President called on Pella, Minister of the Budget and the Treasury, and told him to try to form a government. And Pella, realizing that the political situation was confused and that consultation with the party leaders would consume time, and considering that urgent matters of state were pending that, especially the budget had to be approved, decided to establish what he called a 'business government.' He selected the ministers who would assist him and presented them to the President on August 15. He held the portfolios of Foreign Affairs and the Budget, in addition to that of Prime Minister. All the Ministers were members of the Christian Democracy Party.

On August 19, Pella presented his government's programme to Parliament. He asserted that his government was meant to weather the crisis and, presenting the principles he wished to serve as a basis for his programme, affirmed that it was the duty of all patriotic Italians to help overcome the crisis. Seeing that party disputes had wearied and disturbed the people, all the political parties which desired and worked for Italy's development as a Western democratic state, except the Communists and their fellow-travellers, saw to it that the new government was confirmed. As a result, Pella's 'business government' lasted until December 6, 1953.

In a report I sent the Emperor on September 1, I expressed these views, "I make bold to report that, as far as I can see, the attitude of Pella's government with respect to Ethiopia will neither be better nor worse than that of the previous government. As I have reported to Your Majesty, it has been said that it was Pella who was especially responsible for preventing the resolution of the question of war reparations. It is a matter for speculation whether he would change his former position now that he is Prime Minister and has direct responsibility, and when he has announced that his government would only serve for a short time and attend only to urgent matters. On the other hand, one wonders if he will modify his narrow outlook as Treasurer and view the matter in a wider perspective as Prime Minister responsible for matters of state in general and for foreign and economic policies in particular. The Italian Ambassador in Addis Ababa will perhaps be directed to present to Your Majesty's government the attitude of the new government on the matter."

His Majesty said in a letter he wrote on September 8, "Since the new Prime Minister had served in de Gasperi's government, it is difficult to say that his policy will differ widely from that government's. Nevertheless, there are bound to be differences between one person and another, and you will perhaps detect them as you make an effort to follow up matters carefully, especially as concerns the question pending between us. And in the course of your pursuit, you will explain that the question of reparations between us and Italy is in a confused state. Continue to discuss on the basis of the demand and the negotiation initiated during Ato Yilma's visit."

I look back at the Italian political situation of that period because the Italian authorities had used it as pretext to prevent the development of Italy's relationship with Ethiopia and the resolution with serious intent of questions pending between them. The Emperor was displeased with this, and the Italians in Ethiopia were made to be aware in various ways of their government's lack of concern and to urge on it the especial detrimental effect that it would have on their interests. For his part, the Italian Ambassador was so distressed about the pressure and difficulties he said were encountered, not only by ordinary Italians but also by their diplomats that he resorted to the Foreign Ministry and the other government departments to lodge complaints, but he was dismayed that there was no one to help him. He was in such straits that he returned to Rome in September, 1953, and stayed for one month reporting the difficulties he had faced to Prime Minister Pella and the other government officials and urging the settlement of the question of war reparations. He met Pella two or three times to explain the matter to him and later came to the Embassy to inform me that he was going back to Ethiopia with fresh instructions. He recounted the hardships he said his compatriots and himself had endured in Ethiopia. Here is a summary of his complaints: He was in great distress because things were taking place in Ethiopia to upset and harass the Italians and the Italian government while he was making efforts to obtain a formula which might lead to an agreement; so much so that it was threatening to get in the way of his efforts to get something done. Saying that it was not easy to enumerate all the vexations encountered by the Italians in Ethiopia, he mentioned five incidents which he said had disturbed the Italian government directly. They were the demolition by bomb of a monument set up at Asab for the Italian Sapeto; the delay in obtaining an 'exequatur' for the newly appointed consul in Addis Ababa and the refusal to grant him a re-entry visa after a visit to Italy; the refusal to recognize their consul general at Asmara unless his letter of appointment was changed from 'Asmara, Eritrea' to 'Asmara, Ethiopia;' the requirement for Alitalia aircrafts to land at Gura Airport and not at Asmara due to their heavy weight, and the demand that Ethiopian Airlines act as agent for Alitalia; the refusal of a visa to Angelo Machia, an Italian foreign Ministry courier who was to carry his government's dispatches to Asmara and Addis Ababa.

I told him that it had been over ten months since relations between our two governments had deteriorated; ever since Ato Yilma went to Rome and his government treated him with indifference. I had tried to warn the authorities of his government in clear terms that it was in no one's interest to drag on the matter, but I had seen no sign of their giving heed to my warning. They disregarded the hand of friendship and goodwill stretched out to them. What was upsetting him now was a result of that reaction. And it was to be feared the situation might get worse if his government did not reconsider its attitude at an early date.

After trying to persuade me that the main reason for the delay was the political crisis in Italy, he said that he was now striving to obtain a formula for an agreement; but if vexing news of incidents of the type he had enumerated were to come daily from Ethiopia, his government might say to him that those people did not appear to desire any agreement and that he was pestering them to no purpose. So, would I please help him to see that nothing was done in Ethiopia to worsen the situation; he knew the Emperor would listen to me. I told him that I would report to my government what he had told me but I was fearful lest it only be the kind of cajoling already given me. He protested it was no cajolery this time and that he was hoping to take something tangible to Addis Ababa and we separated on this note.

I sent the Emperor on October 24 a detailed report of the two conversations I had with Ambassador Tacoli. In a letter he wrote on November 4, His Majesty said, "We have noted you conversations with Ambassador Tacoli. As you know very well, We have exerted every effort to welcome them with a hand stretched out in friendship and to forget the past. But on their part, the outcome has not been satisfactory; only words of mouth. We have sent you Our speech on the occasion of Coronation Day so that you may know it before they ask you. It is they who compelled us to pronounce these words to our people. Ambassador Tacoli returned to Addis Ababa on November 3 and you will be informed if there is anything he has to present to Us."

In the Speech from the Throne to Parliament on November 2, 1953, on the anniversary of Coronation Day, the Emperor expressed his disappointment with the attitude of the Italian government as follows, "In Our speech of last year, We informed the Parliament of the beginning of negotiations of particular importance for the establishment of good relations with another country. On that occasion, We stated that We hoped that these discussions would be carried on in an atmosphere of cooperation and understanding and that they would result in a spirit of friendship and comprehension by which, in the future, the mutual interests and dealings of the two countries would be guided. We undertook those discussions in a spirit of sincere friendship and optimism founded, not only on the advice of friendly countries abroad, but also on a firm determination to create this friendship, whatever the obstacles. Unfortunately, the mission did not receive the welcome which it had reason to expect, and, after giving manifold proofs of its patience, was obliged to abandon its efforts.

"A programme has been pursued abroad darkening the future of Our relations and attacking the sincerity of Our spirit of collaboration as well as Our firm determination to work, indeed to make all necessary sacrifices, for the welfare of Our loyal subjects of Eritrea, within the framework of the settlement achieved. We are not in agreement with the assertion that the difficulties have stemmed from psychological obstacles in Ethiopia. Quite on the contrary, the gestures have come from this side. Ethiopia stretched out a friendly hand, but found no hand stretched out towards her. Ethiopia wishes to adopt a new basis for her relations and it was on this new basis that, in Our speech of last year, We referred to the republic of a new country. However, Ethiopia which wishes to forget the past, in the interest of charity as well as progress, can, unfortunately, only note that, on the contrary, the past seems to weigh heavily upon the minds of others."

On November 20, the Emperor wrote, "We have met the Ambassador since he came back. Although what he told Us orally and gave Us in writing are different, We are sending for your information, copies of the minutes of the discussion and the 'aide-memoire' he has presented. We shall inform you of what may follow." The Amharic minutes of the discussion with Ambassador Tacoli when he was received in audience by the Emperor on November 12 read in part as follows, "Ambassador Tacoli: I have been in Rome and reported to my government the discussion I had last July with Ato Aklilou on the question pending between Ethiopia and Italy. But nothing could be done because it was the occasion of the election of the Prime Minister in Italy. I have since met and discussed the matter with our Prime Minister, H.E. Mr. Pella, and the other officials, and I am glad to report that now they all have a mind that the pending question should be resolved. Even though there are some people who dislike its conclusion, it is known that there is goodwill on the part of the officials and the people. I have had conversations with what are called parties of the right and they have responded favourably. Prime Minister Pella has indicated the necessity of strengthening the relations between Italy and Ethiopia. It would help to bring the question to a close if Italian private property were taken into consideration. The Italian government is bound to have reservations on this matter on the bases of law and the peace treaty. I can start negotiations early if someone is assigned for the purpose.

"His Majesty: It is also Our wish that relations between Ethiopia and Italy be maintained. It is good that you went to Italy and returned to help resolve the question between our two countries. We have done all We could personally and on the part of Our government to forget what the Fascists had done to our country. But what the Italian press is doing is designed to drive the two countries apart and not to pull them together. As for your request to have someone with whom to confer, We think Ato Aklilou will be back in a few days; in case he is delayed, someone will be instructed to meet you. This matter which has become an obstacle to the relations between the two countries has to be settled. We thank you and Mr. Pella for your efforts in this regard."

The 'aide-memoire' presented by Ambassador Tacoli in French read in part, "Having been called by my government to Rome in mid-September, I have reported on Italo-Ethiopian relations and in particular on the question of reparations after the discussion I had last July with H.E. the Minister for Foreign Affairs, Ato Aklilou. During the discussion, we exchanged views on the possibility of Italy effecting payment by the lump ('prestation forfaitaire') for all the economic, financial and other matters related to the peace treaty. We also recognized the necessity of settling all the pending problems in order to normalize relations and achieve an early renewal of friendship between the two countries. Several points had been clarified with a view to arriving at the desired objective as quickly as possible. The Italian government sincerely wishes to resolve as soon as possible all the pending questions referred to above and to establish the best of friendly relations with Ethiopia. It does not believe there are any insuperable obstacles to prevent the achievement of full agreement.

"On the question of reparations in particular, with a view to the immediate possibility of strengthening the bonds between the two countries, the Italian government affirms its readiness to seek with the Ethiopian government a formula leading to the settlement of all the clauses of the treaty of peace.

"The Italian government is fully confident that the negotiations could proceed on new lines in a spirit of understanding and friendship. It would however, reserve its position on the interpretation of the treaty, which it hopes will not arise, should the negotiations not achieve the desired result.

"All that remains now is to resume negotiations to arrive at points of agreement both on the amount the Italian government will have to pay and on the form and modality of payment. To this end, the Italian government has concrete proposals to present, and I am ready to submit them to the Ethiopian government." Having noted the minutes of the conversation and the 'aide-memoire' the Ambassador had presented to His Majesty, I wrote on November 28, "The fact that the Ambassador has said that he had proposals to present but did not reveal them makes me wonder whether it was meant to enable him to say he had started negotiations and then drag on the process by occasionally throwing out a few points at a time. I think, however, that Your Majesty's Speech from the Throne which was pronounced after his consultation with his government may have disturbed his plan of action."

In a letter dated January 1, 1954, the Emperor wrote, "We have written you about the discussion We had with Ambassador Tacoli on the question of war reparations. Ambassador Tacoli has since had a long conversation with Ato Aklilou and has presented a proposal that the Italian government was prepared to pay the Ethiopian government 15 million United States Dollars by the lump ('forfait'). He has said that the reason for their deducting 10 million Dollars was that the Ethiopian government's demand for reparations had been found to be excessive beyond measure and that the property left here by the Italians could be compared with the amount asked for reparations. He has also claimed that the reason why the Italian government had shown willingness to pay 15 million Dollars was because of its desire to maintain its friendly relations with Ethiopia and that it would not have been obligated by law to pay it. After a proper reply had been given to the Ambassador's baseless claim, he has been told that an answer would be given him after his proposal had been considered. What is now thought is to examine the manner of payment before a reply is given whether we accept or reject his proposal. A commission has been appointed and started to study the modality of payment. Ambassador Tacoli has requested that the process of the matter be treated confidential."

In a memorandum I wrote the Emperor on January 13, I said, "I have no views to present for the moment except to wish success to the negotiations just started. I am wondering whether the recurrence last week of the political crisis in Italy might be an obstacle to the discussion initiated in Addis Ababa. It may perhaps be a convenient excuse for the Italians to put it off, since it will be difficult for them to know if the government to be formed will agree on this matter with that led by Signor Pella."

After Signor Pella, a member of the Christian Democracy Party, had set up in August 1953 what he called his 'business government,' discharged urgent matters of state and laboured to get Trieste restored to Italy, he found his own party divided, with some supporting him and others opposing him. He therefore submitted his resignation to the President early the following January (1954). The President instructed a member of the same party, Amintore Fanfani, to try and form a government. Even though Fanfani presented an elaborate programme to Parliament, hoping to set up a solid-based government, he was unable to obtain the necessary majority to confirm him in office. He resigned his mandate on January 30, three weeks after he was appointed.

The President conducted the customary consultations with leaders of the various parties for one week and directed on February 8 another member of the Christian Democracy Party, Mario Scelba, to form a government. As the three small parties (Liberals, Republicans and Saragat Socialists), which used to work with the Christian Democracy Party and had refused to give it their support for several months, had now agreed to cooperate with it again, Scelba's government was confirmed, and he reported to the President that he could form a government. Its formation was then announced and Scelba presented his programme to Parliament on February 18. A long debate ensued and was concluded on March 10. He obtained a slender majority and a legal government was obtained. The political crisis was over.

After general elections were held in early June 1953, a political crisis was in evidence in Italy which lasted until early March 1954. As a result the leadership of the government was so precarious that one witnessed a panorama of five prime ministers succeeding one another during a nine-month period. But since all the men charged to form a government (de Gasperi, Piccioni, Pella, Fanfani and Scelba) were members of the Christian Democracy Party which had the largest number of members in Parliament their policy had not deviated from that which had been pursued under de Gasperi's leadership. The claim of the Italian authorities that the political crisis was the main reason for the inability to improve, with serious intent, the relations between Ethiopia and Italy was therefore not based on fact. The truth was that the Christian Democracy Party had chosen to make the question serve its election propaganda and had then considered a change of policy during the crisis to be detrimental to its politics.

In a report to His Majesty on March 19, 1954, with reference to the confirmation of Scelba's government, the end of the political crisis and Italy's relations with Ethiopia, I wrote as follows, "I have already reported to Your Majesty that as far as Ethiopia is concerned I did not think that the policy of the new Italian government would show a marked shift. In the present state of Italian politics, whoever the men may be that alternate to hold power, it is the Christian Democracy Party which generally directs policy. It is therefore evident that the party's foreign policy will hardly be changed. Since the administrative officials in the various government departments are not subject to change like the political leaders, the latter are led in what they say and do by the former. Prime Minister Scelba's statement on the Italo-Ethiopian relations is thus based on the advice of the bureaucratic officials, and I have reported to Your Majesty on several occasions the views of these officials on Ethiopia.

"Even though it does not appear that the attitude of the Italian officials has changed perceptibly with respect to Ethiopian-Italian relations, I humbly report that I have been able to observe during the past few weeks that the matter has begun to be viewed in a new light by persons who follow the questions between the two countries in general, and especially by journalists and leaders of opinion. In the first place, the newspapers have restrained themselves from showing that feeling of hatred and contempt which they were used to evince whenever they mentioned Your Majesty's or Ethiopia's name. This was clearly seen after two newspapers had published an article falsely, and maliciously slandered Your

Majesty and a protest made to the Italian Foreign Ministry and after Your Majesty had warned the Italian Ambassador that the publication of such documents was not helpful to the relations of the two countries. Moreover, it is known that the Italians resident in Ethiopia have made strong representations to their government and the authorities to restrain the press, because hostile articles on Ethiopia were harmful to them in the first place.

"More than anything else, the Speech from the Throne which Your Majesty pronounced on Italy on November 2 last has led the Italians, the leaders of the press in particular, to realize that Ethiopian-Italian relations were not improving, as the people generally thought, but were actually deteriorating. Very few newspapers dared to print what Your Majesty had to say on Italy. The eyes of many leaders of opinion were opened on reading the remarks and realized they were in fantasy, far from reality, and they smarted under the words. I have observed that they were particularly vexed by the fact that, while Your Majesty had very friendly words for Yugoslavia, Italy was not mentioned even once in the course of Your remarks. This change of attitude of the Italian leaders of opinion in the past few months was due to the policy which Your Majesty's government had followed in the past year with respect to Italy and the fact that Your Majesty made it abundantly clear in the Speech from the Throne. I venture to state that it was a policy of wisdom which will lead to the realization of the desired result. In writing thus however, I would wish to bring to Your Majesty's attention, as due from a subject and an Ethiopian, that I do think the apparent change of attitude of the Italians is a tactical move, a 'change of mind,' and not a 'change of heart,' not a policy based on determining to forget past grudges and working with due respect to the right and freedom of the Ethiopian people.

"Even though it is gratifying to note that relations between the two countries are beginning to show an improvement, it is imperative to be vigilant day and night so as not to be taken by surprise with this apparent show of goodwill. I am taking the liberty to remind Your Majesty of this because, being here for the time being, I believe it to be my duty and not because it is hidden from Your Majesty whose attention has been engaged by it for the past 37 years, ever since I was a child."

The Emperor wrote on March 24, "We have noted your report on actions taken in the two Chambers concerning Scelba's government. We have also noted that he has obtained a majority vote and will proceed with his task. But with regard to their policy on Ethiopia, since the leaders are from the same Christian Democracy Party who are guided by the permanent employees from inside, it becomes a veneer with no change and your observation is justified. Although the motive for the discontinuance of their vilification campaign in the press is to serve their own interest, what they now disseminate around the world will show that we are in the right and there is reason for hope that it will serve our long-term interest, seeing that we always prevail by dwelling on the truth. In particular, it is clear that the article that Gregorio Consiglio has published in the newspaper, 'Africa,' is helpful to us even though he wrote it for the benefit of his own country.

"Since it was Our duty to enlighten Our people with facts that could not be concealed, We are gratified that Our Speech from the Throne has had a good effect. Nevertheless, as you have reminded Us, however pleased We may be with this, We are not oblivious of the fact that We have manifold tasks to perform, and We shall ponder over them deeply. Negotiations are still proceeding on the reparations and We shall inform you of details of their progress in the near future."

After March 1954, the Italian political situation appeared to be quiet for several months and there was nothing new to observe as far as Ethiopia was concerned. The Emperor visited the USA, Canada and Mexico in June. He was accorded such a gratifying and respectful welcome and the United States government gave him such an open reception accompanied by goodwill and friendliness, noted by all the world, that many Italians appeared to be offended with the American government, thinking that it was an open reproof of their past misdeeds. They were so resentful that when the Emperor visited Yugoslavia and Greece later, the leaders of opinion, especially the Fascists, vented their feelings of hatred on the Emperor and Ethiopia as well as on Marshal Broz-Tito and Yugoslavia in the newspapers. This feeling of the Italians having spread as far as Addis Ababa, the Emperor wrote on October 6, "It has become apparent to us that, since our return from America, the Italian Ambassador Tacoli is performing his duty with absolute indifference and that he is avoiding discussion of some matters with Us. You may indicate this indirectly to the Italian Foreign Ministry when you have occasion to talk to them. It seems that the attitude of the Italians to our recent visit to America and our prospective visit to Europe can be detected from Tacoli's action and demeanour. On the occasion of Our presence in England, We are unable to forget that you were there during the period of exile and are now separated."

Seeing that discussions had been going on from time to time in Addis Ababa on the war reparations, I wrote to the Emperor on August 6 and said, "If there is a chance of the question of the war reparations coming to a successful conclusion, I venture to recommend that the question of the plundered objects and the monument be finalized at the same time." I then proceeded to express the view that otherwise the matter could be dragged out and would perhaps never be settled. In a letter dated August 17, the Emperor wrote, "Discussions are proceeding with the Italian Ambassador on the objects plundered from Ethiopia and the monument together with the reparations. The question of reparations is being tackled with success; the details will be sent you when it is all settled. All that you write on the internal and foreign politics of Italy is very useful and you will continue to write to Us from time to time."

On the question of reparations, it has been indicated above that His Majesty had written me on January 1, 1954, that, on his return from Rome, Ambassador Tacoli had had a discussion with Ato Aklilou when he had presented his government's proposal to pay 15 million Dollars and deduct 10 million Dollars because the Italian government had found the Ethiopian government's demand for reparations to be excessive and because the property the Italians had left behind in Ethiopia could measure up to the amount demanded in reparations; that it had been decided to study the manner of payment before a decision was to be made as to whether the proposal should be accepted or rejected, and that a commission had been appointed and begun the study.

Having pronounced his Speech from the Throne on Ethiopian-Italian relations and appointed a commission to study the Ambassador's proposal, the Emperor, in June 1954, visited the US, Canada and Mexico, and in October, Britain and Western European countries. The Italian leaders of opinion and the press, taking note of the highly respectful and friendly welcome he had received wherever he went and regretful that Italy was not one of those countries, had restrained their feelings of hatred and stopped their usual insulting remarks. It seemed that the tour had revealed to them the moment of truth more clearly. Even the Italian newspaper which had written with such lack of decency when the Ethiopian delegation had visited Rome in connection with the war reparations and which had written, "What reparations are we to pay? Are we expected to pay reparations because we had poured out our blood and wealth to civilize the country," was now unhappy that the Emperor's tour did not include Italy, and it wrote, "How could we exclude ourselves from obtaining greater benefits for the sake of 25 million Dollars? Let us remove the obstacle that separates us from Ethiopia and hasten to take our proper place in economic and commercial matters." This view reflected the feelings of Italians who were growing apprehensive as they watched the realities of the time. It was for this reason that Signor Gaetano Martino, a member of the Liberal Party, who was appointed Foreign Minister in September, 1954, had told me more than once that he was determined that the question of war reparations should be settled quickly. Although they could not conceal their horror at the thought of paying reparations, even the Fascist newspapers were urging that payment be made and the obstacle removed.

In a memorandum I sent the Emperor on December 3, I wrote, "What has aroused them more than anything else is the wonderful welcome accorded to Your Majesty in all the European countries visited, thus showing that Ethiopia is not a country to be treated with indifference these days. What seems to haunt them with so much chagrin is the development of Ethiopia's relations with the Netherlands and West Germany in such a short time and the fear of the extent to which the door would be opened to them in technical know-how and trade. They are moreover vexed because they feel they are treated like colonial people in that they are debarred from competing directly in tenders for contracts and are compelled to work as sub-contractors for those who win the tenders.

"It is therefore the desire of the Italian government as well as the Italians at present to be in a position to compete on an equal footing before Ethiopia gives away all its development work to its friends. From what the Director General for Political Affairs and Ambassador Tacoli had told me, it would appear that their acceptance of the greater part of the proposal made by Your Majesty's government and their hope that modes of agreement would be found for the other points is because the Italian ministers and the officials of the various ministries are intent on seeing this obstacle removed."

The Emperor wrote on December 17, in reply, "As we write you this letter, Ato Aklilou has just had a discussion with Ambassador Tacoli. He has indicated his agreement to the proposal put to him from this side, except for some minor points. He has even said about the Aksum monument that they would have one made if we wished or restore the monument itself, if we did not wish. The agreement will be sent you in advance as soon as it is finalized.

"From the newspaper cuttings you sent, it would appear that Our European tour has hastened the process. It is true that We have made every effort in the course of Our visits to make friends, hire technicians and invite people with capital, even if on a modest scale to come and work here, and this has begun to bear fruit. The work started by the Yugoslav technicians is gratifying. We are writing you some of these things, however briefly, so that you know them beforehand."

In a memorandum to him dated January 5, 1955, I wrote on the Aksum monument, "With reference to Ambassador Tacoli's remark to Ato Aklilou that they would have a monument made for us if we wished or restore our monument if we did not wish, what he told me when we had a conversation here was not concerning the Aksum monument but about the statue of the lion which they had removed from the Addis Ababa railway station and which they had claimed had been lost when the Americans and the British had occupied Rome. Since the statue of the lion had been made by the French, he said that a replica could be made from the model. What makes the Aksum monument highly valuable is its antiquity and no replacement could be given for it, in the humble opinion of Your servant."

The Emperor wrote on January 12 in reply, "With regard to the Aksum monument, it is obvious to all that the reasons they advance leave an impression of prevarication; however, the Ambassador here has informed Ato Aklilou that the monument will be brought back. It is our firm determination that this monument be restored."

After this, I submitted two detailed memorandums to the Emperor on the discussions I had had in February with the newly appointed Secretary General, Ambassador Rossi-Longhi, and with the new Director General for Political Affairs, Ambassador Magistrati, on Ethiopian-Italian relations, on the indifference shown by the former Foreign Ministry officials, especially by Count Zoppi, the former Secretary General, to hinder the improvement of relations between the two countries and that as a result the question of the war reparations had been dragged out. In the memorandum I sent His Majesty on March 5, I expressed my views as follows, "It appears that, since Signor Martino has been appointed Foreign Minister, more consideration is being given than hitherto to questions that concern Ethiopia. After the Minister changed his assistants with the consent of the cabinet, the new officials seem to follow his views and to show a desire to remove the misunderstanding that has proven to be a hindrance to the relations between the two countries. They have tried to give me the impression that the discussions in Addis Ababa have not been finalized until now because the Imperial government has not been earnest enough. But I could not refute this view, being unaware of the state of the discussions. As the Director General for Political Affairs has told me that we should have a discussion on the question after he had studied it, I humbly beg to be informed of the state of the discussions so that I should not be placed in an awkward position by not having what to answer him, and if there is anything I should transmit to the government from this side."

By order of the Emperor, a memorandum showing the state of the discussions was sent me from the Ministry for Foreign Affairs with a cover letter dated March 16. The main points of the memorandum are as follows: The Italian Ambassador proposed that, out of the war reparations of 25 million Dollars owed by his government, 15 million Dollars be paid. Prior to accepting or rejecting the proposal, the Ethiopian government appointed a commission to study the matter with the Italian Ambassador on the technical basis.

After due negotiation, the commission arrived at an accord as follows:
1). Since the peace treaty stipulated that Italy pay the war reparations with materials made in its industrial plants and with services, projects were presented which it was desired Italy should execute as war reparations. Selections were made from a number of projects presented and it was agreed that the Qoqa electric power project, a limited number of ships and a complete cotton plant were chosen. Italy was to supply them. 2). It was proposed from the Italian side that, in accordance with the peace treaty, Ethiopia supply the raw materials needed for the projects. Ethiopia affirmed however that, since Italy had asked that the amount for reparations be reduced, it should procure the raw materials for the work itself. 3). That, since Italy had agreed to pay one million Dollars for

the money despoiled from the Bank of Ethiopia, the amount be added to the 15 million Dollars to be paid as reparations and a total payment of 16 million Dollars be made. 4). That the amount due for reparations be paid within four years of the ratification of the agreement, and that the mode of payment be as follows:

1. On the date of ratification, 5 million Dollars;
2. In the course of the first year, 4 million Dollars;
3. In the course of the second year, 3 million Dollars;
4. In the course of the third year, 3 million Dollars;
5. In the course of the fourth year, 1 million Dollars.

Total: 16 million Dollars

That the construction of the Qoqa Dam be completed in the course of the first three years and that of the ships and the cotton plant during the last two years.

In addition, it was set out in the memorandum that, in view of the fact that Italy was obligated by the peace treaty to restore the objects removed from Ethiopia, lists of ancient artistic works of art had been supplied to the Italian Ambassador and that, 1). the Italian government had indicated that, since it could not locate His Majesty's library, it was prepared to purchase a number of books and replace it; 2). that it had made a search for but had not been able to find the statue of the lion taken from the railway station and that it could not hold out hope of its being found and, as it was not an ancient work of art, the Italian government was prepared to have one made from a model as desired by the Ethiopian government; 3). that when the Aksum monument was removed from Ethiopia, it had been broken to pieces to make it easier to carry away by freight and that it would not only be of little use if it were dismantled again and shipped back to Ethiopia, but it would also distress the Italian people. The Italian government had therefore indicated its readiness to present instead a monument, a commemorative structure, a hospital or any other thing desired by the Ethiopian government. In case the monument was left in Italy, and so as not to make it appear that it was a spoil of war, an inscription should be placed on it as follows: "Presented by the people of Ethiopia to the people of Italy in token of friendship," and that the structure the Italian people would give in replacement be inscribed, "Gift of the people of Italy as a token of gratitude for the gift of friendship made by the Ethiopian people to the Italian people"; 4). that, as it was difficult to know the whereabouts of the other objects in the lists and, since they were so numerous, the Italian Ambassador had asked whether there could be an alternative way of settling the matter. The Ethiopian government had responded that it would consider any proposal the Italian government would put forward; that objects that were found be restored forthwith, and that a commission be appointed to look for the objects and return them as soon as they were found.

As soon as I was informed of the state of the discussions in Addis Ababa, I had a long conversation on March 23 with the Director General for Political Affairs, Ambassador Magistrati, and the Head of Section, Minister Cardio, with reference to the objects of art. Since it appeared from information we had both received from Addis Ababa that a general mode of agreement had been found on the question of war reparations, we felt that it would be better to discuss matters concerning the historical and artistic objects removed from Ethiopia to Italy. The main items for the conversation were the lion statue, the Emperor's library, the documents of the former Emperors, the Aksum monument and the objects of value despoiled from Ethiopia in general. This is a summary of the conversation.

After the lion statue was transported to Rome, it was placed at the foot of the memorial built to commemorate the Italians who had died at Dogali. When the Americans and the British occupied Rome in 1945, the Allied Commission which was in control of Italy ordered that the statue be removed from there and returned to Ethiopia, and it was removed forthwith and handed over to the Commission. They claimed that they had no knowledge of its whereabouts since. I said in reply that if they had given the statue to the Commission their government could find out from the former officials of the Commission, and if it could not be found, it should be possible to ask the Franco-Ethiopian Railway Company to make one from the model from which the statue was made.

They then explained that they had been unable to find the books that had been in His Majesty's library and the old State documents; that if the Emperor wished they were prepared to purchase books which could serve as replacements. I retorted that His Majesty's books were despoiled by no one and that Badoglio took charge of them when he took over the Palace, that, even though the library books could be replaced, it was impossible to find replacements for the documents of the former Emperors, that the legacy of ancestors could not be bought for money, and that, if the looted objects were not found and returned even in part, no genuine reconciliation could ever be achieved.

Ambassador Magistrati agreed with me in this and said that, if they did not make an effort to try and find something that would create confidence, he did not think the signing of the agreement alone would dispel mistrust. He therefore ordered that a request be sent to the Prime Minister's office that, until his return from America in early April, the departments concerned meet in a commission and do all that was possible to locate the objects.

Finally, the Aksum monument was discussed and Minister Cardio said that, as the Secretary General, Ambassador Rossi-Longhi had told me, they were prepared to restore the monument if the Ethiopian government insisted that it be returned; but that their Ambassador had informed my government that, in accordance with the peace treaty, the Ethiopian government had to pay for the freight and that my government had replied that it would not accept his view since there was no such stipulation in the section of the treaty that dealt with Ethiopian matters. According to experts' reports, freight charges would be about 300 million Lire.

I rejoined that it was not for us to pay for the freight but for those who took away the object. We did not ask the monument to be taken to Rome; one should not forget that it was removed by force. I asked why they found it to be so heavy to take it back when they had paid for the freight to carry it to Rome. He said that was for the experts to say; it was done because Mussolini had ordered it; money had no value in those days, the only concern was to carry out his orders; but now they had found it to be beyond their modest means. He then expressed the wish that the monument might remain in Italy and that Ethiopia be given whatever it desired instead.

I said that I regretted there was one thing they had failed to appreciate; the Ethiopian people did not consider the monument simply as a dressed stone; it was for us a reminder of 2,000 years of history and for that reason could not be exchanged for money; it was not a thing to be given away for a hospital or for any other thing. It was to be deplored that they should ask to retain it in exchange for something because it indicated that they had no concern for the feelings and dignity of our people. Why did they not realize that the Ethiopian government and people could not give away for money what was a symbol of their dignity and a legacy from their ancestors. The monument was taken away as a spoil at a time when our people had fallen. It gave us no joy but afflicted our spirit to contemplate the manner of its despoliation. We desired that all that we considered as a sign of insult should be obliterated now that we stood on our feet and that our rights were recognized. It seemed to me to be good in all respects if they did not keep on offering pretexts and thus add insult to injury, but restore the monument to us as a pledge of sincere friendship.

Observing that I had spoken with feeling, they agreed with me that they should make every effort to find as many of the objects as they possibly could. We then discussed some technical matters which had arisen in Addis Ababa on the manner of payment of the reparations and separated.

I expressed my views on this conversation in a memorandum I sent the Emperor on March 25, "The impression I got from this conversation was that the strategy of the Italian government officials in connection with the objects is not to find and restore them, but to close the matter by simply stating they could not find them, and induce us to be convinced that, since they could not be found, we had better forget about them. I therefore venture to suggest that, in the course of the discussions, the matter be impressed on the Italian Ambassador so that he could urge his government, and that he be convinced that unless the objects were restored, the agreement by itself would not yield the desired feeling of friendliness. If this were to be done, it might help to get back at least the historical documents removed from the Palace. I have had occasion to remind

Your Majesty that I do not feel the matter of restoring the objects of art will ever be effected unless it is settled together with the question of war reparations. I still consider that the signature of the agreement should be conditioned to the restoration of at least the principal objects. I fear we shall get nothing if the two questions are separated."

The Emperor wrote on April 1 in reply, "We have noted from your report of March 26 the conversation you had with the officials of the Italian Foreign Ministry about the objects despoiled from here during the war and the views you presented to them. It is very good. As you say, the negotiations on the war reparations here are nearing conclusion. What has proven rather difficult at present is the question of the plundered objects which we have pressed them hard to restore to us. The following is what has finally been presented to them on the matter and is being considered:

"1. That the Italian government deliver the Aksum monument and the objects it admits to be in its possession;

"2. That a fresh list of selected irreplaceable historical, artistic, and other objects valued for their commemorative nature be made from the lists already presented by Our government and that searches be undertaken until they are found or until it was definite they could not be found; and if found, that they be immediately returned to Ethiopia; that a commission be appointed to look for the objects, (this could be the commission you said has been set up);

"3. That the Italian government pay a fixed sum for the other replaceable objects that could be bought or made;

"It is necessary to consider that it would be detrimental to keep in abeyance the conclusion of the matters on which agreement had been reached. What is your view on this?"

I expressed my opinion in a memorandum I sent the Emperor on April 14, "The reason why I said in my memorandum of March 26 that the signing of the agreement should be conditioned to the restoration of at least the principal objects was in the hope that they would be made to undertake to send back the Aksum monument and the other objects they admitted to have found, and not to suggest that the conclusion of the agreement should be delayed until all the despoiled objects had been restored. To expect that would be tantamount to preventing the conclusion of the agreement. It would therefore be good if the agreement on the reparations and the restoration of the objects were to be signed on the basis of the three points set out in Your Majesty's letter. Now that the time for the conclusion of a comprehensive agreement on the question of the reparations is at hand, I humbly submit that it be signed as soon as possible to avoid the risk of an unexpected hitch due to delay and to dispel the impression of unwillingness to sign it on the part of Ethiopia. Obstacles may also crop up if those in power are suddenly removed and replaced by others owing to the chronic change of position of the Italian authorities." In a letter he wrote on

April 20, His Majesty said, "We have noted your clear statement on the question of the war reparations. As your view coincides with Ours, the Foreign Ministry will continue discussion on that basis."

The negotiations continued under these circumstances with the Italian Ambassador throughout April, 1955, and the Ambassador reported to his government that he was pleased with the words of the Emperor when he was received in audience. And His Majesty wrote in a note he sent me on May 12, "The negotiations are nearing the end and we shall let you know as soon as they are completed." As the discussions both on the war reparations and the despoiled objects of art thus came to an end, I considered my mission to Italy terminated and awaited the Emperor's summons to return to my country. The agreement was signed in Addis Ababa on March 5, 1956, after I went to London. I reckoned the reason for the delay was because Ambassador Tacoli had died before signing it and the new Ambassador had to take time to be acquainted with the matter.

Having lived in Rome for two and a half years by December 1954, and neither my wife nor I having returned home during that time, we were home-sick and weary of the Italian climate. Moreover, as I had heard that my father had been seriously ill the previous year, I had a desire to take him to Addis Ababa for medical treatment. I had reported this to the Emperor and requested permission to return to Ethiopia for a short time. His Majesty had written on December 30, "As you know, negotiations on the question of the war reparations are proceeding in earnest; you should therefore have patience for a little while and you will return here as soon as that is over." At the conclusion of the agreement, he recalled this and had a telegram sent to me on June 20, 1955, which read, "By command, you are to hand over the work to Major Mesfin Yebegashet as Chargé d'Affaires a.i. and return with your family: Aklilou." My wife and I were elated and I knelt down and praised my God that the time had arrived for me to return home, having in three years peacefully completed the difficult task assigned to me in Italy. In the course of my diplomatic tour of duty in foreign lands, I had never experienced such a thankless task devoid of pleasure like the mission to Italy. As discussed above in detail, the Italian authorities and the leaders of opinion, the Fascists in particular, who had been full of rancour for a number of years for having lost Ethiopia, were extremely angered and embittered that the Ethiopian government had demanded that Italy pay reparations to Ethiopia. It aroused in them such feelings of uncontrollable hatred and contempt that they were impelled rashly to ask that our National Day (May 5), for us commemorative of Ethiopia's resurrection and for them reminiscent of Italy's defeat, should not be celebrated in Rome.

However, as the months passed after the demand for war reparations was presented, they realized the futility of their hostile attitude and that in the long-run it was bound to hurt the Italian nationals in Ethiopia and Italy itself more than anyone else. They were therefore obliged to agree to pay the reparations and to restore at least some of the main objects of art they had despoiled, such as the Aksum monument and the lion statue.

The amount of money paid for reparations was designated for the construction of the Qoqa Dam and hydroelectric projects on the Awash river and the hydroelectric and cotton plants on Tiss Abbai falls near Bahr Dar. I could not find out whether ships were built for us; perhaps the funds were not sufficient, not even for the project on the Tiss Abbai falls.

They had often told me during our discussions that they could not find the lion statue but were prepared to have one made for us. I had as often told them it could be found if only they searched for it. I had at the same time set someone to look for it and came to know that the statue had been hidden somewhere in the City, and I drew their attention to it. They brought it out of hiding after a number of years and sent it back. It was erected near its former site at the Addis Ababa railway station and the Emperor unveiled it on December 4, 1971, at an impressive ceremony.

The Aksum monument which they undertook to restore after a lot of arguments had not been sent back at the time of writing (1993). Since I was away from home on some other duty for over three years after the agreement was concluded, I was not able to follow up what had been done in connection with the restoration of the monument or of the objects of art, or of the documents of the former Emperors with which the Emperor had been greatly concerned. The non-restoration of the monument remains a mystery for me!

As soon as the handing over of the Embassy in Rome was completed, I took leave of the Italian authorities and fixed the date of my departure from Rome on July 15, 1955. I announced that my family and I would travel to Athens by Alitalia. The Italians who heard this, the officials of the airline in particular, were pleased and a bouquet of flowers was presented to my wife as we boarded the aircraft. We spent about four days in Athens and took Ethiopian Airlines for Asmara where we stopped for two days. We returned to Addis Ababa on July 22. Relatives and friends met us at the airport and welcomed us with joy. We gave thanks to our God for enabling us to regain our native land.

I visited Foreign Minister Aklilou in his office on my return to Addis Ababa. On the mention of the agreement with Italy, he exclaimed, "You have made us work, Man!" As mentioned above, when I was appointed to Rome, I had requested the Emperor that instructions be given me concerning my work. He had ordered Ato Aklilou twice to provide me with them but he had not given me anything. I had to report this to His Majesty when I took leave of him, but seeing nothing could be done, he had told me to present my views on matters that might arise while I was in Rome and he would send me directives.

Following this directive, I continually sent him detailed reports, along with my views, on the questions that arose between the two countries. As the Emperor was deeply concerned with the payment of the war reparations, seen at that time to be the main question outstanding between Ethiopia and Italy, he had received with pleasure all the reports and views I had submitted and, after considering them with his advisers, seen to it that Ato Aklilou stressed my views, in the course of his discussions with the Italian Ambassador. His Majesty had also informed me without interruption what had been done on that side. One important thing that gave me special pleasure and inspired me in my work was the fact that the Emperor had sent replies to my reports often within ten days and sometimes within one week, sharing his views with me and giving me directives. It was considered by Ato Aklilou that I had made them work, because the Emperor, prompted by the views I had continually submitted to him, had made him and his assistants work without respite until the negotiations on the war reparations and the restoration of historical and artistic works had been concluded in agreement.

NINE

London: Ambassador Plenipotentiary
1955 - 1959

I stayed in Addis Ababa for five months after my return to Ethiopia from Italy. I brought my parents from Wollega and they stayed with me. Medical treatment was given them.

Some of the Emperor's high officials who had been ill at ease for many years about my living and working in Addis Ababa repeated the stratagem that was seen at the time of my return from India. They had been busy preparing a post for me abroad and persuaded the Emperor to approve their recommendation. Since these persons held key positions in the structure of the government, they were in daily contact with the Emperor and at times aroused his anger. On these occasions and whenever their work was found to be unsatisfactory, he used to reprimand them and say, "Don't forget there is Amanuel," as if to say he could replace me in their respective positions.

This might have been a suitable stick for him to beat them with, but it aroused in those persons feelings of hatred for me; so much so that they constantly schemed how they could get me to live far from Addis Ababa. They had shown that it would be dangerous for them to let me live in Addis Ababa and be a close servant of the Emperor in the Autumn of 1943, after I returned home from Britain. While I was away to visit my parents in Wollega, soon after, they had caused the post in the Foreign Ministry, which was perhaps intended for me, to go to one who was their partisan and had tried to keep me down by causing me to be commanded to work under him. Upon revealing my resentment, I was rescued from the low position to which I had been relegated, through His Majesty's consideration, and assigned to serve in the Ministry of Education for three years, the Emperor himself being my immediate superior. They had constantly plotted to have me removed from that post and schemed to prevent my appointment after that to any position for two years. They had been relieved when I was sent to India.

Although their plan to have me sent to Egypt on my return from India was thwarted by an unforeseen event and I was appointed to a post abroad not of their choosing, the fact that I was sent to Italy after a wait of nine months had allayed their fears until my return home. Since the Emperor was aware that the strong plot to prevent me from getting too close to him in my work dated from 1943, it was too obvious both to him and to me that due to the situation then obtaining and his internal policy, I could not take over any of the positions held by them, and the mention of my name was only meant to keep them in permanent suspense. The factors that militated against it were the part of the country where I was born, my evangelical faith, the fact that my views were almost always at variance with theirs and that I lacked relatives or supporters in Court circles.

Even though the principal official who from the beginning had been continually and subtly opposed to my being too close to the Throne (we used to work together during the exile) was removed from power in 1955 when I was in Rome and his partisans had fallen out with him on other matters, they were at one as concerned me. They therefore pursued the same line and prepared a post for me abroad before my return from Italy; it was London. And there was another matter which made it inevitable. The official who was Ethiopian Ambassador in London at that time and who had lived there for many years conceived the idea that, for him to get relief, it was essential for me to replace him. He therefore implored the Emperor to appoint me to London and allow him to return to Addis Ababa. This was a welcome support for those who had made it their aim to keep me away from Addis Ababa. They pretended to praise me saying, "There is no one more suited than Amanuel for the post since London is a city where he had lived for many years." They thus obtained the Emperor's sanction that I should go to Britain. But, reckoning that I would not be happy to go abroad again (and since I had been given the epithet of 'headstrong'), they advised His Majesty that he himself inform me of it instead of the Minister of the Pen, assuming that I would not oppose the Sovereign's direct command. The Emperor therefore summoned me to his presence alone one morning and, recalling what I had done in Rome, told me that he had decided that I go and serve him in London.

Even though no one had ever told me about it, I had had a consciousness for a number of years of the intrigue that was being carried out against me so that I did not live in my own country. I therefore decided, despite the suddenness of the command, there and then to express my discontent and said with feeling, "How could You send me to a land where I had lived for so many years in difficult circumstances; where my right hand had been paralysed from too much writing and the condition of the climate? My right hand with which I serve is still hurting. How can I serve You if it is disabled again?" - The Emperor who had not expected my remarks was taken aback momentarily and said, "Are you embittered to this extent?" - I replied, "Why shouldn't I be embittered, Your Majesty? I can be of no service to You if I fall ill." - He then said, "You go now since We had decided on it earlier. If you express the desire to return home, even after three months, We shall let you come back." Thereupon, I bowed and retired from the presence.

Knowing that it was unrealistic for one to serve for only three months at a post like London, I determined to endure a stay of three years and then request to be recalled home. In truth, I was not averse to going to London as ambassador and I knew it was difficult to change the decision. When I went to India, my two children who were infants and the other two who were born later had to learn to speak English from the beginning and had gone to an English school when I was transferred to Italy. I knew they would benefit greatly if they were to go to school in England. (My two daughters studied in Britain until they graduated from the University). I ventured to express my views to the Emperor to give notice that I would not go abroad after my return from London. It would appear that His Majesty appreciated it and no one ever mentioned my being sent abroad after my return home from Britain in 1959.

In this connection, my conscience impels me to state the relationship between His Majesty the Emperor Haile Sellassie and myself with respect to my work during the period I was in government service. The Emperor had occasion to get to know me at the time when he was in exile (1936-1940) in Britain, since I happened to be working in his Legation. He also knew that, due to the great disaster that had fallen on Ethiopia, I used to go around and speak at a number of English meetings about the plight of our country. He was present at one of the meetings and had been pleased and felt pride on hearing what I had to say. On returning to his Throne, he had deigned to reveal this to me in writing and in other ways. He had repeatedly told me that, over and above the reports I had sent him from London when he was in Khartoum and after he returned to Addis Ababa, he had derived both pleasure and benefit from the many reports I had written him from the countries to which I had been sent. I had also had the impression that he had been gratified with the service I had rendered to the Country and the Sovereign as one of the ministers in the departments to which

I had been assigned after the end of my diplomatic tour of duty. Though unable to repress the intrigues that were constantly devised against me, he had been my supporter and protector because he knew I had no friends around him. He had helped and encouraged me in all I had done. He had never left me at the mercy of those who hated and slandered me. And above all, even though he was aware I am not highborn and endowed with wealth, he had shown the regard and goodwill he had for my family before the whole Ethiopian people by consenting to the marriage of his grandson to my daughter. There were many Ethiopians during his reign who boasted that they were of noble birth and had great wealth; but it was known that very few were vouchsafed this honour.

November 2, 1955 was the 25th anniversary of the Coronation of Emperor Haile Sellassie and elaborate preparations were in progress to celebrate the silver jubilee. It pleased His Majesty that I should be in Addis Ababa on the occasion. He therefore summoned me to his presence one day and told me to stay until after the celebrations. A letter dated October 31 and signed by the Minister of the Pen was sent to inform me that I had been appointed Ambassador Extraordinary and Plenipotentiary in London. Before my departure for Britain, however, something happened that I had never thought of or expected.

The Lutheran World Federation (LWF), 'a communion of churches' all over the world had planned a conference for delegates of about one million Evangelical Christians, known as Lutherans, who lived on the African Continent with a view to getting them to meet and become acquainted with one another and strengthening their unity in the Faith. It had decided that the conference be convened in November, 1955, in Tanganyika (now Tanzania) in the town of Marangu situated on the slopes of Mount Kilimanjaro. The Norwegian bishop, Dr. Fridtjov Birkeli, who was Director of the LWF Department of World Mission, was charged to visit the African countries where the Lutherans lived and invite them to participate in the conference.

Most of the Evangelical Christians in Ethiopia at that time were considered to be Lutherans because they had entered the Church through the preaching and teaching of Swedish and German Missionaries. Even though the time had not yet come when those Christians were to get together and assume the entity of a church, they had been formed into congregations in a number of places. The chief of them was the congregation that had been established in Addis Ababa by the SEM and the leadership of which had been taken over by the Ethiopian believers after the Italian war of aggression. It had been named 'Mekane Yesus-Ethiopian Evangelical Church.' There were also congregations in Eritrea which were established when the missionaries first arrived in Ethiopia.

On his visit to Addis Ababa, Dr. Birkeli met the leaders of the Mekane Yesus Congregation, the elders of the Congregation in Asmara, and the Mission Directors and explaining the Federation's plan, invited them to send their delegates to Marangu to take part in the conference. They accepted the invitation and, when selecting the delegates, my name was mentioned and a suggestion made that I be one of them.

I have indicated in Part 5 above that I had become a member of the Mekane Yesus Congregation on my return from Britain in the summer of 1943 and that, as president of the congregation, I had laid the foundation stone of the new church building just before my departure for India (1949). I had resumed my membership and worshipped there on my return from India and Italy. Although I was not one of them in 1955, the leaders had determined that I should go to Marangu as one of the delegates and introduced me to Dr. Birkeli. I told them that I had been appointed to go to Britain but was prepared to attend the conference if it was the Emperor's wish. On hearing this, Dr. Birkeli requested an audience of His Majesty and, explaining that the Christian conference that was scheduled to be held in Tanganyika was the first ever in African history, be-sought him to go and address the historic conference in his capacity as head of the Ethiopian Church and since Ethiopia was an ancient Christian country in Africa. On being told that the Emperor could not be present at the conference, he requested that I be allowed to attend it before my departure for London, and to send a message to the conference. This was granted and he reported to the leaders that he was glad to have obtained his wish. His Majesty also told me that he had granted me permission to go and ordered that my air passage be paid. A message to the conference was prepared.

Ato Emmanuel Gabre Sellassie who was president of the congregation that year (1955) was the leader of the delegation. Seven of the delegates were Ethiopians, two of whom came from the congregation in Eritrea. There were two missionaries, one each from Sweden and Norway. They were Pastor Per Stjarne, who had served in Ethiopia for almost 50 years, and Mr. Johannes Sandved, one of the first Norwegian Missionaries in Ethiopia. We left by air for Tanganyika on November 10 via Nairobi, Kenya. The conference lasted from November 12 to 22. The story will be narrated in Part 15 below.

On return from Tanganyika, I stayed in Addis Ababa until December 15 and left for London with my family arriving in Cairo in the evening. We had to stay in Cairo for three days waiting for an aircraft to take us straight to Britain. We boarded an Indian airliner on December 19 which stopped at Geneva airport after a flight of eight hours and continued its flight to London. The city was overcast with fog on that day and the aircraft had to land at Herne Bay. We arrived in London by train on December 20.

The Chief of Protocol came to our Embassy the following day and informed me that Her Majesty Queen Elizabeth II was going to Sandringham on holiday and I would have to present my Letters of Credence after the Christmas holidays.

I went to the British Foreign Office on January 3, 1946, and met the Permanent Under Secretary, Sir Ivon Kirkpatrick, the Chief of the African Department and the Head of the Ethiopian Section. The Under Secretary told me that the only active matter at that time pending between the two governments was the Somali question and that the officials of the two governments had been meeting in Harar to discuss the difficulties that had arisen from the agreement that had been concluded on the question. I replied that I had heard about the meeting of the officials before I had left Addis Ababa but, since I had been travelling, I did not know the outcome. I then reminded him that there was in addition a difficult problem that needed clarification concerning the Ethiopians who lived in Kenya and that we would have to discuss it in due course. I then called on the Assistant Under Secretary in charge of African Affairs. He also told me that the relations between our two governments were good and that he would do all he could that understanding was obtained on matters that might arise from time to time. I assured him that, since it was the objective of my mission, my efforts would also be directed to that end. On leaving him, I met the official in charge of Ethiopian affairs and his assistant. We had a similar exchange of views and goodwill.

On January 24, I went to Buckingham Palace to present my Letters of Credence to Her Majesty the Queen. We conversed for some time after the ceremony when the Queen said that she understood I had been a teacher. I replied that I had taught for a few years after I left school, that I was secretary of our Legation in London during the War and that I had been sent to India and Italy. The Queen asked whether I liked my work in Italy. I said that it was not easy because I was the first to be sent there when relations were being re-established after a lot of bloodshed. It was difficult to forget the past, and I had found that to be more difficult for the Italians, especially for the officials. The Queen then said that the Italians were temperamental; they might have been upset by the change of circumstances. Her Majesty proceeded to say that she did not think my task there would be difficult as there had been no such bloodshed between us. I replied that was the case; there was nothing but friendship between us, and it was my hope that my mission would be a success. Her Majesty then commanded that my colleagues be admitted and they made obeisance and retired. My wife was then introduced and paid her respects. The Queen asked her about her children and we withdrew from the presence. My next task was to write letters to the members of the Diplomatic Corps announcing my arrival and that I had started work. I next made a round of visits to them which took several months due to their large number.

I saw more clearly after I began work that, as the Under Secretary for Foreign Affairs had warned me soon after I arrived in London, it was the Somali question that was clouding Anglo-Ethiopian relations. And it had not been resolved when

I returned to Ethiopia after three and a half years. Here is the story: The British had relinquished most of the Ogaden after the War, but for various reasons, they had retained the district bordering on Somaliland and Somalia called the Haud and the 'Reserved Area.' The main reason they had advanced for this was that the area was most important to the Somalis under British protection for grazing purposes. But as the Ethiopian government had made strong demands to the British government for its restoration, the British government had decided to give it back, and an agreement had been signed on the occasion of the Emperor's state visit to Britain in November 1954. The British Somalis were disturbed on hearing this and, venting their supposed hatred for Ethiopia by repeated peaceful demonstrations, sent petitions first to the British government and later to the UN General Assembly to give them back the territory. As their petition was not considered by the General Assembly, they passed through London in January 1956 on their way home from New York and the press took up their cause and widely publicized it. They met the Colonial Secretary and demanded that the British government undertake to give them freedom forthwith like Somalia and make preparations for the two territories to be merged and given independence. The minister gave them a cordial welcome and sent them away with expectations.

Some members of Parliament had alleged that Ethiopia had failed to properly carry out the terms of the 1954 agreement concluded between the two governments and had tried to accuse it in Parliament. The British press had also worked hard to depict Ethiopia as oppressor and despoiler. Seeing the matter was causing apprehension, an Englishman had written to tell me that, in order to save Ethiopia's reputation, it would be useful if the Ethiopian government were to cause a brochure to be prepared stating the true state of affairs and countering the propaganda let loose on Ethiopia. I took up the suggestion and submitted a report to the Emperor in which I stressed that it was clear that, apart from the accusation on the Somali question, there were persons who were bent on tearing away the Ogaden from Ethiopia if possible, and that it was essential to oppose the defamatory and harmful propaganda.

The Ethiopian government had asked the British government to allow it to open a consulate at Hargeisa but had had no response for six months. The Foreign Ministry then sent word that I repeat the request. So, in February, I went to see Under Secretary of State Sir Ivon Kirkpatrick and, informing him that the delay was disturbing my government, urged him to give us a reply. He put me off by saying that he had not followed the matter and would have to study it. He would let me know either directly or through the African Department. A few days later, the chief of the department telephoned to say that, as he was occupied with some other matter, the Under Secretary had directed him to give a reply to my request.

I therefore went to the Foreign Office on March 5 and we had a discussion. The official told me that, since the two governments were longstanding friends as well as war allies, it was believed that all matters tending to disturb their political relations from time to time should be eliminated, and that the British Ambassador had been received by the Emperor the previous week and requested that a mission led by Mr. Dodds-Parker visit Addis Ababa and have a discussion with a view to getting clarified all the matters that had arisen between the two governments. He then said that His Majesty had accepted the idea in principle. Since the Italian government had a strong desire that the former Italian Somaliland should be granted its independence in the near future, what the British government wished to achieve through the mission was to consult together as to what the status of all the Somalis would be as a result, as well as some matters affecting the two governments. On the question I had posed to Kirkpatrick, he informed me that, due to the difficulty that had arisen from the grazing area and the matters connected with it, the hatred of the Somalis against Ethiopia had been aroused and the governor of Somaliland had therefore stood firm that the consulate should not be opened for the time being.

I rejoined that Ethiopia's purpose to open a consulate in that territory was to help cool down the feelings that were said to have been aroused and to explain to the Somalis the attitude of our government. The 'exequatur' had been delayed for over six months and they were delaying it still further by connecting it to the matter of the mission they were proposing to send to Ethiopia. I then told him that, it was my view that the issuing of an 'exequatur' for which, contrary to international practice, we had waited too long and the early presence of our consul at Hargeisa would help move the task of the mission forward. He kept repeating that the Somalis did not like us and that they feared opening the consulate would aggravate their hatred for Ethiopia; they needed time to explain the matter to the Somalis.

I replied that it was difficult to understand their attitude. Not long before, His Imperial Majesty's liaison office had been opened in Mogadishu and, even though the administrators there were Italians with whom we had had bloodshed, nothing had been heard of hatred for Ethiopia or of disturbances; we had found it difficult to understand why, from what they told us, it was only their Somalis who hated us. He replied that we had had no clashes on the Somalia border, but as their Somaliland was concerned, there had been periodic clashes and difficulties which had greatly aroused the people's feelings of hate; time was needed to cool them down, and the recent meeting in Harar had not helped to resolve the matter as they had hoped.

I reminded him that the recent clash was made between their own Somalis and that Ethiopia had had nothing to do with it; it was hard for us to understand why Ethiopia should be hated every time their Somalis clashed. I then asked whether it was because we allowed them to come and go in our country at will that their

Somalis hated Us. He said that they were like children and now that the spirit of nationalism had been greatly aroused, it was making them restive; they therefore thought it would be better if the question of appointing a consul were to be discussed with their delegates in Addis Ababa together with other matters.

I reported to the Emperor on March 7 this discussion with the official and advanced the following comment, "I gathered from this official's words that what is exercising them is the question of the Somalis and the grazing area, and that they will have no rest until the agreement recently signed between the two governments, which they strove to get modified without success at the Harar meeting is interpreted and carried out the way they desire. Although it is difficult to grasp, as they contend, why of all the Somalis, the British Somalis should hate us so much, it appears that the British are determined to use that as a cover to see to it that Ethiopia gets neither peace nor rest in that connection. I say this because when I asked him whether the Somalis, being our neighbours, would never have a peaceful relationship with us, he replied he did not think they would ever have one."

Another matter I discussed with the chief of the African Department was with reference to a racial discrimination law passed in Kenya which had resulted in mistreatment, imprisonment and acute suffering of Ethiopians who lived in Nairobi and other towns of Kenya. The Ethiopian government had from time to time made representations to the Kenyan administration and to the British government that the law should be amended to enable Ethiopian nationals to enjoy the rights granted to nationals of other free nations. The official said that there was perhaps some good news in that regard. He then proceeded to tell me that, due to the consultation they had had with the Colonial Secretary on the matter, the law affecting Ethiopian nationals would be amended and that a draft law was being prepared which would free them from the discriminatory law. They were hoping that their delegation would discuss it with the Ethiopian government when it visited Ethiopia.

On April 11, the Emperor wrote in reply to my report, "With reference to the appointment of a consul at Hargeisa, We note from your report that you replied effectively that there were no sufficient grounds for the argument advanced by the official of the Foreign Office that the Ethiopian consulate should not be opened at Hargeisa. It is astonishing that the British government should oppose our opening of a consulate at Hargeisa when we have allowed it to open consulates in a number of places in Ethiopia. Since We were aware that the main reason why they asked for the recent meeting in Harar was to thwart the agreement concluded in 1954 on the 'Reserved Area,' We had warned that nothing be done to change or to amend the agreement during the discussion. The Foreign Ministry will now advise the British Embassy that we do not wish to renegotiate the agreement on the 'Reserved Area' with the visiting delegation. Keep reminding them to enact, as promised, a new law which will save from oppression the Ethiopians living in Kenya."

Mr. Dodds-Parker who was a member of Parliament and Parliamentary Under Secretary at the Foreign Office asked me to meet him and I went to the Foreign Office on March 29 for a discussion. He informed me that he was going to Addis Ababa by way of Libya and Hargeisa; he was due to arrive in Addis Ababa on April 10. He then said that, even though it was possible to communicate through diplomatic channels, they considered it to be useful that politicians should also meet directly sometimes and exchange views. I replied that direct communications and discussions helped to expedite matters, and expressed the hope that his Ethiopian visit would be attended with success and be conducive to a better understanding. He said Muslim aggressiveness was preoccupying our two governments in that part of the world; it was likely that the former Italian colony, Somalia, would be an independent state before long; who was to replace the Italians when they withdrew? The Egyptians had begun to be troublesome in several respects; they might try to install themselves in Somalia; that would not suit either of us. This was no news to us since the Muslims had tried to destroy us for a thousand years. The Russians also might try to have their finger in the pie as was their habit. The object of his visit was to have consultations on these and other similar matters. I replied that it was no doubt a matter for preoccupation. It would appear that although the Somalis might attain political independence, the resources at their disposal at present would not be adequate enough to enable them to achieve economic independence. Of necessity, foreign financial assistance would have to be provided, and whoever supplied the finances would undoubtedly be in political control. As he had just remarked, we had contended against the Muslims for a thousand years; the last battle we fought with them was when we beat the Dervishes off. We had had a measure of rest from them for about 60 years since. It was certain that they would try to gain by subtle modern stratagems what they failed to achieve by war. I then proceeded to tell him that one thing that was disturbing and saddening us was the propaganda being spread that the Somalis did not like Ethiopia. Ethiopia was a country in which various ethnic groups lived, including Somalis; all her nationals had equal rights; our common interests would be best served only by living in unity and harmony. The geographical position of our country compelled us to live in unity, and we found it hard to understand why it was being said that the British Somalis did not wish to live in friendship with Ethiopia.

He said that was one of the questions he desired to discuss when he got to Addis Ababa. The British Somalis wanted their assistance until they told them to leave their country; what was disturbing them was that the Haud district had been separated from them; in their view, that district was a part of their own country. I replied that the district was administered together with Somaliland for only about 14 years after the War; it was necessary not to forget that it was a part of Ethiopia before the War; the British Somalis used to cross over periodically and graze their herds at that time and there was then no claim or disturbance as was now the case. It was my view that they were being taught all that by foreigners. He might remember the 'Greater Somalia' plan advanced by Bevin and Sforza and it would appear that there were still people who were intent on carrying out that plan.

On March 30, I reported to the Emperor on the discussion and added the following comment, "From my observation in the countries to which I have been and from what I see here, there are two types of officials in the administration of governments. One type of official is the one who plans and conducts broad policies with other governments without being involved in details. He is the political official who is replaced periodically. The other type of official is the one who is concerned all his working life with pursuing his government's policies in detail and who is able to influence, for better or for worse, the policies of his government by the advice which he advances. From what I have observed in the British Foreign Office as in the Foreign Ministries of other countries, the second type of official appears to a foreigner to be difficult and one whose task is to be sly and devious. As the ambassadors and diplomatic staff who live in other countries are the same type of officials they are capable in unison with them to improve or worsen the policies of their governments with other governments. My previous report was based on the discussion I had with the second type of official whose duty it is to offer plausible arguments which make it difficult for him to see other aspects of a matter. The first type of official like Dodds-Parker, being a politician, is able to look at the relationships of his government in a wider perspective. This may perhaps make it easier to discuss and arrive at an understanding with his type. But since he is followed by the second type of official wherever he goes, who tries to influence him on most matters, even to the extent of putting words in his mouth, it is doubtful whether much could be accomplished."

Before going to Ethiopia, Mr. Dodds-Parker stopped in Somaliland to consult with the British officials. He spoke more or less as follows to the people who met him with a peaceful demonstration, "We have realized that you are a people who have been wronged; we have found a remedy to cure your ills. Her Majesty the Queen of England supports your views and aspirations, and will meet your wishes as she promised to your delegates. The British government has declared to your delegates its determination to work for the unity of the Somali people. It has also announced to the world the future status of the Somali people."

He then proceeded to Addis Ababa to present his government's views to the Ethiopian government and began discussions with the Foreign Minister on April 12, 1956. He told him that his message was to request the consent of the Ethiopian government that the Haud and the 'Reserved Area' be detached from Ethiopia and joined to British Somaliland. Ato Aklilou declared that it was impossible to accept this request which was designed to achieve the British plan for a 'Greater Somalia.' He then told him that, if the problem was getting worse, it was mainly Britain's fault.

Dodds-Parker dropped the whole thing the following day and agreed that the Harar meeting, which had been held due to differences in the execution of the agreement, be resumed! They then had a long discussion on some of the difficulties that had arisen in execution. Since there was no formula on which they could agree, however, they had to part without anything being achieved.

It was thought at the time that the British government dared to ask Ethiopia, through Dodds-Parker, to cede a part of its territory to Somaliland in the hope that it would please the British Somalis and that, when it was united with Somalia, the new independent government would be induced to be a member of the British Commonwealth. This British hope became obvious when the Deputy Colonial Secretary, Lord Lloyd went to Somaliland in May 1956 and announced to the Somalis and the world at Hargeisa that the two Somali territories, together with the Ogaden, the Haud and the 'Reserved Area,' should be included in the 'Greater Somalia' plan.

The British officials, who entered the Haud and the 'Reserved Area' for purposes of control during the grazing period, were disappointed at the failure of the Dodds-Parker mission and made it their main task to disturb Ethiopia in every possible way. The British would not take heed of the repeated representations of the Ethiopian government to desist from every activity which was contrary to the agreement. They also persisted in refusing to permit the opening of the Ethiopian consulate at Hargeisa. As a result, the Ethiopian government ordered that the British consulate in Harar be closed.

It was considered that an important step had been taken towards the realization of the plan for a 'Greater Somalia,' when the two Somali territories were united in June, 1960. In the event, the new Somali government did not become a member of the British Commonwealth. And as the 1954 agreement, which had been a cause of a number of disputes, was cancelled, entry was denied to the British into the Haud and the 'Reserved Area,' and farther into the Ogaden, to cause mischief.

As I had been appointed to be Ethiopia's Envoy Extraordinary and Minister Plenipotentiary in the Netherlands, in addition to my duties in Britain, I went to the Hague on November 21, 1956, and presented my Letters of Credence to Her Majesty Queen Juliana. I spent ten days making a round of visits to get acquainted with the government authorities and the foreign diplomatic representatives before I returned to London. While in the Hague, I learned that the Wonji Sugar Works were functioning satisfactorily but that the rice project had not been started for various reasons. I again visited the Netherlands for a few days in January 1959. When I was recalled at the end of my diplomatic mission, I did not find it convenient to travel to the Hague and take leave of the government.

This additional task was given me not because there was a lot to do in the Netherlands but because it was considered to be useful to have diplomatic relations with friendly countries. Since it is found, for economic and personnel reasons to be onerous for countries like Ethiopia to open embassies or legations in all the independent states, many governments of the world use this method, taking account of their capabilities. Even wealthy states benefit by this practice.

During the period I was in Britain, several difficult questions appeared which threatened the peace of the world. The Egyptian government which was led by Colonel Gamal Abdel Nasser, claiming that the Suez Canal was Egyptian property and should revert to it, took it over suddenly in August 1956. The Canal had been opened a century earlier and had fallen into the hands of the governments of Western Europe, especially Britain and France, who greatly benefited from it. The British and French governments were enraged and invited eighteen governments who were said to be beneficiaries of the Canal to a conference in London. They met twice in consultation and established an association of the users of the Suez Canal. They sent the Egyptian government rules and regulations for the administration of the Canal. The conference appointed and sent a delegation led by Mr. Robert Menzies, Prime Minister of Australia. The Ethiopian Foreign Minister was one of the delegates. The delegation's mission was a failure because the Egyptian government refused to accept the plan and to cooperate with the proposed Canal Users' association.

On September 11, Mr. Menzies called the ambassadors of the 18 governments to a meeting and, informing them that the delegation's mission was a failure, presented a report on the question. The ambassadors met again on October 1 and 4 and constituted the association. The British Foreign Secretary, Mr. Selwyn Lloyd was elected chairman. It was decided to set up a council composed of all the members which was to meet every six months. An executive committee consisting of seven of the members was appointed to assist the administrator and follow up the working of the association. It was decided that the members of the committee should be the United States, Britain, France, two governments to the west of the Canal, Norway and Italy - and two to the east of the Canal - Iran and perhaps Ethiopia. Since Ethiopia, Iran and Japan had not then indicated their desire to be members of the association, it was decided that the seventh chair remain unoccupied. I used to go as Ethiopia's representative whenever the council met and several ambassadors expressed hope that Ethiopia might occupy the seventh chair. I had to reply that, since Ethiopia was not even a member of the association, I could not occupy the committee chair.

In a report I wrote to the Emperor on October 5 on the matter, I expressed my views thus, "From what I have observed from time to time and from discussions I have had with Eastern ambassadors, it appears that one reason why Western governments are trying hard for Ethiopia to be a member of the executive committee is because it suits their propaganda, as was the case when the Menzies delegation visited Cairo, and not because they are concerned for the interests of Ethiopia or any Eastern country. I have heard complaints from Eastern ambassadors because of their realization of this, since it is obvious that the great powers always try to achieve their aims by making use of the small powers. The main evidence for this is the fact that the three great powers determined and announced the establishment of the association and invited the others to the second London conference only to be informed of their decision and endorse it. In these circumstances, it would be advantageous, in the opinion of Your humble servant, if Ethiopia would defer its membership of the association and wait and see how it will function and what the outcome of the debate soon to take place in the Security Council of the United Nations will be. It would seem that the benefit to be gained from membership of the association at present, apart from the possible political difficulties that might ensue, would not be worthwhile when viewed against the financial outlay it would entail and the shortage of personnel. In addition, it is known to everybody that nothing can be done without Egypt's consent, and since Egypt has so far shown no sign of its willingness to cooperate with the association, it would appear that nothing can be done with the association, at least for the time being." The Emperor wrote on October 12, "Seeing it is possible to join the association at any time, We have elected to defer membership in line with your recommendation."

Britain and France accused Egypt before the UN Security Council because of its seizure of the Suez Canal, but it came to nothing after a long debate, due to the veto of the USSR. Likewise, nothing tangible came out of the discussion the British Foreign Secretary had with the Egyptian Foreign Minister. Egypt's apprehension was thus relieved, and as the Egyptian government continued to send troops to the Sinai Peninsula to kill people and destroy property and the armed forces of Syria and Jordan declared their firm military support, it was feared that war would soon be started not only against Israel but also against the Western powers. The Israeli government, wishing to forestall Arab action, began the invasion of the Sinai district on October 29. On the following day, the British and French governments delivered an ultimatum to Egypt and Israel to stop fighting. They also demanded that the troops of the two great powers occupy the Canal as arbitrators for the time being. Israel declared it would stop hostilities if Egypt did the same. Egypt refused to accept the ultimatum declaring that, as a victim of aggression, it could not hand over the Canal and her own territory to other states.

The Security Council met urgently in New York and, declaring unlawful the invasion of Egypt by Britain and France, passed a resolution ordering them not to fight Egypt. Most of the Council members, including the US and the Soviet Union, supported the resolution, but Britain and France vetoed it. The UN General Assembly met on November 1 and demanded that war against Egypt be stopped. The British Parliament had a fierce debate on the question. The Labour Party campaigned strongly that Prime Minister Eden should resign and the British people was divided in two. There was serious apprehension that the war might spread all over the world. However, Eden insisted they would not stop before the Canal was recaptured. He later made it known that they would be prepared to hand over the task of arbitration to the UN should it set up a police force. But Eden's main aim was to take over the Canal.

President Eisenhower and the American people were outraged because Britain and France had started their war of aggression against Egypt without informing the American government. And since the British government did not notify even the Commonwealth governments, many of them were greatly disturbed; it was only the Australian and New Zealand governments which attempted to support and justify the act of aggression. Their peoples were however as divided as the British people. The Soviet Union was so strongly opposed to the action of the two governments that it proposed to the US that they send a military force to Egypt to counter the three aggressors. However, America did not accept the proposal for fear it might separate it from its Western allies and trigger a world war. A resolution was passed by the UN that an international police force be established to safeguard the security of the Middle East and dispatched to Egypt to take over the Canal from the British and the French forces.

Seeing that the whole world was opposed to his policy and that his government was faltering, Eden consulted with the French government and, at the behest of the UN General Assembly, announced on November 7 that he had agreed to stop the fighting. The Israeli government, under strong pressure from President Eisenhower announced on November 8 that it would comply with the demand of the UN to relinquish, on the arrival of the international police force on the Suez Canal, the Egyptian territory it had occupied by invasion.

In a report to the Emperor dated November 9, I advanced the views I held at the time, "The aggression perpetrated on Egypt by the two Western powers is extremely to be regretted and it is greatly to be feared that the small nations will run the risk of being subjected to the same type of aggression at any time and for any reason whatsoever. What aggravates the fear is that the people and government of Britain who, even if feared and mistrusted by many peoples, were looked upon by the majority of mankind as standing for justice and the due process of law and for the rights of the individual, should be found committing an act of violence of the kind inflicted on Egypt.

"On the other hand, Colonel Abdel Nasser and his colleagues, after having declared that they were determined to afford welfare and a better chance in life to the poor common people of Egypt, the world watching them with goodwill and the expectation that the Egyptian people might really have a fair deal, abandoned their declared policy and, posing as leaders and champions of the Arab peoples and the whole of Africa, interfered left and right in the private affairs of other nations, inflicting wounds on great and small alike, like biting dogs. It was clear that in due course they would be exposed to danger. It was obvious in particular, that their dispute with Britain and France, following their forcible and sudden seizure of Suez Canal, would not be beneficial either for Egypt or for its neighbours, and that it was bound to disturb the security of that part of the world. Now the expected has happened and the modern weaponry Egypt had acquired from here and there at great cost has been destroyed by British and French bombs to no one's benefit and much of the rest captured by the Israeli forces. Egypt will be compelled to spend vast sums to replace all that which will further erode its economy, already thought to be weak, and make nothing but a dream the hope for development and prosperity held out by Abdel Nasser when he seized power. It would appear, moreover, that there are people among the Egyptians who dream of the overthrow of Nasser's regime and who, taking advantage of his predicament, may try to subvert his government either on their own initiative or egged on by foreign governments. It looks therefore as if Nasser's government which has sown the wind is beginning to reap the whirlwind."

The British political parties and people were deeply divided due to the invasion of Egypt by Britain for the Suez Canal. The US government and many of the member governments of the Commonwealth were also deeply disturbed because of the invasion of Egypt by Eden's government without their knowledge. The countries of Western Europe and the Middle East were equally very much upset. The British people faced grave difficulties, not only due to the political disturbance but also because of the economic disruption. President Eisenhower ordered an oil embargo on Britain and France unless they relinquished the Canal. Oil shortage was experienced not only for vehicle traffic but for factories and heating of homes because, in addition to the blockage of the Canal, the flow of oil by pipe through Syria to the Mediterranean was interrupted. Many politicians and leaders of opinion as well as many newspapers therefore strongly demanded that the two aggressor governments pull their troops out of Egypt without delay. The UN General Assembly also strongly urged that the aggressors, including Israel, leave Egyptian territory. On account of this pressure on the British government, the Foreign Secretary on December 3 announced in Parliament that it had agreed with France to remove their armed forces quickly from the Canal Zone. And the American government ordered that the oil embargo be lifted. In the meantime, it was announced that, because he was tired and his health was impaired, Prime Minister Sir Anthony Eden had gone to Jamaica for three weeks on the advice of doctors that he should go where he could be in the sun. Since the difficulties of the British people grew more acute not only politically but also economically and in living conditions during November and December, and because relations between Britain and its friendly nations had deteriorated, there were insistent demands that Eden should be replaced by some other person. He therefore tendered his resignation to Queen Elizabeth on January 9 and retired.

In a report I sent to the Emperor on January 14, 1957 on Eden's resignation and on the ministers who replaced his government, I wrote, "From reports received from abroad, it appears that many governments are pleased with the change of Prime Minister and Macmillan's appointment. It is said that many believe it will be beyond the power of any British government and quite impossible for the Conservative government to restore the impaired prestige and authority of Britain in the whole world and especially in the Middle East. As the British themselves admit, since most of its accumulated wealth had been squandered in two world wars, Britain no longer possesses the power to ensure the respect of its worldwide authority and interests as formerly. But many British people were reluctant to accept this situation so disappointing to them. The fact that they had to stop the fighting they had started on Egypt before gaining their objective and the difficulties that followed this blunder have proved to be harmful to the British people more than to anybody else, entailing as it did not only a political but also an economic crisis, and indicating clearly that today's British power is not the same as obtained in the reign of Queen Victoria. This has aroused the hope that henceforth it will pursue its policies not according to its desire but according to what is possible to achieve considering its present position. It is clear that, as evidenced by the clashes and disturbances taking place between Yemen and its Aden Colony, Britain will have yet to face more difficulties in the countries of the Middle East, and the new government is expected to face more troubles in that part of the world."

In a letter dated January 30, the Emperor wrote, "We have noted your detailed report concerning Sir Anthony Eden and the other Ministers. We have a good understanding of the situation because you have written the details with such clarity. Your views on the inside workings of the British government are penetrating, educing what revolves in the consciousness of everyone, if not recorded."

In the course of my sojourn in London, the Kashmir question which had been a bone of contention between India and Pakistan ever since their independence flared up again. The reason for the renewal of the dispute was because the government and assembly of Kashmir on February 26, 1957 opted for the total integration of the state into India for consideration like other provinces. They notified the government of India of the measure and promulgated a constitution to confirm it. The government of Pakistan was so unhappy with the act that it accused India before the UN Security Council. With the exception of the Soviet Union, the Security Council, including Britain and the US, supported Pakistan's plea and passed a resolution demanding that India delay the integration of Kashmir. This greatly disturbed the government and people of India. They complained that the United States and Britain were offending India because it would not join them like Pakistan in the Baghdad Pact and in the South East Asia Treaty Organization (SEATO), and that Pakistan was trying to stand up so boldly against India because America had supplied it with war materials in abundance. Speaking on several occasions, Prime Minister Nehru protested bitterly that it appeared that the British, not satisfied with having divided India on their departure, were now intent on dividing what was left of Indian territory under the guise of religion. The Indian politicians and the press also spoke and wrote against the British government with such violence that it was disturbed in its turn. It was said that the people of India had demonstrated no such feelings of hatred for Britain since India became independent. The fact that the Prime Minister of Pakistan for his part went around speaking about his people's gratitude to the British for their support was considered to have been made deliberately to inflame all the more the differences between India and Britain. The British press united in depicting India, and especially Mr. Nehru, as blameworthy with respect to Kashmir. A number of Indians and newspapers urged that India withdraw its membership of the Commonwealth, but Prime Minister Nehru did not accept the suggestion. The dispute between the two governments was thus seen to be worse and their quarrel bitter.

According to reports current at the time, the British felt deeply affronted by Mr. Nehru at the time of their humiliation when, after the British government struck at Egypt with armed might in October 1956, the Indian leaders, and Mr. Nehru in particular, attacked with violence the British government's action in the meetings of the UN and led others in compelling the British and the French to withdraw their troops before attaining their aim in Egypt. It appeared that they decided to support Pakistan in the Security Council because they disliked Mr. Nehru's action who had always been preaching on the necessity of observing international law and whom they considered to be sanctimonious. They also felt it would give them an opportunity to criticize him if he failed to carry out the wishes of the Security Council and thus take their revenge.

Because many newspapers and leaders of opinion engaged in a violent campaign against India and its Prime Minister, the government of India became apprehensive and the Foreign Ministry and the Indian diplomatic representatives abroad made every effort to explain India's position on the Kashmir issue to other governments and to convince them that it was Pakistan and not India which infringed international law and the UN Charter by invading Kashmir; that the main reason why Pakistan desired to possess Kashmir was because its people was largely Muslim, but that India did not wish that a people should be divided on religious grounds; that it was greatly to be feared that, if India consented to a plebiscite in Kashmir, it would not only hinder the progress and well-being of a people that was not yet able to appreciate what was in its interest, but it would also become a cause for the repetition of the carnage between Hindu and Muslim that was so evident when India was divided, not only in Kashmir but also in India and Pakistan.

With this in view, Mrs. Pandit, who was Mr. Nehru's sister and High Commissioner of India, visited our Embassy and we had a long discussion on the problem. I told her that I had stayed in New Delhi for several years beginning in 1949 as Ethiopia's representative and had closely followed the dispute as well as visited Kashmir. I then remarked that, because the matter had dragged on for a number of years, the world had appeared to have lost sight of the genesis of the problem and that it was India that first took the case to the Security Council; that the Western powers had supported Pakistan because its policy happened to suit their purpose for the time being and that I believed India's position was basically the right one. I finally told her that, speaking personally, I subscribed to India's view that no people which are ethnically one and the same should be divided merely for religious differences.

Even though Mrs. Pandit did not ask that I should present the matter to my government, I took it for granted that she came to share it with me with that in mind and I presented a detailed report to the Emperor on March 13. His Majesty wrote in his letter dated March 23, "With reference to the dispute between India and Pakistan on Kashmir; We have not forgotten what you had written earlier and have again written; We often consider it. Since Kashmir has supported India's position on its own free will and proclaimed it through its constitution, it would appear there would not be ground for much controversy. When the time comes for us to be involved, We shall support India. It would seem that the Indians have the right to be offended with the British...Although what Mr. Nehru says from time to time may wound the British, it looks that in some cases he is doing so in self-defence. It has to be left to future observers where the cry of the bloodshed between India and Pakistan will lead. Realizing that you had gone into the question in depth, We read on occasion the reports you had written Us when you were in India. You can tell Mrs. Pandit when you meet her that we shall support India's case whenever we have the opportunity. You may also tell her that We have told the government of India that We owe them a debt of gratitude because, even though the Asians and the Arabs had helped Us in our dispute with the Somalis, the Indian delegate had given us assistance in a special way, as though he were one of our people."

In March 1957, the US President Eisenhower and the British Prime Minister Macmillan met in the British Colony of Bermuda, situated near North America, to discuss matters affecting the interests of the two countries. As indicated in this Part above, the American government had been strongly disturbed and opposed Britain and France because they had tried to force Egypt by military might the previous October to bend to their will, without consulting the US government. As a consequence, they were unable for several months to cooperate as previously with mutual understanding and confidence. This situation proved to be convenient for their adversaries but became dangerous for the peace of the world. After Prime Minister Eden, who was the leader of the fight for Suez was discredited and relinquished office and Mr. Macmillan replaced him, the American government relented and, in an effort to improve relations, President Eisenhower and Mr. Macmillan, accompanied by their Foreign Ministers, determined to meet and have a consultation on the Island of Bermuda.

After the two heads of government had conferred for three days, they indicated that their differences had been greatly reduced and published a communiqué detailing the matters on which agreement had been achieved. They pointed out that, although they were in general agreement on the points they had discussed, they were unable to agree on the details of some of the matters under discussion. These were the main points on which they agreed: 1). that they valued highly the agreements on collective security within the framework of the UN and the North Atlantic Treaty Organization (NATO) which they declared was the corner stone of their Western policy; 2). that it was in the interest of the two powers that European unity should be developed within the framework of NATO; 3). that they agreed that Britain should have closer relations with Europe than previously; 4). that they agreed to the plan that free trade should be developed in the European Common Market; 5). that the US government was agreeable to working in the military committee of the Baghdad Pact; 6). that they supported the right of the German people to be reunited in peace and freedom; 7). that they condemned the policy of oppression the Soviet government was perpetrating on the peoples of Eastern Europe while expressing their feelings of sympathy for the Hungarian people; 8). that they were in agreement on the necessity that all the UN resolutions on the Gaza Strip and the Gulf of Akaba should be operational as quickly as possible; 9). that the execution of the resolution passed by the Security Council on October 13 was of high importance and that they were agreed to support the UN Secretary General's efforts in this regard; 10). that they had announced the declaration they had agreed on in connection with the testing of the atomic and hydrogen bombs; 11). that they agreed that the US give some guided missiles to Britain to promote common defence and common economic policies.

Even though it was known that there were matters on which the two parties did not agree, they did not include them in the communiqué. The main points were China and Britain's desire to reduce its military forces in Europe. The Americans were opposed to Communist China in those days and were bent on injuring it as much as possible. The British, having recognized the Chinese government and desiring to extend their commercial relations with China, tried to persuade the Americans not to oppose them but were unsuccessful. The reduction of the British troops was sanctioned to be effected gradually.

Although there was no complete agreement on the Suez Canal, their agreement as indicated in Point 9 above was taken to be a good sign. The UN Secretary General Dag Hammarskjöld was then negotiating in Cairo on the Canal, the Gaza Strip and Akaba and they desired to know Egypt's explicit views on the matter. Since the Suez Canal had been cleared of all obstacles at that time, the problem had arisen as to whom the Canal fees should be paid. The Western powers had proposed to Egypt through Dr. Hammarskjöld that all the fees should be deposited with the World Bank, half of it to be given to Egypt to run the Canal and half to be retained until the question of the Canal was settled. But Colonel Nasser had earlier notified the powers that all ships passing through the Canal had to pay all the fees to Egypt.

Another matter on which the two governments did not agree was the American government's insistence that all political problems around the world, especially the intractable questions of the Middle East, should be discussed and settled in the forum of the UN. On the other hand, the British government had argued that, since it had proved to be extremely difficult to achieve anything in the Security Council due to the multiplicity of the Russian veto and, because the so-called Afro-Asian group of countries were basically suspicious of the policies of the Western powers and often opposed them, nothing worthwhile could be done in the General Assembly; the great powers should therefore not allow that their responsibility to keep the peace and security of the world be thwarted by the animosity and ignorant actions of the small states. Unhappy because the UN forum had been transformed and had not turned out to be as they had originally planned it to be, viz. merely a cover for the great powers to impose their will on the weak nations, and because the Afro-Asian nations had been unwilling to be used as instruments and puppets, and unable, due to their current limitations, to revert to their ancient policy of power politics for which they longed, the British and the French had desired to obtain the support of the American government to exert pressure on the governments uncongenial to them. The American government however had not been willing to accept this British policy for fear that, if it did so, the Eastern nations would all turn to the Soviet government and become all the more hostile to the Western powers. President Eisenhower and his assistants had not agreed with the idea of ignoring the UN because they had realized that, despite its many imperfections, the organization was the main instrument for opposing the Russians and for strengthening relations with the countries of the East, thereby securing world peace.

The Emperor wrote on April 3 in reply to a report on the matter which I had written him on March 27, "We were very pleased to read your detailed report on the discussions that took place between the American President and the British

Prime Minister as well as the views you expressed on them. Even though We hear about it from here and there, you have discharged your duty well in stating it in such a comprehensive manner. You have observed that it is obvious that whenever the Americans, the British and the French reach agreements, they do not overlook the Afro-Asian group. Don't you think, though, that the European Common Market will adversely affect Ethiopia and countries like Ethiopia which have started the Afro-Asian policy? Should you have a document dealing with the Common Market, We feel it will be useful if you make an abstract and send it to Us with your comment." I sent him on April 26 a report of my understanding of the Common Market together with my views.

The Suez Canal which was blocked when Britain and France began to attack Egypt in October 1956 was cleared through the efforts of the UN and opened the following April. The Egyptian government, taking advantage of the event and desiring to reassert its claim that the Canal was Egyptian property, sent to the UN Secretary General on April 24 a declaration it had prepared on the administration of the Canal with a request that it be registered at the headquarters of the UN. The points presented with respect to the running of the Canal were as follows: 1). That Egypt recognizes the Protocol signed in Istanbul in 1896 concerning the Canal; 2). Any increase on the Canal dues shall be fixed not to exceed 1 percent in a period of 12 months; an increase over and above that shall be settled through consultation or arbitration; 3). The Canal shall be administered in conformity with what is requisite for modern ships; 4). The Canal would be administered by the Egyptian Suez Canal Authority; 5). Five percent of the gross income would be paid as royalty to the Egyptian government as owner of the Canal; 6). Twenty-five percent of the gross revenue of the Canal would be set aside for the improvement of the Canal; 7). Should any dispute arise in connection with the execution of the regulations of the Canal, a complaint should be lodged with the Canal Authority and then with the Tribunal of Arbitrators; 8). Any claim for compensation pursuant to the nationalization of the Canal should be referred to arbitrators in accordance with international practice; 9). Any dispute arising on the 1896 Protocol or on the declaration should be settled on the basis of the UN Charter; 10). It was Egypt's wish and decided policy that the Suez Canal should be an instrument of peace and prosperity for the peoples of the world. The declaration and the obligations contained therein would be registered at the headquarters of the UN.

The US government tried unsuccessfully that the Egyptian declaration be in line with the six guiding principles passed by the UN Security Council in October. It therefore asked that the Council convene and discuss the declaration. The Council met on April 26 and the member governments expressed their views. Some of them criticized Egypt for what it had done; others urged that, since the Canal question was a fait accompli, Egypt's declaration should be put into operation. Even though the American government was not fully satisfied with Egypt's declaration as it did not conform to the six guiding principles, it expressed the view that it would be better to see it in operation and argue with Egypt in case it was found to be defective.

The British government which, unwilling that the Canal should be run under the authority of a single government, had initiated an unsuccessful military operation against Egypt in conjunction with France, decided to make use of the Security Council's six guiding principles, which it had ignored when it attacked Egypt, and to try to unite against it all the countries that were users of the Canal. It therefore called the 'Canal Users Association' to meet in London on April 30 to consider the Egyptian declaration as well as the debates of the Security Council. It also invited the members to suggest items they wished to be discussed at the meeting. The consensus obtained from the meeting was however that, in conformity with the American government's recommendation, there was no alternative to accepting Egypt's declaration for the time being and trying to make it operational. The French alone declared that it was their firm decision not to allow their ships to pass through the Canal.

The inclination of the members of the Association on the matter was so painful for the British government that it requested that the Security Council meet again and debate the question. But it was left in abeyance because many members were of the opinion that no useful purpose would be served and that it might even be harmful.

A brief summary of the six guiding principles adopted by the Security Council on October 13, 1956, is as follows: 1). The Canal should be used freely and openly without overt or covert discrimination, including the political and technical fields; 2). Egypt's independent nationhood should be respected; 3). The operation of the Canal should be detached from the policy of any country; 4). The payment of dues and fees should be determined by agreement between Egypt and the users of the Canal; 5). A suitable proportion of the revenue of the Canal should be used for its improvement; 6). Disputes on matters unsettled between Egypt and the Suez Canal Company should be settled by arbitrators to whom necessary powers should be given, and suitable arrangements should be made for the payment of awarded amounts.

In a report to the Emperor on the matter dated May 3, I commented, "It is clearly seen that the reason why the British government desires the Security Council to meet again on the question of the Suez Canal is because it wishes Egypt to give an undertaking not to withdraw at will the declaration it had presented to the United Nations and consider that as an international obligation for it to use as a cover to allow its ships to use the Canal. The British and the French, due to their impatience to follow the process of negotiation to the end, not only incurred the strong criticism of the world but lost their rights and advantages for a negotiated settlement, thus suffering a severe loss of prestige in the eyes of the world and the Egyptians. It is obvious, moreover, that the apparent disappearance of the interests of other countries in the proper operation of the Canal which had begun to show signs of improvement had greatly disappointed many governments and peoples."

As soon as he received the above mentioned two reports, the Emperor went into deep mourning due to the accidental death of his son, Prince Makonnen, Duke of Harar, and so I did not receive a reply indicating his views.

A missionary society, called 'Egypt General Mission,' which had been established to proclaim the Gospel among Egyptian Muslims through educational and health care institutions and which had been expelled by the then Egyptian government under pretext after it had worked for 60 years, asked me to approach the Imperial government on its behalf to grant it permission to send the medical doctors and teachers to work among the Muslims in Northern Eritrea so that its long-standing experience of working among Muslims might not be lost. I presented a memorandum to the Emperor on May 29 and His Majesty wrote thus on June 11, "We are agreeable in principle to granting permission if the mission is prepared to assume another name before coming here. It would be necessary for it to send someone to discuss with the Ministry of Education and Bitwoded Andargachew (the Representative in Eritrea) as to where the schools should be built and other conditions." I informed the officials of the mission accordingly and they wrote back to say that they were willing to change the name to 'Middle East Mission' and that, if it was acceptable to the Ethiopian government, they were prepared to send someone to Ethiopia and discuss the conditions of their work. I wrote on July 4 to inform His Majesty of this. The Emperor wrote on July 15 to say that the changed name was acceptable. The mission sent someone for a discussion and was granted permission to work among the Eritrean Muslims.

I have recounted above in this Part, how after the War the British had restored to Ethiopia by agreement in 1954 the district of the Ogaden bordering on Somaliland called the Haud and the so-called 'Reserved Area,' and how the British Colonial Secretary and the Somaliland administration, in addition to pursuing aggressive acts in connection with the grazing area, had made so bold as to ask and failed to get the district detached from Ethiopia and given to Somaliland.

The British government, through its Ambassador in Addis Ababa presented in May 1957 a 'note verbale' to the Ministry of Foreign Affairs, declaring that it had abandoned its 'Greater Somalia' policy for another. The Ministry asked me to investigate and report as to how this had happened. I wrote on June 21 that change had been taking place since the Autumn of 1956 in the policy of the British government with respect to the Somali problem and that in so far as I could observe and understand, the reasons were as follows:

"1. The fact that Mr. Dodds-Parker's mission, which had visited Addis Ababa when Sir Anthony Eden was Prime Minister, had failed due to the firm negative response of the Imperial government and that it led the British authorities to realize clearly that Ethiopia's position was irreversible in that regard; that they could not claim as formerly that Ethiopia was incapable of administering its outlying territories and ensure their security because the Ogaden was being administered so well that they had seen there was no room for manoeuvre and that they had been heard off and on to complain about the efficiency of the administration. They had therefore been convinced that if the slandering and aggressive actions of the British Officers in Somaliland and of some Somalis were continued, the dispute might go beyond the grazing area and become a cause for Ethiopia and Great Britain to clash on the world stage, leading to the further deterioration of their friendly relations.

"2. The seizure of the Suez Canal by Egypt and the failure of the military action launched against it as well as the unforeseen hardship experienced by the British had greatly weakened Britain's influence in that part of the world and clearly shown the waning of British power and authority which for a century had awed the countries of the East. It had become progressively clear that Aden Colony and the Somali coast and territory, which had been occupied not for their economic value but because it was thought they should be held for their strategic positions so as to keep Egypt and the Canal in British hands, to control the Red Sea which led to the entrance of the Canal from the east and to protect the approaches to India from a rival power, were becoming burdensome to the British. Since the Yemen government which had lain low, unable to dispute about occupied Arab land during the predominance of British power, now observing the awakening of the peoples of the Middle East and the weakening of British power, is claiming that Aden Colony and several sultanates surrounding it had originally been Yemeni territory forcibly occupied by the British government and striving to get them back even by military means, it is known that the British government has concluded that it will be forced in due course to withdraw from Aden and the surrounding territory. Moreover, they are coming to the realization that the value of the territories like Aden and Berbera, which had been occupied not for their economic potential but as means of easy access to India and Egypt, had been greatly diminished after the achievement of independence by the two countries, and that in particular they were gaining no benefit from their Somali territory which has become a financial burden and a source of dispute. It also seems that, since the Arabs in Aden and the surrounding territory have begun to agitate that the British leave their country and as the Somalis are proclaiming their dream of being liberated from the British in the near future, either to unite with Somalia or gain independence in some other way, they are beginning to see that it is absurd to quarrel with Ethiopia whose friendship can afford them greater advantage, for the sake of a territory they will not hold permanently.

"3. When Sir Anthony Eden resigned due to the failure of his Suez Canal policy, the Conservatives, who had put pressure on Eden to the point of militarily attacking Egypt and who are still impelled by the old spirit of imperialism, were weakened due to the abortion of their policy and the resignation of some of their leaders when Mr. Macmillan formed his government. One of these is Lord Lloyd, the former Under Secretary in the Colonial Office, who last May went to Somaliland in the name of his government. He was the one who showed signs of intimidation and threat to H.E. Ato Aklilou when they met in London in August 1956. (Mr. Dodds-Parker was also dismissed from his post of Under Secretary in the Foreign Office at the same time).

"After it became obvious that the influence such Conservatives exerted on the direction of government policy had been weakened and their views become less weighty, because British power could no longer have sway over that part of the world after the conflict with Egypt, the strategic value of Somaliland also decreased. It appears therefore that the present British government has concluded that the territory will be of no use to them but only a financial drain and a cause for difficulties, and determined to leave it as soon as possible. Consequently, it is apparent that they have made a final decision to get it merged with Somalia soon after it becomes independent in a few years and relieve themselves of further responsibility. To this end, they have set up for the first time a legislative council in accordance with the programme Lord Lloyd announced to the Somalis last year to enable Somaliland to begin to administer itself. It is known that the aim is for the Somalis gradually to take over the government of their country and decide their own destiny themselves whether by merging with Somalia or joining Ethiopia. According to some sources, the security of that part of the world will be better served if both Somaliland and Somalia are joined to Ethiopia by federation or in some other way. Considering its past activities, however, it is not possible to ascertain from here to what extent the British administration in Somaliland will go along with this decision and help in its execution. Realizing that the spread of education among the Somalis is the real instrument to get them to administer themselves properly, it is planned to develop the educational programme and bring a number of Somalis to this country to be trained in various fields of administration. A scheme is afoot to bring over 400 Somalis for training in a number of occupations until 1960."

In a report I sent the Emperor on the same date, I enclosed a copy of the letter and stated the following additional views, "As I have tried to explain in the letter, owing to the forcible occupation of the Suez Canal by Egypt, the strategic importance of Somaliland has been diminished and the British have abandoned their plan of uniting all the Somalis under their protection as rumoured, because the Suez Canal conflict has made abundantly clear the extent of the hatred for them by the peoples of the Middle East. It is my humble view that this has induced them to realize that the period of their influence and hegemony in that region of the world is at an end and has served as a signal for their decision to withdraw their political hand.

"Moreover, seeing that the British people is suffering under economic pressure due to the waning of their power and the depletion of their wealth, it is apparent that they have determined to reduce the annual budget of the armed forces, and are striving to limit the military installations spread around the world and to cut the number of troops, thereby lightening the burden of the people. It is becoming progressively clear that they have made it their basic policy to restrict all their large-scale operations and gradually bring them into line with Britain's current capability. There are also indications that they wish to relinquish in due course places such as Aden and Berbera held solely for prestige."

The Emperor wrote on July 2, "We have noted in your report the reasons you have adduced in reply to the message you received from the Foreign Ministry as to what prompted the British government to abandon the policy it has pursued hitherto with respect to the question of a 'Greater Somalia;' they are good observations. The result of Our visit to India and the discussions that had been carried out with the Americans and the French from time to time are also additional factors. Nevertheless, since the sincerity of a change of policy by the British can only be convincing when put into operation, we have to be constantly alert."

Dr. Kwame Nkrumah, Prime Minister of Ghana, who was on a visit to London for the Commonwealth Prime Ministers' Conference, came to see me at the Ethiopian Embassy on July 1. He told me that he had written earlier to the independent African governments (eight at the time) and asked them to meet in Accra and discuss the problems of the world, especially the questions affecting Africa, and that the conference should take place in October. I replied that I was in agreement with the idea but that I thought it would not be suitable to meet in October since the African governments were not much acquainted with one another in those days and that if they were to meet in such haste, the matter being new, it was bound to be publicized all over the world by press and radio and more might be expected of the governments than they could perform; that as they would not have enough time to deliberate and decide on the questions, it would give those who might not have Africa's interests at heart a good opportunity to denigrate them and might become a barrier separating the governments. It would therefore be better, in my view, if the governments would meet as it were in camera and thrash out the questions on which agreement could be reached before they met in conference.

Dr. Nkrumah expressed agreement with my remarks and said that the conference was only meant to be a matter of formality to be followed by a declaration and not to go into the substance of the problems. He realized all the same that it was necessary to discuss them in private and arrive at an understanding. He then said that since other African Ambassadors he had met had expressed views similar to what I had stated, he agreed it would be better to proceed on those lines and asked me how I thought it should be started.

I replied that since the idea was initiated by his government, it was preferable for it to prepare a memorandum and send it to the other governments with a draft agenda of items it wished to be discussed; they would then consider it and give their views. If government ministers were to travel from country to country for the purpose, they would be conspicuous and followed by the press. The task should therefore be undertaken by diplomatic representatives who would have to make a thorough preparation and identify what could or could not be achieved.

Dr. Nkrumah agreed to the proposal and said that, since all the African governments had diplomatic representatives in London, he thought they should be charged with the execution of the task and it was his intention to present a memorandum and a draft agenda through the High Commissioner of Ghana in London.

As I had promised that I would acquaint my government with the substance of our discussion in the meantime, I presented my views to the Emperor in a report I sent on July 4, "It is my hope that the opinions I expressed to the Prime Minister are in line with the views of the Imperial government. The Moroccan diplomatic representative here had also mentioned to me a few weeks ago that the government of Morocco was intending to call a similar conference in Morocco and I had given him a reply similar to what I told Dr. Nkrumah. He had accepted my suggestion and we had agreed that it would be better if governments met and became more acquainted with one another before such a conference was publicized and convened.

"Morocco and Ghana, being nations that have recently achieved independence by means of nationalism and anxious to assert before the world the equality of their leaders with the leaders of other independent nations, it would appear that they wish to demonstrate their skill in international affairs. Even though it is proper to rejoice with the African peoples in regaining their lost freedom one after another and to show them goodwill, and although they are aware that there are many obstacles in their way, it is my humble view that, being new to the responsibility of government, they do not fully realize like Ethiopia that it is beneficial for a weak people to take responsibility seriously and proceed warily. It is therefore necessary to advise them in every possible way to advance deliberately and not to attempt to do things with undue haste and precipitately."

In his reply dated July 12, His Majesty wrote, "We have received your letter and noted the visit of the Prime Minister of Ghana and the discussion you had with him. We consider the views you expressed as though uttered by Us and We are pleased. During Our visit to India, We had a discussion with Mr. Nehru for over an hour and We spoke on the same lines concerning Afro-Asian questions. As suggested, it is felt to be of great benefit to consider the proposed agenda in our several ways so that it would be something to be demonstrated in action and not just for show. The reply you have given to the diplomatic representative of Morocco is as good as that given to Ghana."

The governments having thus agreed that their representatives in London be charged with the preparation of the agenda of the conference, the Ambassadors held their first meeting in the Sudanese Embassy on August 15, 1957, and considered and agreed on the following points put forward by the Acting High Commissioner for Ghana on behalf of his government:

1. That the conference be convened in Accra on January 28, 1958, and continue for one week.

2. That the conference be attended by the Heads of Government.

3. That the number of each delegation be not more than five and that the Ghana government be responsible for accommodation, hospitality and the cost of transportation in Accra.

4. That no observers be allowed either from political organizations or dependent territories due to their large number and to avoid delay and complications, since permission had to be sought from metropolitan powers, and that the press also be excluded from the conference.

The Ambassadors then considered the draft provisional agenda in four points and agreed that the Ghana government present a memorandum elaborating the agenda to enable the other governments to express their views on it and finalize it in a spirit of understanding. They agreed before they rose that the next meeting be held at the Ethiopian Embassy when the representative of Ghana had received the memorandum from his government. They submitted the results of their first meeting to their governments and requested their approval.

The four-point draft provisional agenda presented by Ghana was as follows:

"1. Exchange of views on foreign policy, with special reference to the African Continent, the future of dependent territories in Africa, the racial problem; and the steps to be taken to safeguard the independence and sovereignty of the independent African states.

"2. Examination of ways and means of promoting economic cooperation between the African states, based on the exchange of technical, scientific and educational information, with special regard to industrial planning and agricultural development.

"3. On the cultural level, the formulation of concrete proposals for the exchange of visiting missions between the various countries, both government and non-government, which might lead to first-hand knowledge of one country by another and a mutual appreciation of their respective cultures.

"4. Consideration of the problem of international peace in conformity with the Charter of the United Nations."

The second meeting of the Ambassadors took place at the Ethiopian Embassy on November 8. The main decision made at the meeting was that the provisional starting date of the Accra conference be set at April 8, 1958, in view of the Sudanese Ambassador's request that it be convened after the general elections in the Sudan. This was referred to the governments and accepted by all of them. It was reported that the memorandum from the Ghana government on the draft provisional agenda had not been received and it was decided to consider it when the Ambassadors next met at the Tunisian Embassy.

The third meeting of the Ambassadors was held at the Tunisian Embassy on December 21 to consider the memorandum sent by the Ghana government and an item on subversive activities which the Liberian government had proposed to be added to the agenda. The Ambassadors agreed that the memorandum was comprehensive and explicit but, as they had sent it to their respective countries, they had to wait for the comments of their governments. With respect to the item presented by Liberia, some Ambassadors contended that, as the question was purely internal, the governments should not discuss it at Accra. On the Liberian Ambassador's explanation of the reason for presenting it for consultation, followed by an exchange of views, it became evident that the matter did not concern persons who lived in a country and strove to change a legal government but foreign organizations or governments desirous of subverting a government and getting it replaced by a government that suited them. Finally, the Liberian Ambassador was requested to present a memorandum explaining the views of his government, and it was decided that the fourth meeting be convened at the Liberian Embassy on February 10, 1958.

In compliance with the Foreign Ministry's instructions in December that the 'Principles of the Bandung Conference' be placed on the agenda of the Conference of Independent African States, I sent to the Heads of Mission in advance copies of the Principles and they were discussed on February 4, at the fourth meeting held at the Liberian Embassy. It was agreed that they be placed on the agenda for reaffirmation by the States. The item was included in point 4 of the agenda.

The Liberian Ambassador presented the memorandum requested at the third meeting and, after considering and amending it, the Ambassadors agreed that it be placed on the agenda as point 5 under the title 'Foreign Subversive Activities in Africa.'

A request presented to the Ghana government by the Sudan government on behalf of Somalia that it be allowed to attend the Accra conference as an observer was discussed. Even though the Ambassadors were not opposed to the idea, they were of the opinion that, if the door was opened for one country, it would be necessary to do the same for others like Algeria and Nigeria. It was therefore agreed not to allow Somalia to attend the conference.

A memorandum was presented by the Ghana government for consideration at the conference on an African maritime belt, i.e. the extent of territorial waters over which a state exercises complete and sovereign rights to the exclusion of other powers. The Ambassadors, while agreeing that the subject was a vast one which needed much study, decided to place it on the agenda for an exchange of views at the conference. It was therefore included as point 6.

On the Ghana High Commissioner's suggestion that permanent machinery be established, I expressed the view that it should be left to the conference to decide. The Heads of Mission supported me and it was included in the agenda as point 7 under the heading 'The Setting up of a Permanent Machinery after the Conference.' The meeting then adjourned after deciding that the final meeting be held on March 24 at the Ghana High Commission.

The Tunisian Ambassador informed the Heads of Mission in February that he had been instructed by his government to request for the addition to the provisional agenda of the Algerian problem which it had found to be necessary. The Libyan Ambassador also wrote to the Heads of Mission in March that he had been ordered by his government to support the request. Since the Moroccan Minister also supported the two Ambassadors at the fifth meeting, the remaining Ambassadors accepted the request and the matter was included in point 1 of the agenda as 'the Algerian Problem.'

The Chairman for the day who was the Ghana High Commissioner then asked the Heads of Mission to give final approval to the provisional agenda. Having agreed earlier on all the items, they confirmed the Provisional Agenda of the Accra Conference in seven points. Finally, the Ambassadors agreed to issue a communiqué on the preparation of the agenda by the Heads of Mission in London of the independent African states after a series of meetings which started on August 15, 1957. They announced that the participating countries were Egypt, Ethiopia, Ghana, Liberia, Libya, Morocco, Sudan and Tunisia, and this was thought to be the final meeting of the Heads of Mission.

Early in April, however, the Tunisian Ambassador informed the Heads of Mission of his government's request that they consider at a special meeting two items, viz. the presence of an Algerian delegation at the conference and the acceptance of Arabic as an official language of the conference. The Ambassadors met on April 10 at the Tunisian Embassy and, after a long discussion, agreed to recommend that the question of adopting African languages as official languages for future conferences be decided by the conference itself, and in view of the previous recommendations regarding the admission of observers and the shortage of time, it was felt that the question of the presence of an Algerian delegation should be left for the Accra Conference to decide.

Thus it was that the league of African peoples later known as 'The Organization of African Unity' (OAU) was initiated in London.

PROVISIONAL AGENDA OF THE ACCRA CONFERENCE

1. Exchange of views on foreign policy, especially in relation to the African Continent, the future of the dependent territories of Africa, the Algerian problem, the racial problem, and the steps to be taken to safeguard the independence and sovereignty of the Independent African States.
2. Examination of ways and means of promoting economic cooperation between the African States based on the exchange of technical, scientific and educational information, with special regard to industrial planning and agricultural development.
3. On the cultural level, the formulation of concrete proposals for the exchange of visiting missions between the various countries, both government and non-government which may lead to first-hand knowledge of one country by another, and to a mutual appreciation of their respective cultures.
4. Consideration of the problem of International Peace in conformity with the Charter of the United Nations and the Reaffirmation of the Principles of the Bandung Conference.
5. Foreign Subversive Activities in Africa.
6. The African Maritime Belt.
7. The Setting up of a Permanent Machinery after the Conference.

I have indicated in Part 6 above that my wife, Woizero Elleni Alemayehu, had been well-trained in her youth in traditional housecraft. We found this to be very useful during our sojourn abroad (1949-1959) on diplomatic mission. When we left for India, she prepared the red pepper well and took some of it with her, leaving the bulk of it at home with the request to a friend to send it to her when needed. She therefore prepared our national dishes for us while in India whenever we had a desire for them.

Whenever we returned to Addis Ababa to await transfer from one diplomatic post to another, she again prepared a substantial quantity of pepper, leaving the bulk of it at home and taking some with her. Knowing that 'teff' was an essential ingredient of Ethiopian food, we used to take along one quintal (100 kg) of 'teff' flour and ask friends to send us more by boat when it was almost finished. As a result, we often enjoyed Ethiopian food, especially on Sundays.

When we were in Italy, she used to get a lamb slaughtered and prepared in accordance with our national tradition, all the dishes that are consumed during the Easter festival, including 'dulet.' We used to invite to the feast the Embassy staff, the teachers and students of the Ethiopian College in the Vatican, and Ethiopians who were in Rome. Ethiopians who visited us in the course of their travels in Europe and America used to experience special pleasure when we treated them to 'injera and wott' at the Embassy. My wife trained the Italian women who were employed at the Embassy to bake 'injera' and make 'wott' in some measure and they assisted her in the work.

On transference to London, we again took prepared pepper and 'teff' flour and had more sent from home when necessary. Since there were many Ethiopian students in Britain in those days and we realized that they longed for their national food, my wife suggested that we entertain them, and made elaborate preparations for the Christmas of 1957 and 1958. She trained some Spanish and Portuguese maids who worked in the Embassy to help her. We had a clay baking disc brought over by air from Asmara to bake 'injera.' Not less than 100 students were invited to the Christmas parties on each occasion. Some students who studied in Germany and France and who had heard of the party turned up on the second occasion.

On the day the party was to be given, my wife would start baking 'injera' at 5 a.m. with the help of the maids and prepare the various Ethiopian dishes. When the students gathered at 7 in the evening, they would scarcely believe their eyes looking at many dishes of 'wott' spread out on the tables. After presents were distributed in accordance with the custom of the land, the young people would be invited to go to the table and help themselves to whatever they desired. They would pile up their plates with the food and eat until they were satiated. They would then spend the evening dancing and be asked at midnight to have a second meal when they would help themselves to no less food than previously. They would resume dancing; some would stay up until the small hours. My wife would ask them to have breakfast before their departure and they would eat as much as they were able, and go away happy. We also would be very pleased watching their happiness.

My two daughters, Ruth and Sarah, were diligent in their studies and growing in body and mind. This meant that the time was nearing for them to go to boarding school in line with English tradition. The school in London which my two sons, Amenti and Dawit, attended was rather expensive and I began to feel that the fees I would have to pay when Ruth and Sarah had to go to boarding school would be beyond my means. I therefore sent a memorandum to the Emperor in December 1957, requesting him graciously to allow Ruth and Sarah to be sent to a boarding school at the expense of the Ethiopian government as was being done for the young people who were studying in Britain.

His Majesty wrote, "We have noted what you wrote concerning the schooling of your children; it was due to your difficulty. It is known that We are helping on Our part many poor children. It is not overlooked, however, that We are also paying for the children of some well-to-do parents. If they are at a stage to be admitted to Miss Swain's school, We shall pay for your children whom you have helped so far as much as you could in their schooling. You can ask the Ministry of

Education to which instructions have been given that the fees be paid from the time they are admitted to the school."

The girls were sent in September 1958 to Clarendon School in North Wales to enable them to take advantage of this good fortune. Ruth was 11 years old and Sarah 10. Miss Swain, the headmistress, was a friend of Ethiopia and she welcomed the girls with pleasure and looked after them well until they left the school. Several Ethiopian girls, beginning with Princess Aida Desta, had previously attended the school.

On completing her secondary course, Ruth was admitted to Leeds University in 1965 and, on obtaining (at age 21) her Bachelor's degree in Political Science, returned home in August 1968. Sarah entered University College London, after her divorce, and earned in 1973 a Bachelor's degree in Anthropology. We brought home with us Amenti and Dawit in July 1959 and sent them to the English School in Addis Ababa. Amenti was admitted (at 14) to the Haile Sellassie I (now Addis Ababa) University and graduated in 1969 with a Bachelor's degree in Geology, with great distinction. He worked in the Ministry of Mines for several years and then went to Canada. He obtained his master's degree from Edmonton University and returned home in 1973. Dawit pursued a course at the Addis Ababa Commercial School and was later sent to the United States where he was admitted to California Lutheran College (now University). He received a Bachelor's degree in Public Administration and returned home in 1974. Ruth married on April 16, 1977, Ato Assefa Birru, a law graduate of McGill University in Canada. They have two sons, Thomas and Daniel.

My wife was unhappy due to the changeable London weather and the humidity as well as from the lack of sunshine. As this was followed by rheumatism, we became apprehensive that she might fall seriously ill. We therefore decided that she should return to Addis Ababa for a few months, and she left London on March 25, 1958. I availed myself of the occasion to send a memorandum to the Emperor on March 19 in which I wrote that, when I was commanded to go to Britain for a second time in 1955, I had reminded him that I could not get rid of the ailment with which I had been affected during my previous sojourn in London, that I had pointed out the fear that it might get worse on my return there and that, since I could get no relief even for one hour from the tingling pain in my right hand and arm which extended to the spine on my right side and since I had the feeling that the pain was getting worse, the doctors had advised that the only thing that could be done to lessen the pain was for me to live at a place where there was sunshine. I therefore requested that I be allowed to return home because I was afraid that my arm might again be rendered useless.

His Majesty wrote on April 5, "We have received your memorandum explaining in detail that the condition of your health is leading to suffering owing to the

London weather. We do not wish that your health be impaired and we shall allow you to come back. We shall inform you of the time of your return."

In July 1958, a political change took place in Iraq in a most horrifying manner. The government was overturned. The king and the prime minister were suddenly massacred with their families. The Emperor who had heard the news sent me a letter on August 6, "You have not written us details of the happenings in the Middle East, especially in Iraq, as well as your views."

I sent him a rather long report on August 28 and explained that the reason for the delay was because there was no way one could obtain information on the state of the country due to the fact that the military officers who had seized power had sealed it off completely, so that there was no way of getting news except for brief announcements given on the radio on and off. Another reason for my hesitation to report on the matter was because I had had the feeling that he was not pleased with a report I had presented, insofar as I could follow it from Rome, even though it was not part of my duties, on a similar change which had happened in Egypt in July 1952, and which had resulted in the deposition and expulsion from the country of the king and his family. Since it seemed that the report had given him no pleasure, I did not wish to displease him again by reporting on the events in Iraq.

As far as I could follow it from London, the main reasons for the subversion of the government in Iraq were as follows. Egypt and Syria had determined to form a union under one government called the 'United Arab Republic' with Colonel Nasser as President. The government of Iraq, led by Nuri es-Said was politically at odds with Egypt and Syria and, seeing that the Egyptians were becoming more powerful by this process and concerned lest Jordan also might fall into the hands of Egypt and thus isolate Iraq, had decided to obstruct Egypt's progress, and caused to be signed in great haste in Amman a federation with Jordan. It was stipulated that the two countries be united in foreign affairs and defence but not in internal matters for the time being. This was not seen to be a lasting federation by the Western powers but a device meant merely to oppose Egypt and Syria; the main reason for this view was that it was a federation between the kings and their ministers and not the majority of the two peoples. Moreover, the almost one million Arabs who had fled from Palestine and settled in Jordan, impelled emotionally and through the propaganda of the Egyptian radio did not appear to desire the leadership of Iraq but of Egypt.

As the aspiration of the Arabs was growing in those days and as Colonel Nasser was believed by the majority of Arabs to be the protagonist of that aspiration and as he caused it to be spread around by the press and radio that Iraq, Lebanon and Jordan as well as Saudi Arabia were the friends and tools of the Western powers which throughout the centuries had oppressed the Arabs and hindered the achievement of their unity, the leaders of those countries had found themselves in a compromising situation vis-a-vis their peoples.

Educated young people who desired that the outdated administrations of their countries should be reformed and that law and justice should be equal for all, but who had no share in the government, as well as the junior military officers were planning, like the young Egyptian officers, to overthrow those governments and set up the type of government they desired. In the same way that the young Iraqi officers were plotting to overturn the Iraqi government, a section of the young officers of Jordan was also conspiring to overthrow the Jordanian government and kill King Hussein. In the event, the king was not killed nor his government subverted, because the conspiracy was exposed two or three days before the assassination and the conspirators were arrested. But since the police and the security had no desire to save the Iraqi government, the king and the prime minister perished with their families.

I explained all this in detail and expressed my views as follows, "It is known that Nuri's government, after having determined to spend 70 percent of its 300 million Dollar oil revenue, had made several plans to raise the people's standard of living and executed some of them. It was estimated that it would have taken about ten years before the programme could have been completed and the entire people reaped the benefit. But as it was reported that, while working for the future welfare of the people, Nuri's government had exerted strong oppression on them morally and robbed them of their political freedom, it became extremely detested by the people. This reaffirms the truth of the words Moses wrote several thousand years ago, under the guidance of the Spirit of the Lord, that man does not live by bread only is immutable. It would appear that even if the promise that was given by the government were to be fulfilled overnight rather than in ten years, it would have been inevitable, given the nature of Iraq's political rule and the impetuous character of the Arabs, that his political adversaries would have tried to overthrow him. Even though unsuccessful, they had tried it once or twice before. Forgetting that, unlike animals, humans cannot be perfectly happy with just eating and drinking, Prime Minister Nuri who had spent his long life administering his people according to his own lights, failed to meet their needs, whether he knew them or not, and seemed to be unwilling to identify himself with the current struggle for Arab unity. For this he suffered the death penalty at the hands of his own people in a horrifying manner. Not only that, he became the cause for the obliteration from the face of the earth of the young king who could not be said to have done wrong, of the royal family and of his own relatives."

In a letter dated September 5, His Majesty wrote, "We have noted that your letter about the events in the Middle East was delayed to enable you to confirm the facts. As the British Ambassador to Iraq and other British persons who experienced the difficulties have returned to England, you can write to us further if you obtain more information.

"Furthermore, you made a good observation when you stated in your letter that Prime Minister Nuri Said had left good work behind by initiating a ten-year programme to spend 70 percent of the country's wealth for the benefit of the people, since India and other countries have also been working according to set plans. However, as your quotation from the Bible at the end does not appear to be appropriate to the detailed description you gave above, it would be helpful if you tried to enlighten Us on the matter."

In a memorandum I sent him on September 25, I tried to explain the statement as follows, "I wrote about the happenings in the Middle East last July on the basis of what I observed and heard from the distance. I tried to compare the good things Prime Minister Nuri es-Said was said to have done for the benefit of his people with what he was said to have done to their detriment during the long period he had ruled Iraq. I also briefly considered, as much as I could, the reason why the people who had lived under his authority had massacred him and the king with their relatives and concluded that it was because they felt that the harm they had done outweighed the good they had done for the people. Even though the Prime Minister had spent the bulk of the country's wealth on permanent work to improve the physical condition of the people, he had grieved them by exerting heavy pressure on their spirit, thereby obliterating their sense of gratitude. For instance, he deprived them of political freedom. Although there was a parliament, there was no right of free election and only persons whom Nuri favoured could be elected. People who dared to present opposing political views were debarred from election, often made to suffer in prison and driven out of their own country.

"In addition, Nuri's government, it had been reported, had been cruel and oppressive, especially towards the end; justice had not been impartial between the rich and the poor; Nuri had no compassion for the poor people because he despised them; he had wasted a part of the country's wealth on his supporters and for recruiting spies who pursued the people; he had dispersed the parties that had been organized to fight for the rights of the people and, declaring them illegal, had persecuted them when found working underground; he had suppressed the freedom of the press and had prevented anything to appear in the newspapers or broadcast on the radio, except what he and his supporters desired. Owing to this, the people harboured extreme hatred for Nuri and Emir Abdullah who had been the regent of the country for many years. Although the armed forces who possessed weapons were the spearhead, it has been reported that, after the fall of the authorities, the common people led the way in burning down the palaces and in pursuing, capturing and killing Nuri. In the circumstances, while it is not denied that Prime Minister Nuri had used the bulk of the country's resources for the future development of the nation, it is believed that his oppressive rule, his contempt for the people and the favour he showed to the wealthy and the landed classes were some of the factors that made him hated unto death.

"His firm friendship with the Western powers, especially Britain, which are said to be the enemies of Arab freedom and unity, and his hostility to Colonel Gamal Abdel Nasser whom most Arabs extol as the champion of Arab freedom and unity has identified Nuri as the enemy of Arab dignity and interests, and as a tool of the imperialists. Cairo and Damascus radios therefore continually proclaimed that he should be removed from the face of the earth, and, by constantly attacking him, the Egyptian and Syrian presses captured all the modern educated Iraqis who are proud of being Arabs, imbued with the spirit of nationalism and prone to believe that all who show friendship to the Whites are traitors and enemies of their peoples. I humbly submit that the reason why I quoted from the Bible in my earlier report on this matter was because I thought it to be appropriate, taking into consideration all that I have indicated above and the fact that Prime Minister Nuri, while making endeavours for the physical well-being of the people, had apparently given no thought to their spiritual interests and needs.

"Since the First World War, and especially in the past 25 years since Iraq became independent, many schools had been opened and modern learning from the West had spread among the people; many young people had gone to Europe and America in pursuit of further education and on their return home could not help being disappointed on comparing the social development and advanced learning of those peoples with the miserable poverty and ignorance of the Iraqi people. Their impatience to be on equal terms with them and their eagerness to acquire modern science induced them to neglect the beliefs and culture of their ancestors to such a dangerous extent that they became entirely divorced from religion. They replaced the worship of God with the worship of nationalism, modern science and fleeting benefits. Their consciences were so numbed and their spirits poisoned that they made it their aim, in their haste to reach their goal, to mercilessly destroy anything that they saw to be an obstacle in their path.

"It would appear that Nuri who had witnessed the change that had come over the contemporary people of Iraq and who had not only witnessed but led them as Prime Minister was at fault in trying to rule them by methods that obtained 50 years earlier, even though he was born when the Turks governed Iraq and brought up in the atmosphere and educational institutions of that period. This was the reason why I indicated in my previous report that he received the death penalty at the hands of his people because he failed to satisfy their true needs, whether he knew them or not.

"It seems to me that his treatment of the people may be likened to trying to require a 20-year old youth to live like a child of seven. A father who, while amassing wealth and property for his son's future life, hedges him in with various restrictive rules when under his authority will drive the young man to consider it as oppressive even though the father may believe he is doing it in his son's lasting interest. It has been observed from time to time that the tension thus created would increase between them until one of them would have to suffer the consequences. Even though Prime Minister Nuri might be seen as a considerate father of the Iraqi people, he was strong-willed and only tried to make them follow his wishes rather than understand and meet their needs. It was most unfortunate that he should be looked upon with contempt and suffer horrifying death instead of receiving gratitude and encomium. I humbly report that, since it had been obvious that he was unwilling to change his set policy, observers had been led to believe that his actions would one day be followed with such dire consequences."

Iraq is thousands of kilometres away from Britain and it was no part of my duties to concern myself with the affairs of that country, but the Emperor knew that, due to the development of the mass media, it was convenient for me to follow political and other events around the world from London. He had often told me that he had been gratified with the many reports I had sent him from Britain, India, Italy and America. He had therefore commanded me in July 1958, to report to him in detail on the political events in Iraq and to give my views on them. I had written him from Rome in 1952 on the political changes in Egypt because I knew he was expecting it. I had sensed from his reply to my report on the political changes in Iraq that he was not pleased with my views; and on presenting at his order the facts which were the basis for my views as detailed above he gave me no reply.

I should state here that I reported in such detail not only for its news value but because I had the feeling that Nuri es-Said's political methods and the steps taken by the Iraqi people to overthrow his government and assassinate the king and himself together with their families arose from its loathing of his policy and the methods he used, and that it might serve as a grave warning to Ethiopia's political leadership and governance. The fact that, contrary to his habit, he gave me no reply clearly showed me that there was no similarity of views between us on this question. The impression was left on me that he did not wish to find fault with my views directly and in writing because he did not deign to reveal his feelings on the matter.

Even if I had had the realization that it was no easy matter, that it could even be dangerous, to proffer to the Emperor Haile Sellassie, who ruled the country with unrestrained authority, a warning on something that appeared to be a fault, I nonetheless used to send him without reservation, during my stay abroad, my views on some political problems and the manner of their execution in the hope that he would compare his own methods, with those presented to him and be willing to rectify what might appear to be faulty. I could not know to what extent he compared the political methods and shortcomings of the foreign governments with his own political methods and shortcomings, but judging from the two grave political crises that engulfed Ethiopia later on, it did not appear to me that he gave the matter serious thought.

The governments of Britain and the USA had agreed to approach the Ethiopian government with a view to informing it that it had been planned to merge former Italian Somalia and British Somaliland at an early date and to ask it not to oppose the merger since it was designed to oppose Egypt and the Soviet Union and not to carry through the 'Greater Somalia' plan. A démarche was accordingly made in January 1959, first by the US Ambassador in Addis Ababa and then by the British Ambassador. It has been indicated above that ever since Mr. Ernest Bevin, the former British Foreign Secretary, had enunciated that it was British policy to establish a 'Greater Somalia,' the British government had periodically raised the matter and the Ethiopian government had as often vehemently rejected it. Suspecting that there was something else at the back of the démarche, the Emperor and his government were deeply disturbed by the request and strongly opposed it. Observing Ethiopia's strong negative reaction the British and American governments tried to persuade the Ethiopian government that their aim was not to reactivate the 'Greater Somalia' plan or to ask Ethiopia to cede a part of its territory to Somalia but that, since they were themselves not opposing the union of the two territories if they wished it, it would be a good thing if Ethiopia also did not oppose it. The Ethiopian government however persisted in the view that the two great powers were intent on putting pressure on Ethiopia, affirmed that their move was not proper and informed the world in detail of their scheme and overbearing manner. It also declared openly that the British government, having attempted and failed several times to achieve anything on its own, was trying again to put pressure on Ethiopia with the help of the American government.

Faced with the determined opposition of the Ethiopian government, the American and British governments, in an attempt to give clarifications, stated that they had no intention of putting concerted pressure on Ethiopia or harming its interests; that they had no desire to reactivate the 'Greater Somalia' plan; that seeing that British Somaliland was being assisted towards independence and that it would be difficult to oppose the union of the two territories, should they so desire in due course, it was only proper to consider this in time so as to ensure that other governments do not advance opposing views, and that Ethiopia should also agree to this in its own interest. Moreover, recalling that the Ethiopian Foreign Minister had announced in February 1959 that the Ethiopian government would not oppose the union of the two territories and that this was in accord with their policy, they expressed their regret that an unnecessary misunderstanding had arisen between them, and declared that it was their hope that the friendly relations between their two countries and Ethiopia would be further strengthened.

I had been successively reporting to the Foreign Ministry by telegram the opinions that were being aired in the British press and I followed it up as follows in a report to the Ministry dated February 26, "It will be remembered that I have been sending brief reports by telegram of what has been published in the newspapers soon after it was reported that H.M. the Emperor had summoned the American Ambassador and the British Chargé d'Affaires to convey to them the views of the Imperial government. As far as can be ascertained from here, it is the view of the British public that, even though the political programme offered to the Somalis by Mr. Lennox-Boyd had been given too late and it would be impossible to execute it properly in the two years that remain, it is useful in that it is becoming obvious that it is no longer possible to close the door and keep the Somalis in the dark as hitherto. Since the realization of a 'Greater Somalia' plan will involve the inclusion of a part of Northern Kenya and of Jibuti as well as a part of Ethiopian territory, they appreciate that Ethiopia and France will be strongly opposed to it. They convey to the public the notion that even the British government will not support the idea. The main reason advanced for this is that it will entail its handing over of a district of Kenya to the Somalis. They therefore argue that Mr. Lennox-Boyd's statement to the Somalis that they would support the union of the British and Italian Somalilands and assist in its realization does not mean that it is supporting the establishment of a 'Greater Somalia,' and that the British government has made this clear to the governments concerned when it discussed the question with them. As it now appears, they do not seem to be in a hurry to take over French Somaliland and the Somali district of Kenya for the time being, since what is uppermost in the minds of the British and the Somalis whenever they raise the 'Greater Somalia' question is to detach from Ethiopia and include in Somalia and British Somaliland the Ogaden district, especially the Haud and the grazing area, which they regard as vital to the life of Somalia. And as it looks that the people who stand behind the British Somalis and incite them against Ethiopia have warned them not to mention the question of taking over these two districts, as seen from here, they do not appear to be claiming Jibuti and the Somali area of Kenya so much. The report that, when they presented the démarche to the Ethiopian government, the American and British governments had assured the French government that French territory would not be affected seems to confirm this opinion.

"In the short run, it seems to me that the British have attained one of their aims, which is to make it appear to world opinion that Ethiopia and the Somalis have fallen out with one another and that Ethiopia is opposed to the independence and hostile to the union of the Somali people which is African, while Britain and America support them.

"Although the telegrams sent by H.E. the Foreign Minister may have been necessary, it is my view that argument by telegram, especially with the British Somalis, should cease as they solve nothing and merely arouse feelings. The reason is that, while the British have so far said nothing on this question in public, they are revealing their intentions by causing the Somalis to dispute with us and elicit our thoughts thereby. It does not seem to be a good augury for our future relations with the Somalis that the British, who have so far prevented them from making any contact with us as their protected persons and have stopped for the past three years our consul from being sent to Hargeisa, should now let loose on us these tools of theirs to communicate with us directly and lay claim to our territory. If our quarrel is with the British and the Americans and not with our Somali brothers, as is evident from the telegrams of H.E. the Foreign Minister and discussed in our newspapers, it would appear that our long-distance communication and our public debate with them is being followed by severing relations before we have even met. The British Somalis are still under British tutelage and they do not seem to have any sense of responsibility; I feel therefore that, for the time being, it would be better to deal with the British on matters that concern that territory."

I sent a copy of the report to His Majesty the Emperor on the same date and added some more observations as follows, "I humbly convey to Your Majesty my deep disappointment that the British have changed their tactics and, realizing that their word is no longer feared and heeded in that part of the world as formerly, have enlisted the assistance of the American government to resume their policy of exerting pressure on Ethiopia, after having in the past 15 years tried secretly and openly and failed to detach Ethiopian territory and attach it to their own territory. The démarche, that the British and the Americans have presented to Your Majesty's government purports to show that it was planned to allow former Italian Somalia to be united to British Somaliland in order to oppose Egypt and the Soviet Union and not to confirm the 'Greater Somalia' plan and that therefore Ethiopia should not oppose it. I believe it was well that their hypocritical action has been denounced before the world when it is considered that the British had asked two or three times before, albeit secretly, that a part of Ethiopia be detached and joined to their territory, and that it has been found that their word has proved not to be credible. Although the British had been told that their request for a part of Ethiopian territory to be ceded to them could not be entertained, the fact that, considering the British people to be its friends, Ethiopia had not wished to expose the overbearing attitude and cupidity of their government before the world had encouraged that government to try again to attain its aim in a roundabout way and with American help.

The government appears to be perturbed for the time being because it had not expected Your Majesty's government would be so upset and embittered with this latest importunate request; and the exposure before the world of details of its past actions of craft and bullying tactics has been so disturbing that it is trying to keep the news hushed up as much as possible.

"In this 20th century, when their alien rulers have recognized that even all the weakest African peoples deserve freedom and liberate them one after another and when it is declared that even the Somalis, who are never expected to be self-sufficient, are to be given independence in the near future, and when Yemen is claiming Aden to be its own territory and is fighting for it, it is to be wondered at why the British government is constantly provoking Ethiopia. Even though it is not possible to know all the reasons, I make bold to present to Your Majesty some thoughts as I conceive them.

"When in 1957 the British Ambassador informed Your Majesty's Foreign Minister that his government had abandoned the 'Greater Somalia' plan, I had indicated, in trying to comment on the reasons that had led the British government to take this decision, that following the independence of India and Egypt and in view of Egypt's seizure of the Suez Canal, the strategic value of Aden and its district and of British Somaliland which had been occupied to prevent it falling into the hands of a rival power, had gradually been reduced. The British dependencies like Aden, Malta and Cyprus which were primarily occupied for strategic reasons are losing or gaining in importance depending on the tempo of dependent peoples around the world regaining their independence. For instance, when five years ago a British Minister had announced that Cyprus would never be taken away from British hands it provoked a riot and the death of many persons. But in the wake of Egypt's occupation of the Suez Canal and Jordan's expulsion of the British, the strategic value of Cyprus has been greatly diminished and it is now making ready for independence. Cyprus' strategic loss has apparently enhanced in British eyes the value of Aden and Somaliland which had lost in importance due to the independence of India and Egypt. The fact that after the Suez conflict the British have transferred the headquarters of their Middle East Command to Aden and Kenya and their expulsion from Iraq following its revolution has given greater strategic value to the Horn of Africa which lies between Aden and Kenya.

"Seeing that Britain's paramount interest at present is to be found in Kuwait and the Bahrain Islands in the Persian Gulf and that 80 percent of the oil vital to British life is to be obtained from Kuwait, and seeing that Nasser and the Saudi government as well as Iran are striving to take over the islands and the adjacent territories, the British government, determined to hold on to those territories and their oil wealth as long as possible, has moved its military headquarters from Cyprus to East Africa and caused the Commander-in-Chief to have his seat in Aden. I therefore, humbly submit that the main reason why the British with American help are impelled to try to establish themselves not only in their Somali territory but also in Somalia is their interest in the strategic value of those territories and not their consideration for the Somalis or their preoccupation for their freedom and well-being. It is doubtful that they will alter their present policy as long as their interest in the Gulf endures.

"According to unofficial reports, the main reason why they desire to have the Haud is not for the Somalis to graze their herds but rather because, apart from its inaccessibility to foreigners and its distance from the sea, the Haud is nearer to the Persian Gulf, the centre of their interest, and to the Soviet Union, the target of their intrigue, by about one thousand miles than is Kenya. They reckon therefore that it will help them if they can build a large air base there. Perhaps, the Americans are assisting them in this because they assume it will be useful for them in their policy of containment of the Soviet Union. In view of the fact that the Americans have not been able to obtain sites for the construction of air bases for assault on Russia from any government from Syria to India, and further back not only Egypt but the Sudan and Ethiopia also do not appear to have looked with favour on the matter, it is probable that, taking advantage of Somalia's independence and financial plight, the two great powers have agreed that it was important for them to get a strategic foothold on the Horn of Africa.

"Moreover, as it is generally believed that there is oil in the Horn of Africa, one wonders whether, in case they lose the oil in Iraq and Kuwait some day, the British entertain the hope of prospecting and finding a replacement in the Somali territories and the Ogaden. In any event, knowing that former Italian Somalia and British Somaliland will unite after a while and become an entity, created for the convenience of the British like Jordan, in spite of the fact that it will be unable to exist even for one year without British and American financial aid, but intent on realizing their plan, the British have for 15 years importuned Ethiopia for a part of its territory, not because they have any regard for the well-being of the Somalis but because, even if they knew that Ethiopia was not willing to accommodate them, they desired to get hold of that portion of Africa from which they hoped to obtain several benefits and, by giving the Somalis an annual subsidy, trick the world into believing that they obtained the right by fair means. Now that the question has come to the open, therefore, it seems to be helpful to find support by informing the leaders of states who stand up for freedom and the rights of weak peoples of the views and the struggle of Your Majesty's government through diplomatic channels and the UN headquarters. That the British also will make an effort to get supporters all around should give an impetus to this.

"It would appear, the more the Asian and African governments, convinced of the basic craft of the British and American governments, reproached them openly, distanced themselves from them and made efforts to procure assistance from the Soviet government, the more these great powers showed an attitude of persuasion and regard, and hastened to assist them with weapons and finances, while they intrigue against and exert pressure on Ethiopia which has approached them as friends. And when comparison is made between the abundance of money the American government is showering on countries which show it feelings of opposition and the amount it has given Ethiopia by way of aid, it does not only appear as if it feels assured of Ethiopia's friendship and need therefore not bother about it but has also emboldened it to ask Ethiopia to cede to aliens a part of its own territory and a section of its own people. I would therefore make bold to recommend that it would be in the lasting interest of Your beloved country if, following the example of the Sudan, the Imperial government were to reconsider and modify its policy vis-a-vis these governments."

The Emperor wrote on March 13 in reply to this report, "You have shown Us in your report that you have followed up and thoroughly grasped that, on the Somali question, America was exerting pressure and Britain, the initiator of the process, was attempting to get the matter settled through a third party. On receipt of the démarche of the British and the Americans, We received the Ambassadors of the two countries and had discussions with them. After setting out the reasons for our rejection to the American Ambassador and recalling at length the long-standing and continuing friendly relations between us, we asked that his government find a way of withdrawing its proposal, since there was no reason why it should be involved in the matter. The Ambassador gave Us last week his government's response both orally and in writing. We are sending you a copy of his note to be kept confidentially.

"We have realized that, it is persisting in pursuit of the prey for the British to attempt to achieve their aim indirectly through former Italian Somalia after their Ambassador had personally assured us both orally and in writing that they had abandoned the 'Greater Somalia' plan.

"It is well-known that we are prepared to support the independence of the two Somali territories, but, because it involves the cession of a part of Ethiopia, we are opposed to the 'Greater Somalia' plan; and we are astonished that the Colonial Secretary should issue a statement, as reported by Reuters, pretending that they had no intention to ask for the cession of Ethiopian territory. You will have found the statement there.

"It can be said that, on one hand, they realize that God's good time has arrived for Africa to be free as witnessed by their actions in recent years, and that it is not possible to stop the process; and, on the other hand, they are reluctant to face the fact. As you have pointed out in your letter, it should have been enough to convince them that not only Africa but territories in Asia and Europe which had served as stepping stones for the occupation of Africa have either been freed or are preparing to regain their freedom. To pretend that they are acting in the interest of the Somalis when in fact they are asking the cession of Ethiopian territory to satisfy their wish to get Somalia to join the Commonwealth is a great betrayal or weakness that should weigh heavily on one's conscience. America's role in this spectacle is a matter for surprise.

"Our confidence in and friendship with the Sudan have been somewhat tremulous recently due to their revolutionary government and we are waiting to see the outcome. As regards your reference to the attitude of the Sudanese government, you will see in the near future the initiation of what is now under consideration."

His Majesty's response to my suggestion at the end of my letter that, his government would do well to follow the example of the Sudan and reconsider, in the interest of his country, its policy concerning these governments, indicated the extent to which he had been affronted by the overbearing manner of the American and British governments, and that he was considering the necessity of turning away from them and looking for the friendship and assistance of another great power. Aware that, in view of the political situation obtaining in the world at that time, there was no alternative to approaching the Soviet government; he communicated with that government and visited Russia for the first time a few months after he had written to me. Explaining his predicament, he asked for support and military equipment. Although not disposed to meet his request in full, the Soviet government gave him a friendly welcome and agreed to advance a credit for 400 million Roubles which no doubt displeased the two overbearing powers for a time.

In the event, the American government, which had been gradually changing its political stance vis-a-vis the Ethiopia government, indicated its unwillingness to afford it assistance to withstand the dangerous threat it was facing from Somalia. The relationship between the two governments had deteriorated rather than improved in the following 15 years, and the American government had apparently not been happy with Ethiopia's internal situation and offered him no hope when the Emperor visited Washington in the summer of 1973 for the last time to ask for military equipment. He then went to Russia for a second time to request the Soviet government for aid, but it turned him down in favour of Somalia which was ideologically similar to the Soviet Union at that time.

In this situation, the Emperor could nowhere obtain the aid he desired and, even though great difficulties were cropping up in the country, he did not appear to be willing to change his policy; the Somali war preparations and threat were becoming more real; he was advanced in years and the efficiency of his government was deteriorating markedly. When the rebellion which was later termed 'abiot' was set in motion in February 1974 to overthrow the government, the armed forces acting as the spearhead, his ministers were dismissed and taken into custody with the senior generals. The Emperor himself was dethroned after some months and kept in detention. After eleven months, his death was announced in August 1975. Thus ended the rule of the Emperor Haile Sellassie after 58 years.

Eleven months passed since the Emperor wrote, "We do not wish that your health should be impaired and We shall allow you to come back. We shall notify you of the time of your return home." I grew apprehensive about the state of my health owing to the constant tingling pain in my right hand and arm as well as in the spine on my right side. I was therefore impelled to send a reminder to His Majesty and wrote on March 6, 1959, "I humbly refer to what I wrote in detail in March 1958 concerning the pain I feel in my right hand and arm as well as in my back. The pain has since increased and I feel more fatigued as a result. Even though my wife had to return to Addis Ababa last year for a short stay, the weather of this country being absolutely unsuited to her and it being our fourth winter here, she is suffering from debility and has had to enter hospital twice since she came back from Ethiopia. She has been so ill since January that she had to be admitted to hospital for five days last week to undergo an examination. We realized that her main trouble is that she has no strength to withstand the climate of this country. In the hope of regaining health and strength, we have been forced periodically to seek medical advice which has increased our financial burden on top of the rising cost of living. As I had occasion to remind Your Majesty orally when I took my leave to go to India, I believe there is no one except my sovereign Master who cares to remember me and bring my difficulties to Your notice. I would therefore humbly request Your Majesty's good pleasure to terminate my mission to this country before our situation gets more serious."

The Emperor wrote on March 17, "We are very sad that the state of your health of which you had written Us previously, and that of your wife, has since deteriorated. We shall inform you of our quick decision on the matter." About two months later, the following telegraphic message was sent me from the Foreign Ministry on May 12: "I am to inform you that Your Excellency is commanded to hand over the Embassy to Ato Kebede Abebe as Chargé d'Affaires ad interim and return to Addis Ababa with your family: Blatta Dawit Ogbazgi, Minister of State."

As soon as I received this message, I completed the work in hand, transferred the Embassy to Ato Kebede and took my leave of the officials of the Foreign Office. I left Ruth and Sarah at boarding school and, taking along the other members of my family, left London on June 24. We stopped at Asmara for three days and arrived in Addis Ababa on June 29. This marked the end of my diplomatic mission and exile. The Emperor was then on a tour to Egypt, the Soviet Union and five other European countries. He returned to Addis Ababa after two months, on August 24, 1959.

WORLD TOUR OF THE CROWN PRINCE

After my return to Ethiopia, I stayed for three months awaiting the Emperor's return from his tour and to be given an assignment. His Imperial Highness Crown Prince Merdazmach Asfa Wossen and his wife, Princess Medferiash Worq Abebe, were due in the Autumn of 1959 to visit a number of countries and government personalities around the world and many persons who had heard of the matter were presenting memoranda to the Emperor to be included in his suite. I had heard nothing about it until a few days before their departure and, as I had no wish to go abroad again, I would not have asked to go along even if I had known about it. Nevertheless, the Emperor's choice fell on me and I was summoned to be told of it. He also commanded me to find out if my wife wished to go along. As she had been thoroughly weary of life abroad, she indicated that she had no desire to leave Ethiopia again and she remained at home. I was called 'His Imperial Highness' Escort of Honour and Adviser' and got ready to accompany him.

The purpose of the tour of Their Highnesses was not political and diplomatic but, since the Prince had had no chance to visit foreign countries for many years, the Emperor had consented that he travel to some friendly countries as a tourist and visit their cities and the ancient centres of their civilizations. It was also the Emperor's wish that he meet the leaders of those countries. With this in view, he travelled around the world for over two months from west to east and back to Germany. Apart from the countries he stopped in briefly, he visited five major countries (the US, Canada, Japan, India and Germany) and Hong Kong. He saw some of the wonderful development and industrial activities and public buildings.

Even though his visit was not official, I was commanded to accompany the Crown Prince with the intention of helping him with advice and assisting him when he met and talked with the authorities and newspapermen in his capacity as Crown Prince. My other duty was to see to it that the couple were comfortable wherever they stayed.

The Crown Prince and Princess started on their travels on September 29, 1959, after 'Mesqel.' The Emperor and Empress were at the airport to see them off. Many dignitaries and ladies were also on hand to pay their respects at the airport. My suitcase was left behind due to the bustle; but as we crossed the Atlantic by liner from England to the US, I was able to purchase a suit and some underwear on board. The suitcase was forwarded to New York.

The world tour of the Crown Prince and Princess and my duties ended in Bonn on December 4. I took my leave of Their Highnesses at 5:30 p.m. on that day and returned to Addis Ababa by air early the following morning. The Crown Prince and Princess went to Austria for ten days and arrived back in Addis Ababa on December 13, 1959.

TEN

Addis Ababa: Chief of Political Affairs in His Majesty's Private Cabinet
1959 - 1961

Not long after my return to Addis Ababa after accompanying the Crown Prince on his tour around the world, I was summoned to the Palace on December 21, 1959, and the Minister of Pen informed me in the presence of two observers that by His Imperial Majesty's gracious will and command I had been appointed Chief of Political Affairs in His Majesty's Private Cabinet with the rank of Minister. Although I could not understand at the time what was implied by this appointment and what its consequences might be, it appeared that it was given a high estimation since many persons, including members of the Imperial family, came to my house to express their good wishes.

The terms 'His Majesty's Private Cabinet' and 'Chief of Political Affairs' were new to our country, and it is desirable to stop here briefly and discuss why it was necessary to introduce them. Not to mention the history of the Gonder Emperors, if we look at the history of those who reigned since the days of the Emperor Theodore, we observe that each monarch had chosen at will persons he desired to serve him in civil or military capacities, and conferred on them titles such as Ras, Bitwoded, Dejazmach, etc., down to the lowest rank. There had been no civil service trained to work in the various branches of government as had been the practice in Western countries for several centuries. Titles were not hereditary as in Europe but granted by the Sovereign as he saw fit up to that of Ras to those he favoured and believed to be faithful to him, irrespective of their social status, and he appointed them to rule over large provinces. The Emperor Theodore's appointees could be taken as typical examples, Ras Ingida, Fitaurari Gebrié and Balambaras Galmo. They were all commoners. It is to be remembered that Theodore himself was a man of the people who attained to the dignity of emperor. On his death, those who survived the wars and their children reverted to their former status among the people.

Similarly, in the reign of the Emperor Yohannes, officials like Ras Alula who rose to high rank and their children returned to the people and were lost sight of on the accession of the Emperor Menelik. Menelik, besides his near relatives, selected men like Ras Gobana, Ras Bitwoded Mengesha Atikem, Fitaurari Habte Giorgis Dinegdé and many others from whatever ethnic group or region of the country, gave them titles up to Ras and used them to help him in the administration of the country. Toward the end of his reign, he felt fatigued due to advancing years and illness and began to appoint ministers in the traditions of the states of Europe. This procedure was however only meant to introduce a new method and did not prove to be as effective as in Europe. And since the appointees understood neither the titles nor the function, the Emperor had to govern the country as formerly until he fell seriously ill.

On Menelik's illness, a struggle for power occurred and the government showed signs of instability. As Ras Bitwoded Tesemma who had been appointed regent of the Empire died a year after he ousted the Empress Taitu from power and Lij Iyasu, the Heir to the Throne, could not concentrate on affairs of state, the council of ministers endeavoured to administer the country. After Lij Iyasu was deposed, the people were disaffected with the rule of the council and conspired against it. They submitted a petition to the Empress Zauditu and to Ras Tafari Makonnen, the Heir to the Throne. With the exception of the war minister, Fit. Habte Giorgis, all of Emperor Menelik's ministers were dismissed and banished for a limited period.

After the dismissal of the ministers, Ras Tafari and Fit. Habte Giorgis, in spite of occasional differences of outlook, shared power in the administration of the country for a decade. On the death of the War Minister in 1926, the Heir to the Throne, gradually eliminating Menelik's dignitaries who were opposed to him, assumed full power in 1928. On the death of the Empress Zauditu in early April 1930, he succeeded to the Imperial throne under the name of Haile Sellasie I. Following the tradition of his predecessors, the new Emperor selected persons who suited him and, granting them high titles and positions, assigned them to departments of state and provincial administrations. He organized the council of ministers on an improved basis and, granting them powers and duties, caused them to serve the country on modern lines. As indicated above, since there was no civil service to carry out the day to day affairs of the country in the various branches of government and since the Emperor was disposed to pursue the details of administrative work, he had to receive all that was submitted to him from all directions and give directives. As the activities of the government expanded and he advanced in years, it became more and more difficult for him to read and digest all the memoranda and petitions he received from all directions. The fact that the ministers continually presented for his decision all the important matters they had planned and decided on individually and collectively made the task all the more burdensome for him.

From 1954 onwards, whenever he visited countries in Europe, America and Asia, the Emperor brought home and put into practice certain ideas he thought would be of benefit to the workings of his government. Accordingly, having visited Yugoslavia several times and established a close relationship with Marshal Broz-Tito and being of the same age, it was inevitable that he should observe how the Marshal discharged his heavy duties. It would appear therefore that he determined to follow his method of work after his visit to Tito in 1959. The method was to designate persons he trusted to read the numerous official documents submitted to him daily, make abstracts of the main points and present them with their views to expedite his decisions. He thus decided to appoint persons he trusted to study and analyse memoranda on matters submitted for his decision on political, economic, social, security, defence, judicial and Church affairs, and caused a new office, called 'His Majesty's Private Cabinet,' to be established.

Apparently, he had considered and decided some time earlier that I should work in this Cabinet and, soon after my return from the tour around the world, other persons chosen to serve in the Cabinet and I were summoned to the Palace and assigned our various duties. The reason why I stated earlier that I could not understand at the time what was implied by the appointment and what the consequences might be was because I was not in the country when the matter was mooted and considered, and I had no inkling of it. I was therefore completely unaware of what awaited me when I was summoned for the appointment.

We attended on the Emperor the following day and he read to us the directives which we thought were extremely serious at the time. The main points read as follows: "We chose you to be assigned to the sections allotted to you to relieve the routine work which takes such a big share of Our time. Your responsibility is not to be taken lightly. You are charged to be the assessors and observers of what others do; and Our decisions will have to be based on the detailed analyses you present to Us. You should realize what heavy responsibility this entails."

The offices of the Cabinet were to be in the building called 'Duc Bet' (Duke's House) in the precincts of the former Upper Palace (now the University). The building was so called because it was constructed for the use of the Italian Prince, the Duke of Abruzzi when he came to Ethiopia in 1928. It took some time, after we were given the directives, to arrange our offices and get persons transferred from the other offices to assist us. Ato Befeqadu Tadesse was designated to assist me with the title of director general. It was my impression that he worked diligently for the success of our task.

Owing to the fact that the Cabinet was new to the structure of the government, however, the ministers did not look at it with favour. As a result, they showed us no spirit of cooperation; but knowing that the Emperor was bent on it, they did not dare to oppose it openly. Besides, it would seem that they had the feeling that the danger to them would be minimal as long as we were restricted to our offices to read the documents passed on to us and present our views to His Majesty. We also were at a loss what to do being shut off in our respective rooms, being in contact with nobody except the Emperor. We therefore met in twos or threes to discuss the matter and agreed that it was necessary to make His Majesty aware that, unless we were to meet from time to time to consult together on our common task, we would not be of much use to him.

We had understood that it was Lt. Col. Worqneh Gebeyehu, Chief of Security, who more than anybody else, had supported the idea of setting up the Cabinet and as he was influential, some of us asked him to call a meeting of the members of the Cabinet. The meeting was held and we had a consultation on our difficulties. We then asked him to request His Majesty to grant us an audience so that we could ask for directives. The Emperor summoned us to his office and listened to what we had to say. He then told us that it would be good if we met from time to time and had discussions concerning our work, and that we could periodically elect a chairman from our membership. We retired from the Emperor's presence with satisfaction. We had a meeting soon after and an election took place. I was elected chairman, General Isayas Gabre Sellassie vice chairman and Col. Worqneh Gebeyehu, executive secretary. The ministers felt strong apprehension on hearing this lest we should compete with the council of ministers in influencing the Emperor by uniting our efforts. They therefore exerted themselves more than ever to hinder us in our work.

In addition to analysing and presenting abstracts of documents sent to us and proffering our views, we got together to study and submit memoranda to His Majesty on matters which concerned political, economic, social and administrative subjects as well as defence. We also prepared briefings, supported by maps and charts, on pressing problems of the day and endeavoured to present them to the Emperor in the presence of the ministers. As Col. Worqneh strongly believed in this type of presentation, the maps and charts were prepared in his office. A briefing took place before His Majesty on May 6, 1960, on the difficulty which was apparent in the Ogaden, the ministers attending. The Emperor was gratified and he rebuked some of the ministers, calling them by name (including Ras Abebe and Tsehafé-Tizaz Aklilou). They appeared to be dismayed and their hatred of the Cabinet increased proportionately. The tension was such after the briefing that, judging by their looks, they would have taken a violent action against us had it been possible. We learned later that some of them expressed their deep sorrow to the Emperor at the humiliation they had suffered and pleaded with him that they might not be reprimanded again in our presence. For our part, observing that the Emperor was pleased with our briefing, we desired that it be continued and sent Col. Worqneh to obtain His Majesty's permission. He tried hard but was unsuccessful and our briefing programme had to come to an end.

Although we were allowed to elect our officers to facilitate our work, we faced several obstacles. We acquainted the Emperor with them and were ordered to consult together and report as to how we could render better service. We therefore submitted the following memorandum on March 30, 1960: "Firstly, realizing that the main reason for the creation of Your Majesty's Cabinet was to assist in routine work from close quarters, we humbly submit after careful study the conclusion we have arrived at. The directive given us by Your Majesty reads: 'We chose you to be assigned to the sections allotted to you - to relieve the routine work which takes such a big share of Our time.' In line with these words, our study has led us to the conviction that it will only be possible for us to assist Your Majesty in lightening the routine work if the following points were put into effect by Your Majesty's strict orders.

"a). To help lessen the routine work, the documents, except those that are strictly confidential or those meant only for Your Majesty's eyes, should be distributed to the Cabinet members concerned as soon as they are presented to Your Majesty and after analysis each member should be allowed, according to the urgency of the matter, to explain briefly the content of the documents in the form of briefing or in writing. This will save the time spent in reading each document twice and allow the time saved to be used for other purposes. It will also enable the person who collects the relevant facts, studies and analyses the subject matter to submit it orally in a short time and obtain a decision, thus obviating the effort and saving the time spent in writing and reading. For the record, however, each study and analysis should be put in writing to enable someone to read and understand the factors that led to the decision.

"b). According to the procedure followed so far, Your Majesty's orders have been needed to transmit two things through the Ministry of Pen in the discharge of our duties:

"1. To transmit for execution by the relevant department matters which have been studied and for which decisions have been secured or Your Majesty's orders or decisions on questions that have been submitted.

"2. To require the party or the department concerned to supply additional evidence and clarification to help in the study of a question already submitted, before a decision is secured.

"As concerns the first point, it is clear that it is the duty of the Ministry of Pen to transmit as in the past Your Majesty's decisions after due consideration. But, we are of the opinion that it will delay all the more the work on the documents given us and add to the routine to present to Your Majesty all the details and obtain orders whenever it becomes necessary to call for additional information or explanation from the departments concerned to enable us to make detailed studies before we present our considered views on the documents we receive from Your Majesty.

"Moreover, as it is stated in the regulations given to each section of the Cabinet that 'it has the duty of making inquiries to find out whether orders by His Majesty the Emperor to the departments have been executed, and report,' it is evident that it would greatly facilitate the work for us to be in direct communication with the departments to which orders have been given. According to the present practice, however, we have to obtain Your Majesty's orders to communicate through the Ministry of Pen for every item of work.

"If, as pointed out above, the present procedure of Your Majesty giving instructions through the Ministry of Pen is to be continued, rather than relieve the burden as intended, Your Majesty's Cabinet will add tedious and time-consuming work. We therefore humbly submit, after much deliberation, that it is our conviction that the work will be considerably expedited if Your Majesty's final instructions were to be given that one of the following three recommendations Your Majesty wishes be put into operation and given us in writing.

"1. Realizing this difficulty as soon as we started to perform our duties, and in order that the Cabinet might obtain a standing in relation to its contacts for study and so that its aim and service might be recognized, we requested that a special seal might be given us. Your Majesty granted our request but, for reasons we have not been able to comprehend, we have not secured the seal as of yet. We therefore entreat humbly Your Majesty graciously to command that a seal be given us to utilize it together with the signatures of two or three officials of the Cabinet authorized by Your Majesty.

"2. If it be considered that a special seal is unnecessary and to enable us to obtain information and additional clarification as well as ensure that Your Majesty's orders have been executed, we request that the Ministry of Pen (a) transmit without delay the draft letters we send it; (b) that it accept as authorized and pass on for execution the decisions given directly to us on matters we present to Your Majesty.

"3. In case this is found to be unacceptable, that Your Majesty's decisions be transmitted over the signatures of two or three members of the Cabinet authorized by Your Majesty and with the seal of the Ministry of Pen, not as final orders, but to call for information in writing.

"Secondly, the other directive that heavily weighs on our minds is the following: 'Your responsibility is not to be taken lightly. You are charged to be the assessors and observers of what others do, and our decisions will have to be based on the detailed analyses you present to Us. You should realize what heavy responsibility this entails.' Convinced that this directive has the highest priority, we humbly submit that we can be worthy of the tasks for which we have been chosen only if we are allowed, by obtaining a seal as we have recommended or in some other way, to communicate and consult with the various departments and receive additional information when necessary on the documents submitted to Your Majesty, so that we can study them thoroughly and present lucid recommendations for Your Majesty's decisions."

As indicated in the memorandum, even though His Majesty had consented that the Cabinet should be provided with a seal, he had changed his mind in the meantime and when I reported in person that we had not been able to obtain it, he said, "What use is the seal to you?" This was the end of the matter! It was my judgment that the reason why the Emperor had changed his mind was due to the strong objection on the part of the Deputy Prime Minister who was also the Minister of Pen. He had apparently argued strongly with the support of the officials of the Ministry and others that it would do away with the powers and duties of that Ministry as the sole channel for the transmission of Imperial orders if the Cabinet were given a seal and allowed to share those powers and duties. And since the alternatives we had recommended in our memorandum were also not allowed, it became impossible for us to perform our duties properly and relieve the Emperor of his burden as had been intended. Nevertheless, we never ceased to read the documents passed on to us and submit abstracts with our views.

The Cabinet plant which was imported from Europe to Ethiopia was poisoned by the atmosphere of Ethiopian politics and intrigue and withered away instead of thriving. The experiment seemed to me, following the analogy used by the Lord Jesus Christ, like sewing a piece of new cloth on an old garment. The Emperor temporarily took a liking for the idea of working through a private cabinet and tried to make it operational. But he did not seem to have considered in depth whether it would fit in with the Ethiopian political and administrative structure of the day as it had with the political and administrative structure of some other country; neither did he appear to have expected the difficulties that were to follow. Even though he liked the idea, because of old age or some other reason, he did not seem to me to have possessed the will or the strength to overcome the hatred the persons around him had for the new method of work and for the persons assigned to do the work, as well as the intrigues they were continually hatching. The Cabinet could not function as successfully as expected because those individuals had struggled hard to weaken and eventually to eliminate the new cloth before it tore wide open the old garment and made it useless.

I would mention in this connection that, whether by design or accident, many of the persons chosen at first to head the sections of the Cabinet were born outside Shoa, in other parts of Ethiopia. The officials of the Ministry of Pen were men born in Shoa, indeed in the so-called Amhara Shoa. The man who was Minister of Pen in those days and his brothers as well as his predecessors in that office and their like were obsessed with the notion that the State belonged to Shoa and that they were the ones who were most loyal to the Throne! I had had the conviction, ever since I returned home from England in 1943, that they had determined and striven to reserve all the key positions, if not all the power of the State, for natives of Shoa as a monopoly. A glance at the lists of appointments of ministers, governors general and district governors from 1941 onward is sufficient evidence for this. The difficulties encountered by the Cabinet workers did not therefore appear to be strange to me. What I could not understand was why His Majesty, who was aware of this, chose to assign me to work in this Cabinet. The mere fact that the majority of the Cabinet section heads were born outside Shoa Province was reason enough for the secret intrigues of our adversaries. That this was no guess on my part but pure fact was shown in a note I was compelled to present to the Emperor at the time. There was no response to it.

One year elapsed while we struggled to discharge the functions entrusted to us, in spite of many obstacles. Then, in the middle of December 1960, an unexpected grave danger faced the Emperor and his government which incidentally proved to be an additional factor to weaken the Cabinet. In the course of the night of December 13, while the Emperor was away on a state visit in Brazil, the Commander of the Imperial Guard, General Mengistu Neway, and his younger brother, Germame Neway, caused the Guard to rebel. The Chief of Security, Lt. Col. Worqneh Gebeyehu, and the Chief Commissioner of Police General Tsige Dibu, joined them in the rebellion. The Crown Prince and Ras Imru together with a number of ministers were arrested and detained in the Upper Palace. The Crown Prince was made to declare over the radio that a new government had been formed and that they had taken power. It was widely reported that the Prince was compelled to do this at the point of a gun. The so-called proclamation made by the Crown Prince was repeated ad nauseam on the radio.

Not aware of what had happened during the night, I proceeded as usual to my office which was in the precincts of the Upper Palace and found the gates closed and guarded by troops. Having been denied entry, the Palace servants were standing around. The Empress happened to be staying in her villa on the Entotto road. I asked the soldiers to allow me access to my office but they told me it was not possible. On hearing that Col. Worqneh was in the Palace, I asked one of the soldiers to tell him to secure a permit for me to go to my office in the afternoon and returned home. After lunch, I asked again for entry to the Palace and was told that it could not be allowed and that Worqneh was not available. On my return home, my wife and friends reproached me for going to the Palace a second time. For my part, I was intent on performing my duty and could not see that I was perhaps exposing myself to certain death. Several ministers and dignitaries, who had argued with the troops and had been allowed in, lost their lives when, after their defeat and before their flight, the rebels gunned down all those who were under detention. I tendered heartfelt thanks to the Lord my God for delivering me from this danger in view of my lack of judgment and naivety.

The then Commanding Generals of the Army, Generals Merid Mengesha and Kebede Gebre, were determined to oppose the Commander of the Imperial Guard and his fellow rebels. The Commander of the Air Force also stood with them. The Patriarch pronounced an anathema against the rebellion. His words of excommunication were scattered all over Addis Ababa by aircraft. The inhabitants of the City were extremely distressed by the rebellion for a few days, and they felt helpless.

On the first day, December 14, the two sides exchanged views before noon but could not reach any agreement. The Imperial Guard therefore made preparations to attack the Army. On December 15, General Mengistu incited College students and caused them to demonstrate in the streets in support of the rebellion. He also utilized the radio all day to enlist public support. On the same day, General Merid concentrated Army troops by air in Debre Zeit and brought the tank corps to be brought there from Nazret and kept on the alert. In an effort to capture General Merid and his fellow Generals, the Imperial Guard marched to the Fourth Army Camp and opened fire at 2:30 p.m., but had to retreat because they could not occupy the Camp. Gunfire continued all night in the centre of the City. Whoever possessed a firearm let it off, and considering the intensity of fire it seemed that the whole City was in ruin. The main reason for firing was that many people desired to warn off those who had a mind to loot and their adversaries; they were also making an effort to contain their fright. As a result, many perished by stray bullets.

On the third day, December 16, the Army launched an attack in its turn. The offensive was so strong that the troops pushed their way to the Upper Palace and Jubilee Palace where the rebels were entrenched and the tanks smashed the Palace gates. On seeing this, the leaders of the rebellion lost hope, machine-gunned the detainees and fled from the Palace. Fifteen ministers and high ranking officials were killed, three were wounded and two escaped unscathed.

As soon as he heard the news of the revolt, the Emperor interrupted his Brazilian visit and took to the air to return to Ethiopia. He stopped briefly in Liberia and Khartoum, and as soon as General Abye Abebe, the Emperor's Representative, assured him that Eritrea was free of the rebellion, he proceeded to Asmara and spent the night of December 16. On hearing that the rebels had been defeated and had fled, he returned to Addis Ababa by air on December 17. The people were elated and welcomed him with loud cheers and ululation. On the following day, he reassured by a radio address the inhabitants of the Capital who were in great straits. On being asked by foreign correspondents whether he would modify his political programme because of the rebellion, the Emperor made it clear that no modification would be made!

Of those who took part in the rebellion with Mengistu and his brother, Col. Worqneh Gebeyehu took his own life; Gen. Tsige Dibu and a number of officers and soldiers were killed during the fighting. Mengistu and Germame escaped from the City but were pursued by the Police and overtaken in a few days near Mount Zuquala. They were just on the point of being captured after an exchange of fire when Germame fired and wounded his brother. He then took his own life. Mengistu was arrested and, after staying many weeks in hospital, was condemned to death by a court of law and hanged in March 1961 in one of the public squares.

The structure of the government at the ministerial level was disrupted due to the assassination of quite a number of ministers, ministers of state and vice ministers. It became inevitable, therefore, that the surviving ministers take charge of one department each until new ministers were appointed. On December 22, I was assigned ad interim, in addition to my Private Cabinet post, to administer the Ministry of Community Development of which General Mulugeta Bulli had been the incumbent. I worked in that Ministry for about two months.

The rebellion stirred up by Mengistu and Germame against the Emperor Haile Sellassie was smothered for a time like a fire, but was not extinguished. The truth of this was revealed in 1974 when the revolt termed 'abiot' was set in motion. It became instrumental in ending the reign of the Emperor and the collapse of the ancient Ethiopian regime.

On Diplomatic Missions

1. Republic Day in Ghana

While I was working in His Majesty's Private Cabinet, I had occasion to go on two diplomatic missions abroad in June and August 1960. Ghana, the West African nation which had been liberated from Britain in 1957 and administered as a Dominion with Dr. Kwame Nkrumah as Prime Minister, had elected to be a republic under presidential rule. The Emperor desired that I should be present at the inauguration ceremony as his representative and I proceeded to Ghana by air on June 26 accompanied by Ato Ayele Moltotal, a director general in the

Ministry of Foreign Affairs. We arrived in Accra in the evening of the same day and stayed at the Ambassador Hotel. I toured the City on the following day. On June 28 before noon, I visited the University College and Achimota College. I called on the Foreign Minister in the afternoon and asked him to arrange an appointment for me to meet Dr. Nkrumah and then went to Tema to see the new port which was under construction. As I was informed that Dr. Nkrumah would receive me in the course of the morning of June 29, I went to his residence and presented His Majesty's letter and presents. I also gave him the Emperor's greetings and good wishes.

July 1 was Republic Day on which the ceremony of Dr. Kwame Nkrumah's assumption of office as the first President was to be observed and I went to State House to attend it. The report I submitted to the Emperor on July 8 after my return from Ghana indicated what I saw and heard at that time. I shall therefore quote it in part as follows:

"The government of Ghana has expended large sums of money to celebrate its Republic Day and proclaim its complete independence to the whole world. As someone who has followed the matter from the inside told me, half a million Pounds had been spent up to the inauguration day in preparation for the occasion. Since the festivities lasted six days and 750 guests had been invited for the majority of whom travelling expenses were paid by the Ghana government, it would appear that up to a million Pounds had been spent. It was evident that the large number of guests, the vast preparations, the shortage of staff and their lack of experience had together brought about a lot of difficulty. Many of the guests had to stay in the hotel for about two days before anybody visited them. For instance, the delegate of the Sudan who is a cabinet minister had no one to attend to him and was able to get a car only after repeated demands. On June 29, 400 guests were invited to the dinner party given for the farewell of the British governor general. Many of the guests were not on the list and therefore had no place at the dinner table. They had to go away disappointed. They had sent me an invitation card but had reserved no seat at the dinner table. But as soon as they saw their mistake, I was given the seat of one of their ministers. They had seated side by side the delegates of Pakistan and India, and when the Pakistani who was a general expressed anger, they offered the Indian delegate a seat at another place. Mr. Krishna Menon in his turn got so angry that he would not eat anything. When the Egyptian delegate found out that no place had been reserved for him he went away in a fit of pique and would not be persuaded. Likewise, the delegate of Mali returned in anger to his country the following day because he was not given a seat. The Egyptian was vexed the whole week because he met with disappointments at all the receptions he had attended and left for his country before the end of the festivities.

"What appeared to us delegates to be a short-coming was that at every reception the chairs were primarily allotted to the ministers of Ghana and their wives; and instead of reserving what was left of the chairs for the guests, whoever arrived first was allowed to occupy them. Protocol was observed only at the assumption of power by Dr. Nkrumah. It can be said, in short, that there was no such thing as protocol in Accra. The impression left on the observer was that both the occasion and the celebrations were too much for them. They had spent a lot of money but, because they did not know how to use it wisely, the bulk of it could be considered as wasted. It was evident that they offended rather than pleased a number of their guests, especially the delegates of governments, whom they had brought over at considerable expense. In my view, they were only concerned in making the world know that they had established their republican government and reaffirmed their independence.

"They appeared to be at pains to impress on the Africans, especially on their neighbours, that Nkrumah is a great and wise leader, the initiator of African freedom and the champion of African unity. It does not appear, however, that there are many Africans who would accept this judgment of the Ghanaians. The leaders of Liberia, Nigeria, Togoland and Cameroon have shown in various ways that they were not prepared to accept Nkrumah's leadership. The Prime Minister of Nigeria went to Accra only on the day following the main event, and it is said that he acted thus deliberately. The President of Guinea, Secou Touré, on the other hand, had to be present throughout whether he liked it or not. And the Ghana-Guinea Union was the subject of discussion in every speech. It is reported, nevertheless, that even Secou Touré is becoming discontented with Nkrumah's leadership.

"As I have observed above, the government of Ghana had prepared the celebrations on a grand scale which turned out to be beyond its capability. I humbly submit that a more self-confident and experienced government could have reduced the expenses by half and seen its guests depart in a more contented mood."

2. Conference on the Congo Crisis

I received orders from the Emperor during the second half of August 1960 to go on another mission. Due to the crisis encountered by the government and people of the Congo (now Zaire), it had been suggested that, in addition to the assistance the independent African countries had extended them through the UN, the heads of state of those nations should meet on August 25 under the chairmanship of the Congo government to assess at close quarters the difficulties faced by the country with a view to affording them more aid. But, seeing that the time was short, it had been decided that the governments meet on the same date in Leopoldville (now Kinshasa) at the Foreign Minister level. For reasons not revealed to me, His Majesty commanded me to lead the Ethiopian delegation, and I left for Leopoldville at 6:30 a.m. on August 24 from Debre Zeit Air Base by an Ethiopian Air Force flight, accompanied by Ato Asrat Yinesu and Ato Getachew Mekasha. After brief stops at Entebbe and Stanleyville (now Kisangani), we arrived, after a flight of almost 12 hours, at Leopoldville airport. General Iyasu Mengesha, who was then commander of the Ethiopian troops in the Congo, sent us his car and we went into the City and stayed at the Stanley Hotel. No official of the Congo government turned up to meet us, the reason being, as Foreign Minister Bomboko informed us later, that he could not go to the airport due to the pressure of work and that he had no one to send. I had occasion to observe in the course of the conference that there was in fact no official of the Foreign Ministry to be seen besides himself. We were able to ascertain during our stay that the other government ministries were in a similar position; they had not been organized.

Even though it had been planned that the conference should be started early on August 25, the opening session was only convened at 4 p.m. because the Congo government was not ready. Prime Minister Lumumba made the opening speech. The points he raised in his speech were that, even though the enemies of African freedom had struggled to divide the African peoples, the Leopoldville conference had demonstrated the futility of their efforts; that the struggle for freedom of countries like the Congo, Angola, Algeria, Kenya, Nyasaland and Rhodesia had begun after the first conference of the independent African states was held at Accra; that the purpose of the conference was to hasten the struggle and declare to the whole world that there was nothing to prevent its success. He recalled that the conference was convened to clear the way for the heads of state to meet quickly and it was expected that they would support heartily all the efforts that were being made for the whole of Africa in general; that, to ensure true freedom, it was important not to be involved in the entanglements of either the Western or Eastern powers; that it was necessary to do away with differences in language and outlook that the colonialists had imposed; that commercial relationships should be developed and Africa's position defined vis-a-vis the European Common Market; that decisions should be made with respect to mutual armed cooperation and the establishment of a powerful radio station in Leopoldville. He asserted finally that Africa was only opposed to attempts again to push it down to the position of dependency and despoil it, and said that the government and people of the Congo could not adequately express their feelings of joy at the presence of the delegates and concluded, "Bound by one spirit and one aim, and united in one purpose, we shall make Africa a truly free and independent continent."

The heads of delegation of the various governments then rose one after another and conveyed the greetings and support of their governments and peoples, and expressed their sentiments of solidarity and brotherliness with the government and people of the Congo. In the same spirit, I presented the brotherly greetings of the Emperor, of the Ethiopian government and people and the gratification felt by our people when the Congo secured its independence; that, when soon after independence the Congo people faced difficulties, the Emperor and his people had sent Ethiopian troops without hesitation to help restore peace and security; that it was their fervent hope that peace and concord would soon prevail in the Congo, and that it was the hope of the Emperor's delegates that the conference of the brotherly African states would help reassure peace and bind our peoples together all the more closely in love and friendship. The conference adjourned soon after the statements of the delegation leaders was over.

On the first day of the conference, while the leaders of the delegations were making statements, a considerable number of Lumumba's opponents and President Kasavuba's supporters were demonstrating against Lumumba. The intention was to disrupt the conference by making a great deal of noise. We learned later that security men fired and injured many persons. Meanwhile, it was reported that Kasavubu had gone to Brazzaville across the Congo river opposite Leopoldville, to tell his friends that the demonstration was off; that the demonstration had taken place with the President's knowledge and at his orders because it was considered that the conference had been convened in Lumumba's interest and to enhance his prestige; that it had been planned that Kasavubu should open the conference but had to be dropped because Lumumba was unwilling to yield precedence to him and that the President had allowed the noisy demonstration because he was provoked. The President's trip to Brazzaville was meant to give the impression that if the conference had been discontinued it could be claimed that he was not responsible since he was away from the city and if it had continued its session it would be said that he went on a pleasure cruise. In any case, he played host that evening at the dinner party given for the delegates at the President's residence.

The conference resumed its session in the forenoon of August 26 and Congo Foreign Minister Bomboko was elected president of the conference. It was decided that only the delegates of the independent and dependent countries should attend the conference. The heads of delegation of Tunisia, Ghana, Liberia and Ethiopia were then elected vice presidents and the head of the Moroccan delegation was elected rapporteur.

Since Prime Minister Lumumba had expressed a desire to meet the heads of delegation at 4 p.m., the conference was suspended and the leaders went to see him. He remarked soon after we met him that, as he had urgent business to attend to, he could not stay with us more than five minutes; if we wished to tell him anything we should inform Bomboko who would convey it to him, and then left us! The heads of delegation who had been loath to interrupt the conference to go and meet him could not but deplore Lumumba's behaviour. As revealed later, Lumumba acted thus, not because he had more urgent business to do but because some of the heads of delegation had that morning met and warned him that the deterioration of relations between the Congo and the UN had become critical. After a lot of argument and to evade giving his reply at once, he had promised to give his views in the presence of all the heads of delegation but, after consultation with his advisers, he had decided not to give a reply.

On August 27, the leaders of the conference, viz. the heads of delegation of the Congo, Tunisia, Ghana, Liberia, Ethiopia and Morocco met and prepared the conference agenda which was as follows:

1. Review of the Situation in the Congo;
2. African Aid to the Congo;
3. Cooperation between the Congo and the United Nations;
4. Meeting of the Heads of State of African Independent Countries.

The conference was then called into session, discussed the agenda, and adopted it after making some modifications in wording.

The delegates expressed their views on the first item and, reaching the conclusion that the Congo's main problem, in their estimation was the secession of Katanga which might lead to bloodshed, asked what the Congo's views were. Expressing Ethiopia's standpoint, I stated that the rivalry between Congo's leaders and their differences of outlook appeared to be the main difficulty. Since every human being was transient while the nation was permanent, I urged that they find points of agreement and strive for the lasting good of their people. A number of delegates spoke in the same vein. But when the conference resumed its session on the following day, August 28, the Congo delegates made light of the Katanga problem and declared that they would destroy the rebel Chombe by force of arms. Seeing that it was useless to be more concerned than they were, the discussion was closed by passing a resolution.

The next item, 'African Aid to the Congo,' was then discussed by all the delegates. Recalling that the African governments had made available urgent assistance at the request of the Congo government, they expressed the hope that they would continue to afford it the assistance and that it would be increased and accelerated.

The conference continued its session on August 29 when there was an exchange of views on the item, 'Cooperation between the Congo and the United Nations.' Since it was the government of the Congo which had requested the UN for help in its predicament and as the majority of the countries giving aid were African, they strongly urged the government to cooperate in unison with the UN to restore peace and security to its country. Recalling Lumumba's visit to Stanleyville on August 27 and reminding the conference of the assault on UN workers and the fact that it was the responsibility of the Ethiopian troops to keep order in the city, I recommended strongly that the Congo government consider seriously that such incidents were not repeated. The other delegations also conveyed their feeling of apprehension in similar words. For their part, the Congo delegates claimed that such incidents occurred for the most part because the UN officials did what they pleased without consulting the Congo government and flew all over the country carrying white persons which made the people very apprehensive lest

Belgian Commandos might suddenly fall upon them. They explained that had the officials shown a desire for cooperation the situation would not have been so tense. The counsel tendered was thus concluded and the conference passed the third resolution on the subject.

The conference resumed its session in the afternoon of August 29 and the heads of delegation expressed their views on the fourth item, 'Meeting of the Heads of State of African Independent Countries.' While all agreed in principle that the heads of state should hold a meeting, none of the delegates, with the exception of the Congo and Guinea, wished to fix at that time the date and the place of meeting. The Congo and Guinea delegates contended that it was essential that the meeting take place before the UN General Assembly met on September 20, 1960. With the exception of the Egyptian delegate, all the other delegates stood firm on the view that the time would be too short for their heads of state to consider the decisions taken at the conference and to weigh up what their meeting would be expected to accomplish. They should therefore be given the option of consulting one another through diplomatic channels or by other means and decide on the date and place of meeting; it would be disrespectful to our leaders for us to fix beforehand the date and venue in view of their heavy responsibilities and possible commitments at the time. But, as the delegates of the Congo and Guinea persisted in arguing to the point of being wearisome that the meeting-place should be in Leopoldville and the date September 20, the conference, which it had been hoped would be concluded on August 30, had to debate the issue from early morning to 3 p.m. Finally, seeing that the majority of the delegates would not budge and as it was desired to avoid giving the impression that the conference was divided, the delegates of the Congo and Guinea were obliged to abandon their point of view and it was left to the supreme leaders to fix the date.

The conference was thus concluded, but since the whole day had been spent on debate, Bomboko suggested that the final meeting with Lumumba which had been arranged for that day be postponed to the forenoon of the following day, August 31. The conference agreed and asked Bomboko to request Lumumba to receive the heads of delegation in advance.

Lumumba met the heads of delegation separately at 11 a.m. on August 31 and the Tunisian Foreign Minister Mokadam, opening the discussion, said that the reason for wishing to meet him was because the disagreements that had arisen between the government of the Congo and the UN officials had caused apprehension and if the frequent incidents were to continue they might be followed by more hostile actions and disagreements which might be harmful to the Congo and to Africa. He therefore urged strongly that the dangerous clashes be halted. Then, recalling the unfortunate incident which had taken place a few days before the conference in Stanleyville where the Ethiopian troops were stationed, I asked him to give strict orders that the Congo troops did not repeat such acts so that their African brothers might not be involved in bloodshed with the Congolese and that animosity and disunity might not be allowed to reign instead of friendship and unity.

At this point, Bomboko reminded the meeting that the rest of the delegates and other people were waiting in the conference hall and it was suggested that the discussion be suspended and continued after the conclusion of the conference. Lumumba agreed that the meeting be resumed at 4 p.m. at his residence and we all moved to the conference hall.

At this last session of the conference, the heads of delegation rose one after another and thanked the Congo government for its hospitality and reaffirmed their governments' firm intention to give it assistance. Lumumba then made the concluding speech of the conference in which he told of the enthusiastic welcome accorded him by huge crowds on his visit to Stanleyville a few days earlier which he said confirmed that the people strongly supported his government and, recalling that the Congo had at one jump passed from complete subjection to complete freedom, he reaffirmed that he requested UN assistance because Belgium had invaded the country after independence had been achieved and because they desired to contain the conflict and obviate difficulties. In doing this they had placed their confidence in the Organization. Continuing, he stated that the reason for the differences apparent between the government of the Congo and the UN was because the Organization's authorities working in the Congo had at no time consulted with them in accordance with the instructions of the Security Council. After claiming that the incidents would not have occurred had the spirit of cooperation been created between the two parties from the start, he declared that they had in all seriousness requested that the UN cooperate with the armed forces of the Congo in their task of restoring peace to the country. He then thanked the UN for the wonderful work they had performed in the Congo and all the countries which, promptly responding to their request, had afforded the assistance needed and, recounting the provocative acts perpetrated by Belgium in Katanga, asserted that political freedom by itself had no meaning without economic and social development. Finally, he wished the delegates a safe return to their countries and asked them to convey their sincere thanks to their governments and peoples, and concluded saying, "We shall safeguard Africa's honour and freedom united as members of one family."

The heads of delegation proceeded to Lumumba's residence as appointed and resumed the discussion begun in the morning. Lumumba declared that the UN representatives had from the start considered the Congo as a country occupied by armed forces and not as one to which they brought aid, and as he had indicated earlier the origin of the misunderstanding and souring of their relationship was due to the fact that the UN had failed to consult with the Congo government on any matter. He adduced at length reasons for their falling out with Dr. Hammarskjöld before his return to New York and asserted that the misunderstanding would get worse unless the UN changed its behaviour. In response to the strong appeal made to him not to allow the continued ill-treatment of the Organization's workers by the Congo troops, he revealed that he had given strict orders to the armed forces that very day to refrain from provoking conflicts. Then followed Mr. Monji Selim, Tunisia's representative on the UN Security Council, who had given much assistance to the Congo at UN Headquarters and who had acted as Lumumba's adviser on his visit to the US; he raised a number of points in detail and offered Lumumba advice to help him avoid pitfalls.

After a frank discussion lasting three hours, it was decided that the heads of delegation together with Foreign Minister Bomboko visit the office of the UN to report the outcome of the conference and discuss as to how the two parties could reach an understanding. Thereupon, the delegates took leave of Mr. Lumumba. At 10 p.m., the heads of delegation of Tunisia, Ghana, Liberia, Ethiopia and Morocco went to the UN headquarters with Mr. Bomboko and met Mr. Cordier, Dr. Hammarskjöld's Special Representative, Generals von Horn, Cotan and Iyasu as well as other senior officials. The Moroccan head of delegation who was rapporteur of the conference told them the salient points of Lumumba's complaint. For his part, Mr. Cordier related the difficulties faced by the Organization in the Congo, and it was agreed that the two parties overlook the past and try to work in harmony and a spirit of understanding. Since the UN considered the control of the airports to be essential for its work and Lumumba also regarded it to be equally important for him to control them personally, they agreed that Cordier present a draft agreement for discussion to Bomboko on September 2. The delegates expressed the hope that agreement and harmony would be achieved by the two parties and the meeting concluded at midnight after a discussion lasting two hours.

I returned to the hotel to fetch my luggage and headed for the airport with my companions. We boarded the Ethiopian Air Force airplane at 3 a.m. on September 1 and flew to Juba via Stanleyville where we left the Sudanese Vice Minister and his assistant. We then continued our flight and arrived at Debre Zeit Airfield at 7 p.m. in the evening. I paid my respect to the Emperor who was at Debre Zeit and proceed to Addis Ababa, arriving home at 9 p.m. On September 3, I presented to His Majesty a report of the proceedings of the conference as related above together with my comments as follows.

"I observed during the seven days I was in the Congo that there is a government in name only. As indicated above, Foreign Minister Bomboko was the only official of the Ministry seen at the conference. I understood that the other departments also have hardly any workers except the ministers. In brief, the government has yet to be organized. Prime Minister Lumumba desires to be involved in and do everything, but since this has proved to be beyond his ability, the work is not conducted satisfactorily. As a result, not only his own people but all those who have gone to his aid are nonplussed. Being Minister of Defence as well, Lumumba is in command of the armed forces and goes around giving orders to the troops. General Iyasu told me that Lundala who has been named general is at a loss of what to do; if he had his way, the troops would not have been allowed to roam around and disturb the peace; but since the politicians, in effect Lumumba, give direct orders without his knowledge, he is helpless. The situation in the Congo shows that, even though it has been more fortunate than any other African country in obtaining prompt and full aid from the United Nations in its hour of distress, it is to be feared that it may have to face a situation fraught with more danger because it is unfortunate in its present leadership. There is no doubt that Lumumba is an intelligent person, but he does not at all appear to be suitable for the leadership of a state; his mind and his actions seem to be too fast and incoherent. And because his close advisers are steeped in communist ideology and had been pursuing revolutionary activities for many years, the way they talk and act, they appear to be still engaged in a revolutionary struggle, even though they have achieved their purpose in the Congo. Moreover, since the Congo's political leaders are at variance with one another, some desiring it to be a unitary state and others a federal one, it does not seem that the country will have peace soon unless a solution is found in agreement for this controversial issue. Until then, it is inevitable that the people continue to be plagued by strife; and as long as Lumumba holds the reins of power, it seems certain that there will be strife.

"It became clear to all the delegates at the conference that the reason for the desire to convene an African heads of state conference is to enhance Lumumba's prestige and convince the Congo people and the political leaders who oppose him that he has attained the position of a great leader. This was why the majority of the delegates were opposed to fixing the meeting-place and the date of the conference of the heads of state. In the opinion of Your servant, unless there is compelling reason for a meeting and until it is prepared very carefully beforehand, it will not be in anybody's lasting interest to meet just for the purpose of propaganda.

"Another unpleasant fact which I had occasion to observe while in Leopoldville is that the Congolese hardly seem to appreciate the aid extended to them by the United Nations. They appear to take as their due all the assistance that has been given them; in fact, they give one the impression that we should consider it a favour that they have allowed us to tender them aid! As concerns Ethiopia, my observation and the feeling I got were that there is antipathy against the Ethiopians, the leaders of this sentiment being Lumumba himself and his close advisers. The main reasons for this seem to be their notion that we are not a revolutionary people, too close to the West and therefore of no use to them. Nevertheless, in my humble opinion, it is wise to continue the assistance as long as it is needed without regard to their narrow attitude of spirit and mind in the knowledge that it had been and is being given in the lasting interest of all humankind in general and of the African peoples in particular."

3. The All-Africa Lutheran Conference

I had received an invitation to attend, as one of the delegates of the EECMY, the Second All-Africa Lutheran Conference to be held at Antsirabé in Madagascar in September 1960. With His Majesty's consent, I proceeded to Nairobi in the forenoon of September 4 to join the other delegates of the Mekane Yesus Church who had left in advance. We boarded an Air France airliner with 63 other passengers in the evening of the following day and, stopping en route at Dar-es-Salaam, flew all night and arrived in Tananarive early on September 6. We stayed at the Hotel Colbert overnight and travelled by train to Antsirabé. The conference was convened on September 8 in the College Lutherien and lasted until September 18 when I returned to Addis Ababa. The story will follow in Part 15.

ELEVEN

Addis Ababa: Minister of Posts, Telegraphs and Telephones
1961 - 1966

I have told above that due to the assassination of a number of ministers, arising from the rebellion of Mengistu Neway and his brother, the surviving Ministers had to take charge of one department each until new ministerial appointments were made. After two months, on February 14, 1961, a general cabinet reshuffle was made. The Emperor's close advisers and persons of influence, realizing that the time had passed for them to be appointed to the departments, and wishing 'to see their eyes with their own eyes,' as the Amharic saying goes, saw to it that their young sons and the sons of their peers were assigned to the ministries they chose for them. They also made their protégés to be placed in the departments they desired for them.

Since it had become evident that I would no longer go to diplomatic exile and as I had been given the rank of minister when I was named Chief of Political Affairs in His Majesty's Private Cabinet, it was inevitable that I should hold one of the ministries. This gave a good opportunity to those who had tried hard not only to weaken but to eliminate His Majesty's Private Cabinet to secure my removal from there. This was evidenced by the fact that while the other heads of the Cabinet offices were allowed to retain their positions in the Cabinet when they were assigned to other posts, I had to relinquish my post there when I was appointed to the Ministry of Posts. A few of us who had no partisans or supporters were assigned to the departments no one else cared for. It fell to my lot to go to the Ministry of Posts, Telegraphs and Telephones. In those days, that ministry was considered to be one in name but not in fact, not only by the authorities but by the public at large. And because all those assigned to it were offended men, the story went to the effect that anyone appointed to the Ministry of Posts was a person to whom it was desired to apply the Amharic proverb, 'invite him lest he should complain, push him off lest he should eat.' The intent was to call him a minister in name only and then see to it that he is not allowed to get involved in weighty matters of state and in counsel lest his views should upset those who claimed that power belonged to them.

I have recounted in other Parts above that I had no part in their cabal; so I was not surprised by this appointment, neither was I offended. But I determined that they should not be allowed to deceive themselves into thinking that I was not aware of their scheming and, soon after I started work in the Ministry, I took occasion of a visit to the Prime Minister to discuss some matters to tell him about a report that was circulating in the City at that time. I said he must surely have heard it; he inquired what it was and I told him that people were saying that, from Lorenzo Taezaz (1942) to Amanuel Abraham (1961), the persons appointed to the Ministry of Posts were those whom it was desired to keep as nominal ministers because they were not congenial to them and it was not convenient to get rid of them altogether. He professed that it was just a rumour devoid of truth. I rejoined that reports never circulated for nothing; the public observed everything and expressed their views without fear. I added that, even though I had been transferred to a derelict department, I was neither offended nor resentful; he should know one thing, however, that I would not leave that despised ministry until I had made it an object of envy. I worked in the Ministry of Posts for five years and, not long after I left it, it became a department to be wished for.

The Ministry of Posts, Telegraphs and Telephones was established in the reign of the Emperor Menelik. In those days, single telephone lines extended from Addis Ababa to all parts of the country and the governors reported the state of the country to the Emperor every morning through the head of the Post Ministry. He was the official who was granted an audience before the others every morning. The first question from the Monarch was, "How did My people pass the night?" The official reported all he had heard from the various districts. It was after this that the dignitaries and other officials were allowed to appear before him for discussion and consultation on various matters all morning. In later years, however, it became a department whose value was not realized, called a ministry in name only, and not desired for appointment unless compelled to.

I had observed, in the course of my sojourn abroad, that the Post Office was not a department to be despised but one which was popular and appreciated. In addition to being a source of revenue more than many ministries, I had noticed that it gave service to the public like a bank and was an important means of communication. I had realized when I lived among them that the British people who were fond of communicating by mail highly regarded the Post Office. It was true that until recently the section of the Ethiopian people that could write and send letters by post was minimal. I saw clearly that, as education spread and the number of people who could write increased, postal communication would correspondingly increase. I thereupon concluded that it was very important to be ready for that occasion. I therefore determined and placed my views before the Emperor that, in addition to building and opening small post offices which could serve for a time in the rural areas at places deemed to be necessary, a post office building should be constructed in Addis Ababa which would give full service for at least a century, in view of the fact that, besides the government departments and commercial establishments, the number of diplomatic missions and international organizations was increasing from time to time. His Majesty had a similar feeling on the matter and he graciously assented to my proposal and afforded me assistance until the completion of the project. Whenever he thought the work was slowing down, he telephoned or summoned me to the Palace to urge me on.

The authorities of the Ministry of Posts who preceded me, fully aware of the deplorable and disgraceful condition of the Post Office, had from time to time presented requests for funds to enable them to improve the service and to construct a new Post Office building. But, under the pretext that there was no money, many years had to pass before anything was done. Convinced that no allocation would ever be granted control; it was to obtain His Majesty's permission to retain the proceeds of cancelled postage stamps sold to philatelists on the first day of issue and deposit them in the bank for the construction of a new post office building. The Emperor gave permission and on my transfer to the Ministry of Posts in 1961, I found that a start had been made to collect money by this means. I was pleased that this opening had been found and I intensified the business of collecting funds by philatelic sales. Aware that Ethiopian stamps were in demand abroad, I saw to it that many kinds of stamps were printed at short intervals and sold to philatelists. I had portraits of ancient emperors, empresses, bishops and men of learning drawn by prominent artists and printed in the form of stamps. The next step was to get stamps printed depicting the most beautiful and varied birds of Ethiopia. The stamps were very popular with philatelists and were sold in large numbers. In consequence, the building fund increased so much that it amounted to almost four million Birr in three years.

I reported the situation to the Emperor and requested that a building plot be granted for the construction of buildings for the Post Office, the Ministry of Posts and the Board of Telecommunications. His Majesty directed me to look for a suitable site and to report. I requested that a broken area crossed by the Qurtummi stream on Churchill street, a notorious quarter occupied by women of ill repute, be granted and that orders be given to the Mayor to give equivalent plots to the owners in exchange. I undertook to pay for the houses and the trees found on the plots in accordance with the estimates presented severally by the Municipality and the Ministry of Public Works, it being understood that the basis of payment would be the higher estimate of either department.

The Emperor had also been looking for a suitable plot and remarked that the site I had indicated was crossed by a stream and did not appear to him to be suitable. He had therefore thought of giving me the level plot which was later named 'Mesqel Square' and then changed to 'Abiot Square.' (It has since been given its first name). I pointed out that the site I had in mind was near the square in lower Churchill street which was becoming more central and on which the National Bank building stood, and requested that it be granted rather than the one later to be Mesqel Square. I added that the architect could make it suitable for the construction of the buildings. Thereupon, His Majesty readily gave his consent and the Mayor, Kentiba Zaudé Gebre Heywot, was summoned and commanded to give in exchange equivalent plots around the stadium nearby to those who had plots on Churchill street and to those who owned plots at the back their equivalents elsewhere. The Mayor cooperated willingly and I was able to take possession of the area in a short time on payment of the estimates for the houses and the trees. The work of preparing the site for construction was effected soon after the houses and the trees were auctioned off. The channel of the Qurtummi stream was diverted slightly to make the site more suitable for foundation work. A reinforced concrete watercourse was constructed from Churchill street to the boundary of the site to allow the stream to pass underground. The narrow valley was then filled with earth and became level ground. Before continuing the story of the construction of the buildings, I shall stop here briefly to describe the condition of the postal administration of the period and the steps taken to improve it.

As pointed out above, the postal administration and service, having been neglected for many years, were in a pathetic state in 1961. After the expulsion of the aggressor and the restoration of the Ethiopian government (1941), a number of persons were employed in the Post Office and the Ministry of Posts, and a short proclamation was promulgated in 1942 to re-establish the postal service. But, as the ministers who were appointed to the Ministry of Posts from time to time had taken offence in the belief that they had been set aside and had therefore given no thought to the work, 20 years passed before any sign of improvement could be noticed in the postal service. The employees who could obtain work in the other departments had left the Post Office and only those stayed who would not leave because they liked the work and those who had nowhere to go. The salaries of the letter sorters and the so-called secretaries were 50 to 90 Birr. In those days, these were the salaries of errand boys and not of secretaries in the other departments. So, as soon as I was transferred to that ministry, the workers pestered me orally and in writing to do something to ameliorate their lot.

The Post Office was operated in a building constructed for commercial purposes some 40 years earlier by an Indian merchant named Mohammed Aly. In my school days, it was regarded as an admirable building. The post office which was in the Arada quarter was burned down when the Italians occupied Addis Ababa (1936), and they confiscated Mohammed Aly's building and turned it into a post office. The Ethiopian government in 1941 continued postal service there. The offices of the Ministry of Posts were located in the houses behind the Post Office building which had served as residences for Mohammed Aly and his staff and as store-houses. Mohammed Aly's bedroom was the minister's office.

Mohammed Aly's building which had appeared to me to be a marvellous piece of construction when I arrived in Addis Ababa from the country in 1925 seemed to me to be outdated in 1961 and not at all suitable for a post office. The corrugated iron sheets with which the building was covered when it was built were so old that leaks spoiled the mail. I therefore made it my first duty to get the building covered with new corrugated iron sheets. I was so weighed down with the feeling that the work was not properly done and the employees were in distress that I submitted to the Emperor a detailed report of what I had observed. When we discussed the problem, I hazarded the view that the workers were in a pitiable condition and that it could be considered that there was no post office. I then recommended that adequate funds be granted to operate it properly or that it be closed down altogether.

His Majesty who was well aware of the condition of the Post Office said that he would tell me something I did not know about the Post Office. He then related the story of a postal sorter who was in dire need because his salary was so low and had to resort to taking a large number of letters to his house, peel the stamps from the envelopes and sell them. He stacked the letters under his pillow, mattress and bed. There were constant complaints from persons whose letters had been lost or had not arrived at their destinations. The officials became suspicious of the sorters and ordered an investigation which led to this particular employee. On persistent questioning, he admitted that he was the offender who caused the letters to be miscarried by peeling the stamps and selling them. He then led them to his house where mail was found to fill a small truck.

The Emperor then gave orders that Tsehafé-Tizaz Aklilou and Ato Yilma

Deressa be summoned to the Palace the following morning and commanded me to be present at the time. The three of us stood before His Majesty the next day and the Emperor ordered me to repeat what I had told him about the Post Office the previous day. I described in detail its predicament. His Majesty turned to Aklilou and commanded, "Go and give him money." He suggested that Ato Yilma be ordered. The Emperor turned his back on Yilma and glaring at Aklilou repeated sternly, "Go and give him money." As soon as we left the Emperor's presence I asked Aklilou, "Well! When will the money be given me?" The two men exchanged words and I was told to meet them the following day in the Prime Minister's Office. When we met at the appointed time, I asked them why the employees working in their departments were paid double the amount given to my employees for the same kind of work, seeing that they were all Ethiopians. The reply was now that they had been ordered to give me the money they had to pay it. It was agreed that the finance officers of the Ministries of Finance and Posts should meet under the chairmanship of the Prime Minister's Private Secretary to equalize the salaries of the employees of the Ministry of Posts with those of the other departments and report. I sent my finance officer the next day and my employees were allotted the same salaries as the others without discussion. There was rejoicing when the money was brought from the Treasury and paid to the employees. It was the talk of the town for a time, and it was said, "Amanuel has sprinkled them with Amanuel's holy water." (This was a reference to the popular mineral water at the springs of the Church of Mitaq Amanuel, near Ankober, which was believed to cure a number of ailments).

As it shows the condition of the postal service at that time and reflects the views I had on it, I shall quote in part from a memorandum I presented to the Emperor in July 1962: "Your Majesty, the Ministry of Posts, Telegraphs and Telephones was established at the time when the ministerial system was introduced to Ethiopia, but it now appears to be one of the few departments lagging behind in growth and development. Ethiopia having become a member of the Universal Postal Union many years ago, is more or less fulfilling the obligations undertaken by the member governments, especially as regards postal service to foreign countries; but there is a great deal to be done with respect to internal postal service. There is lack of equipment with which to do the work; many of the employees do not possess the know-how or the ability to discharge their responsibilities, and consequently the salaries of some of them are no better than those of errand boys and watchmen. This leads them to dishonest practices and they use the sale of the postage stamps entrusted to them for their personal needs. This has created problems for the government and for them, and has become a drawback on the service. The public, observing their practices, have not been able to give them credibility and are transmitting the modest number of letters through relatives and friends. As a result, the post offices opened in the various towns are there only in name and of no use either to the government or the public and, since their expenditures exceed their revenues, they have proved to be harmful.

"Ever since I was commanded to administer this department, I have discovered that the main reason for the loss and the harm done has been that, although it is not denied that the Ministry of Posts is a department that can render service both to the government and the public, it has not been provided with adequate funds and organized as it should be. Even though the postal employees should be persons trained in postal work, able to command public confidence and given adequate salaries, many of them do not possess the knowledge and the experience, and are there just because they have nowhere else to go. Nevertheless, while the revenue of the department is more than the annual revenue any other department earns for the state, the budget allocated to it is the least of all. While the annual revenue of the Ministry of Posts is two million Birr, the amount allotted to it is one million Birr; and because this budget has not been altered year after year and has even been reduced as of late, the department has not been able to make progress; in fact, it has deteriorated because the employees are disheartened and not working willingly, owing to the inadequacy of their salaries and the loss of hope for any increment. I therefore humbly beg of Your Majesty to graciously give due consideration to the Ministry of Posts so that it can get out of its pathetic situation."

I submitted in the same memorandum a request that all the annual postal revenues be wholly granted to the Ministry of Posts to enable us, primarily, to construct buildings for the post office on the site given by the Emperor on Churchill street since it was bound to take a rather long time to collect funds from philatelic sales; and, secondarily, to provide full equipment to the post office to enable it to give adequate service. I wrote as follows: "Seeing that postal communication will be much in demand, like the other means of communication, as Your people becomes more mature with education and as international relationships are more developed, Your Majesty has granted a large site on Churchill street for the construction of the postal and telecommunication buildings worthy of Your Capital City and adequate for the future service expected from these departments. We are now in the process of taking delivery of the building site. We have more than 300,000 Birr in the bank obtained from the philatelic sales granted for the construction of the Post Office building. Nevertheless, excluding the telecommunication building, it is estimated that two million Birr will be needed for the Ministry of Posts buildings alone. This means that we shall be obliged to wait for four or five years to start building, if we have to depend on philatelic sales only; and, since after construction has been completed we shall need more funds to run the postal service on modern lines than the budget at present allocated to the Ministry of Posts permits, I humbly beseech Your Majesty to graciously consent that all future postal revenues be used, primarily, for the construction of the buildings and then for the extension of the postal service, as is the practice in other countries.

"After having observed the problem closely, I have arrived at the conclusion that this is the only remedy if it is desired that the Ministry of Posts should build its own offices and extricate itself from its current difficulties. The Post Office Proclamation promulgated in June 1942, apart from being too brief, has become obsolete. I therefore humbly submit a draft law in Amharic and English, after several months of careful study, to serve for the present and for some years to come. In addition to setting out in detail the terms enjoined by the Convention of the Universal Postal Union for the proper administration of the postal service, we have added an article in the draft law which reads as follows: "The Post Office is hereby established as an autonomous government department and shall defray from its own revenue all expenditures for the purpose of this proclamation." Should this be granted, it will do away with the difficulties of the Ministry of Posts and the postal service which I have tried to elucidate above. On the basis of the draft law I am now presenting, it will be possible to give up-to-date postal service to Your people and to all the peoples of the world in the new Post Office building. I therefore humbly beseech Your Majesty to assent to this recommendation, with Your accustomed foresight, so that it could be discussed in the Council of Ministers and proclaimed after the required legal measures have been taken."

The draft law submitted to the Emperor was passed on to the Council of Ministers and after a long delay was sent to Parliament which after a debate passed it into law. The Emperor assented to it and it was published in the 'Negarit Gazeta (official gazette, journal)' on July 26, 1966. I had earlier issued in the 'Negarit Gazeta' the 'Postage Rates Regulations, 1961,' pursuant to authority vested in the Minister of Posts, Telegraphs and Telephones by the 1942 Post Office Proclamation.

When the draft law was discussed in the Council of Ministers, the Minister of Finance attempted unsuccessfully to oppose the proposal that the Post Office be a self-supporting department financing all its expenditures out of its revenue. He presented an amendment to be inserted in the law that any uncommitted balance at the end of each fiscal year be paid into the Central Treasury. I opposed the amendment as it stood since it would negate the independence of the Post Office, adding that it might be acceptable if a clause were appended to his amendment to the effect that should the Post Office have a deficit it would be covered by the Ministry of Finance. My suggestion was supported and our two proposals were put together and incorporated in the law, thus ensuring independence in financial matters for the Ministry of Posts and the Post Office.

The amendment reads as follows:

"6. Revenues: Budget.

"1. The Post Office shall collect and shall, subject to the other provisions hereof, dispose of all funds collected by it for the performance of services hereunder in accordance with the annual budget prepared by it and approved by the Minister.

"2. The annual budget of the Ministry, after being adopted in accordance with the law, shall be financed out of funds collected and retained by the Post Office pursuant to paragraph (1) of this Article 6. Any balance remaining uncommitted at the end of each fiscal year shall be paid into the Central Treasury of the Government, and any deficit shall be covered out of the ordinary budget of the Government."

As the proceeds of the sale of philatelic stamps were increased and in the expectation that all the revenue collected by the Ministry of Posts would be granted, I judged that the time had come for the buildings to be constructed on modern lines and determined to invite tenders from eminent architects on the international level to present designs for the construction of the buildings, including the telecommunication building. In addition to the architects who were in Ethiopia, I sent out invitations in May 1963 to architects in Europe, America and Asia who were disposed to take part in the competition. Thirty-seven architects from 16 countries competed and presented designs of buildings they thought would be suitable for the site. To help me in the scrutiny and selection of the designs, I enlisted the cooperation of about half a dozen professors who taught in the University of Addis Ababa. I acted as chairman and we met several times to examine the designs and documents. Three designs considered best were selected on February 28, 1964, and prizes were given to the winners. Of the three, Kovacevic and Straus, Yugoslav architects, were awarded the first prize and it was decided that the buildings be constructed in accordance with their design. The buildings now stand in the centre of Addis Ababa, lending grace to the City and performing their postal and telecommunication services in the interest of the public.

As soon as the selection process was completed and the winner of the competition was known, Architect Kovacevic came to Addis Ababa and set up his office to supervise the construction work to the end. A service agreement was signed with him in March 1964. The site was prepared for construction under his direction. He presented the specifications and the bill of quantity in April 1965 and contractors were invited through the press. They presented their estimates for construction work within the specified period. I called a meeting of the learned men and the tender envelopes were opened in the presence of a representative of the Ministry of Public Works, when the estimates were recorded. There were nine competitors and the lowest estimate (about eight million Birr) was offered by the Ethiopian Building and Road Construction Company (ETBURC). It was decided that it be given the building contract. I came to know that ETBURC was in the habit of presenting the lowest estimates at competitions but that its performance was often less than satisfactory. I therefore made it clear that I would not give it the contract unless it gave as guarantor a dependable construction company for the quality of the work and for its completion in accordance with the estimate given and within the time set for construction. ETBURC presented a well-known Italian construction company named Mantelli as guarantor which accepted responsibility for the good performance of the work. The contract was signed on February 8, 1966, and the work was executed under the strict supervision of Architect Kovacevic.

Although I was transferred to the Ministry of Communications soon after the construction of the buildings was started, I was gratified that the new Minister of Posts, Telegraphs and Telephones, Ato Salah Hinit, followed the plan very carefully and, in cooperation with the architect, carried out the work to its conclusion. The Post Office draft law, after a delay of three years in the Council of Ministers, was sent to Parliament in the year I left the Ministry of Posts (1966). Being new to the matter, Ato Salah asked me to help him in presenting the draft law to Parliament and I accompanied him there several times to explain the purpose of the law to the members article by article. Parliament adopted it and it became law with the Emperor's assent. I was overjoyed to see the idea I had conceived for the Ministry of Posts and the Post Office, when the Emperor commanded me to administer the Ministry, had been fulfilled and I offered praise to the Lord my God.

As soon as construction was completed, His Majesty the Emperor inaugurated the buildings on November 1, 1969. The impressive inauguration ceremony took place at the entrance of the Post Office building and was attended by members of the Imperial Family, Ministers, dignitaries and other persons. The Minister of Posts presented a report on the construction of the buildings. He stated that the total amount spent for the work was 8,100,000 Birr. Out of the total, 2,905,000 Birr was for the Post Office building and the internal equipment; 1,860,000 Birr for the Ministry building; 2,415,000 Birr for the telecommunication building, and 920,000 Birr for the colonnade and the arrangement of the compound. I was gratified that this compared well with the estimate presented when tenders were called for. I was also glad that the architect kept the promise he had given before construction work was begun when His Majesty, on visiting the site and inspecting the plan, cautioned against the expenditure exceeding the estimate. The architect was awarded a decoration at the inauguration ceremony. At the end, the Emperor spoke and made a tour of the buildings.

The Emperor, who had closely followed the steps that had been taken from the time when the plan for building was initiated, who had encouraged me when he thought I had slowed down and who had readily afforded me every assistance I had requested of him, spoke thus with reference to my efforts, "We thank Ato Amanuel Abraham who had laboured to get the plan of the buildings ready for tender and who later had initiated the construction work to be started."

TWELVE

Addis Ababa: Minister of Communications 1966 - 1969

I spent five years endeavouring to improve the postal administration, to make that important public service take its proper place in the structure of government and obtain a building worthy of the service it gave. It became known in early April 1966 that consultations were in progress to make changes and appointments at the cabinet ministerial level. The Emperor had determined to introduce a new administrative order by granting the Prime Minister and the cabinet more powers and duties in the direction of affairs. It was reported that he had confirmed Tsehafé-Tizaz Aklilou in the office of Prime Minister and authorized him to select cabinet ministers to be approved by the Emperor. Accordingly, Aklilou invited to his office successively persons he thought would be suitable for the ministerial posts to work in cooperation with him. Seeing that Tsehafé-Tizaz Aklilou had been authorized to choose his own colleagues and that there had been no love lost between us since 1943, I reckoned that the days of my work in the cabinet were drawing to a close, and I awaited the announcement of the names of the new ministers. Nevertheless, he invited me to his office one morning and asked me to join his new cabinet which was to function in accordance with the new order. He recalled that we had known each other for 30 years (since 1936) and had been in government service ever since; we were secretaries in Paris and London respectively, and informed me that he had thought of asking me to take over the portfolio of the Ministry of Communications at that juncture when the Emperor had deigned to give more power to the cabinet.

I was at a loss to know why he mentioned our acquaintance of 30 years on that occasion. Knowing that he had intrigued against me with his cabal for many years to have me wander from country to country and had made a point of offending me whenever I was sent to the UN General Assembly, and believing that his offer did not originate from him, I replied as follows: "As this is the moment of truth, I wish to tell you some home truth. I do not believe you would make me a member of your cabinet willingly because you have no friendship for me; I would not have cared to work with you either, but you are now inviting me to work in your cabinet because it is the wish and command of His Majesty the Emperor. His Majesty got to know me and asked me to serve him when he was in exile in a foreign land and enduring difficulties. I will tell you the decision I then made considering the circumstances, it was to work for him as long as he needed my service and to withdraw the moment he told me to quit. I accept your offer because you are telling me that it is His Majesty's wish that I continue to serve him. There is one more thing I want to tell you and that is that the Emperor is now allowing the door of authority to be kept ajar. I feel it is up to us to get the door opened wider or for it to be slammed in our face." I concluded by saying that I desired to complete my task in the Ministry of Posts which no one had cared for and would therefore request that I be allowed to remain there and finish the job. Although he did not expect my remarks, the Prime Minister received it calmly and made no effort to refute them. All he said was that my work in the Ministry of Posts had been done, that someone else would see that the construction of the buildings was completed and that he would now ask me to take over the Ministry of Communications. I agreed to accept the portfolio of the Ministry of Communications and we parted company.

He had apparently reported to the Emperor what I had told him and when on the following day I went to pay my respects, His Majesty beckoned me and asked, "What was it you said to Aklilou yesterday?" I replied, "Your Majesty, as he has no doubt told You everything, I have nothing to add." He pressed me to tell him but I was adamant and only said that I had told him that my task at the Post Office had not been finished and that I would rather have liked to remain there, but that on his insistence I had agreed to move to the Ministry of Communications. The Emperor remarked that it showed my Christian conviction. Thereupon, I bowed and retired. I have never been able, though, to fathom this cryptic remark of his.

The Prime Minister invited the other ministers to his office and proposed to them to join him in the new administrative order and they all accepted his proposal. The appointments were announced and on April 11, 1966 the ministers were received in audience by the Emperor 'to kiss hand.' His Majesty then spoke as follows: "You have been told of the appointments for which you have been chosen. The Prime Minister has selected his colleagues and you have been called upon to cooperate with him in the respective duties assigned to you. We have spoken about many things before. It has now become imperative to follow the trend of the times and to work in line with the people's intelligent forethought and educational advance. The main thing to remember is that you or the people you have to lead cannot throw the whole burden on one man. The entire people have responsibility to Ethiopia commensurate with the opportunities had and the positions held. In choosing you for such duties, we are adding to your responsibilities and, since Tsehafé-Tizaz Aklilou's responsibility is becoming more onerous, you have to set a good example of cooperation to the whole people."

Ever since the government was restored in 1941, the Department of Communications had been joined to what was called the Ministry of Public Works and Communications and had existed in a neglected condition like a poor relative. All the officials appointed to that ministry concentrated on the Department of Public Works and disregarded the Department of Communications; so much so that it never had a decent building for its offices and was frequently moved from one old building to another. Since any employee whom the minister did not wish to work in the Department of Public Works was sent to the Department of Communications, it became a place to which unwanted employees were relegated. This led to the demoralization of the employees and made it a department where it could hardly be said the public was properly served.

Not long before the new cabinet reshuffle was made, a building constructed by the invader, was found near Mexico Square and the offices of the department were moved there after a struggle. The building had been left derelict for many years and had to be properly renovated. On its being made a separate ministry, funds were granted to repair the building. Pending the renovation, I worked in the office of the Minister of Public Works while the new Minister of State of that ministry worked in another office in the same building. The renovation of the Ministry of Communications building was completed in six months and I moved there. I studied in depth during that period the plight of the department and the employees.

The minister who immediately preceded me had issued regulations in accordance with the law proclaimed when the government was restored. They were: 'Vehicle Size and Weight Regulations (1962)' and 'Transport (Amendment) Regulations

(1963).' Generally speaking, however, it appeared to me that the condition of that department was no better, even worse, than the state I had found in the Ministry of Posts on my transfer there. Realizing, therefore, that my first task was to prepare and get promulgated the basic law for the administration of the department, I enlisted the assistance of a young American Peace Corps lawyer (William Jacofsi) and had the law and the regulations prepared in line with the directives for the Ministry of Communications in the new administrative order. As soon as Jacofsi had the draft law and regulations ready, we got together to examine and discuss them. I would give him ideas that I felt would better serve the situation in Ethiopia and he would make redrafts and bring them. We would again consider them together and upon agreement I would render them into Amharic. It took me two weeks to translate the draft law and regulations, working in a secluded place. I submitted to the Emperor the Amharic draft of the law as soon as it was ready. His Majesty read and sent it to the Council of Ministers. They discussed it and on approval passed it on to Parliament in 1967. It took more than a year to debate and pass it into law because a number of the members of Parliament conspired to block its passage. They were determined to oppose the law for the following reason.

The vice minister who had been appointed to the Ministry before my transfer was widely criticized for not giving licences to persons who desired to run buses, smaller vehicles and heavy trucks for the transport of people and goods from town to town and from province to province unless he was given in advance many thousand Birr for his private use. As a result, he had been exposed to public odium. Those members of Parliament believed that they had found a good opportunity to air this public grievance openly by trying to block the law. They thus strove to get it rejected in Parliament and the first year was spent in debating the issue.

I requested the Emperor to send a message to Parliament to consider the draft law again in the course of the next parliamentary sessions and it was sent back on the opening of Parliament in November 1967. The members who were out to block the passage of the law offered as their reason for doing so that the vice minister was robbing the people by taking bribes and that they would not discuss the law unless he appeared before them for questioning. I was then attending Parliament to explain the law and argued that I was there as the minister responsible for the law and that it was the first time I was hearing that a draft law presented to Parliament would not be considered unless a vice minister was also present. What I had heard at various times was that the ministers demonstrated their contempt for Parliament by not appearing in person but sending their vice ministers or directors general. Now, since it was being insisted that a vice minister should be present even though a minister was among them, I was departing and would not return to Parliament. They should know that they were assuming the responsibility for that. I then made a movement to leave when the President requested me to stay. The members were taken aback and a number of them stood up to make noises.

When quiet was restored at the request of the President, some members rose to explain that the reason for their demand that the vice minister should appear before them was not because they wished to slight the minister but to ask the vice minister why he was despoiling the people by taking bribes. They therefore requested me not to leave and to bring the vice minister along. I told them that I would ask him to come to the next session, but that the motive that gave rise to their complaint was that there were no laws or regulations in the ministry. To block a law prepared with much effort would not be to the benefit but to the detriment of the people. I then strongly urged them to consider the draft law so that it could be promulgated without delay. The members accepted my proposal and resumed the consideration of the law.

When the vice minister appeared before them at the next session, no less than ten members sprang to their feet and overwhelmed him with questions and abuse. He read a lengthy statement by way of a reply and left after being told that he should be present at the next session when they would produce more evidence to prove that he had taken bribes. Not wishing to appear before them again, he went into hiding. When they saw me in Parliament next, they asked me to produce my deputy. I had to tell them they had better ask the Prime Minister since the responsibility to send a government official to Parliament had been given to him. I then requested them to proceed with the consideration of the draft law. Seeing that there was no escape, the members continued to debate on the law. The vice minister never returned to Parliament; but since he was a near relation of the Prime Minister's he and his relatives were displeased when they heard the news of his humiliation in Parliament. Nevertheless, not long after that, perhaps to cause people to wonder, the Prime Minister had him appointed Minister of State in the Ministry of Communications!

Earlier on, my ears and my heart had ached from constant complaints that the vice minister was personally collecting every morning written requests from some persons who stood at the entrance to the ministry to obtain licences to run transport vehicles from place to place. Convinced that he had been dispensing licences as he chose, ignoring people who had sent in requests months earlier and issuing them to others within 24 hours, I called the vice minister to my office one morning and cautioned him against personally receiving requests for licences from any person; all requests should be registered in the archives where the date and the hour of receipt should be stamped on them and considered by a committee I had appointed with him as chairman. I stipulated that the committee had to act on the basis of 'first come, first served' and report to me whether a licence should be issued or not. This stopped the excessive collection of bribes from people seeking to obtain licences, but I could not be certain that it was stopped altogether. He and his relatives were greatly displeased with my action and began to plot how to oust me from the Ministry. In any event, he was tied down for two years by this action.

After repeated visits to Parliament to explain the intent of the law, the members adopted it unanimously. The Emperor gave his assent and it was published on December 4, 1967, in the 'Negarit Gazeta' under the title, 'Road Travel and Transport Proclamation (1967),' to be effective after four months (on April 3, 1968). 'The Road Transport Administration Order (1967)' was decreed the same day in the 'Negarit Gazeta.'

On completion of discussions on the law, complimentary remarks were exchanged with the members. Some of those who had conspired to reject the law said that there were members who had been determined not to allow the law to be passed by Parliament but that I had prevailed over them, and the law had been accepted. What they wished me to know on our separation was that they were giving me the law in trust to make it operative. I thanked them for the confidence placed in me and said that it was not possible for me to accept the trust, seeing that I had no contract with the Sovereign or an appointed time with the Creator. Nevertheless, since I had worked hard to secure acceptance for the law, I could give them my word that I would see to it that it would be put into full operation while I was in the Ministry. The members insisted that they had given me the law in trust and we separated after an exchange of words of goodwill.

After that, regulations based on the law were successively presented to the Council of Ministers who, after discussion, approved them for submission to the Emperor. He assented to them and they were published in the 'Negarit Gazeta' in the course of 1969. The validity of the two regulations issued by my predecessor on the basis of the 1943 law, viz. 'Vehicle Size and Weight Regulations (1962)' and 'Transport (Amendment) Regulations (1963),' was confirmed by legal notice entitled 'Road Travel (Confirmation of Validity) Regulations (1968)' and published on March 7, 1968. They were regarded as issued under the new law and their effectiveness was made to coincide with that of the new law. I then had the following regulations to be published in the 'Negarit Gazeta' on February 22, 1969:
1. 'Road Traffic (Speed Limit) Regulations (1969);'
2. 'Motor Vehicle and Trailer (Identification and Inspection) Regulations (1969);'
3. 'Motor Vehicle Operators (Licence) Regulations (1969).
And on March 24,
4. 'Road Travel (Delegation of Authority) Regulations (1969).'

The vice minister and his relatives, who watched the Ministry beginning to function on the basis of the new law and realized that the door to bribes which had been wide open was being closed and the gain to which they had been accustomed was decreasing, made an effort to get me transferred three years after I was appointed to the Ministry. Prime Minister Aklilou who was aware that the Emperor would not listen to any tales directed at me, changed tactics and, rehearsing about my being assiduous in my duties, strongly recommended to His Majesty that I be appointed to another run-down ministry to put it in order. He thus secured His Majesty's consent for my transfer to the Ministry of Public Health. The directive in the new order of government which stipulated that the Prime Minister had to consult with a Minister before his appointment whether he was willing to accept the post offered was forgotten, and I was summoned to the Palace one morning in February 1969, and told by Aklilou in the presence of two observers that I had been appointed to be Minister of Public Health. Even though I had never cared to pursue their machinations against me and there was no one to tell me, I had sensed that something was afoot and, deciding then and there to expose their malicious action, I told him that I would like him to know and would request him to submit to His Majesty that I was not prepared to accept the appointment because I had heard that the ministry was not a peaceful place but one rife with misunderstandings and animosity. He said that it was chosen for me because it was judged to be congenial with my character. I rejoined by asking him whether he had ever visited the Menelik II Hospital where it was reported that the patients were made to sleep on straw mattresses and eat a quarter of an 'injera'. I then went on to ask if that suited my character and added that it was not possible for me to accept the position.

He proceeded to inform other officials of their appointments and then reported to His Majesty that I was unwilling to accept the appointment. I was summoned to the presence soon after the appointees had 'kissed hand.' I paid my obeisance but was greeted with the angry question, "Amanuel, what is the matter with you?" I replied, "There is nothing the matter with me, Your Majesty; I simply cannot serve You in that department since I hear reports that it is a place of intrigue and hostility, and I do not like intrigue but work." He repeated the very words Aklilou had used earlier, "It was judged to be in line with your character." - I saw at once that Aklilou had induced him to consent to his recommendation by arguing that as a Christian I would see to it that patients were looked after humanely, and said, "Your Majesty, it will be difficult for me because I hear there is no harmony in the ministry and my health is not strong enough. Your Majesty will perhaps remember that my right arm and hand were disabled when I was in London." - He said "Yes, We do remember that." I continued, "Well, they still tingle and hurt; what purpose will it serve if I fall ill due to strain from quarrels in that department?" - Then, the motive behind the intrigue hatched by Aklilou and company suddenly flashed through my mind and I said, "There is something more I may bring to Your Majesty's attention." - He said, "Go on, say it." I continued, "I have spent three years in preparing the law and the regulations for the administration of the Ministry of Communications; I have rendered them into Amharic and copied them with this my weak hand; I have made efforts to expound them and get them to be adopted; the regulations are now in the press at the 'Berhanena Selam Printing Press' to be published in the 'Negarit Gazeta.' The effort now being made is to stop their publication." (It should be noted here that his relative was promoted to be Minister of State that very day)! Aklilou remarked, "The regulations are ready and the next minister will put them into operation; there will be no difficulty." I retorted, "Your Majesty, it took me three years to prepare the law and the regulations and to get them accepted; it will take the next minister three years just to read them; this means that all the efforts will be wasted." - The Emperor exclaimed, "You are to remain there. That is all!" - Aklilou stood there like a ramrod, apparently unable to utter a word. I bowed and retired.

The remark I had made that the minister who would succeed me would take three years to read the law and the regulations was incidentally proved to be true one day in the Council of Ministers. When the famine in Wollo was at its height in 1974, the Council met to discuss as to how the government departments and the public transport organizations could be made to cooperate in transporting grain to the province. The minister who had taken over the Ministry from me in 1969 was in attendance with the Road Transport Administrator who had been appointed later and they were asked to explain what had been stipulated in the law and the Road Transport Administration Order with respect to the problem at hand. Since both of them had not read them in four years, they had nothing to say! The Prime Minister then turned to me and said, "Ato Amanuel, please explain it to us since you know it well." - I took the 'Negarit Gazeta' from the Secretary and, reading the relevant articles, gave an explanation to the Ministers.

Convinced that Aklilou and his relatives were so disappointed at the failure of their plot to get me moved to the Ministry of Public Health that they would not rest until they had presented another misleading advice to get me out of that ministry, I called to my office as soon as I returned from the Palace the Administrator of Road Transport, Ato Negga Fenta, who had been appointed in accordance with the Road Transport Administration Order, and told him that I had a feeling that my term of office in the Ministry was drawing to a close. I encouraged him to get busy so that we could prepare and present without delay the 'Special Commercial Vehicle Registration Regulations' on the basis of which the Road Transport Board could operate. The draft regulations were made ready in three months and I presented them to the Council of Ministers. Although there was a gesture of opposition, the Ministers approved them and they were published in the 'Negarit Gazeta' on June 24, 1969, with the Emperor's assent.

The law and the regulations concerning land transport were basic and are still in force (as of 1993), except for minor modifications necessitated by the exigencies of the time.

I was gratified that my duties in the Ministry of Communications were completed with the publication of these regulations, and I awaited the time when another plot hatched by my adversaries would come to light. It happened ten months after their attempt to have me assigned to the post of Minister of Public Health. I was appointed to be Minister of Mines on December 8, 1969.

In addition to my duties in the Ministry of Communications as indicated above, I had to direct the following principal departments from the time I took over the Ministry in April, 1966: (1) the Marine Department; (2) the Civil Aviation Department; (3) the Land Transport Department; and (4) the Road Transport Administration. The departments, except that of Land Transport, had a board each to discharge policy matters with the Minister of Communications as chairman.

The minister also acted as chairman of (1) the Ethiopian Airlines; (2) the Ethiopian Shipping Lines; (3) the Administrative Council of the Franco-Ethiopian Railway Company; and (4) the Road Transport Board. A general manager or administrator ran the activities of each principal department. The office of the chairman of Ethiopian Airlines was in the Ministry of Communications. The boards of the Ethiopian Airlines, the Ethiopian Shipping Lines, the Civil Aviation Department and the Railway Administrative Council met in the offices of those organizations.

The Marriage and Divorce of Sarah and Commodore Iskender

During my term of office in the Ministry of Communications, an unexpected event took place which involved my family. Commodore Iskender Desta, the son of Ras Desta Damtew and the Princess Tenagne Worq Haile Sellassie came with a request to my wife and me to consent to his marrying our second daughter, Sarah. Having completed her secondary education in Britain the previous year (1966), Sarah had expressed a desire to go to Geneva for six months to improve her French before her entrance to the University. I went with her to Switzerland and left her in the care of the family of a friend, (Dr. Arne Sovik).

The Emperor stopped in Geneva in early May 1967 on his return from a visit to the US and Canada and Commodore Iskender was in his retinue. Iskender found Sarah there on May 5 and proposed to her to marry him. She accepted his proposal and two days later he took her to His Majesty to pay her respects.

He had reported to the Emperor earlier about their agreement to marry and His Majesty had readily given his consent. Iskender had telephoned his mother to tell her that he had decided to marry Ato Amanuel's daughter who had accepted his proposal and that His Majesty had graciously given his consent. His mother had expressed her happiness and her gratification that her father had agreed to it.

On returning to Addis Ababa, Iskender came to our house on May 12 to request us to give our consent. We were taken aback because we had had no previous inkling of the affair and asked whether Sarah had agreed to marry him. He assured us that she had accepted his proposal and that the Emperor and his mother had given their consent. We told him that we had decided long ago that our children would be free to marry whomever they pleased after the completion of their education, and that we did not wish to place obstacles before them if they were in love; nevertheless, we had found his request to be difficult for us since Sarah was young (she was 18) and had not completed her education; it would be advisable, therefore, that they exercised patience until she finished her studies at the University. He protested that he could not wait that long; he would like them to be married without delay and it would not be difficult for her to continue her studies at the University here. We told him we did not feel that married life and studies would go together; wouldn't they reconsider the matter? But he insisted that he could not wait. Sarah wrote on May 7 from Geneva to say that she had accepted Iskender's proposal to marry him and that she had paid her respects to the Emperor. She added that she loved Iskender and would be happy to marry him, but they would have to wait three years because she desired to complete her studies.

This sudden event landed us in a dilemma and we became apprehensive. We were aware that it was considered a high honour for our daughter to marry the grandson of the Emperor. Commodore Iskender was a naval cadet in the British Navy during our sojourn in London (1955-59), and he stayed with us at the Embassy during his holidays like a member of the family. (There was no thought of marriage then because Sarah was only between 7 and 10 years old). But, as we had had occasion to observe during his stay with us that he had an impetuous and inconstant nature, it appeared to us risky that he should so hastily wish to enter into such a serious matter as matrimony. Nevertheless, apart from the knowledge that it would not create a good impression both at Court and on the public if it became known that we did not desire our daughter to marry a member of the Imperial Family, we conceived a feeling that our daughter, being of age, must have known what she was doing when she accepted his proposal before-hand. We therefore considered the matter settled and bowed to the fait accompli.

Ten days later, on May 22, the Princess Tenagne Worq and Ras Andargachew Messai sent General Abye Abebe and Ras Mengesha Seyoum to our house as go-betweens with a request, in accordance with tradition, that we give our daughter in marriage to Commodore Iskender. They informed us that the Princess his mother and Ras Andargachew as well as his sisters were delighted to hear the news and that it was hoped the wedding would take place the following September in the Orthodox Church. I told them that it gave us great pleasure and was an honour seeing that they had both agreed to marry; it was not a matter of concern to us where the wedding took place. I then inquired whether the Emperor's consent had been obtained. They replied in the affirmative, adding that they could not have come if that were not the case. They were then served with champagne and left.

Sarah returned from Geneva as soon as her school was closed for the European summer and they were engaged on August 1. The couple had agreed that she should pursue her studies here and she submitted her application to the University. Even though she was accepted by the University, she was compelled to withdraw soon after because she was faced with difficulties owing to the unstable situation of the period in the University.

It had been planned that their wedding take place in September, 1967. But because of the death of Ras Mesfin's son, Jarra, who was a relative of Iskender's, it was postponed until forty days following his demise. The wedding ceremony was performed in St. Mark's Church on October 28, 1967 in the presence of the Emperor, the Imperial Family, princes, ministers, dignitaries and ladies. His Majesty gave a wedding breakfast at Jubilee Palace; my wife and I offered a wedding luncheon to many hundred guests at Ghion Hotel; the Princess Tenagne Worq and Ras Andargachew gave a wedding dinner to about a thousand guests at the Villa of the Empress on Entotto road. Soon after, the newly-weds left by air to spend their honeymoon in London. They returned to Addis Ababa in December.

Sarah became pregnant while they were in London and the two families were delighted. It became apparent after a few months, however, that there was difficulty between the couple. In April 1968, six months after their wedding, Commodore Iskender and I happened to be travelling to Western Europe, each on his own business. The airliner stopped at Asmara airport and we were stretching our legs on the tarmac when he said, "Sarah and I are in difficulty because we are unable to understand each other. We may have to separate." "So soon!" I exclaimed, "Didn't you get married protesting you were in love?" Iskinder smiled as was his habit and said nothing more. On my return from Europe, I discovered that the matter had grown more serious, but Sarah hardly said anything about it. Her mother and I one day went to visit the Princess Tenagne Worq and she burst into tears as soon as we met, and said, "Iskender and Sarah are going to be separated; we are very sad about it." And we returned home very depressed.

Soon after that, Iskender began to importune his mother and relatives to secure him a divorce. Sarah affirmed that she did not believe in divorce; if a husband and wife had a quarrel, they separated for a time and then got reconciled; that was her conviction. She added, "I am pregnant with his child and cannot leave my house; he will have to wait until I give birth to the child." Thereupon, he left the house and went to live in Jubilee Palace.

Sarah was delivered of a baby girl on August 5, 1968 and named her Naomi. She was christened Fiqerte Marqos (Beloved of Mark) 80 days after birth in line with the national tradition. Commodore Iskender was not present both at the birth and the baptism of the child. Her grandparents on both sides did all that was necessary.

As soon as the baby was born, Iskender pressed his marriage witnesses, Dejazmach Kifle Ergetou and Fitaurari Sahle Dilnessahu (later Dejazmach), to secure him a divorce. They tried to persuade him to abandon the idea of divorce, but finding him adamant, they approached me to explain the situation. I was sad at heart and told them to get together with Sarah's marriage witnesses, Bitwoded Asfaha Wolde Mikael and Bitwoded Zaudé Gebre Heywot to constitute a panel of family arbitrators to consider the problem and settle it in accordance with the requirements of the law. The panel met several times and examined the matter. They could not discover the cause of the quarrel, but because Iskender persisted in obtaining a divorce, they granted it to him on February 19, 1969, by virtue of the authority vested in them by law.

I requested the family arbitrators to see to it that Iskender be required to provide funds to enable Sarah to complete her studies since he was responsible for the interruption of her University education to marry her with undue haste. They believed the demand was reasonable and recommended it to his mother and His Majesty both of whom acceded to it. The arbitrators decided as follows with regard to property: "We recognize that husband and wife have no property in common to be divided between them in accordance with their marriage contract. Nevertheless, considering the dissolution of their marriage and the injury suffered by the respondent (Sarah), we have decided, in conformity with Article 692 of the Civil Code that the petitioner (Iskender) gives her 2,000 sq m of building plot from his property in Addis Ababa and 50,000 Birr for the construction of a house. Moreover, 20,000 Birr is to be paid to the respondent to enable her to complete her interrupted studies." The amount for Sarah to pursue her education was paid to me without delay.

With respect to the child, the arbitrators ruled, "We have decided that the child who was the issue of this marriage be in the care of her mother, Woizero Sarah, and that the petitioner pay 200 Birr a month toward her maintenance. It will be in order, if they both agree, that the child be looked after and brought up by a third person."

As soon as the instrument of divorce was signed on February 19, 1969, Sarah left the baby in the care of her mother and me and proceeded to Britain to resume her studies.

After spending some time looking for entrance somewhere and preparing for her studies, she was admitted to University College, London, in September, 1970 and took a BA degree in Anthropology in June, 1973. She returned home in August and on December 22, 1973, married Dr. Asmarom Legesse, Professor of Anthropology in the US. They departed for the US in September, 1974 and have lived there ever since.

We have considered Naomi as our fifth child since her mother left her in our care when she was six months old. Her father had paid 200 Birr monthly toward her maintenance until February, 1974, and her mother provided adequate funds later.

Naomi was fortunate in obtaining a scholarship in 1974 when she was six years old from the American Community School (later International Community School) in Addis Ababa. She lived with us until 1986 when she completed 12th grade at 18 and graduated with distinction. We sent her to the US in September to join her mother and pursue her college education. We are deeply thankful to the Lord for Naomi Iskender Desta's life and good fortune.

THIRTEEN

Addis Ababa: Minister of Mines 1969 - 1974

As indicated in Part 12 above, I was appointed Minister of Mines on December 8, 1969. I was summoned in the morning to the Palace and Prime Minister Aklilou informed me that by the gracious will and command of His Imperial Majesty I had been appointed Minister of Mines. I saw in a flash that the plot he and his clique had been devising for ten months had come into the open and said, "When will you ever stop persecuting me, Man! And why do you make me curse the day I entered this government?" I then pointed to the Parliament building opposite to His Majesty's office where we were, and added, "Why don't you send me there?" Aklilou murmured, "I have not been commanded to do that." I then requested him to submit to His Majesty that I was unwilling to accept the appointment.

He informed other persons who were in line to learn of their appointments and proceeded to the Emperor's office to report that I had refused to accept the appointment. I was told to wait until the appointees had paid their respects. On that very day, the Ministries of Posts and Communications to which I had devoted my time for almost nine years of my life were joined together and Lij

Endalkachew Makonnen was appointed to the new ministry. A committee had been appointed when I was in the Ministry of Posts to study the restructuring of the government departments and had reported on it. As the Prime Minister had not wished at that time to agree to some of the committee's recommendations, the Ministry of Communications was not joined to the Ministry of Posts to which some other person was assigned when I was appointed to the Ministry of Communications (1966). In 1969, however, the two ministries were merged in the hope of gratifying Endalkachew! In view of the tradition of the land for someone to toil in the field, ploughing, sowing, harvesting and breeding livestock, while someone else enjoyed sumptuous food and tender meat without lifting a finger in producing them, it might be said that this was nothing to wonder at. I contend, nevertheless, that it was one of the main factors which contributed to the overthrow of Ethiopia's age-old polity.

Soon after the appointees had 'kissed hand,' I was summoned to appear before the Emperor who exclaimed in an angry tone, "Amanuel, what has happened to you these days?" I replied, "Your Majesty, nothing has happened to me; I am just tired, wearied; I am tired of being pushed around from one department to another every three years. I am not an engineer and know nothing about mining; why am I ordered to go to that department?" His Majesty remarked, "But it is an important work." I rejoined, "Is an important work given to someone who knows nothing about it? What qualifications do I possess for it?" His Majesty then said, "What does it matter to you if no work is done?" I took that to mean, "You need not do any work, just take Our orders," and interjected, "But Your Majesty, I do have a conscience!" He said nothing more after that, and Aklilou and I stood silently. Aklilou, who had desired to see me exert myself for three or four more years on a task I knew nothing about, had convinced the Emperor in private that mining which they had neglected for a generation, ever since the invader had been driven out of the land, was such an important work that only Amanuel could perform it. He therefore left the argument to the Monarch and just stood there listening! I had expected the Aide-de-camp (ADC) would be summoned any moment to arrest me, but he made no appearance. I bowed and left.

My name was included as Minister of Mines when the appointments were announced that day and I took it as confirming my appointment. The snare that Aklilou and his clique had set for His Majesty to fall out with me had held and the Emperor was offended with me. For my part, I was deeply hurt at the ill-treatment inflicted on me periodically, under the guise of appointment, by listening to the advice of men who hated me, without stopping to consider whether it was given in good faith. The thought revolved in my mind for several days of not doing any work, seeing that the Emperor had told me that it did not matter if no work was done. I shared the thought with my wife who said simply I had better forget it because I could not live without doing any work; I would soon go to the office. Sure enough, I could not sit idle. I took over the Ministry of Mines as soon as I handed over the Ministry of Communications to Lij Endalkachew.

I went to the Palace the following morning, to pay my respects as usual but, contrary to his habit, there was no response from the Emperor. I decided there and then not to go to the Palace anymore and stayed away for three weeks. His Majesty had always liked to see his officials go to the Palace and greet him every day or at least three or four times a week. If someone who was accustomed to do that did not appear before him for any length of time, he would feel ill at ease and inquire his ADC's why he was not to be seen; was he disgruntled or ill? But he was aware of the reason for my absence for so long.

Seeing that the machinations of Aklilou and his relatives had led to my falling out with His Majesty, I visited some of the persons who were in exile with me in Britain and several members of the Imperial Family to acquaint them feelingly that they had caused the Emperor to be offended with me and that I was deeply hurt. I warned them that if I got involved in any accident, it would be the action of Aklilou and his relatives. They appeared to be saddened; one of the Princesses actually wept and said, "Ato Amanuel, have all your services come to this?" From what I heard later, those persons sought favourable opportunities to approach the Emperor and report that I was very distressed because of the intrigue against me and that, when he realized that the advice he had been given was done in bad faith, he had remarked that he had been misled. All the same, he could not bring himself to own it to me. (The king does no wrong)! On the other hand, he desired to dispel the ill feeling and I was summoned to the Palace one morning. As soon as I bowed in greeting, he bade me good morning and called, "Amanuel, come here!" He was smiling and affable as he had been whenever we had met before, and began to discuss and commend the Amharic programmes of Radio Voice of the Gospel (RVOG) to which he was in the habit of listening every evening. We conversed on the subject for several minutes after which I bowed and took my leave. The ill feeling was done away with and concord restored.

Even though I was entirely strange to my new task, I realized that I had to pursue and master it, since it was considered to be so important as to warrant my being commanded to discharge it. And until I was able to perform it with confidence, I gave instructions orally and in writing to the vice minister and the section heads to carry on with their duties as usual and to bring important matters for my decision. I then requested them to bring me the files according to their importance so that I could study them.

The Office of Mines was raised to the status of a ministry in 1958 and it was properly administered as such when the minister was given full authority and directives in 1966 when the so-called new administrative order was granted. Earlier, it was for many years a branch of the Ministry of Finance and was later administered at a disadvantage by being joined to the Department of State Domain. Mines meant in those days the Yubdo platinum mines which had been worked for many years and the Adola gold mines started during the period of the Italian war of aggression. The main function of the office of Mines was to see that the gold and platinum obtained from the two areas were sent to the Central Treasury, and so it was obvious that no serious attention had been given to the development of mining for 30 years. The Directors of Mines who had been assigned to the office periodically had spent their tenures of Office disgruntled for lack of adequate funds and organization to perform their duties. And what appears to be an indication that the Minister of Finance gave no thought to the work was the story, circulated at the time, that whenever he was displeased with an employee of his ministry he used to order his transfer to the Office of Mines! This is proof enough that the lot of that office was similar to that of the former Department of Communications.

As I grew more accustomed to the work and working of the Ministry of Mines, I became convinced that priority had to be given to getting the basic law on mining promulgated. To this end, I found that my predecessor and the vice minister had for the most part prepared a draft law. After spending some time studying the draft and as soon as the English text was ready, I spent several weeks in preparing the Amharic draft with some of the officials. My aim was to get the sense of the English text rendered into Amharic as much as was possible and assimilate into my mind the spirit and objective of the law. In consequence, I found no difficulty in explaining and clarifying the draft law to the Council of Ministers and to Parliament. Detailed mining regulations based on the draft law had also been prepared. (It is fair to state in this connection that Ato Teshome Gebre Mariam, the vice minister, had laboured in compiling both the English drafts in cooperation with foreign experts).

The draft law was considered and accepted by the Council of Ministers and sent to Parliament in 1970 with the Emperor's consent. It was studied by the legal committee of Parliament for several months and presented to the Chamber of Deputies which approved of most of the draft but found itself unable to accept the section dealing with 'quarry substances' (gravel, sand and stone) and therefore did not adopt the law. The draft was accepted by the Senate but could not be passed by a joint session of the two Chambers. A report explaining the situation was thereupon submitted to the Emperor. His Majesty sent a message to Parliament to reconsider the draft law and I attended the sessions when it was debated a second time. A compromise agreement was at last found on 'quarry substances' and Parliament adopted the law by acclamation. It was published in the 'Negarit Gazeta' on March 12, 1971, and the Mining Regulations were issued on June 24 of the same year.

This was how the Government and Parliament arrived at an agreement on 'quarry substances.' Since many of the deputies were landowners and derived benefit from the sale of gravel, sand and stone in the towns as well as the countryside, they were apprehensive lest they should lose the right to sell them for their own use if quarry substances were defined as minerals and argued against acceptance of the proposal. Seeing that quarry substances were needed by the Highway Authority for road construction and by government departments for building schools, hospitals, dams, airfields, and many other constructions, it was not considered possible to buy quarry substances from the landowners for all these purposes. In particular, it was argued that it was unthinkable that loans should be obtained from the World Bank and other international organizations to pay landowners for quarry substances. It was pointed out further that the construction of roads across the property of landowners was bound to enhance its value and give them higher returns; it was reason enough for the government not to pay anything. The debate grew to be more and more heated, however, that it became necessary that a compromise should be offered. Accordingly, I presented the following proposal at a joint session in the Chamber of the Senate:

"We all know that Ethiopia is not poor in stone. If we visit Northern Ethiopia in particular, it is hard to see anything else but stone. It does not seem to be advisable therefore to be at variance among ourselves over something inexhaustible. I propose that it would be wise if agreement were to be reached, on one hand, for the Imperial Government to use quarry substances freely for the construction of roads, government buildings, schools, hospitals, and similar constructions deemed to be necessary for public service and, on the other hand, for landowners to sell quarry substances found on their estates for their own use." The members of Parliament were so elated to hear this that they demonstrated their pleasure with applause. It was said to be the first time that the members applauded, except at the annual opening of Parliament by the Emperor. I immediately went to the Palace to report to His Majesty that Parliament had unanimously adopted the law. The Emperor said, "This is a great thing." The Highway Authority was especially pleased with the agreement because a large number of law suits against it that were then pending before the courts fell through soon after the publication of the law in the 'Negarit Gazeta.'

Under 'definitions' in the law, it was stated, 'Quarry substances shall mean gravel, sand and stone in their natural state and such other substances as the Minister may, by regulations, so declare.' The compromise agreement reached with Parliament on the matter and included in the law reads in part, "Exploitation:

"1. Subject to the rights of third parties, the owner or possessor of any land shall have the right to mine and use quarry substances therefrom without a quarry licence.

"2. No person shall extract minerals other than quarry substances from a quarry.

"3. The right of the Government, any sub-division or agency thereof to extract from the sub-soil of any land quarry substances, without any payment therefrom, for the construction and maintenance of highways, roads, bridges, ports, dams, irrigation canals, airports, schools, hospitals and any other Government work, other than for commercial purposes, shall not be affected by the provisions of this Proclamation, provided however, that:

- "1. The above provisions shall not offset the obligation of the Government, any sub-division or agency thereof, to pay, in accordance with law, compensation to landowners for land, but not quarry substances, permanently expropriated by the Government or to pay compensation for all damages caused by the Government or for both, as the case may be.
- "2. The Government, any sub-division or agency thereof, shall not mine quarry substances from land currently being quarried, primarily and not casually, for commercial purposes unless it pays compensation for interference with such commercial activity."

After being left in a state of neglect for many years, the Ministry of Mines was made to stand on a firm basis and the development of mining was begun in earnest. Taking note of the promulgation of the mining law and regulations a considerable number of foreign organizations and companies came to Ethiopia and were given permits to prospect for and explore various kinds of minerals.

I saw that the time had come to get in touch with the authorities of friendly countries and ask them for financial and technical assistance to accelerate the development of the country's mineral resources and made a tour, with the vice minister, Ato Teshome Gebre Mariam, five months after my transfer to the Ministry of Mines, in Canada, the US, and Europe from May 9 to June 13, 1970. On my return, I presented a report to the Emperor spelling out the purpose of my visit as follows:

"1. Convinced that the mineral potential of Ethiopia could only be ascertained by making a proper study of the country's natural resources, it was necessary to meet with the authorities of several governments and ask them to give us free grants as much as they were able.

2. To invite companies with adequate organizations and capital to be granted permits by the Government to exploit some of the minerals the existence of which had been proved through prospecting and study up to 1970.

3. To encourage the companies that had been given mining leases by the Government and that were exploring for minerals to redouble their efforts using improved equipment. With this purpose in view,

1. The Canadian Government

a). promised to make available no less than one million US Dollars worth of technical assistance to explore the mineral potential of the Omo Valley and the provinces of Illubabor, Kafa, Gamo-Gofa and Sidamo, in part;

b). agreed to grant scholarships to ten young men in 1970 and more from time to time for the better training of our technical personnel in geological science;

c). decided to detail some experts to help develop the Department of Geology and an expert to help organize the Geological Survey.

2. The United Nations

a). I persuaded the United Nations Development Programme (UNDP) that better returns would be obtained if, on completion in June 1971 of the exploration for minerals in Wollega and Sidamo which it had operated in cooperation with the Ministry of Mines, it would continue with its assistance for about three years on the same basis and scale on which it had operated previously and cooperate with us to complete the work. The request was accepted and it was agreed that a team would be sent out to evaluate what had been done and present an estimate of additional expenditure that would be needed.

b). It accepted my request for experts and laboratory equipment to strengthen the Geological Department.

c). In response to my request that instructors and educational material be given us to intensify the training of young geologists that the Ministry of Mines had undertaken in cooperation with the Haile Sellassie I University, it promised to send someone without delay to study the details.

3. The British Government

a). I requested the British government to give us technical assistance to confirm with up-to-date equipment the promising mineral exploration that the Ministry of Mines was conducting in Eritrea, Tigrai and Begemder. It agreed to give us technical aid worth about 800,000 Birr in the course of 1970.

b). Owing to the obsolescence of the equipment for mining gold at Adola (Kibre Mengist), I asked the Government to aid us with equipment and services to the amount of 1.5 million Birr to be charged to the credit that it had promised to advance to Ethiopia. It indicated its favourable response to the request.

4. The French Government

I requested the government's assistance in completing the equipment and set-up of our laboratory with a view to expediting the exploration for minerals. It promised to provide us with equipment worth about 250,000 Birr.

5. The German Government
Seeing that it had been ascertained that the geological formation of the Provinces of Hararghé and Balé gave promise of the presence of minerals, I asked the German government to undertake a full survey and exploration of the area in the form of aid. The authorities, accepting the idea in principle, promised to give us assistance upto the amount of two million Birr. They also agreed to give technical aid in geothermal exploration.

In addition to the effort made to obtain assistance from foreign governments to help us in the task already in progress to determine the country's mineral potential, I invited no less than 20 heads of companies and businesses to bring out their capital and expertise to participate in the development of copper found in the Asmara area, nickel, platinum and gold in Wollega and nickel thought to exist in Sidamo. I explained to them the general situation in Ethiopia as well as the laws and traditions of the country. Many promised to send their agents soon to study the mineral potential at close quarters. To this end, an exploration licence was granted to a German company, Preussag, to explore for minerals in the Red Sea area, in Ethiopian territorial waters and in the depth of the sea beyond.

Apart from inviting new companies to come to our country and cooperate in the development programme for mining, I visited and urged the companies which had been granted mining leases and were participating in development work to expedite their activities. Most of the companies engaged in mineral exploration in Ethiopia in those days were petroleum companies. They were:

1. 'Mobil Oil Company' which, in cooperation with 'Esso,' had discovered natural gas in the Red Sea at a depth of three kilometers but had found the problem of exploitation insuperable and was unable to contain the pressure for lack of equipment. The gas burned for several weeks until the hole caved in. It stopped drilling, claiming that it was necessary to study the evidence that had come to light consequent upon the discovery of gas. I had a long discussion with Mobil's officials requesting them to expedite their study and resume drilling quickly. They promised to acquaint me with the step they would take in the course of that month (June) and informed me soon after that they were unable to resume drilling.

2. 'Gulf Oil,' which had spent 20 million Dollars in seven years in the exploration of petroleum to the South of Mobil (in the Red Sea), announced that it had decided to stop its activities and relinquish its lease, claiming that it had obtained no result.

3. A company called 'Baruch Foster' had been given a licence in 1966 to explore to the south of Gulf but had failed to do satisfactory work up to 1970. Consequently, I had to inform it that we had been compelled to revoke its licence.

4. An Israeli company had presented an application for a licence to explore for petroleum to the south of this company. We negotiated a prospecting permit to be considered by the Council of Ministers.

5. A company called 'Ethiopian Potash' had been given a mining lease to exploit potash. After spending one million Dollars, however, it decided that the potash was not the type it had looked for and informed me that it had decided to stop mining!

6. 'Tenneco,' the American petroleum company, which had been granted a licence in July 1969 to explore for petroleum in Hararghé, Balé and Sidamo had requested that the area which two companies called 'Sinclair and Elwerath' had explored previously be granted to it additionally. Believing it to be useful, I granted it an exploration licence. After exploration and investigation lasting two and a half years, Tenneco carried out a drilling programme in Balé and the Ogaden from February 1972 to February 1974. It discovered gas in abundance and was exerting itself to find oil in similar quantities when it had to stop drilling, collect its equipment and return to America owing to the revolt that was stirred against the Government in February 1974. The search for oil and gas which had been started in all seriousness was thus interrupted indefinitely.

7. A British company called 'British Canadian' which had been given a licence to mine sulphur in Dalol (Afar area) and to prospect for gold in Asossa district assured me that it was coming to Ethiopia that very month (June) to start its activities.

Many of the private capitalists I met in the course of my tour had told me that they were gratified with the stable situation that then prevailed in Ethiopia while they felt apprehensive that the periodic political disturbances in the neighbouring countries might affect its security. The fact that the companies which had been granted leases in the Red Sea area to exploit oil and potash had relinquished their leases and withdrawn had left an impression on me that it was not only because the result of their explorations were not satisfactory but also because the situation in Eritrea had given them cause for apprehension. Nevertheless, the majority of the company officials with whom I had discussions told me that they had obtained better information on Ethiopia due to my visit.

On the recommendation of my friend, Dr. Paul Empie, the Board of Trustees of Muhlenberg College had informed me that it was prepared to confer on me an honorary degree. I therefore took the opportunity of my presence in the US on the business of the Ministry of Mines to travel on May 30 by air from Washington to Allentown, Pennsylvania where the College is situated and Dr. Empie introduced me to the College authorities. Dr. Empie was at that time chairman of the LWF Commission on World Service and, as I was a member of the Commission, we had become friends through working together for some years. He had recommended to the Board of Trustees of Muhlenberg College, his

Alma Mater, to award me an honorary degree. The President of the College had informed me in December 1967 that the Board had voted to confer on me the honorary degree of Doctor of Laws and invited me to be present in Allentown to receive it in the summer of 1968. I was not able for two successive years to attend the Commencement but, finding myself in America in the third year, I was awarded the degree with three other persons on Sunday, May 31, 1970.

In June of the same year, I received an invitation from Concordia College, Louisville, Missouri, to receive an honorary award with five other Church leaders invited from Africa, Europe and Asia, after attending a meeting in the US. As I could not go to America twice in one month, it was arranged that the General Secretary of the Mekane Yesus Church, the Rev. Gudina Tumsa, represent me and receive the award on my behalf. The award was in the form of a medal on the obverse of which a design representing the Lord was depicted and the words 'Christus Vivit' (Christ lives) inscribed. On the reverse was a representation of the College seal. It was to be worn around the neck with a ribbon. I understood that the award was conferred on a lay Church leader whom it was desired to honour.

As soon as the powers and duties of the Ministry of Mines were determined by law and regulations, it was divided into three departments which were; 1). the Administration Department, 2). the Geological Survey and 3). the Mining Controller's Office. The Geological Survey was set up by my predecessor, Major Aseffa Lemma, for the first time in Ethiopia and was fairly well supplied in personnel and equipment. It made quite good progress in four years. He was assisted in this by the UNDP which started in 1967 mining exploration in Western and Southern Ethiopia in cooperation with the government. The Ministry acquired modern geological equipment of great value in the process. Moreover, the UNDP was requested to make available experts who would help develop the Geological Survey and six persons who had wide experience in geological science were sent to reinforce the Department.

Major Aseffa, who had been convinced that it was essential to make the country self-sufficient in this field as fast as possible, initiated a scholarship programme for young persons disposed to study geological science in Addis Ababa University. A good few young men who took advantage of this were awarded Bachelor's degrees in geology and began to participate in mineral exploration.

On my transfer to the Ministry, I found it to be a serious matter to prepare potential leaders for the Geological Survey. I therefore had some graduates from the Addis Ababa University who evinced signs of leadership to proceed to Canada to benefit from the scholarships granted by the Canadian government. The young men acquitted themselves quite well in their studies and returned home within three years having earned their Master's degrees. They further strengthened the Geological Survey.

In addition to the activities mentioned above, on the basis of the exploration and detailed investigation carried out by the UNDP in cooperation with the Ministry, minerals had been found which it was hoped would be of great value. Some of the more important findings were the following:

1. Copper which had been discovered in the Asmara region by the Geological Survey and the exploration and mining rights of which had been granted to the Nippon Mining Company of Japan at the beginning of 1971. The company made a detailed exploration of the area for two years and, after making more than a dozen drill holes in the Adi Nefas and Debaroa areas, found that the copper content of the gravel was far above average. It therefore undertook to build a factory in 1975 near Debaroa, 30 km South West of Asmara, and to start mining and refining the copper for the world market. The project was aborted, however, owing to the revolt against the Government. The mineral is still lying underground!

2. The Geological Survey exerted itself to prepare a geological map of Ethiopia for the first time by sending teams of geologists to Tigrai, Sidamo and Wollega to make detailed investigations. Moreover, the Geological Survey, in conjunction with the UNDP, did commendable work in exploring, investigating and recording hot springs and steam in the desert and low lying areas of the country stretching from Dalol through Tendaho to Langano. This gave an impetus to start in April 1974 detailed investigations to find out whether electric power could be generated by means of the hot springs and steam.

3. As indicated above, I had requested the Canadian government to give us technical assistance in mineral exploration and geological mapping in the then untouched areas of the country, the Omo river valley, Illubabor, Kafa, Gamo-Gofa and a part of Sidamo, by using modern expertise and equipment. The Government had responded favourably and sent out experts and the necessary equipment in September 1973. It was expected that it would complete its task and present a final report in two years.

4. The Government of Japan had been asked to make geological surveys and detailed investigations of gold, copper, nickel and similar minerals in the Asossa and Kurmuk area as well as an estimate of the platinum, nickel and gold occurrences in the Yubdo and Nejo areas. The Overseas Technical Cooperation Agency of Japan made the survey and investigation between April 1973 and May 1974 and presented reports. It had to discontinue its activities, however, because of the revolt against the Government.

5. The Hydrogeology Section was established in the middle of 1970. Its activities had been given considerable emphasis because of the great need for additional water supplies in the country for irrigation and town water supplies. The main aims of the Hydrogeology Division were as follows:

    1. Production of a hydrogeological map of Ethiopia.
    2. Production of a comprehensive report on the hydrogeology of Ethiopia.

3. On the job training of Ethiopian nationals at all levels.
   4. Advising Government and private agencies on siting boreholes and wells and on other hydrological problems.

Additionally, within three years of the publication of the Mining Proclamation and Regulations, the Ministry of Mines issued prospecting, exploration and mining licences and renewed old licences in line with the new Regulations to a large number of Ethiopians and foreign capitalists to exploit mineral substances such as hot springs, mineral springs and salt as well as quarry substances like sand, lime and stone. It was stipulated in the law, with especial reference to gold and salt, that "individuals who have been traditionally engaged in the exploitation or utilization of minerals and obtain their livelihood therefrom" were not to be required to register their mining rights. It was enacted, moreover, that "the right of persons to own or possess precious minerals raw or refined up to fifty (50) troy ounces shall not be prejudiced."

In the Regulations issued on June 24, 1971, under the heading, "Powers delegated to the Controller," it was stated as follows: "The Controller is hereby delegated with all the necessary authority to administer the provisions of the present Regulations unless otherwise prescribed." Accordingly, the Office of the Controller was set up in 1972. The British government detailed an expert for one year as technical assistance. The expert arrived in November of the same year and helped organize the Controller's Office. Ethiopians were assigned to perform the task.

Seeing that the Geological Survey was developing fast, I determined that it should be separated from the Ministry's offices and given its own building. I therefore bought a building plot to the south of Mexico Square and the Ministry of Mines, near the road leading to the Mekanisa quarter. I had a plan prepared for the building of the Geological Survey, but had to leave Government service for good in February 1974 before I saw the completion of the plan. The three departments of the Ministry of Mines exerted themselves to hasten the development of our mineral resources and I regularly reported to the Emperor the results obtained until February 1974.

As the activities of the Ministry of Mines were seen to gather momentum, it was evident that people of goodwill were gratified while those who had left it in oblivion for so many years and persons of ill-will were observed to begrudge the progress of the department which they had held in contempt and to which they had no wish to be appointed because it could bring them no immediate personal benefit in its former state. And the officials who had caused me to be commanded to undertake the task under the pretense of appointment, and who had hoped that I would fail in administering the department and perhaps be discredited, became jealous at the sight of its progress and tried hard to malign and cause me injury through persons who were their willing tools. The vice minister whom I had found in the Ministry on my transfer there became in due course their chief instrument for the purpose. He had appeared to be sincerely cooperative for two and a half years beginning in 1970. After that, a change in his attitude and action was perceived. The reason was that he had become reconciled with the Prime Minister who had been offended with him.

It was an open secret that Prime Minister Aklilou was making every effort to draw to himself a considerable number of University-educated young men, holding out to them prospects of appointment to offices and other privileges. He gave parties, through the intermediary of his brother, for select groups of young men and consulted with them on various matters to obtain their views and try to secure their loyal support. On one occasion, in the course of a heated discussion, my vice minister, who was a law graduate and held the position of attorney general in the Ministry of Justice, apparently made unexpected remarks on a matter under discussion which caused disappointment. Soon after, he was ordered under the guise of appointment to be a High Court judge in Asmara. He was so upset that he made up his mind not to accept the order and went to work privately for eight months.

At this juncture, Major Aseffa Lemma, who had become Minister of Mines in 1966 and was looking for a lawyer, secured His Majesty's consent in July 1967 that he work in the Ministry of Mines as vice minister. It would appear that the Prime Minister was displeased and I had occasion to observe that the vice minister met several times unexpected difficulties surreptitiously aimed at him. He often came to me in distress to tell me of the rights and benefits he claimed he had lost. I placed his requests before the Emperor several times and they were granted. He also pleaded with me to help improve his position and remuneration seeing that his peers and his juniors had outstripped him. I took him to see the Prime Minister in October 1971 and asked him to listen to his grievances and see that his requests were met. The vice minister recounted his bitter grief to him.

Prime Minister Aklilou, who had apparently been fated to try to frustrate my work underhand, found an opening to meddle in the affairs of the Ministry of Mines. His relative, whom I had tried to restrain while I was in the Ministry of Communications from despoiling the public too much and who had nursed feelings of deep hatred for me since, acted as intermediary for the vice minister to get reconciled with Aklilou. He was restored to favour, promoted to be minister of state and his salary was made equal to that of a minister. From then on, the man who had appeared to be modest and energetic began to reveal the other side of his character. He would not often stay in his office; and, when he happened to be in, he would make noises that as minister of state his authority was equal to that of the minister. Accordingly, he went to the extent of corresponding on important matters without consulting me. Whenever I had to go abroad on business, he acted as my replacement legally and took every opportunity to vent his grudge by harassing the department heads for working in conformity with my directives.

Considering all this, I called him to my office and warned him of the consequences; but as he chose to persist in his ways, I gave instructions, with a copy to the Prime Minister, that no official letter he wrote was to be stamped with the seal of the Ministry. Aklilou, who was not disposed to show his opposition to me openly, did not react to the letter. He did make a point of reporting to the Emperor, though, that I was not working in harmony with the minister of state. So, I was summoned to the Palace one day and His Majesty said in the presence of the Prime Minister, "It is reported that there is no agreement between you and your assistant." I responded, "Your Majesty, he and I do not at all understand each other; I cannot work with him because he strives to mislead and deceive me. It would seem to me to be better if either he or I were removed." I added looking at Aklilou, "I have already recommended that several times to my chief." His Majesty turned to him and began by saying, "So it is you…" I bowed and retired as he began to speak.

In reality, the Emperor knew the matter very well. The Minister of State was in close contact with persons who attended on the Emperor, especially with the principal ADC and told him regularly all sorts of stories, relevant or irrelevant (often irrelevant), which the ADC rehearsed to the Monarch every morning as he proceeded to his car to go to his office. As soon as His Majesty arrived at the office, I would be summoned to the Palace and the Emperor would say in a discontented mood, "Say, how is this mining business proceeding? It does not appear to be performed properly." Since I had reported regularly in writing the state of the activities, especially Tenneco's drilling for oil, I had to tell him that there was nothing hidden from him. Toward the end (early 1974), I felt tired of being summoned and cross-questioned at least twice a week and since, apart from the fact that he was eager to hear the news of the discovery of oil, I felt that he was implying that he was not satisfied with my work, and wishing that he should be aware of my own feelings of dissatisfaction, I said one day, "Your Majesty, I had told You at the very beginning when I was ordered to do this work that I was not competent to undertake it. But since it was a command, I have tried to do what was in my power. As my work does not appear to be satisfactory, it would be a good thing if someone else were commanded to perform it." The Emperor retorted, "Did we act wrongly then?" I got the impression that he was telling me indirectly that he had done well to appoint me to do this task. If that were the case, I saw no reason why I should be summoned and questioned in a discontented mood so often. Nonetheless, it was clear that his composure had been disturbed by the whispering campaign which the man who was supposed to be my assistant was conducting through the ADC.

On another occasion, he talked to me with such apparent impatience that I had to remark, "Your Majesty, I simply have not been able to perform in three years this mining work which was neglected for thirty years." The Emperor rejoined, "That of course is the penalty we have to pay." It is true that we are being punished to this day (1993) because our natural resources which lie hidden underground have not been secured and used for our benefit. If, in addition to the assured discovery of abundant gas in the Ogaden and Balé, the Tenneco Oil Company had had the chance to continue its drilling activities after 1974, Ethiopia would perhaps be the owner of oil and natural gas today. Would that it may one day attain that end!

A few days after our conversation on the disagreement between the Minister of State and myself, I heard that His Majesty had summoned him to his presence and severely reprimanded him. But it so happened that the end of his reign was drawing to its close and all the cabinet ministers had to relinquish office in February 1974 while we both were still in the Ministry of Mines.

The six months preceding February 1974 were especially difficult and trying for the Emperor and the Ethiopian government. Owing to the drought in Wollo Province many people had been famished and several hundred thousand persons had perished. Although the famine was caused by drought and not the Government, it was severely blamed for hiding it while so many people died for lack of food. Moreover, units of the armed forces began to mutiny, particularly, in Negelle-Borena and Asmara, complaining that they were suffering from too much hardship and neglect and for other reasons. The economic situation had weighed heavily upon the people, especially on the town dwellers and salaried persons. As a result, industrial workers, teachers and taxi drivers disturbed the Government by going on strike. There was a strong agitation that the Prime Minister and some of the ministers should be dismissed. University and secondary school students roamed about the streets in demonstration, shouting slogans and demanding that the condition of the people be ameliorated and that land be distributed among the tillers. They clashed with the police and many were injured. On one occasion in February 1974, while going home for lunch, the Prime Minister was surrounded by a mob with shouts that upset him. His guard had to fire into the air before the mob dispersed. The Prime Minister was not hurt but he was shaken. The incident brought home to him more than ever the deterioration of the political situation.

Seeking to pacify the troops, the Emperor sent military officers to Negelle and Asmara. The troops put under detention those sent to Negelle and other officers had to be sent to persuade them to release the detainees. The officers sent to Asmara were likewise detained. After a few days, one of the detainees was held as a hostage and the rest were allowed to return to Addis Ababa with the emissaries of the troops who submitted to the Emperor the grievances of the army.

In the meantime, the political situation in Addis Ababa was getting worse; the Prime Minister was increasingly threatened as crowds of people took to the streets calling vociferously for his resignation as well as that of the ministers. Some persons spread rumours that Aklilou would be killed unless he relinquished power forthwith. In this situation, the Prime Minister decided to tender his resignation to the Emperor on February 27, 1974, and called the cabinet ministers by telephone to assemble at Jubilee Palace at 6 p.m. I was then at a meeting of the Mekane Yesus Church Officers and interrupted it to go to the Palace. I inquired on arrival the reason for the meeting and was told that it was because the cabinet was going to offer its resignation to His Majesty! I was puzzled somewhat because I had had no inkling of it in advance; but as I was aware that political tension had been rising for some time, I was not overly surprised. All the same, it was strange to watch the Prime Minister suddenly gather his colleagues before the Sovereign and entreat him to relieve them of their duties.

Even though I had been convinced before it was promulgated that the so-called new administrative order would not last and my conviction had been confirmed by the Prime Minister when he had me commanded, without consulting me in line with the directives he had been given, to move to the Ministries of Health and Mines, it was an action hard to understand that he should disregard with ease the concept of collective responsibility, which had been proclaimed with serious intent and much publicity, and request the Emperor, without seeking and weighing the views of his colleagues, to release them in a state of panic and with undue haste. On hearing his entreaty, the Emperor asked, "What is it that causes you to ask for a release. They are after Us, not you." - Seeking to flatter the Monarch as was his habit, Aklilou said, "Your Majesty, You are the life of Ethiopia, who will hurt you?!" - The Emperor enjoined, "Very well then, go and prepare a communiqué." - Ras Asrate Kassa, who arrived on the scene later, remarked, "There is no precedent in Ethiopian history for the Emperor's servants to resign their offices; the Emperor appoints and dismisses them. It would therefore be appropriate to say that the Sovereign has dismissed them." - His Majesty retorted, "Go along with them and draft what should be announced." Thereupon, a few men got together and prepared the announcement. It was read out and His Majesty ordered that it be announced over the radio. This was done at 8 p.m.! He then commanded that the emissaries of the troops in Asmara be shown in. The ministers bowed and proceeded to their homes. On my way home that evening, I felt as if a heavy burden had fallen from my shoulders at the thought of leaving the Ministry of Mines.

Large crowds were milling around in the squares and the streets that evening, shouting, "Down with Aklilou." One minister who was conspicuous by his absence when the cabinet was dismissed was Lij Endalkachew Makonnen, Minister of Posts and Communications. It was reported that he was then directing the demonstrations from his office with some other individuals who were plotting with him against the Government. He was a member of Aklilou's cabinet but was at the same time working hard for its fall with a few persons who were supposed to be his relatives and friends but whom he deserted later.

On the following day, February 28, the Emperor personally announced on the radio that Lij Endalkachew Makonnen had been appointed Prime Minister! This appointment, rather than improving the country's political situation and solving the problems that were besetting the people with difficulties, made them worse, and six and a half months later, brought in its train the end of the reign of the Emperor Haile Sellassie I.

FOURTEEN

Addis Ababa: In Detention 1974 - 1975

On the dismissal of Prime Minister Aklilou and his cabinet colleagues at his earnest request and the appointment of Lij Endalkachew Makonnen as Prime Minister, the Emperor confirmed his choice of a new cabinet. The former ministers stayed without work. For my part, even though I had no government work, I was quite busy as President of the Mekane Yesus Church. Even then, my former colleagues and I continued to resort to the Palace to pay our respects to the Emperor as usual and His Majesty received us and had discussions with us as if nothing had happened.

Easter was celebrated on April 14 that year (1974) and since it was traditional to go to the Palace and wish the Sovereign a Happy Easter, and as I saw no reason why I should discontinue the practice, I donned my national dress and went to pay my respects with many other people. The ADC gave me room among the dignitaries. I saw not a single other former cabinet minister there. It so happened that it had been decided that the Emperor was to announce on the occasion that Prince Zera Yaqob, son of H.H. Merdazmach Asfa Wossen, was to succeed to the Throne after the Emperor. It appeared to me that the consensus was that, even though rather late, it was good that the announcement was made on that occasion.

I went to tell His Majesty after Easter that being no longer in Government service, I was going to Wollega to visit my parents. The Emperor asked, "How old is your father?" - I said, "He would be about 87 years old; he is rather old!" - His Majesty remarked, "We have also aged!" - On that note I bowed and took my leave. It was the first time I had heard the Emperor speak about getting old! He was 81. Even though I did not know at the time, it was the last audience I was to have with the Emperor. On returning from Wollega, I was taken into custody before I saw him again. The Emperor was deposed a few months later and, after almost a year's detention, it was announced on August 28, 1975, that he passed away on the previous day!?

The new Prime Minister was not pleased to see the former ministers chatting with His Majesty. It was an open secret that a number of the former ministers had felt chagrined at relinquishing their positions and were criticizing Endalkachew and the new cabinet, in consequence. Endalkachew grew apprehensive and, seeing that his administration did not appear to be popular, acted in collusion with the chairman of the first 'Derg' and commander of the airborne troops stationed at Debre Zeit, Lt. Colonel Yalemzewd Tesemma, for the army to take steps against the former ministers. Under the pretext that the armed forces were displeased with the trend of events, he compelled the Emperor to follow his bidding. He caused that demands be presented to His Majesty that the former Prime Minister and Cabinet be placed out of harm's way since they had angered the army and he was unable to discharge his duties while they were about. Aklilou and as many of the former ministers as could be mustered were made to appear before the Emperor on April 26 and told by the Minister of Defence, Gen. Abye Abebe, that they were to be taken into custody by the armed forces. They were then led to the Camp of the Fourth Army.

I heard later that Aklilou protested to the Emperor with deep emotion and said "How could You condemn us to death after we have served You for so long," and that the Monarch did not utter a word! On the same day and on the following day, the ministers who could be found and the senior army officers were arrested in their homes and taken to join them. On April 28, they were transferred to the Officers' Club of the 17th Infantry Regiment in the Gofa Quarter to the south of the City. It was reported that the original plan was that they be kept isolated at the Galila Palace Hotel, near Qoqa Dam, 100 km from Addis Ababa.

I was away in Wollega with my daughter Ruth while this event was taking place in Addis Ababa. I had spent the day on April 27 at the dedication of the Mekane

Yesus Trade School in Nejo and we were listening to the evening news broadcast when we learned that the former Prime Minister and cabinet ministers had been taken into custody by the armed forces and their names were read out. Not hearing my name, Ruth remarked innocently, "Were you not with them?" I said, "Since I am here with you, how could I know why my name was not mentioned," and we left the matter at that. Another former minister whose name was not mentioned was Dejazmach Kassa Wolde Mariam because he was also in Wollega.

On their rounds to pick up the ministers, the troops had been to my house to arrest me, and my wife had informed them that I was away in Wollega to visit my parents and invited them into the house to look if they wished. The officer did not accept the invitation and asked her to tell me to telephone them. He then saluted and left with the soldiers. Qes Gudina Tumsa, General Secretary of the EECMY, sent me a message to say that he thought it was advisable for me to return to Addis Ababa without delay. I had planned to return to the City by car, but instead I took a small aircraft on Tuesday, April 30, and returned to Addis Ababa before noon. On arriving home, my wife informed me that troops had come for me and on hearing that I was not in town, had asked her to tell me to telephone as soon as I returned. I told her that my name had not been mentioned the previous Saturday evening when the names of the former ministers were read over the radio, and she remarked that I had better get in touch with them in any case. I was at a loss whom to contact since I knew no one of the new officers. It then occurred to me to telephone the Minister of Defence, General Abye Abebe, and I rang up his home at 2 p.m. and asked him why the troops were looking for me. He said because it was considered I should join my companions. I told him that I had just returned from Wollega and that his troops would find me at home. He said that General Wolde Sellassie Bereka would ring me up and tell me where to go. That was the end of the telephone conversation. General Wolde Sellassie, who was Chief of the General Staff, telephoned 15 minutes later to ask what time would suit me to proceed to the Gofa Quarter. I told him I had just returned from the country and asked whether the soldiers could be sent at 5 p.m. to give me time for a bath. The General replied it would not be convenient because the compound where the former ministers were held would be closed at 5 p.m. It was agreed that they come to my place at 4 p.m.

A major and a soldier arrived by jeep at the appointed time and I walked to the jeep carrying a small suitcase. The officer said, "No, Sir, please take your own car." As the driver was away, I got into the car of friends who were visiting us. My wife said she wished to go along with me to see where I was staying. We followed the jeep and proceeded to the Officers' Club. My companions could not believe their eyes on seeing me and all fell on my neck and kissed me, including Aklilou. One or two of them remarked that they had not thought I would join them. I said that I had no idea that would happen when I went to see my parents in Wollega and do the work of the Mekane Yesus Church, and I added "What do you mean? Was I to run away from the country? What wrong have I done to do that? Have I not served with you, appointed to offices and awarded honours? How can I now be separated from you?" I then entered the club building and found the bed allotted to me in a rather small room which I had to share with five other men.

The Officers' Club in the Gofa Quarter had a pleasant compound with lovely flowers and shrubbery. On entering the club, one found a nice lounge with armchairs. There were four or five rooms at the back with beds for the former ministers. My bed was in the room to the left as one goes into the lounge. The location of the club was pleasant. The building looked out on the little Aqaqi river and the Furi and Wechecha mountains. It was convenient to sit in the sun outside and read or write.

Our wives and relatives brought us food three times a day. Those in one room shared the meals and there was so much to eat that we had to send back the leftovers. Since relatives and friends visited us on Tuesdays and Saturdays every week and books and newspapers as well as radio sets were sent us from home, we had no feeling of being shut in except that we could not go to town. The number of persons kept in custody in the club house in May 1974 was 25. Of these, 18 were ministers, 5 lieutenant generals and 2 provincial administrators.

My fellow-workers in the Central Office of the Mekane Yesus Church appealed to the Minister of Defence to allow me to continue my task of coordinating the efforts that the Church was making to provide relief to that section of our people suffering from the effects of drought and to deal with correspondence initiated with donor agencies. Permission having been granted, I was taken by a major to my office every week, beginning on June 12, on Mondays, Wednesdays and Fridays, to work until 12 noon and returned to the detention camp. My wife and I could not help noticing that this gave rise to feelings of envy on the part of my companions, and especially their wives. There was no single instance, however, when I went to my house; the officer always conducted me from my office straight to the club house.

It was apparent that our detention was becoming more rigid after the first 'Derg' was superseded by the second 'Derg' which took over control on June 28, 1974. The original plan that we be made harmless and kept under the eyes of the military for a time was done away with and we were regarded as prisoners. Our number increased as other officials were arrested and brought over to join us. An order was given on July 9 that no newspapers were to be delivered to us and that radio sets were to be sent back to our houses. Visitors were allowed to come and see us on Saturday mornings only.

The fact that we were transferred on July 16 from the Gofa Quarter to the Fourth Army Camp was an indication that control was growing tighter. To bring home to us that we were just ordinary prisoners, the following instructions were issued on August 9: 1). All the books in our possession were to be sent home; 2). We were all to be shaved; 3). We were to get out of the room one by one to receive our food; 4). We were to be given an airing for only 30 minutes a day; 5). We could only have a bath once a month; 6). The troops were to determine the number of persons who were allowed to go to the WC at a time. The prisoners sent their books home and had their heads shaved, except Abba Habte Mariam Worqneh who refused to surrender his Bible and to have his hair shaved, claiming that a monk could only be shaved by another monk. I too was exempted, seeing that I had no hair worth shaving. The major who had escorted me to the Central Office of the Mekane Yesus Church failed to turn up on August 21 and I took it that it was no longer desired that I go out. I last visited my office on August 19.

Two months after the appointment of the Endalkachew Cabinet, the former ministers and generals together with some provincial administrators, who had been kept under military detention in contravention of the Constitution and the laws of the land, feeling that they had been forgotten, addressed a letter on June 11 signed by all concerned to the Defence Minister, General Abye Abebe, requesting him for an interview. He replied on June 15 in a letter addressed to Tsehafé-Tizaz Aklilou and said: "It has been determined that a commission be appointed and a law enacted to examine the happenings. The law has now been passed by Parliament and the members of the commission are being selected. The affair will take shape when the commission is appointed and starts work. I should be grateful if Your Excellency would communicate this to all concerned, since I would not be able to give you any more information if I came to see you." We then consulted together and agreed that it was proper to present a petition signed by all of us to the Emperor to place our complaint before him. We therefore wrote on June 23 as follows:

"Your Imperial Majesty, It is now over eight weeks since some of us appeared before Your Majesty on April 26, 1974, when H.E. Lt. General Abye Abebe stated that we were to be given into the custody of the armed forces. We have been detained in the Gofa Quarter ever since. Even though our consciences could not accept this illegal action which deprives us of our human rights in such a deplorable manner after a long period of service, we complied with Your Majesty's wish and were detained by the military.

"In a radio address on May 5, 1974, Your Majesty confirmed to the whole Ethiopian people that the Constitution and all the current laws are still in force. In the knowledge that the detention and imprisonment by the armed forces to which we are subjected are contrary to the statement, we have patiently waited from day to day expecting to be released.

"As no official came to discuss our situation with us during the whole six weeks that we had been separated from our families, we sent a note on June 11 to H.E. Lt. General Abye Abebe requesting an interview with him on the matter. He replied on June 15 that a law had been enacted by Parliament on the matter and that it would take shape when the commission to be appointed on the basis of the law started work. Since the law was promulgated not only for us but for all the employees of the Imperial Government and since nowhere in the law is it stated that the persons involved in this matter would have to be kept in custody at a specified place, we who are in detention reiterate that we are denied our constitutional rights and are enduring acute suffering day and night together with our families who are compelled in addition to provide us with food. We therefore humbly plead with Your Majesty to consider this and give orders that our rights are protected like that of any other Ethiopian and we be released forthwith."

Although no response was received from the Emperor to the petition, an investigating commission was appointed as General Abye had informed us, and on August 27, Dejach Solomon Abraham was taken away first for investigation. Ato Mulatu Debebe was taken away on August 30 and Ato Getahun Tesemma on August 31, as were Dr. Tesfaye Gebregzi, Ato Negusé Habte Wold and Ato Tegegn Yetesha Worq on September 5, and Dr. Seyoum Haregot on September 10. They were not returned to our Room but taken to Detention Room 8.

Lij Endalkachew Makonnen was dismissed in the third week of July 1974 and Lij Michael Imru replaced him as Prime Minister. Endalkachew and a number of his Cabinet ministers were arrested and brought to join us. According to the report we received at the time, Endalkachew pleaded earnestly on his arrest not to be taken where we, his former colleagues, were and was kept elsewhere for about a month. But they brought him to join us in the end. We had of course all been offended with him because of the unjust treatment he had inflicted on us, and some of the men among us could not hide their feelings of hatred. He and I happened to be together in Room 2 when we were removed from the Fourth Army Camp to the Menelik Palace compound, and Lij Endalkachew was among those who took their seats before the hour of the evening prayer. It was my hope that the Gospel message he heard at that time would lead him to true faith and enduring well-being.

Seeing that the number of the prisoners continued to increase after we were transferred to the Fourth Army Camp from the Gofa Quarter, we agreed that order should be given to our prison life in such a crowded room. Steps were therefore taken to constitute an administrative committee. About five persons were elected to sit on the committee and I was made chairman. It was considered important that all the inmates who were in Room 5 at the Fourth Army Camp and in Room 2 in the basement of Menelik Palace, excepting those who were advanced in age, should participate in turn in the administrative work, and elections were made to divide them into sub-committees to serve for a time. There were sub-committees for sanitation and order, for receiving and returning food containers brought from our homes and for other needs. A spokesman was chosen to act as liaison officer to present our requests to the prison administrator and to conduct discussions with members of the 'Derg' when they visited us. Dr. Minasé Haile discharged this task with such scrupulous care and tact that he was commended by both sides.

The committee was careful in nominating persons suitable for each job. We made efforts to examine their temperaments and attitudes before nominating them for assignments, to make sure on which sub-committee they would best serve. Whatever needed doing in the room was thus divided among them and I am gratified to recall to this day that they did everything willingly and in a spirit of mutual understanding and respect. It is my belief that the daily Gospel readings and prayers helped the process in an intangible manner. My other function while at the Fourth Army Camp was to give lessons in the Oromo language to about a dozen of my fellow-prisoners for an hour every morning. The lessons were discontinued when the commission started investigation and we were transferred to the palace compound because many of them were moved to another place.

We were informed on September 3 that, starting from the following day, no food would be brought us from home and that we would be issued prison rations. We decided to lodge a complaint with the 'Derg.' We received breakfast from home the next morning and prison food was sent us at 11 a.m. which we were made to receive standing in a queue. We were told that each person would be given three loaves of bread, 'kik wott' and a mug of tea. As it was almost impossible to chew the 'bread,' it was clear to us that none of us would have survived had the 'Derg' persisted in its decision. All the chairs and tables in the detention rooms were removed on September 5. Persons sent by the 'Derg' told us on September 6 that it had been decided to allow food to be received from home once a day. My wife brought me food on September 8; the others also received theirs. As it was claimed that the instructions were not clear, no food was received the following day. The delivery of food from home was resumed at 12 noon on September 10 and leftovers were used for supper and for breakfast the following day.

It was proclaimed on September 12 that His Majesty the Emperor Haile Sellassie I had been deposed, that Crown Prince Merdazmach Asfa Wossen was to succeed to the Throne as King, that the Constitution had been abrogated, that the Parliament had been abolished and that the former high officials were to be arraigned before a special military court for enriching themselves illegally, for miscarriage of justice and for abuse of power. A loud-speaker was installed outside our detention rooms for us to listen directly to the proclamation. In the course of the morning, the Emperor was brought to the Fourth Army Camp in a Volkswagen car surrounded by troops and a mob shouting and abusing him. Rear Admiral Iskender Desta was arrested on the same day and brought to join the prisoners in Room 5.

Ato Akale Worq Habte Wold was taken to the investigating commission on September 16. Ato Ketema Yifru was taken away on the following day and on September 18, Ato Minasé Lemma was taken to the Military Police Camp for questioning; they were brought back on October 2. On September 19, Ato Ketema Abebe, General Debebe Haile Mariam, Dejach Kifle Ergetou and General Kebede Gebre were taken away for investigation. Tsehafé-Tizaz Aklilou was taken to the investigation commission on September 20 and did not come back. On September 23, nine generals were brought to our Room from Room 6. Thus, even though some prisoners had been taken away for investigation and transferred to another room, the number of the inmates in Room 5 increased to 49 on October 2; and as 11 persons were brought from Room 6 on October 8, there were 60 of us and we were cramped for space. Among those who were added to us were Ras Asrate Kassa and Abba Habte Mariam, but they were taken back to Room 6 the next day. Dejach Kifle Dadi was taken to the commission on October 9 and was not returned to us. On October 10, a team of army television operators arrived with some officers and took films while our families handed us food containers and while we had lunch. The officers spoke to some of us and listened to complaints.

The inmates of Room 5 unanimously agreed that a chapter be read from the Gospel and a short prayer offered every evening at 7:30 p.m. and asked me to read from the Scriptures and lead in prayer. The process was started on Sunday, September 22. I perceived that it would be beneficial if they followed the Gospel reading beginning with the Gospel according to Luke, to be followed by the Acts of the Apostles. It was agreed. The reason for the suggestion was, except for a few persons (one Roman Catholic, two Muslims, and myself), all the inmates were connected with the Orthodox Church and the majority were not accustomed to reading the Bible. I therefore felt it to be necessary that they should get acquainted with the basis of their religion.

Earlier on, some of my fellow inmates had requested me to lead them in reading the Bible and in prayer. I had replied that, since the room was full of persons who differed in outlook, some who professed to be unbelievers, others who had unsettled minds yearning for an early release, and still others who had formed themselves into groups and, to while away the time, played cards and other games in the course of which noisy arguments were heard, it would be difficult to meet and read God's Word and pray quietly in such an atmosphere. Moreover, I told them that I was apprehensive that disputes might arise with those who did not care to hear the Word and that it was not my wish that the Word of God should be made an occasion for differences but for harmony. I therefore advised them to exercise patience until such time as all the inmates had found a settled mind and a quiet spirit. The men who had a desire that prayers be conducted had private discussions with those who it was thought might oppose it and, realizing that the prospect for an early release was growing dim, they agreed that it was time for them to collect their minds and turn to the Lord. Thereupon, they asked me to read the Scriptures and offer prayers. I thanked the Lord that the hour I had been waiting for had come. I read one or two chapters daily, explained the text as much as I was able and concluded with a prayer.

The men grew so interested in the exercise that the majority of them asked their wives or relatives to bring them Bibles and Bible Dictionaries both in Amharic and English which they read and studied with diligence. After prayers, they used to exchange views in groups of three or four on the text of the day. They also came to me for a discussion in the form of argument and to seek clarification. I was gratified to watch this development. I thus continued to read the Scriptures to them every evening, to explain the passages and to conclude with a prayer until the day I was released, January 27, 1975.

Seeing that most of the inmates were members of the Orthodox Church and that the Orthodox priest, Nebure-Id Ermias, was among us, I felt he should participate in the act of prayer. With the consent of the men, he led in prayer at times. It was later decided, at the wish of the majority, that Nebure-Id Ermias should conduct prayers in accordance with the rites of the Orthodox Church for about 15 minutes every Sunday morning. He started the service at 8 a.m. on Sunday, October 13.

On October 11, Captain Demissé Shiferrau, a leading member of the 'Derg' from the Imperial Guard, was arrested and brought to join us. On October 12, three members of the investigating commission came and distributed to us bound forms to be completed, listing the assets and property of each inmate. They put us under oath and made us sign for the accuracy of what we were to fill in the forms. It was made clear to them that it was impossible to write down from memory, shut up in prison, things acquired for over thirty years, and they promised to place the matter before the commission. On October 14, after the evening Bible reading, some people expressed their desire that prayers should be said every morning and, after an exchange of views, the consensus was that Nebure-Id Ermias conduct the prayers in line with Orthodox rites beginning October 15.

We were ordered to get ready to be transferred elsewhere at 2 a.m. on October 23, with the exception of two persons, and we sat all night putting our things together. We were taken to Menelik Palace at 7:30 a.m. and were made to live in the basement under the Throne Room. It was divided in two with boarding. Most of us who were in Room 5 at the Fourth Army Camp were lodged in Room 2. On entering the room, we had the feeling that it was chilly and that the windows were rather narrow. The walls and the ceiling were whitewashed and looked cleaner than the old Room 5. Our feeling of chill disappeared after a few days due to the crowded condition of the room and the heat of the uninterrupted electric light. On November 15, Ato Belete Gebre Tsadiq and Ato Getachew Beqele who were members of the second and third cabinets (appointed after us) were brought to join us. Ato Teshome Gebre Mariam was arrested on November 22 and taken to Room 1.

Around 7:30 p.m. on Saturday, November 23, 27 men were removed from Room 2. Likewise, we observed that men were taken away from Room 1. As it had been reported that a military court was being appointed, we surmised that the men were taken elsewhere pending their appearance before the court. But we were in doubt because they did not take their belongings with them and one or two were in pyjamas. Their personal effects were collected and tied together on November 24 and, though no one told us what had happened to them, we concluded that they had been killed. We were informed through our liaison man, Dr. Minasé Haile, before lunch on November 25 that our companions had been massacred. We were also told that newspapers containing the details would be given us the following day. We read in the newspaper on November 26 that 60 men, including those taken from our Room, had been put to death by political decision of the 'Derg.' It was stated that the Chairman of the 'Derg,' General Aman Mikael Andom, had also been killed. Members of the 'Derg' came at 11 a.m. to preach to us through Major Getachew Shibeshi about the men who had been killed by political decision and to inform us that they had been sent to reassure us that thenceforward none of us would be executed by political decision before his case had been examined by a military court and it was decided that he was guilty. They asked us to inform our families of this to save them from anxiety. The Major swore twice in the name of God to confirm his statement! On November 30, other members of the 'Derg' came on two occasions to reconfirm to Dr. Minasé Haile that no prisoner would henceforth be executed by political decision and that we would begin to appear before a military court in a week or two.

On December 4, two members of the 'Derg' came to inform us that a special military court had been established and that we would be provided with charges preferred against us. They alerted us to look for defence counsel so that the matter would not be protracted. We pointed out to them that it would not be possible for us to appoint suitable counsel before receiving the charges. They made notes and affirmed that we would receive them as soon as possible. On December 12 before noon, representatives of the International Committee of the Red Cross from Geneva visited the prison. They inspected the sleeping quarters and the condition in which we lived. They put some questions to the persons we had selected to speak on our behalf, took notes and left. On December 19, a number of officers who had arrived from Negelle-Borena came to the prison before noon and inspected our sleeping quarters.

We were pleased to learn on December 20 that we could send for our Bibles and books of prayer. We were also informed that permission had been given for us to read the newspapers. We realized that this was the result of the visit of the representatives of the Red Cross. Our evening prayers had not been interrupted in spite of the withdrawal of our Bibles on August 9. Some of the men had borrowed and read clandestinely Abba Habte Mariam's Bible while we were at the Fourth Army Camp. But what proved to be of valuable assistance to us in our evening readings was a Gideon New Testament which belonged to General Haile Baikedagn. As it happened, he was ill in hospital at the time and had his New Testament with him; and when he rejoined us I read from it and prayed. On our transfer to the Palace, Abba Habte Mariam was brought to Room 2 and some persons used his Bible. He gave lessons in 'Zéma' to a few men who desired it and at times led in prayer. Our families were allowed to visit us on Ethiopian Christmas Day, January 7, 1975, and I was happy to see my wife and children as well as my cousin, Ayantu. Though they could not come near to us, we conversed raising our voices.

At 4 p.m. on January 27, while we were outside sunning ourselves, several persons sent by the 'Derg' came to tell six men including myself that we were required to go to the office of the administrator. Observing that some of the inmates were startled, they spoke that no harm was meant. We found some other prisoners in the administrator's office one of whom was a woman, Woizero Lullit Belai. The administrator informed us that the 'Derg' had decided to release us and proffered his congratulations. After a wait of one hour, we were received by the two vice chairmen of the 'Derg' and about half a dozen of their comrades in the council room where the former cabinet had met when the Emperor was in the chair. They rose and approached us to shake hands as we entered the room. We sat around the old table and the first vice chairman, Major Mengistu Haile Mariam, rose and spoke as follows: "My Fathers, we have kept you under detention until now because we were new and your former activities had to be investigated and checked. From today, you may live in freedom as any other Ethiopian." Thereupon, my companions beckoned me to speak. But as I did not wish to speak on that occasion, Nebure-Id Dimetros, Bitwoded Asfaha Wolde Mikael and Ato Salah Hinit expressed pleasure for our release and thanked the 'Derg.' Ato Salah also pleaded with them to release our other fellow-prisoners as well on the conclusion of the investigations. In the end, the vice chairmen and their comrades went to the door and shook hands with each one of us before we left. Nine persons were released on that occasion.

On leaving the room, we asked to be allowed to take leave of our companions and collect our belongings. Some of the soldiers replied that it was getting late and we should go straight home; we could remove our things the next day. We implored them to let us say good-bye to our companions and they yielded. When we told the inmates the good news of our release, we could not help noticing that, while glad of our release, they were crestfallen at their being left behind. We kissed them all good-bye and they carried our luggage as far as the wire fencing. As soon as I got out of the Palace gate leading to Menelik II Boulevard, I met Major Getahun Wolde Giorgis, (a kinsman), who took me to my new house constructed during my detention. My wife and children, together with many friends and residents of the neighbourhood who had heard of my release, welcomed me home with rejoicing. In the course of the following days, many people came to see me and offer their congratulations. What can I offer but praise to the Lord my God, whom I worship with all my heart, for delivering me, according to His inscrutable purpose, from this grave danger and trial!!

In this connection, I would be remiss if I did not acquaint the readers of these reminiscences the great debt of gratitude I owe to my wife and life partner, Elleni Alemayehu, for the service she rendered to me with deep love and patience during the nine months I was kept in custody with my colleagues, the Imperial Ministers. On my detention in April 1974, she gave me inestimable care in bringing me provisions thrice a day for the first four months and later once a day, as well as clean clothes and other requisites two or three times a week. As an accomplished housewife, she prepared the food with more than usual care and brought me more than enough. I often shared it with my companions and had to send back what remained.

While thus preoccupied with my well-being and comfort, she greatly suffered with grief and anxiety, and cried to the Creator day and night. Even though she was convinced that I had done no wrong against our country and people, and never doubted that I would be freed in due course, I heard later that she had fallen ill and admitted to hospital for a few days from her compassionate nature and stress of spirit. She was overwhelmed with joy on the day I was released and returned home in answer to her intercession and sorrow.

I have no words with which to thank my God for giving me Elleni Alemayehu for a life partner and helper. On the analogy of the remarks made by the Emperor Theodore concerning his first wife, Woizero Elleni has cared for me as wife, mother and helper from the day we were united in holy matrimony. For this I offer her heartfelt thanks.

As pointed out in another Part above, on my return home in 1943 from abroad, I had tried to get married to two young women successively and failed. I had then prayed to the Lord to give me a young woman for wife who would be like a relative to me. I had also indicated my yearning to a few friends. The friend who led me to Elleni had told me that she was an orphan who was brought up in hard circumstances and would be like a relative to me. (It came to light later that her mother was living but, as they could not meet for many years due to difficulties of communication, she had been reared by a relation from childhood). Believing that she was appointed by divine grace to be my life partner, I asked her to marry me and she accepted my proposal without hesitation. Our God confirmed that our union had His blessing through the love that has endured between us throughout our married life and the children He has given us. We have lived together now (1993) for over 46 years through thick and thin. I trust His grace will continue to attend us all through the remainder of our earthly lives together.

I would also wish to place on record the great gratitude I owe to the many fellow-Christians all over the world who stood by the EECMY in the unity of the Faith and in constant intercession before the Throne of Grace for my safety and deliverance. I am very appreciative of the concern shown by Dr. Carl Mau, General Secretary of the LWF, and his colleagues in Geneva, who exhorted the member Churches of the Federation to join in intercession. Dr. Mau travelled to Addis Ababa to show his solidarity with my family and the Church in the face of this danger. He visited my wife to assure her of his sympathy and prayers.

I was deeply thankful on being unconditionally released for the sake of the reputation of the Mekane Yesus Church. Had I been killed as a wrongdoer in that situation, a dark spot would have been left on the witness of the Church to the Gospel of Christ, and I would have been held up as one who did great disservice to my people whom I had served faithfully for 42 years and to my Church which I had led during the greater part (22 years) of her young life as a national Church.

Boji Karkaro Hill, Wollega; photo taken in January 1999.

The author's Father, Ato Abraham Tato Gurmu and Mother, Woizero Qanatu Malimo Gama, Addis Ababa, January 1970.

Woizero Gumesh Wolde Mikael, wife of Pastor Gebre Statios, the first Evangelist to Wollega, Addis Ababa, in the 1930's.

Ato Terfa Danki (right) with the author's Father, Boji, in the 1930's.

Dr. Worqneh C. Martin in his studio, London, in the 1930's.

The author with his Father before departing for London, Addis Ababa, 1935.

Tafari Makonnen School, Addis Ababa, in the 1950's.

The Emperor Haile Sellassie in exile, England, 1936-1940.

The author at 25 in London, March 1938.

The author with Ato Emmanuel Gabre Sellassie soon after returning from England, July 1943.

Pastor Badima Yalew, undated; the first Pastor of the Addis Ababa Evangelical Church Mekane Yesus (1941-1966).

The author with Pastor Badima Yalew, undated.

The Emperor Haile Sellassie as Minister of Education at the time, laying the foundation stone for a school in Gulele, 1945.

The author with the Senior Officers, Office of the Imperial Board of Telecommunications, Addis Ababa, in the 1960's.

The author and Woizero Elleni Alemayehu on their wedding day, Mekane Yesus Church, Addis Ababa, January 12, 1947.

The author's wife, Woizero Elleni and children; from left Sarah, Dawit, Ruth and Amenti, Addis Ababa, May 1952.

The author presenting Credentials to the first President of the Republic of India, Dr. Rajendra Prasad, New Delhi, February 1949.

The author presenting Credentials to the Governor General of India, Mr. Chakravarti Rajagopalachari, New Delhi, May 1949.

The author meeting the President of the Republic of Italy, Signor Einaudi, Rome, June 1952.

The author's wife, Woizero Elleni, Rome, June 1953.

The author greeting Mr. Jawaharlal Nehru, the first prime minister of India and his daughter Mrs. Indira Gandhi, at Villa Madama, Rome, July 1955.

The author with his wife, Woizero Elleni, London, 1957.

The author's children in London in the 1950's; from left, Sarah, Amenti, Ruth and Dawit.

Ethiopian students in England and Europe at a Christmas Party given at the Ethiopian Embassy, London, 1956.

The author and his wife, Woizero Elleni greeting guests on National Day at the Ethiopian Embassy, London, May 5, 1957.

The author's daughter Sarah and Commodore Iskender Desta on their wedding day, Addis Ababa, October 28, 1967.

The author's daughter Ruth with her husband Ato Assefa Beru, Addis Ababa, 1977.

The author's grandchildren from left, Thomas Assefa, Naomi Desta and Daniel Assefa, Addis Ababa, in the 1980's.

The author's grandson Thomas Assefa and his wife Katherine Vazquez on their wedding day, New York, August 23, 2005.

The author's wife, Woizero Elleni, Addis Ababa, June 27, 1983.

On the Occasion of the awarding of Honorary Doctorates by the Mekane Yesus Theological Seminary, to the author (center) for Leadership Development.
From left, Dr. Debella Birri, Chairperson, EECMY Seminary Board (Honorary Recipients for Language Development, Dr. Neils Reimer, Rev. Tesgara Hirpo and Rev. Loren Bliese); Dr. Belay Guta, Principal of the Mekane Yesus Seminary, Addis Ababa, January 18, 2009.

The author with his daughter Woizero Ruth, on the occasion of the Symposium on Ethio-India 60 years of Friendship, Addis Ababa, November 25, 2008. He is shown receiving a gift from H.E. Mr. Gurjit Singh, Ambassador of India to Ethiopia, in recognition of being the first Ambassador of Ethiopia to India.

The author with Rev. Bruno Muetzelfeldt, Director, LWF Department for World Service (to the author's right, back-row) and members of the LWF Commission on World Service, Geneva, 1971.

The author with Dr. Emmanuel Gabre Sellassie, the first President of EECMY (1959-1963), at the Mekane Yesus General Assembly, January 1997.

The Addis Ababa Mekane Yesus Church, in the 1960's.

The author with Dr. Emmanuel Gabre Sellassie (center) and Qes Yadessa Daba (right), Ex-Presidents of the EECMY, at the Meeting of the Committee of Mutual Christian Responsibility, Addis Ababa, 1993.

The author at 91 leading the Centennial Celebration of the Addis Ababa Mekane Yesus Congregation, March 2004.

The author with EECMY President Rev. Dr. Wakseyoum Idosa at the Addis Ababa Mekane Yesus Church, April 2009.

In the Service of the Church

The author laying the foundation stone of the Addis
Ababa Mekane Yesus Church (Mother Church), early
1949.

FIFTEEN

In the Service of the Church

1. INTRODUCTION

I have recounted in an earlier Part of these *Reminiscences* the efforts made by my father for me to be brought up in the Christian Faith and doctrine from my childhood. But contrary to his desire and through the Lord's inscrutable counsel I was not to go to a Mission school but to have the privilege of being admitted to the Tafari Makonnen School which was in those days (1925) the newest and most modern school in Ethiopia. The Bible stories that I had learned at home had been so deeply stamped on my mind and spirit that, through the grace of God and the guidance of His Holy Spirit, I grew in the faith and knowledge of the Lord Jesus Christ during the years (1925-1935) I was at the Tafari Makonnen School as a student and at the Asbe Tafari School as a teacher. When I went to live in England in a way which was not of my planning (1935-1943), I have indicated how I was confirmed and grew in the Faith, and how through fellowship with some Christian friends, I was rescued from loneliness and spiritual atrophy (Parts 1,5).

I have also narrated how, on my return home to Ethiopia from Britain in July 1943, I became a member of the Addis Ababa Mekane Yesus Congregation and how I had participated in its administration from 1943 to 1949 and how I had retained membership when I had to leave my country and people again and live abroad for ten years beginning in 1949 and how, when the Church began to have relations with the Lutheran World Federation (LWF), I had on several occasions attended the All-Africa Lutheran Conference as her delegate (Parts 9, 10).

2. MEMBERSHIP OF THE MEKANE YESUS CHURCH AND MY SERVICE IN THE LUTHERAN WORLD FEDERATION

In view of the fact that the Ethiopian Evangelical Church Mekane Yesus (EEMCY) was not instituted as a national Church during that period (1955-1959), the Addis Ababa Mekane Yesus Congregation had been elected to be a member of the LWF at its 3rd Assembly which was held in Minneapolis, USA, in 1957 and it was decided that I should attend the Assembly as a delegate of the Congregation. But even though my official duties in London were advanced to prevent me from going to the Assembly, the Minneapolis Assembly elected me to be a member of the Federation's Executive Committee until 1963. Thereafter, I was elected to be a member of the LWF World Service Commission at the 4th (1963) and the 5th (1970) Assemblies of the Federation and served on the Commission for 14 years.

At the 5th Assembly which was held at Evian, France some of the leaders who wished that I become President of the Federation sent Dr. Hans Lilje, Bishop of Hanover and former President of the Federation, to urge me to stand for election. But I thanked them and declined the suggestion because as a government official I could not stand for election without the knowledge and sanction of the Emperor. I told His Majesty of this on my return to Addis Ababa and he said I should have accepted it; I said it was because I could not know what his pleasure was.

I was again elected to be a member of the Executive Committee at the 6th Assembly of the Federation which took place in Dar-es-Salaam, Tanzania in 1977 and served on it until the 7th Assembly (1984) which was held in Budapest. I therefore served for 27 successive years (1957-1984) in the Federation on behalf of the Mekane Yesus Church.

Since the Emperor held the view that my presence at the assemblies of the LWF was in the general interest of Ethiopia, he showed his goodwill from the time in

November 1955 when he allowed me to go to Marangu in Tanzania and attend the first All-Africa Lutheran Conference until 1974 when his reign came to an end, on the first two occasions by authorizing that my airfare and travel expenses be paid from public funds, and later on by sanctioning my presence at the meetings of the Federation. A proof of his conviction that it was in Ethiopia's interest is contained in a letter he addressed to me when the authorities of the Federation requested his permission for me to go to the Minneapolis Assembly. He wrote on March 5, 1957, "We consider your presence at the Assembly to be beneficial in making our country known; judging from what you had done previously it should be helpful." It appeared, however, that, taking advantage of my absence from Addis Ababa, persons around the Emperor had advanced opposing views and the Private Secretary had to inform me to give up attending the Assembly. Nevertheless, at no time after that was I prevented from participating in the Federation's meetings.

The fact that the Mekane Yesus Church became a member of the LWF at the Minneapolis Assembly and that, beginning in 1958, the presence of her delegates at the various meetings helped to obtain assistance by presenting the situation and the needs of the Church and the country was a matter of no mean importance. It is evident that one of the reasons for the establishment of the RVOG in Addis Ababa was due to the fact that the Mekane Yesus Church was a member of the LWF. For this our Church is no less grateful to the Emperor for his far-sighted and broad views than to the LWF.

While the Emperor was thus looking with goodwill at the Mekane Yesus Church and her work, it has to be recorded that the leaders of the Ethiopian Orthodox Church and some high officials of the government were ceaselessly trying to hinder her work. Not only when I was in the Ministry of Education, but also after 1959, the highest authority in the Church's hierarchy kept accusing me before the Emperor from time to time. I praise the Lord that this in no way brought harm to our Church.

As concerned the government officials, I would cite as an example the attitude of Prime Minister Aklilou. We were talking one day after I had returned from one of the meetings of the LWF when he said I would not have gone if he had known about it. Even though he would have been unable to prevent it since it was His Majesty's wish, his remark showed his thinking and the fact that he gave no value to the benefit the country derived from it. It was clear to me that his main concern was to oppose what I was doing. As I was convinced of this, our years of service came to an end and we parted for good before I ever told him of my travels abroad to attend the Federation's meetings with His Majesty's consent.

3. ESTABLISHMENT OF THE MEKANE YESUS CHURCH

After meetings and consultations over the years, the delegates of the Evangelical (Lutheran) congregations in several parts of the country met on April 23 and 25, 1958, under the leadership of the Addis Ababa Evangelical Congregation and with the encouragement of the Lutheran Missionary Societies and the LWF to deliberate on a draft constitution and establish the EECMY. The constitution was adopted on April 25 but since the delegates of the Wollega congregations requested to be given time to secure the authorization of their congregations their request was granted and it was decided to convene the First General Assembly on January 21, 1959, formally to constitute the Church on the national level.

Qes Badima Yalew was elected interim president, and Ato Hagos Legesse and Mr. Haktor Thorsen, Norwegian Lutheran Mission (NLM) were to be Executive Secretary and Treasurer respectively. I was in London at the time and rejoiced to learn that the EECMY had achieved the status of a national Church.

The First General Assembly of the Church met in Addis Ababa on January 21, 1959, and elected for a term of four years Ato Emmanuel Gabre Sellassie, President, Dr. Herbert G. Schaefer, American Lutheran Mission (ALM) Vice President, Pastor Manfred Lundgren (SEM) Treasurer, and Ato Hagos Legesse, Executive Secretary.

The EECMY replaced soon after the Addis Ababa Mekane Yesus Congregation as a member of the LWF. As related elsewhere, on my return home in June 1959 at the end of my diplomatic mission, I was appointed to serve in 'His Majesty's Private Cabinet' and resumed my membership of the Addis Ababa Mekane Yesus Congregation.

4. ACHIEVEMENTS IN THE FIRST FOUR YEARS

It should be recorded here that three main objectives were achieved during the first four years after the EECMY was constituted as a national Church and elected her Church Officers in January 1959.

1. A Theological institution called the 'Mekane Yesus Seminary' was opened in Addis Ababa in September 1960 in cooperation with the American Lutheran Mission, the Swedish Evangelical Mission, and the German Hermannsburg Mission (GHM). The Seminary's aim is to assist in the extension of the Kingdom

of God in Ethiopia by training and offering to the Church, pastors and Church leaders. It admits young people, gives them tuition in theology and other subjects for four years and graduates them on the bachelor and diploma levels. The Seminary was built on a large site purchased in the name of the Church by the ALM in the Mekanisa area. The school building, the teachers' houses, the student residences and the library were constructed with funds provided by the LWF. The Rev. Gustav Arén was the first Principal of the Seminary who launched it on a sound basis. The educational work is thus proceeding in a quiet and comfortable atmosphere.

2. A programme to extend literacy in Ethiopia was started with funds obtained through the LWF. A request was made to the Government in October 1961 and the Ministry of the Interior was informed through the Ministry of Education that permission had been granted for the Church to open literacy schools in a number of districts. The 13 Provinces (Balé was then a part of Harar Province) were notified accordingly and the programme was launched. It was instrumental in freeing millions of Ethiopians from illiteracy.

3. The Church submitted her constitution and by-laws to the Ministry of the Interior with a request that all the congregations under her authority be allowed to purchase land through designated persons and get it registered in her name according to law. It was also requested that various acts of oppression endured by the believers in the Provinces be made to cease.

The Minister of the Interior, General Abye Abebe, wrote to the 13 Provincial Administrations on December 28, 1962, as follows:

"1. There is no reason why persons should be prevented from buying land in the name of the Church provided it is ascertained that they are Ethiopian nationals.

"2. If it is proven that the members and workers of the church have been unjustly treated, proper steps are to be taken and the situation reported to me. The governors are to be warned that no oppressive measures are to be taken against them in future."

It should also be recalled that, before the establishment of the Church on the national level, the Lutheran Missions had in 1957 built the 'Ethiopian Evangelical College' at Debre Zeit (Bishoftu) on land granted them by the Emperor. The objective of the college was to give to the youth of the Mekane Yesus Church secondary school education and teacher training courses on the college level on the basis of Christian principles. The educational programme was based on the curriculum adopted by the Ministry of Education for secondary school education and included tuition in the Bible. The teacher training course given to the students on the college level was for two years. Being directly concerned with the work of the college, the Mekane Yesus Church later became a member of the

College Board. The college was confiscated by the Revolutionary Government in 1977 and had to stop its activities.[1]

It was thus that the EECMY became a legally registered Church. Her entity and work were recognized and she became well-known all over the country.

5. ESTABLISHMENT OF RADIO VOICE OF THE GOSPEL

Before my return home from Britain in 1959, the LWF had planned to set up in one of the countries of the African Continent a radio station capable of transmitting the message of the Gospel to the whole of Africa, the Middle East and South Asia, and had undertaken a study as to which country would be most suitable. After having ensured that, in addition to being an ancient Christian country, Ethiopia was more suited for this purpose than any other African country, the Federation decided to request the Imperial Government to grant it the special right (franchise) to build a radio station in Addis Ababa. Another foreign Christian Organization had earlier presented a petition to the Government to allow it to build a radio station in Addis Ababa but had been turned down. The Organization had then approached the Liberian government and obtained permission which had left a sense of regret on our Government.

Dr. Sigurd Aske, a Norwegian who had been charged to pursue the matter of establishing a radio station for the LWF, was sent to London by the Executive Committee of the Federation in May 1958 to get the benefit of my views and we had a long discussion. I told him that as the Ethiopian government had already missed one chance, it was my considered view it would not neglect a second chance if a request was presented to it. I then advised that the petition be directly presented to the Emperor. Since another Christian organization had also requested at that time permission to build a radio station in Ethiopia, the LWF sent its petition to Addis Ababa with dispatch. The leaders of the Mekane Yesus Church did all they could to ensure the success of the request.

After a delay of 12 months, priority was given to the Federation's petition and a serious discussion took place at a meeting in November 1959 chaired by the Emperor and attended by the leaders of the Church and Cabinet Ministers as to whether to grant or withhold the special right. The Orthodox Church leaders, including the Patriarch, were opposed to the establishment of the radio station in Ethiopia. The Emperor reprimanded them for their short-sighted attitude and decided that the radio station be built in Addis Ababa. This greatly pleased

---

1 The Ethiopian Evangelical College Debre Zeit was returned to the EECMY on April 17, 2010 by decision of the Federal Democratic Republic of Ethiopia.

the LWF and the Ethiopian Evangelical Christians. The Federation presented a draft agreement and after a negotiation which lasted for one year, an agreement was reached. I had returned to Ethiopia by then and was working as Chief of Political Affairs in 'His Majesty's Private Cabinet.' The English draft agreement was passed on to me. I translated it into Amharic and it was submitted to the Emperor. His Majesty considered it and it was given to the Minister of Posts, Telegraphs and Telephones who, as Chairman of the Imperial Board of Telecommunications (IBTE), was instructed to study the draft with the Board and sign it.

A Cabinet reshuffle took place in the meantime and I was appointed Minister of Posts, Telegraphs and Telecommunications and Chairman of the IBTE on February 14, 1961. The agreement was then ready for signature but the Vice Minister declined to sign it under the pretext that he had not been authorized to do so. Even though I had followed the matter from its inception and had translated the agreement into Amharic, it was other officials who had negotiated and brought it to a conclusion. In the hope that it might not harden all the more the opposition of the Orthodox Church leaders who had been against the establishment of the radio station from the start, I felt I should not sign the agreement so soon after my appointment, and I suggested to the Emperor that it might be better if the signatory were to be the Vice Minister of Posts who was an Orthodox rather than myself, an Evangelical. His Majesty readily agreed and the Vice Minister was commanded to sign it which he did on February 15, 1961.

I have to recall with regret in this connection that the opposition of the leaders of the Orthodox Church never ceased from February 1963 when the RVOG was dedicated until March 1977 when it was confiscated. It was however true that thousands of Orthodox people were happy to listen to the radio and follow the daily spiritual messages and obtain beneficial information for their daily lives. I affirm that His Majesty the Emperor Haile Sellassie was one of the regular listeners to the spiritual messages and various other programmes broadcast daily by the Mekane Yesus Church. I say this from personal knowledge and not hearsay since we often used to discuss the broadcast programmes.

The site of the transmitters was selected at a place 30 km to the south of Addis Ababa and the government rented the land to the LWF for 30 years. A large site was purchased on the outskirts of the City near the Jimma road in the name of the Mekane Yesus Church and rented to the Federation for the construction of the radio studio building and staff residences. The construction work was completed in two years and the radio station was dedicated with an impressive ceremony on February 27, 1963, in the presence of the Emperor. As the Minister responsible, I conducted the dedication ceremony.

In addition to broadcasting evangelistic messages and the daily news, the RVOG continually transmitted programmes on education, health care and development. The programmes were prepared in a number of African and Indian languages in studios abroad and sent to Addis Ababa for broadcasts in the languages they understood; the fame of the radio station spread all over the world and it was highly appreciated. And as the EECMY prepared and broadcast daily Gospel messages and various programmes in Amharic to the Ethiopian people, her service was recognized and appreciated, and her name was revered. As a result of her evangelistic ministry, believers grew in the Faith and many believed in the Lord Jesus.

6. MY ELECTION TO BE PRESIDENT OF THE CHURCH

Some time before the dedication of the radio station, the director, Dr. Sigurd Aske and Ato Emmanuel Gabre Sellassie came to the Ministry of Posts one day to tell me that Ato Emmanuel had been transferred to the radio station as adviser, and that since no one employed at the station was allowed to do any other work, to entreat me to accept the position of President of the Mekane Yesus Church when Ato Emmanuel's term was over in January 1963. I pointed out that it would be difficult for me to undertake additional work as my official duties in the Government occupied all my time. Ato Emmanuel remarked that they would all help, but the desire was that I hold the position. On my acceptance of the request, they held a consultation with the other leaders of the Church and I was elected President for four years on January 25, 1963, at the 3rd General Assembly of the EECMY. It was just four years since the Church had been established on the national level; the membership was about 21,000 and the delegates at the 3rd General Assembly were about 100. After that, I was successively elected four more times and served as President for 22 years, until January 25, 1985. The Vice Presidents during my term of office were Fit. Baissa Jammo, Ato Francis Stephanos and Dr. Emmanuel Gabre Sellassie. The Treasurers were Dr. Herbert G. Schaefer (ALM), Pastor Ernst Bauerochse (GHM), Mr. Omund Lindtjorn (NLM), Mr. Magnar Mageroy (NLM), Ato Hailu Wolde Semaiat, Ato Berhe Beyene, Dr. Olav Saeveraas (NLM) and Pastor Gunnar Oseng (NLM).

7. WHY ARE NON-CLERICAL PERSONS ELECTED TO BE LEADERS OF THE CHURCH?

In discussing my work in the Church, and especially about the Presidency of Dr. Emmanuel Gabre Sellassie and of myself, the question arises as to how we were elected to be leaders of a Church when we did not hold the title of pastor or bishop and when additionally I was a government employee as well as an official, and why it was necessary to establish a Church in this country apart from the Orthodox Church. As I feel there are people who are at a loss to know the reasons, the following elucidation will perhaps be in order.

It should be understood, in the first place, that the Church is a communion of people who believe in the Lord Jesus Christ. All Christians are therefore equal before the Lord God, and they enjoy equal rights and responsibilities. It is abundantly clear from the Bible that there is no difference whatever on that score. "There is neither Jew nor Greek, slave nor free, male nor female, for you are all one in Christ Jesus" (Galatians 3:28). Moreover, as Martin Luther, more than 450 years ago, had forcefully reminded the whole Church that all believers are God's priesthood. This is evident from several passages in the Holy Scriptures: "You also, like living stones, are being built into a spiritual house to be a holy priesthood, offering spiritual sacrifices acceptable to God through Jesus Christ" (1 Peter 2:5). "To him who loves us and has freed us from our sins by his blood, and has made us to be a kingdom and priests to serve his God and Father - to him be glory and power forever and ever. Amen" (Revelations 1:5,6). This is also indicated in the books of the Old Testament (Exodus 19:6 and Isaiah 61:6).

The Amharic word 'cahen' indicates essentially serving God. It is therefore the right and the responsibility of persons elected by the believers at any level of service, including the leadership of the Church, to serve the Most High God and the believers. It is the belief of Evangelical Christians that any believer can serve as a leader of the Church even if he is not called a pastor, bishop or archbishop. It is therefore clear that it is in accordance with the Scriptures that the Church elects a person whom she believes to be a worthy leader to serve as president, and it is on this basis that Emmanuel Gabre Sellassie, Emmanuel Abraham and Francis Stephanos were elected by the believers to be the highest leaders and servants in the EECMY.

It should be emphasized in this connection that the Church can give her leaders the title of bishop and archbishop if she so desires. It is noted that, in a number of countries, Evangelical and Lutheran Churches have adopted this style of administration. Administration being the main duty of a Church president, nothing prevents a member of a Church, even if he is not called pastor or bishop, from being elected president or vice president of the Church, provided his spiritual standing is recognized and the believers choose to elect him.

8. WHY WAS IT NECESSARY TO ESTABLISH ANOTHER CHURCH BESIDES THE ORTHODOX CHURCH?

The main reasons appear to me to be the following:

1. The Ethiopian Orthodox Monophysite Church had been in Ethiopia for over 1,600 years and had been known as the State Church. This led her to believe that the country and the people were her exclusive preserves. As a result, she did not appear to tolerate any other type of Church in Ethiopia.

2. After she had led a separate life for a millennium, cut off from the rest of Christendom, the Roman Catholics came to Ethiopia 450 years ago and tried to destroy her very existence and replace it with the Catholic Church. The Church rose in self-defence and after much bloodshed and the loss of many lives, they were expelled from the country. As a result, the Church came to the firm conviction that, in the interest of self-preservation, there was no alternative to the policy of denying access to Ethiopia of any kind of Christian doctrine which is contrary to her own beliefs and doctrine. It thus became impossible for her to look with favour at any kind of Christian organization.

3. Evangelical Christians, who claim to have come to Ethiopia to teach only what has been revealed in the Bible, say that they do not believe some of the teachings of the Orthodox Church because they are not found in the Holy Scriptures. For instance, they say they cannot accept the teaching that the Virgin Mary, the Angels and the Saints mediate for the salvation of humankind, because it is contrary to the teaching of the Lord Jesus and the Apostles. Our Saviour Jesus Says, "I am the way, and the truth, and the life. No one comes to the Father except through me" (John 14:6). And the Apostle Paul has written, "There is one God and one mediator between God and men, the man Christ Jesus" (1 Timothy 2:5).

4. As is evident from the history of the Evangelical Missions that came to Ethiopia over the years, the missionaries were sent to Ethiopia not to destroy the entity of the Orthodox Church and replace her with another church but to help her leaders and the believers to hear and read the Holy Scriptures in the language they understood and to base their beliefs and teaching on the knowledge of the Gospel in the hope that the Church might experience renewal and carry the light of the Gospel to the many millions of pagans and Muslims who lived around them and proclaim the message of salvation.

Under no circumstances would the leaders of the Orthodox Church wish to budge from the faith they had inherited from their ancestors and they insisted that no change should be made in their faith and doctrine in their lifetime. They therefore made it their business to strongly oppose those who preached the pure Gospel; they excommunicated their believers, refused to baptize them and to officiate at their funerals. Although saddened by this attitude, the Evangelical

Christians organized themselves into congregations, established their own Churches, constructed their own church buildings, trained and assigned persons to serve as pastors and made available to their believers the spiritual ministry denied them by the Orthodox Church. They proceeded to proclaim the Gospel of Christ to millions of their fellow-Ethiopians who had never heard it. The EECMY was instituted in the firm belief that to discharge this duty was acting in obedience to the divine commission given to His followers by the Head of the Church, the Lord Jesus Christ.

9. THE FUNCTIONS OF THE PRESIDENT AND THE DUTIES OF THE GENERAL SECRETARY

When I was elected president of the Mekane Yesus Church in January 1963, the intention was not that I work in the Church Office daily but that I attend and act as chairman of the weekly and other meetings of the Church Officers and perform the functions of the President as laid down in the constitution of the Church, and to represent the Church in her relations with the Cooperating Missions and Churches, and the Ethiopian Government.

During the first few years, the Executive Secretary and his assistant carried out the office work and brought whatever was beyond their competence to the weekly meetings of the Church Officers for decision and direction. The Executive Secretary used to bring any matters that might arise in the interim to the government department where I worked and get my views and instructions. Whenever visitors came from abroad and desired to see me, the Executive Secretary would bring them to my Ministry for a discussion. The Mission directors did likewise when they had something to bring to my notice. It was intended that the Executive Secretary (later General Secretary) be in charge of the Church Office and perform the day-to-day work. In the beginning, he and the Assistant Executive Secretary (later Associate General Secretary) were considered to be Church Officers and elected by the General Assembly. It was believed later on that they should work full-time as permanent employees and, on the recommendation of the Executive Committee, the 7th General Assembly (1971) adopted the idea and the constitution and by-laws were amended accordingly.

Three men were successively designated General Secretaries from April 1958 to July 1979; Ato Hagos Legesse from April 1958 to the end of 1962; Qes Ezra Gebremedhin from January 1963 to September 1966 and Qes Gudina Tumsa from September 1966 to July 1979. During that period, there were six Associate General Secretaries: Ato Gebre-Ab Biadigilign, Ato Amare Mamo, the Rev. Olav Saeveraas (NLM), the Rev. Robert J. Miller (ALM), Ato Tarekegn Adebo from the Kambata Synod and Ato Bulti Aleku from the Western Synod. Qes Gudina was suddenly abducted on July 28 by unknown persons. Strenuous but unsuccessful efforts were made to find his whereabouts and we were compelled to consider him as no longer in this world!

10. THE CONSTRUCTION OF THE CENTRAL OFFICE AND YOUTH HOSTEL

Even though the Mekane Yesus Church had been established as a national Church and her entity and work recognized, she had no proper office for several years. The Addis Ababa Mekane Yesus Congregation, having assumed from the start the leadership for the establishment of the national Church, and its President, Ato Emmanuel Gabre Sellassie, being the first Church President, made a room available in the compound of the Addis Ababa Mekane Yesus Church to serve as an office. Due to the gradual increase of the work, a house was rented in the compound and the Central Office continued its work there. Nevertheless, as recorded in the minutes of their meetings, the question of obtaining a proper office had preoccupied the Church Officers from the beginning. A firm step was taken on the matter when in December 1961, Dr. Franklin Clark Fry, President of the LWF visited Ethiopia. He was present at one of the Church Officers' meetings when the question was raised and it was reported that 200,000 Birr was needed to construct the Church Office building and the LWF was requested to give assistance. Dr. Fry remarked that they liked to put their money on such projects and he would fully support the request. He would work for its success when formally presented to the LWF General Office.

Some staff members of the LWF came to Addis Ababa after I took up the function of President (1963). They attended a meeting of the Church Officers and I reported that the work of the Church was expanding and stressed that the question of constructing the Central Office was becoming more and more urgent. After asking a number of questions concerning the matter, the visitors stated that, even if financial aid were obtained from abroad, it would be incumbent on the Church Synods to make contributions as much as they were able. While admitting that it was proper to do this, the Church Officers pointed out that, since the Synods were in the process of being organized and had to make substantial outlays for evangelism and literacy activities, it would be onerous for them to contribute to the construction funds of the office building. They would, however, endeavour to make available a site in the City, at no cost to the LWF, on which the office building would be set up. This would be the Church's contribution. The visitors reiterated that the Synods should indicate the amount they could contribute for it to be presented to the LWF General Office for consideration. In view of the LWF President's assurance, however, we had no reason to fear that we would not obtain financial assistance.

This being the position as regards the possibility of procuring funds for the construction of the Church Office, we were faced with the problem of getting a building site and, after consultation, we agreed to request the Emperor to grant us a piece of land. I therefore approached His Majesty in March, 1963 with a request that a site on King George street, adjacent to the German School, 30 meters along the street and extending back to the compound of the Addis Ababa Mekane Yesus Church and estimated to be about 3,000 sq m be granted to the Mekane Yesus Church. The Emperor, who liked to get multi-storeyed buildings constructed in the City, indicated that he would give us the site provided we were prepared to construct a storeyed building. He then commanded me to present a sketch of the building and remarked, "We shall also have a look at the site."

Not knowing whether we could obtain the site or not, we had not prepared a sketch of the building. So, as soon as I returned from the Palace, I called a meeting of the Church Officers, told them of the Emperor's command and proposed that we ask Mr. Ingvar Eknor, the Swedish architect who had lived in Addis Ababa for many years, urgently to make a five-storeyed sketch of the facade of the building for us without being concerned with the details. They all agreed to the proposal and I requested Mr. Eknor in their presence to give us the sketch as soon as possible. The architect promised that he would give it to us in a few days. In the meantime, the Emperor, remembering his promise had stopped by the site in the course of one of his tours in the City, had his ADC pace off a distance of 30 meters along the street and made a mental note of what he would give us. After a few days, Mr. Eknor brought a sketch of the building whose facade can be seen on the site. We came together to have a look at it and I presented it to His Majesty. He was pleased with it and ordered the Secretary to write that as much land as I had requested be granted to the Mekane Yesus Church with the title-deed. I received the order from the Mayor of the City in April.

Our original plan was of course not to construct a high-rise building, but realizing that we could not get a site unless we built one, we had to present the sketch. There was adequate space, however, for the construction of the Church Office behind the large building. As we had been convinced for some time of the necessity of building a hostel for University students who came from the Provinces and lived scattered in various districts of the City in an atmosphere suited neither to morality nor to study, we asked the architect to design the building for use by University students, and we decided to ask the LWF Department of World Service for funds to construct the building. It was no easy matter to ask for about half a million Birr to build a hostel when our request for funds to construct the Church Office had not materialized. Moreover, the LWF had never before been asked to grant funds to build hostels. Nevertheless, we strongly pleaded with the Federation that, in view of the situation then prevailing in our Church and in Ethiopia, it was essential to provide this service for the well-being of our young people, and that it was our inescapable duty to erect this building when the Emperor had granted us a site in a central area near the University. The funds were granted. This opened the way not only for the EECMY but also for the Lutheran Churches in Africa and Asia to procure funds from the LWF to build hostels.

Several months elapsed before the specifications for the building could be made ready and funds obtained, so that the rainy season supervened before construction could be started. While passing in that street, the Emperor had observed that nothing had been done on the site. We encountered one day in July, 1963 not far from the site and he remarked, "You received the site with such haste and have done nothing." - The remark was so sudden and it was so inconvenient to explain the reason on the spot, I had to parry the question and said simply, "They say one does not build a house in the rainy season." - His Majesty smiled and said, "The rainy season will soon be over."

I had heard that when people failed to build houses on sites he had granted them, the Emperor would take them back and give them to those who were prepared to build. I felt that his remark had an element of threat in it and exerted myself to get the specifications and the funds quickly.

The specifications and the bill of quantities for the building were ready by the end of 1963 and the funds were obtained through the LWF from the Swedish Christian Welfare Organization, Lutherhjälpen. We then determined to get the construction work started and called for tenders. A contract was signed with the firm Diano and Rizzi for an amount which we considered to be reasonable. The four-storeyed hostel building and the Central Office building behind it were dedicated in September 1966 in the presence of Dr. Fry, President of the LWF and other officials.

The hostel was most comfortable with modern facilities for sleep, study and recreation for 78 students. A fifth floor was added later which made it possible to accommodate more than 110 students. There were, in addition, meeting rooms and offices for the director and the staff. There were also three flats on the right side as one enters the building. Since the plan was to charge the students moderate rents, the ground floor was designed to serve as shops to be rented for additional income to help run the hostel.

As the Central Office building had at that time more rooms than were needed for offices, the 'Yemisrach Dimts' Literacy and Literature Sections were housed in the building. With the establishment of RVOG, the Church had the good fortune of broadcasting radio programmes and a third section called the 'Yemisrach Dimts' Radio Studio was set up in February 1963 to transmit daily evangelistic messages and various other programmes. The programmes were prepared at the studio located in the Mekanisa compound of the Mekane Yesus Church.

As soon as the work on the buildings was completed, I requested the Emperor to visit them and he graciously consented to do so one afternoon at 4 p.m. He went over both buildings and expressed gratification with what he saw. News of his visit was broadcast over the radio, published in the newspapers and viewed on television. I was happy at the progress made and gave thanks to the Lord.

11. FREQUENCY OF THE EXECUTIVE COMMITTEE MEETINGS

Due to the considerable growth of the EECMY and the consequent increase in the volume of work, it had been decided in January 1964 that the Executive Committee, which had been meeting once a year, meet twice a year. As the work of the Church was expanding all the more, it was deemed necessary that more frequent meetings be held and exchanges of views made by the leaders. The Executive Committee therefore resolved in June 1973 that it meet three times a year - in January, May and September. Additionally, it became customary for the Executive Committee to have special meetings when necessary.

12. THE ESTABLISHMENT OF A PENSION FUND

The fast growth of the Church entailed an increase in the number of employees and made it imperative that a pension scheme be established for them. The 5th General Assembly therefore directed the Church Officers in January 1967 to prepare a pension plan and present it to the Executive Committee. After considering the views of the Synods, the Church Officers on several occasions requested the LWF to send them an actuary. An American actuary arrived and, after a study of the situation, prepared a draft pension plan. It was presented to the 7th General Assembly in January 1971. The Assembly considered and approved the plan and resolved that it be put into operation and administered by a Board of Pensions as from January 1972.

13. SECOND REGISTRATION OF THE CHURCH

As recounted above in this Part, after the establishment of the Mekane Yesus Church as a national Church, the Minister of the Interior had written to all the Provinces in May 1961 that the Church had her own identity and was a legal institution. He had sent them another letter in December 1962, enclosing the Church's constitution and by-laws, and confirming that her agents were entitled to purchase land like any other Ethiopian and should not be prevented from doing so. He had also enjoined that her believers and workers were not to be unjustly treated. The Church had on this basis developed her relationship with the government departments and had proceeded with the discharge of her functions. But, pending the promulgation of a law regulating the administration of religious institutions, she had to be registered like any other association.

New 'Associations Registration Regulations' were issued in September 1966 and the Church had to be re-registered accordingly. An application signed by all the Church Officers was submitted to the Security Department on September 5, 1968. The leaders of the Orthodox Church and the government officials who supported them and who were opposed to the Church's existence, and were therefore intent on getting her banned if possible, thought this opportune and made an effort to delay registration by repeatedly putting off their decision. And the government departments which had been cooperating with us went so far as to say they had no knowledge of an organization called Mekane Yesus.

As a result, our work was disturbed and we became apprehensive that it might be closed down. We therefore prepared a petition on October 21, 1968, and I submitted it to the Emperor, and reported that we were facing a difficult situation because the Minister of the Interior, Dejach Kifle Ergetou, and the Chief of Security, General Dresse Dubale, after we had waited on them several times, "have interfered with matters of our faith and required us to change the name of the Church and, going into details, have asked us to leave out some words from and include other words in the constitution." We then expressed the view that "it is our understanding that the authority given to the Security Department by law is to maintain law and order and prevent disturbances, and not to act contrary to the freedom of religion Your Majesty has given to Your people in the Constitution, and to disturb their peace and freedom." We then pleaded with him to give orders that the Church be re-registered to enable her to continue her service.

His Majesty commanded the ADC to summon Kifle and Dresse to appear before him the next day and that I should be present. Accordingly we went to the Palace and attended on the Emperor at 9 a.m. the following morning. I stated the difficulty the Church was experiencing and His Majesty asked them the reason for their failure to register. Obtaining no satisfactory reply, he said in an angry tone, "Go and register!" Thereupon, we bowed and retired.

The Vice President of the Church met General Dresse and his legal adviser on October 23 and they presented to him what they thought should be changed in our constitution. We considered their proposal and, at another meeting which I attended, declared that in no circumstances would the Church's name be changed. We then conceded a few minor changes and demanded that the Church be registered in accordance with the Emperor's command. They entreated us that we at least agree that the Church be styled 'Evangelical Church Mekane Yesus in

Ethiopia' instead of 'Ethiopian Evangelical Church Mekane Yesus.' Feeling it to be harmless, we accepted the proposed change. This and the few minor changes were submitted to the 6th General Assembly in January 1969. The amended constitution and by-laws were then presented to the Security Department and the Church was re-registered and a Certificate of Registration was given us on February 13, 1969, with the wording 'Registered for an indefinite period.' We offered praise to the Lord God for delivering our Church from the intrigue aimed at her destruction.

The General Assembly reconsidered the name of the Church in April 1976 and January 1979, and determined to revert to the former style, viz. 'Ethiopian Evangelical Church Mekane Yesus,' by which she has been known ever since.

I feel it is opportune to relate in this connection the accusation the Patriarch of the Ethiopian Orthodox Church, Abba Tewoflos brought to the Emperor against the Mekane Yesus Church and her President. In the Autumn of 1968, some Evangelical Clerics who were concerned about the fact that secondary school and university students had distanced themselves from the Church and the Christian Faith decided to make an effort to approach them and planned to call a meeting they called 'United Christian Convention' in the YMCA (Young Men's Christian Association) hall, adjacent to Holy Trinity Cathedral. They invited Church leaders to offer words of advice to the young people. They requested me to address the convention and the Patriarch to give the blessing.

The Patriarch was offended and went to see the Emperor accompanied by a bishop and the Administrator of the Cathedral and, in the presence of the Prime Minister and a few of the Ministers, made a complaint against the Mekane Yesus Church and against her president in particular. I happened to be at the Palace but was not aware that he was preferring a charge against me. Just as I paid my respects to His Majesty and turned away, I was called to his presence and as I approached him the Emperor asked me what I knew about the convention. I told him all I knew and added that I had accepted the invitation to speak and that the Patriarch had been invited to pronounce the blessing. The Emperor turned to the Patriarch and asked, "What is it then that you want him to do? He says he has accepted the invitation; it is up to you to accept or not." The Patriarch did not reply to the question but began to recite the wrong he said the Mekane Yesus Church, which he called 'Ato Amanuel's Association,' and the other Evangelical Christians had done. I resented his strange manner of speaking and his repeated reference to 'Ato Amanuel's Association' and said, "Your Majesty, I have no association; could his speech be restrained?" The bishop who was with him said, "It is not proper that these people should plan to meet near Holy Trinity Cathedral." His Majesty rejoined, "What do you mean? The Trinity are for all," and proceeded, "Now listen; it has been granted to the people to worship their Creator as they see fit, and We have declared that religion is the affair of the individual and the nation the affair of all the people." The Patriarch, as though he had heard nothing, kept repeating 'Ato Amanuel's Association' and rehearsing his grievances against me. I reiterated that I had no association and glared at him! The atmosphere grew rather tense and the Emperor appeared to be ill at ease. Noticing this, one of the ministers remarked, "Your Majesty, we have understood the problem; if the discussion could be stopped, we would go out and try to bring about an agreement." The Emperor agreed and we bowed and left the audience chamber. From that day on, my personal relations with the Patriarch were severed for all time. His efforts to get our Church destroyed and to have steps taken against me were thwarted. But his action revealed more than ever the extent to which he detested Evangelical Christians, and this left on me a sense of deep regret.

14. SIGNING OF THE AGREEMENT ON INTEGRATION POLICY

After the establishment on the national level of the Evangelical Church Mekane Yesus in January 1959, the SEM took the initiative in 1961 to put forward to the Church leaders the idea that the Church take over the responsibility for the work from the Missions. At a meeting in the Mission's Entotto compound, the Mission director, Pastor Manfred Lundgren, proposed that the transfer be effected with dispatch. The Church leaders advised that it would be better to postpone the transfer, since the Church did not even have a proper office and was facing a serious staff shortage.

After I was elected President of the Church in January 1963, I went to Helsinki the following August with some of my colleagues, to attend the 4th Assembly of the LWF. We visited Stockholm at the end of the Assembly and in the course of a discussion on various matters with the leaders of the SEM, the question of Mission-Church relationship was raised and I was asked what my views were on taking over the work of the Mission. I replied that it was the aim of the Church to assume responsibility for all functions related to her work but that it was difficult to take over responsibility soon due to shortage of leaders and finances. The Synod leaders held similar views at that time.

Following this discussion, the SEM and the NLM presented their respective proposals on the question in writing. The 4th General Assembly of the Church which was convened at Yirga Alem in January 1965 deliberated on the question and appointed a committee to study the matter in the course of the Assembly and report back. After considering the committee's report the Assembly resolved as follows:

"1. That the draft proposals for the transfer of evangelistic and various other programmes to the Synods, presented by the American Lutheran Mission and the other Lutheran Missions be circulated to all the Synods to study and report back their reactions prior to the Executive Committee meeting in May, 1965.

"2. That the proposal to increase the frequency of Synod representation on Mission conferences be deferred pending the study of the subject by the Mission directors and their colleagues.

"3.That the proposal on the subject of training workers for the Church be accepted with the addition of the words that 'immediate steps be taken.'"

The Synods were unable to present their reactions within the specified period. Some Missionaries alarmed the Ethiopians by spreading rumours that it was feared that it would be the end of Mission work after integration and that, in consequence, neither workers nor funds would be forthcoming from abroad. In the meantime, the ALM decided to transfer responsibility for the work to the Wollo-Tigre Synod and the takeover was effected in June 1966. However, a problem was created since the Synod, as a member of the Church, had no legal identity of its own. It became evident that the integration agreement should have been signed with the Church which was a legal person.

I presented a report to the 5th General Assembly in January 1967 on developments related to integration of Church and Mission up to that time. I also added the following comments:

1. It was to be regretted that coordination of policy and timing with regard to integration schedules had been almost completely neglected. The Synod and Mission leaders were therefore urged to pay more attention to the matter.

2. The meaning of the terms integration, transfer of responsibility, and autonomy was uncertain and failure to define areas of authority was creating difficulties.

3. A gradual and selective integration of the work of the Missions and the Church was to be preferred to an immediate and complete integration.

4. Before a Synod or the Church at large accepted responsibility for an institution or a programme, it should be considered whether it was necessary and vital for the life and work of the Church.

5. The agreements of transfer should be as flexible as possible, providing for a real partnership in finances and personnel.

6. If gradual integration were implemented in a spirit of true partnership, there should be no need to wait until all responsible positions could be filled by nationals.

7. If the Synod leaders and Mission directors were to meet with the Church Officers from time to time and discuss important issues, we should be able to avoid misunderstandings and mistakes by learning from one another and coordinating plans and actions with respect to this important and delicate matter of transfer of responsibility.

The General Assembly considered and accepted the proposals and resolved "that the Synod leaders and Mission directors meet the Church Officers periodically and consult with them on matters of mutual concern related to the work of the Church on the basis of the President's report that coordination of Church-Mission integration would be better served."

Following the General Assembly's directive, the Church Officers prepared a programme outline for discussion between Church and Mission leaders and persons invited by the President. Three successive meetings were held in June and August 1967 and in January 1968. The Mission directors were invited to the Executive Committee meeting which was held in June 1967 and in an effort to dispel apprehensions which were apparent in several quarters, I stated as follows in a report I presented to the Executive Committee:

"We have a feeling that there is some misunderstanding regarding 'transfer of responsibility.' Some seem to think that this will mean that the Mission organizations hand over the responsibility and then withdraw. It is now our task to find expressions and interpretations which can do away with these misunderstandings. It is necessary to state that the intention behind integration is not that the Missions should hand over their responsibilities and go. We believe, however, that it is for the Church to keep pace with developments and find forms for its organizational and administrative set-up which meet the requirements of our time. What we wish to achieve with Church-Mission integration is to make arrangements to secure a peaceful continuation of the work and avoid criticisms of the activities as foreign organizations. When we are now encouraging the Synods to take over the responsibilities for the work it is not because we believe that everything will be easy when we have done that. When we consider the international situation as well as developments in our country, however, we feel that we must not let time pass by without using it."

Twelve persons had been invited to give their views on various aspects of integration during the three meetings. Some said integration was inevitable on theological grounds and others said integration was an unavoidable necessity for the successful discharge of the work. I was one of those who presented a paper, entitled 'How integrate?' in the belief that integration was a necessity for the sake of the work. On presenting it to the Executive Committee on June 10, I submitted that integration was not merely an internal matter which we could handle as we wished; it could not be settled between a supporting Mission and a Synod, nor could it be settled by the Missions and the Church at large alone.

I pointed out some issues the implications of which would affect our relations with the government as far as Church-Mission integration was concerned. They were:

1. If the Missions were to remain separate organizations and were to continue to be responsible to the government alone as had been the case up to that time, it would be clear that the Church would be identified with the Missions, seeing that it was mainly located in the geographical areas allotted to the Missions and the Synod structure of the Church was almost identical with the Mission areas. In that case, the Church would continue to be identified with the Mission and

remain a somewhat diffuse organization in the eyes of the government and the public.

2. Our own Church people themselves would continue to think that the Missions were ultimately responsible for the work; so why bother. If they could not do what was expected of them or even what they had pledged to do, the Missions would do it for them. As a result, a sense of responsibility would not develop as it should and integration would in fact have no meaning.

3. If we continued officially to maintain that Church and Mission were separate and should not be merged, we would be suspected of ulterior motives which we did not wish to bring into the open, since it was no secret that the Missions supported the Church and more and more property was transferred from the Missions to the Church.

4. Knowing that it was a period when there was a strong feeling that Africans, Ethiopians are entitled to do everything, we should consider whether the time had not arrived for the foreign Missions to change their position from that of independent institutions to that of supporters of a national organization.

5. There were also other aspects of an internal nature, such as expensive administration, difficulties in coordination and complicated procedures apparent in the set-up of the time.

I then expressed my personal views thus: "Having said all this, I wish to state that I am not unaware of or would not like to minimize the problems involved in integration. We know that as long as the Missions function as independent organizations the work will proceed smoothly and without too much concern on our part. Moreover, we are not oblivious of the fact that the organizational and administrative structure of the Church is not strong enough and that it does not have the capacity to assume the whole burden. It is also clear that there are programmes and institutions presently run by the Missions which cannot be integrated into the Church and for which the Missions will have to be responsible before the government. An immediate and complete dissolution of the Mission organizations is therefore not feasible.

"Apart from what I have just said about the advantages and disadvantages of the present set-up, we must also recognize the right of the Government to be kept fully informed about developments. In a gradual integration, which we have agreed is the most practical and realistic way, not only property, but programmes and personnel will also be turned over to the Church. It is the right of the government to be informed and even have a say in the transfers. We will find ourselves in difficulty very soon unless we work out a clear policy and get it approved by the Government. Here, it is essential that we establish one policy for the whole Church and not act individually either as Synods or as Missions.

"Finally, I would like to conclude my remarks with a few points which I hope we can discuss and possibly arrive at some conclusions.

"a) Before we go any further, we have to lay down a policy which should be the same for the whole Church and for all the supporting Missions.

"b) Terms of agreement should be worked out between the Church and the Missions and presented to the government for approval as soon as possible.

"c) It is my belief that a gradual integration of the individual Missions into the Church in accordance with an integration agreement will be the best procedure for the Church and for our common task."

The Executive Committee considered this and other papers presented that day and resolved on June 10 that a committee be appointed consisting of Pastor Manfred Lundgren, Qes Gudina Tumsa and Mr. Philip Jacobsen,

"1. To prepare a clear policy for the Church and the Supporting Partners.

"2. To draft an agreement acceptable to the Government.

"3. To indicate priorities for the steps to be taken at the time of integration, and report back in August 1967."

The committee presented a draft agreement at the meeting of the leaders of the Church and the Missions held in August. Many objected strongly to a proposal in the draft that the internationalization of personnel and assistance be encouraged. The Church had declined to accept the proposal from the start. So it was dropped and the committee was instructed to revise the draft and submit it to the Church Officers. I sent the revised draft to the Missions and the Synods with a request that they send their comments to the Central Office.

It had been expected that the meeting of the 16th Executive Committee would consider and approve the second draft, but it became apparent from the various comments that it would be necessary to discuss further some basic principles. The majority of the Missions expressed the view that acceptance of the draft would facilitate future consultations, but the representative of the NLM declared that it was necessary to discuss further the idea of integration. He stated in his letter that, since his Missionary Society was established by the desire of the Christian community and its work was based on the voluntary contributions of the Christians, the Society's ability to assist the Church would be reduced if the process of integration were carried out as stated in the draft; and if the Mission in Ethiopia were integrated into the Church, it would be considered as good as closed; being far away from the scene of Mission, the supporters of the Society might become apprehensive that their contributions would be spent on matters they neither knew about nor could control and would therefore withhold their contributions. However, he did not contend that responsibility and property should not be transferred to the Church. It appeared that he was anxious lest the Office of the Mission in Addis Ababa would be closed down. (The Mission office has remained open on the grounds that the Missionary Society was responsible for the hospitals which were not transferred to the Church).

The drafting committee coordinated with the second draft the comments sent to the President and presented it at the third meeting of the Executive Committee with the Mission directors in January 1968. After a thorough exchange of views on January 19, it became clear that the Theological preamble of the draft was not acceptable to many and it was dropped. The amendment presented by the representative of the SEM, which appears as the preamble of the approved agreement replaced it and the draft was read through item by item and necessary modifications were made. It was then resolved that it be sent to the Synods and the Missions to study and send their comments to the Central Office before March 10, 1968.

The drafting committee submitted the final draft agreement to the Executive Committee and the Mission directors when they met in June 1968. It was again read through item by item and approved after a long discussion. It was then resolved that the Church Officers finalize it together with the Missions concerned. The meeting placed on record its gratitude to all those who had laboured in the preparation of the document.

The preamble of the Agreement on Integration Policy reads in part as follows: "Whereas it is accepted that the time has come for the Evangelical Church Mekane Yesus in Ethiopia to assume responsibility for the work established and hitherto furthered by the Missions, the Church and the Cooperating Missions have agreed on the following Integration Policy." Article 2 of the Agreement defines Integration as follows, "In this Agreement Integration is understood to mean practical arrangements with regard to administrative status, property and responsibility."

In Article 3, under the heading 'Administrative Status' it is written, "Whereas the Missions are operating as recognized organizations, individually responsible to the Government for their programmes and personnel; and Whereas the Church together with the Synods and affiliated Institutions is engaged in the same programmes; and Whereas the Church has developed her own administration;

"1. The administration of the Programmes and affiliated Institutions, established and furthered by the Missions shall be transferred to the Church and its Synods in accordance with schedules already agreed upon or to be agreed between the Church, each Synod and each respective Mission and/or Supporting Agency.

"2. Requests for financial assistance shall be submitted by the Church and/or each Synod directly to each respective Mission and/or Supporting Agency.

"3. Requests for expatriate Missionary personnel shall be submitted by the Church and/or each Synod directly to each respective Mission and/or Supporting Agency and the Central Administration of the Church shall assume responsibility for securing all necessary permits from the Government.

"4. Each Supporting Agency may appoint a Field Representative to serve as liaison between it and the Church, her Synods and affiliated Programmes.

"5. The Church and/or each Synod shall enter into specific agreement with each respective Mission and Supporting Agency regarding property, expatriate personnel, finances, correspondence, new programmes and other administrative matters."

The Executive Committee's directive that the Agreement be finalized in conjunction with the Missions was put into effect on April 7, 1969. It was signed on that day by the representatives of the Church and the Missions and registered at the Imperial High Court after nine months. The reason for the delay in signing it has been recounted above under the section, 'Second Registration of the Church.'

The re-registration of the Evangelical Church Mekane Yesus and the signing of the agreement on Integration Policy gave the Church status and renewed acceptance with the government departments and the public. The Church demonstrated that she was truly a national institution by extending her evangelistic and development activities in a number of the Provinces of Ethiopia more than ever before. This happened within ten years of her establishment on the national level. And since this was an indication of the increase of her membership and the development of her work, it gave us cause to praise our God for his enabling power.

Seeing that the work of the Church was growing fast and that her members were ever increasing, we invited more Lutheran Churches and Missionary Societies to come to our assistance both in personnel and finances. We signed an agreement with the Church of Sweden Mission in October 1972. We later signed agreements for assistance with the Lutheran Church in America, the Christofel Blindenmission and the Norwegian Free Church. The Church strengthened her evangelistic activities by co-ordinating the assistance obtained from these and the older Missions; and the aid she received through the LWF greatly helped to extend her development work. The Missions and the Synods on their part gave final conclusion to the Agreement on Integration Policy by signing agreements of transfer within two years.

Even though the Agreement on Integration Policy had been signed with the Supporting Missions, it was no easy task to put the policy into operation. The difficulty became apparent in connection with the allotment of the annual grants and the placing of Missionary personnel they sent. The Church's position was that all the funds granted by the Missions should be pooled together and that, when the annual budget was prepared, the Executive Committee allot them to the Synods in a way most advantageous for the work and that one Synod should not be allotted too much while another was given nothing. It was also the contention of the Church that the workers sent by the Missions should be posted at places where the Church considered it to be most useful for her work and not only where the Missions wanted them placed as formerly.

It has been indicated above that some of the Missions, the NLM in particular, had been striving that the funds they granted annually should not be spent outside the Synod with which they had traditionally worked, for fear that, if their contributions for evangelistic work were spent elsewhere on matters they knew nothing about and over which they had no control, their supporters would be forced to withhold their gifts. They argued in the same way with respect to the workers.

The Church Officers saw this trend as weakening the aim of Integration Policy and as disrupting the desired unity of the Church. So they determined to invite the Mission leaders for consultation on this and other questions, and a meeting took place in Addis Ababa in January 1973. After a lot of discussion, they agreed to work in accordance with the Agreement on Integration Policy.

On the occasion of the first formal consultation in January 1975, the Church and the Cooperating Partners agreed on the procedure for their future relationship and signed a Cooperation Agreement. The Second Consultation was held in February 1978 in Addis Ababa when the difficulties encountered by the Church in implementing the 9th General Assembly decisions concerning the plan for self-reliance were discussed and an agreement was reached on the following five points:

"1. The Consultation accepts the principle that institutions and projects of the EECMY, such as hospitals, schools and agricultural projects, should not be included in the self-reliance programme of the Church but considered as projects, and that until such time as they are handed over to the Government in accordance with the decision of the 9th General Assembly, the Partners of the EECMY accept responsibility for the financial support of these institutions and projects.

"2. The Consultation recognizes that a certain percentage of the grants from the Cooperating Partners be allocated with a view to fair distribution of available resources by the Executive Committee, especially to less endowed Synods. The Consultation further re-affirms the principle accepted by the EECMY 9th General Assembly that the Synods continue to work toward the goal of self-reliance on the local level.

"3. With joy and amazement, the Consultation has heard reports of continued growth of the Church in Ethiopia, in some areas up to 15 percent or more in a year, and recommends to the Cooperating Partners to support financially and otherwise an eventual allocation to the EECMY of a certain percentage of the total Church budget for evangelistic outreach, especially in new areas.

"4. For the sake of economy and efficiency in the remittance of authorized Synod budgets and earmarked funds for approved projects within the respective

Synods, and in the hope of facilitating the flow of information from the respective areas and projects to the Cooperating Partners the Consultation recommends that the grants so defined be remitted by the Cooperating Partners directly to the Synods concerned with proper notification to the EECMY Central Office.

"5. With reference to the fact that regular consultations, such as the present one, were deemed necessary as early as 1975, the Consultation feels that, in view of the present rapidly changing situation, the next consultation should be scheduled for September of this year (1978); it is therefore agreed that we accept the invitation of the Norwegian Lutheran Mission to host the Consultation in Oslo, Norway, and that one important agenda item of the Consultation be the working out of practical machinery for a coordinating structure for support and information between the EECMY and her Cooperating Partners."

When the Consultation met for the third time in September 1978, a draft Terms of Reference for the coordination of efforts, prepared by the Church was presented. The Consultation amended and accepted it to be referred to the respective Partners for consideration and approval after which it should be ratified at the next meeting of the Consultation. At the fourth meeting, the Consultation was renamed 'Committee of Mutual Christian Responsibility' (CMCR) and it was decided that it meet every year.

The purpose of the CMCR was to provide a forum for consultation and discussion at which the Partners consider together all aspects of the relationship between them. Its function was to provide for the presentation of papers, discussion of broad issues and principles of cooperation and for exchange of information among the Partners. It was agreed that the Committee make recommendations on policy matters and the sharing of resources involving personnel, scholarships, training, finances, etc. Finally, the Consultation agreed to hold its fourth meeting in April 1979, in Christiansfeld, Denmark, at the invitation of the Danish Evangelical Mission. That meeting was termed the first meeting of the CMCR.

At the request of the Church, the CMCR amended thus the Cooperation Agreement at its second meeting in January 1981: "For the well-being, unity and integrity of the whole Church, the EECMY shall allocate given grants or personnel as deemed essential to carry out her responsibilities to the best effect. Any allocation shall be communicated to the Cooperating Partners concerned in accordance with the agreed procedures." Since 1981, the CMCR has met in January of every year in Addis Ababa and endeavoured to solve the problems that face the Church in a cooperative manner.

15. THE CALL OF THE NORWEGIAN MISSIONARY SOCIETY

The EECMY is a Christian community founded and developed with the unremitting efforts and patience of Missionaries from abroad who had come to proclaim the Gospel of the Lord Jesus Christ to sections of the Ethiopian people who had never heard it, and by Ethiopian nationals who in pursuit of this ideal had offered their lives in sacrifice to their Saviour. As such she has became a missionary Church making it her primary duty, in cooperation with foreign Evangelical Christians who profess the same faith and pursue the same aim, to proclaim the eternal Gospel to Ethiopians and make every effort to help them attain faith in the Lord Jesus.

The community which is believed to be the oldest of all the inhabitants of Ethiopia and which now lives in the valleys of the Didessa, the Abbai (Blue Nile) and the Dabbus Rivers and known as 'Sanqalla' to the Oromos and 'Shanqella' to the Amharas is one section of our people which had never heard the Gospel. With a view to visiting this community with the Gospel and community development projects, the Mekane Yesus Church and the SEM had cooperated to settle the Shanqellas on three 'gasha' (120 hectares) of land granted by the Government by command of the Emperor in the Didessa lowlands and near the Wollega highway, at a place called 'Didessa Dimtu.' Work was started through the Central Synod in March 1970 to settle and instruct them in farming, to evangelize them and teach them to read and write. The LWF granted 150,000 US Dollars to run the project for five years. The aim was to settle 500 families.

It was no easy task to approach and to draw the Shanqella population because for many generations the Shanqellas who lived in the Didessa Valley and the Oromos who lived on the highlands had been mutual enemies and slaughtered one another. But, realizing gradually that the approach was made for their welfare and not to harm them, a few accepted the advice that it was preferable to settle and build houses rather than live as nomads all their lives. A village was therefore built for them and they began to receive instruction in farming and elementary education. The land was apportioned to them and assistance given with tractors and farm implements. As a result, they familiarized themselves with the work and were able to harvest maize and other cereals. However, after the change of regime, the provincial officials desired to take over the project and we had to hand it over to them in 1980.

The Western Synod of the EECMY had a very strong desire to carry the Gospel message and elementary schooling to another section of this nomadic community in the Didessa and Abbai valleys which had been utterly neglected, and had started to work among them, but finding itself unable to continue, had brought the matter to the attention of the Executive Committee and requested it on several occasions to find a way of obtaining assistance. We, who were working in the Central Office, also realized the importance of the matter and inquired of the Cooperating Missions whether they were willing and able to help. They indicated they could not undertake the task since they were intent on further developing the work they had begun. We then conceived the idea of inviting other foreign Missions and made inquiries as to which Missionary Society would be suitable. Qes Gudina Tumsa, who was on a study visit to Norway in May 1967, spoke to some friends concerning our hopes and was given the name of the Norwegian Missionary Society (NMS) which had been engaged in Missionary work in Madagascar for over a century. Qes Gudina reported on this when he returned home and we began to gather information concerning the Society. The former General Secretary of the Society, Pastor Scaugé, stopped in Addis Ababa in December 1967 on his way home from Madagascar. He visited our office and, in the presence of the other Church Officers, I told him of our desire and inquired if the Missionary Society would come to our assistance. We considered his response encouraging and I immediately addressed a letter to the Society to set the matter in motion.

The matter was placed before the 16th meeting of the Executive Committee in January 1968 and it was resolved that an invitation be sent to the Society. This was followed by a second letter. Qes Gudina happened to go to Norway again in August 1968 and the Board of the Society asked him to be present at its meeting. He gave them details of the reasons why he thought they should accept our invitation and strongly entreated them to send out their Missionaries to help us carry the Gospel to the Shanqellas. After consideration, the Board indicated to us that it would accept the call in principle and that it would recommend it to the General Assembly of the Society for approval. The General Secretary of the Society, Pastor Valen-Sendstad, the Field Secretary, Pastor Torbjornsen and Professor Staalsett visited Western Ethiopia in April 1969 and observed the living condition of the Shanquellas.

On hearing this, the leaders of the NLM whose Mission had been working in South Ethiopia for a number of years and who had declined to extend their activities to Western Ethiopia were troubled at seeing us extend a call to another Norwegian Mission and showed signs of opposition. We had to remind them that they had refused to accept the call and emphasized that the Church had the right to request assistance for her work from wherever she could find it. They withdrew their objection on our explanation of the serious nature of the matter. We then informed the Missionary Society of this and pleaded with them to accept our invitation. In line with its promise, the Board presented the call to the General Assembly in June 1969 at Drammen, near Oslo. I had been invited to attend the Assembly and I took the opportunity, in the course of my official visits to several

European countries, to travel to Oslo on June 27 and attended a meeting from June 28 to 30.

The item on our invitation was brought up on June 30 and debated on all day when 30 speakers took the floor. Many of the speakers expressed the view that it was impossible to decline the call and that it was an inescapable duty which they could not allow to go by default. Some of the younger speakers contended that the matter had not been adequately considered, that the work already under way in other countries had yet to be completed, and that acceptance of the call should be deferred to be decided on by a special General Assembly after a proper study had been made. The majority of those who spoke for acceptance were persons who had seen long service in Madagascar, South Africa and other countries. After all who had desired to speak had had their say, Pastor Manfred Lundgren, who was a guest at the Assembly, explained in detail why the Society should accept the Church's call and urged strongly that they consider it seriously.

The matter was then put to the vote and 333 persons voted for acceptance while 15 voted against. It was then declared that the NMS had accepted our invitation by a very large majority. I was elated and gave thanks to the Most High. After voting was over, the Chairman of the Assembly invited me to speak. I expressed gratification that the Assembly had accepted our call by such a large majority vote and proffered my thanks. I then informed them that the Ethiopians we were asking the Mission to assist were the Cushites of the Bible who had waited for almost 2,000 years to hear the Gospel of Christ.

As I had to leave Oslo on the following day, the General Secretary of the Society accompanied me to the airport and we had occasion to discuss how the work should be started in Ethiopia. I suggested that the Missionaries be designated quickly and sent out in September 1969 for language study which would enable them to start evangelistic work a year later; that it was our hope that they begin operation in the Shanqella and Beghi areas; that the desire was that a clinic and a four-grade school be built in each area; that, since it was necessary to plan in advance for the training of evangelists, it was to be recommended that they work in cooperation with the Western Synod which was running a Bible School at Mendi. I also expressed the hope that it would be of considerable benefit not only to the local community but to the country as well if they would designate an agricultural expert to help settle the Shanqellas in one or two localities to induce them to abandon their nomadic life and be instructed in farming skills. After listening to my recommendations, the General Secretary said that, since the Assembly's decision had opened the way, they would do everything possible and officially inform me what they intended to do. On this note, I took leave of him at the airport.

The leaders of the Missionary Society accepted my recommendations and quickly appointed workers and sent out two pastors with their families and two nurses in the Autumn of 1969. The Missionaries went to language school in Addis Ababa from January to December 1970 and proceeded to Wollega to begin evangelistic, medical and educational work in the Abbai Valley and at Beghi. The Mission also provided funds for administrative work.

Although the work has repeatedly been disrupted in the course of the Revolution both in the Abbai Valley and at Beghi, the Missionaries, in conjunction with their Ethiopian co-workers, have been able to surmount the trials and troubles with confidence and patience. They are still (in 1993) rendering commendable service to the Shanqella Community and the Oromo population living in and around Beghi town in evangelistic, educational, healthcare and community development work. They have helped many to attain faith in the Lord Jesus Christ, and for all this we are deeply thankful to the Lord of the Church.

16. THE MERGER OF THE KAMBATA CHURCH

The Sudan Interior Mission (now the Society of International Missionaries) had started evangelistic, educational and medical work in Kambata (now Kambata and Hadiya) before the Italian war of aggression in 1935; but its activities had been interrupted due to the war. The Mission was permitted to resume its work after the restoration of the national Government in 1941. In the meantime, the number of believers had increased tremendously. In due course, the Mission laid down certain rules in opposition to the traditions and customs of the population and a section of the believers who were unwilling to accept the rules withdrew and wanted to join the Mekane Yesus Church. They sent representatives to the Capital to solicit the Addis Ababa Mekane Yesus Congregation to receive them. They importuned the Congregation for 12 years. People were sent from Addis Ababa to try and compose the differences but were unsuccessful.

After the establishment of the Mekane Yesus Church on the national level, the 2nd General Assembly decided in January 1961 to receive into the Church about 25,000 Kambata Evangelical Christians and authorized the Church Officers to send persons to study the situation in depth and give them adequate assistance. The Church Officers appointed a committee and evolved a programme whereby the congregations could be assisted to attain synod status. The LWF granted funds for five years to implement the Kambata Home Mission Programme. A native of Kambata, Ato Zekewos Edemo, was designated to lead the Programme.

At the 3rd General Assembly in January 1963, Ato Zekewos reported that land had been purchased at Mishgida, Durami district, for the construction of a school; that ten students had been given scholarships at the Evangelical College, Debre Zeit, at the Mekane Yesus Seminary, and at the NLM Bible Training School, Dilla; that 20 students were being given instruction as evangelists for one year at the purchased site, and that, in addition to the four-grade literacy school, a school had been started to give instruction from grades four to six. The Christians who lived in the vicinity of the school had built and presented two houses to serve as classrooms and Bible school.

The Church Officers designated Qes Gudina Tumsa in February 1963 to visit and guide the Kambata congregations for six months. He organized congregations and evolved a plan for their administration. The Mishgida Mekane Yesus School was dedicated on March 6, 1964 in the presence of five Church Officers and staff from the Central Office, and the grades in the school were increased to eight.

Nevertheless, the Kambata Home Mission Programme was beset by a number of obstacles. As reported to the 4th General Assembly in January 1965, the main reasons were that the Kambata Church had been left without spiritual care for many years; that there were no experienced leaders to guide the Church; that the new synod set-up had created misunderstandings and jealousies among the people and the elders; that the elders who had had positions of leadership begrudged the transfer of authority to others and neglected the work; that the Church had failed in its obligation to contribute funds to run its own programme; that many congregations had maintained an attitude of jealousy toward the school because its service did not extend to the whole of Kambata.

In the face of these difficulties, the Church Officers set up a committee, chaired by Ato Emmanuel Gabre Sellassie, to follow up the work of the Kambata Home Mission Programme and guide it in consultation with them. The committee, in cooperation with the Church Officers, issued detailed directives for the re-organization of the Kambata Church. Ato Jalata Jafaro was appointed to be director of the Home Mission Programme; Ato Galata Woltaji was designated to be headmaster of Mishgida School. This resulted in the gradual elimination of the difficulties and the growth of the work; the task of training workers was also strengthened. The then Executive Secretary of the Church, Qes Ezra Gebremedhin was sent to visit the believers in Kambata and to study the situation of the congregations. He observed that they were at a disadvantage for lack of pastors who could minister the Sacraments to them and ordained a good many of the elders.

After taking note of the development of the Kambata Congregations and the training of a number of evangelists, the 6th General Assembly of the EECMY which met at Aira in Wollega in January 1969, authorized the Executive Committee to recognize them as a synod after ascertaining that the believers were fit for membership. The Executive Committee, for its part, considered the constitution of the Kambata congregations and accepted them as a synod at its 18th meeting on June 14, 1969. As a result, the number of Synods increased to five.

Even though the EECMY was able to administer the Kambata Home Mission Programme for ten years with the help of the LWF and improvements could be observed every year, the Church Officers realized that it was essential for the lasting welfare of the believers and the growth of the Church, that on-going support should be sought. To this end, they asked the Missions working with the other Synods whether they would afford grants also to the Kambata Synod. They indicated that they were not in a position to do so. An invitation was therefore extended, at the suggestion of the LWF World Mission, to the Finnish Missionary Society (now the Finnish Lutheran Mission) to come to Ethiopia and help. The Mission sent its representatives to study the situation and after consideration, accepted the invitation. An agreement was signed between the Church and the Mission in October 1968. Three Missionaries were sent to Ethiopia the following January.

Seeing that it was necessary to set up a permanent center for the Kambata Synod, a piece of land, 90 hectares in extent, near Hosaena on the Addis Ababa road, was purchased for 11,000 Birr. It had to be bought at a time when it was uncertain whether the Finnish Missionary Society would accept our call, but for fear that we might lose the option, we had to take a loan in faith. Our God honoured our faith and we were happy to obtain both funds and workers from the Mission soon after. Not only were we able to pay back the loan but we had a number of office and residential buildings constructed. We have also had a constant flow of Missionaries and workers trained in various skills.

The buildings constructed on the land were ready for occupation within two years of the arrival of the Finnish Missionaries and I travelled to Hosaena with my colleagues on March 28, 1971, to attend the dedication ceremony. The center was named 'Kambata Synod Administrative and Training Center.'

The Kambata Synod (now South Central Synod) was thus set on a firm basis and continued to discharge its evangelistic and development work. We were gratified to note the increase of the number of believers annually and this gave us more occasion to render thanks to the Lord of the Church.

17. PROCLAMATION OF THE GOSPEL AND HUMAN DEVELOPMENT

The membership of the Mekane Yesus Church increased by leaps and bounds in the course of the ten years of her establishment as a national Church. The Church leaders became apprehensive because it became very difficult to provide properly for the thousands of new believers. The 6th General Assembly meeting at Aira in Wollega in 1969 directed that a plan be prepared, and the necessary data was collected until 1971. When the plan was considered it was found that the number of believers had increased by an average of 15 percent annually in three years (1968-1971). The membership had reached 142,000. It was estimated that the members would be doubled and reach 285,000 in 1976. Due to this critical growth, it was shown that it would be necessary to train 137 pastors and 1,000 evangelists. But, as she faced a serious shortage of funds, the Church realized that she would be unable to effect this.

To discharge this crucial responsibility it was determined that there was no alternative to requesting, through the LWF, the Churches in foreign countries which were her partners in the Faith as well as the Welfare Organizations to amend their criteria for giving assistance. The 7th General Assembly which met at Debre Zeit in 1971 therefore resolved that the Church Officers address a message to the LWF. The purport of the message was that, in view of our difficulty and apprehension, the Federation urge the Churches to assist us and try, more especially, to persuade the Welfare Organizations to give proper weight to our plan to extend the Gospel and amend their criteria to include direct support for congregational work, leadership training and construction of church buildings. Accordingly, I wrote a letter to the LWF General Secretary on March 9, 1971.

The initial response from Geneva was that we make a study of our economic situation which we immediately began to do. However, since the Executive Committee was of the opinion that the question should not be seen merely from the economic point of view, it was decided that a document be prepared putting forth the Church's Theological position in some detail. A committee was appointed to prepare the document and report to the Church Officers. The document was considered and signed by all the Church Officers and forwarded to the General Secretary of the LWF on May 9, 1972. He circulated it to the member Churches of the Federation and to the Welfare Organizations. It was translated into several languages and studied carefully. I also wrote to some leaders of the African Churches requesting them to give us the benefit of their views on the document.

The main points raised in the document, 'On the Interrelation between Proclamation of the Gospel and Human Development,' may be summarised as follows:

It had become evident that the Churches and Agencies in the West were readily prepared to assist in material development while there seemed to be little interest in helping the Church meet her primary obligation to proclaim the Gospel. From the African point of view, it was hard to understand the dichotomy created in the West and reflected in the criteria for assistance laid down by the Donor Agencies.

Three issues were dealt with in the document which were:
1. The Church's Understanding of Man and his Needs;
2. The Old and the New Imbalance in Assistance from the West;
3. The Situation obtaining in Ethiopia and its Challenge to the Church.

1. The Church's Understanding of Man and his Needs
In the West, the standard of human life and that of society was normally evaluated in terms of economic growth and material wealth or in technology and production. Two things seemed to have been largely overlooked in this materialistic concept of man's development, namely,

a) that there were values in life beyond those of modern technology and economic betterment without which man's development would never be meaningful and lasting;

b) that man was not only the suffering creature who needed help but that he was also the most important development agent.

In the Church's view, a one-sided material development was a threat to the very values which make life meaningful. Due attention should be given to a simultaneous provision to meet spiritual needs. When we were told by virtue of criteria unilaterally decided by the Donor Agencies what we needed or did not need, what was good or not good for us, we felt ill at ease and became concerned for our future. We realized that, in spite of the affluence of the so-called developed societies, man was still suffering from all kinds of evil and the values which made life meaningful seemed to be in danger of being lost in these societies. We therefore saw the development of the inner man as a prerequisite for a healthy and lasting development for our society. We believed that an integral human development, where the spiritual and material needs were seen together, was the only right approach to development in our society.

The other aspect which in our opinion had been overlooked and for which there was very little room within the present framework of the criteria of the Donor Agencies was the question of man as an agent in the development process. The community which the project was supposed to serve was seen more as an object than as an agent for betterment. This basic approach had resulted in two problems:

a) Too narrow and well-defined projects which require professional expertise and which in turn are bound to be remote from those who should be involved;

b) Too few possibilities of long-term support by way of broad training at the grassroots level.

In order to get the ordinary man involved with a view to becoming an agent in the development process therefore, provision must be made to work with unimportant groups over long periods of time. Within the Church structure this brings us down to the congregational level where this potential is available. The artificial division between Church work and development is an obstacle in the attempt of the Church to develop the manpower potential it has within its congregational structure.

A fresh approach to development aid through Church channels would therefore be to consider man and his needs as a totality. The most urgent and the most important investment need in the EECMY was in manpower development where no division was seen between congregational work and development projects. They must go together because the Creator made man that way.

It was strongly maintained that it was the need that should determine where assistance should be given and not criteria laid down by the Donor Agencies which reflect trends in the Western societies and Churches. The guiding principles ought to be more flexibility to meet extraordinary opportunities in an African Church which does not necessarily share all the views of Western Churches and Agencies.

2. The Old and New Imbalance in Assistance From the West

The old emphasis in the mission of the Church had been on the verbal proclamation of the Gospel. All other activities in the educational, medical, and technical fields were regarded as being of secondary importance or even as 'means to an end.' In the promotion of Mission work, social responsibility or help towards material betterment of the living conditions among the people were usually mentioned only as side-issues of expressions of Christian charity.

The new emphasis was on social action, community development, liberation from dehumanising structures and involvement in nation-building. Proclamation of the Gospel had become a side-issue which should be referred to those who might have a special concern for the spiritual welfare of people. The two should be kept apart. These two extreme positions were equally harmful to the local Churches in Developing Countries which see it as their obligation to serve the whole man. It had been suggested that false piety was responsible for the old imbalance and a sense of guilt for the new imbalance in the assistance to the work of the Church. It seemed that the prevailing view in the West assumed that Evangelical Missions had not in the past paid due attention to the material and physical needs of man and that they were only concerned about the salvation of souls. By this attitude of false piety they created an image of Mission work as being only or at least mainly verbal proclamation of the Gospel.

This was not the true picture. Even though they spent a larger portion of their total resources on social activities, the Missions never reported it or reported it in a distorted form due to false humility and false piety. This attitude must be blamed for the situation which had developed and the misunderstanding that had resulted in the breakdown of the relationships between development and proclamation or between witness and service which were inseparable from the Biblical and Theological points of view. God was concerned about the whole man and this concern was demonstrated in the Gospel. The imbalance in assistance created by some Missionary attitudes had been harmful to the Church in its consequence.

The new extreme position taken by more recently formed Donor Agencies had drawn a line between Mission and Development which was completely artificial. This was reflected in the criteria laid down for the distribution of funds. It was a fact that the Church had always emphasized medical work, education and other community development. But in the early 1960's it was necessary to make all such work all the more visible to accommodate the new nationalism in Africa and refurbish the 'Mission image' in the sending countries. This led to a division of ministry and witness which could not be defended Theologically.

It was providential and foreordained that the national churchmen in Ethiopia should begin to question the hesitancy and the equivocation in the proclamation of the Gospel that was witnessed in some of the Agencies which support our work. When the EECMY felt that the time had come to call the attention of the LWF to this issue, she did it with the conviction that something could be done to bring assistance into balance. It was her firm belief that Christian service was neither 'a means to an end' nor 'an end in itself.' It was an integral part of the total responsibility of the Church. And the division between witness and service or between proclamation and development was harmful to the Church and would result in a distorted Christianity.

3. The Situation obtaining in Ethiopia and its Challenge to the Church

Among the many remarkable things that happened in Africa in the 1960's, the rapid growth of the Christian Church was probably one of the most surprising. This phenomenal expansion of Christianity across Africa was frightening for the responsible Church leaders. What was happening in the African Continent at large was also happening in the Evangelical Church Mekane Yesus. We were alarmed by the development and challenged by the opportunities to such a degree that we had to share our concern with our Sister Churches in the West which we believed had both the desire and the means to help us.

The matter was seen to be so urgent that the 7th General Assembly passed a resolution in 1971 requesting the LWF to approach the Donor Agencies in Europe and the USA with a view to reconsidering their criteria for aid and include direct support for congregational work and leadership training to help the EECMY cope with the rapid growth that was taking place. The earnest wish of the EECMY was that the request be passed on to the Member Churches of the LWF to be communicated to the congregations in order that they might know our problems and desires, and that the LWF might influence the Donor Agencies to review their criteria for allocation of assistance and thus give due consideration to our Evangelical Outreach plan. We wanted to proclaim Christ because we believed it was our responsibility. We wanted to proclaim Christ because our people were hungering for Him. The EECMY trusted that the Theological and Missiological trends in the West would not be the sole determining factors for aid but that African views would be taken more seriously and considered against the background of the situation then obtaining.

In the event, it had to be admitted that the Church's arguments hardly made any difference to the policies of the Welfare Agencies. They could not change their criteria as we had fondly hoped. We had to face the fact that the Governments on which they depended for the funds they dispensed could not be said to be interested in the proclamation of the Gospel as in relieving the physical needs of disadvantaged people around the world. Nevertheless, we were grateful that the aid they had afforded us over the years had helped to meet our desire to care for our people in conjunction with our paramount duty to proclaim the Gospel of Christ.

Even though our aim to persuade the Welfare Agencies to amend their criteria was not attained, we were gratified that our document caused a stir in the Churches of the Lutheran Communion and led them to ponder over and modify their traditional thinking on the relationship between Proclamation of the Gospel and Human Development. One can truly say that the arguments advanced in the document have influenced not only the thinking and action of the Lutheran Churches but also of several other large denominations of the Christian Church.

The membership of the Mekane Yesus Church when she was established as a national Church in 1959 was about 21,000; it has grown to be well over one million in 1993. "This is the Lord's doing; it is marvellous in our eyes."

18. A BOOK ON THE ORIGINS OF THE MEKANE YESUS CHURCH

As it was believed that a history on the inception of the Mekane Yesus Church should be written, the Church Officers spent some time looking for someone to write it and arrived at the conclusion that Pastor Gustav Arén who had served the SEM and the Mekane Yesus Church for many years, was the person they were confident could accomplish the task. The Mission was requested to detail him in June 1969 and agreed to commission him to write the book. He started on it in October 1970 and, after extensive research and with meticulous care, prepared a book dealing with the period commencing from the time in the 1820's when Evangelical Christians came to Ethiopia to distribute the Holy Scriptures and preach the Gospel to 1916 when Lij Iyasu was deposed and had to relinquish supreme authority. The book was entitled, 'Evangelical Pioneers in Ethiopia: Origins of the Evangelical Church Mekane Yesus.' It was printed in 1978. Pastor Arén was awarded the Ph.D. degree by the University of Uppsala in Sweden for his achievement. He is now in the process of preparing a second volume which deals with the history of the Evangelical ministry of the Lutheran Missions and the Evangelical Congregations from 1916 to the establishment of the Church in 1959. It is hoped that the second volume will be published in the near future.[2]

19. MEMBERSHIP IN THE INTERNATIONAL CHRISTIAN ORGANIZATIONS

Although the Church had been a member of the LWF since 1957, she had taken her time in joining the other International Christian Organizations. The question was presented to the 7th General Assembly in January 1971 where it was debated and decided that an application for membership be sent to the All-Africa Conference of Churches (AACC). The AACC admitted the Church into membership in 1974 at Lusaka, Zambia. The Central Committee of the World Council of Churches (WCC) also unanimously decided to welcome her as a member of the WCC in January 1979 at Kingston, Jamaica.

20. BETHEL CHURCH INTEGRATED INTO MEKANE YESUS CHURCH

The inception of Bethel Evangelical Church was marked by the evangelistic and medical work started in 1919 by missionaries of the Presbyterian Church of the US in Qellem district of Wollega. The Presbyterians are also called Calvinists because the first teacher and leader of their creed was a Frenchman called John Calvin who lived in the Swiss City of Geneva for many years in the days of Martin Luther. The essential point of Calvin's teaching was that congregations should be autonomous bodies with freedom to conduct their own acts of worship led by elected leaders and elders (presbyters) from among their own membership who were mature both in age and faith. Due to this and other points of doctrine taught by Calvin, his followers separated themselves from the other Evangelical Christians and became known as Calvinists or Presbyterians. In some countries they are also called Reformed Churches.

The Presbyterian teaching and creed were brought to Ethiopia when the Presbyterian Missionary, Dr. Thomas Lambie, arrived in Wollega, Qellem from

---

2 The second volume has since been published: Arén, Gustav. Stockholm: EFS forlaget; Addis Abeba: The Evangelical Church Mekane Yesus, 1999.

South Sudan in 1919. As is known from world history, 1918 was the year that marked the end of the First World War. As a result of the War, the influenza epidemic, known here as the 'Hidar Beshita' (Spanish flu) spread all over the world and caused the death of millions of people. The Ethiopian people could not escape the epidemic and many people died from it. When the epidemic reached Qellem, on the South Western border of Ethiopia, the then governor of the district, Dejazmach Birru Wolde Gabriel (later Ras Birru), learning that Dr. Lambie was in the vicinity of his district, in the Sudan, invited him to come over to Ethiopia and help in warding off the epidemic. The doctor arrived via Gambela with his wife and opened a temporary clinic at Dhenqa, near Dembi Dollo. A hospital was later built at Dembi Dollo.

Evangelistic outreach was started by preaching to and instructing persons who worked in the clinic, patients under treatment and their friends who brought them to the clinic. The Ethiopians who helped the missionary, Dr. Bergman in preaching the Gospel were Ato Gidada Solen, Ato Mammo Chorqa and many others. The activity of these persons was not limited to the clinic compound; they toured the countryside proclaiming the Gospel to the population on Sunday afternoons and holidays. So many people were able to hear the Gospel in this way that they used to travel to Dhenqa on Saturday afternoons to spend the night there and attend Divine Service on Sunday mornings. Some persons were ready to go out and preach to people who lived in distant places as a result of which the message of the Gospel spread in Qellem district like wildfire until the invasion of Ethiopia by Fascist Italy. Since preaching was done in Oromo, the language of the people, and since the Oromo Bible, translated by Onesimus Nesib, was ready at hand, the people were able to hear and read the Word of God in the language they understood. Moreover, the Mission had established educational and medical institutions, including a school for the blind. (Qes Gidada Solen and Ato Shorro Ambel who were blind learned at the school to read and write in Braille).

As soon as the war began, the American Missionaries left and returned to their own country through the Sudan. With the help of the Italian officials, the Italian Catholic Mission drove out the Evangelical Christians and appropriated their chapel. It would not even allow them to assemble in the compound for prayer and the practice of house prayer meetings was started. As the Italian authorities allowed them to get a plot of land elsewhere and build their own Church, the Evangelicals pooled their labour and funds and built a house of prayer in the central area of Dembi Dollo in April 1937. They called it 'Bethel Church.'

The head of the Orthodox Church in the town prevented them as usual to bury their dead at the church burial place. This led them to the realization that it was time they had their own pastors trained and ordained. As a result, Gidada Solen and Mammo Chorqa were sent to Addis Ababa and, after supplementary instruction was given them by the American Presbyterian pastor (Duncan Henry), they were ordained.[3] They then returned and assumed the leadership of the Evangelical Christians.

The Italian authorities detained Pastors Gidada and Mammo in the course of 1940. They were kept in prison in Jimma for about one year and, after their defeat in 1941, the Italians were on the point of killing all the prisoners when the victorious British troops suddenly appeared on the scene and rescued them. The two pastors were released and returned to their native district. On his return to Dembi Dollo in 1945, it was reported that an American Missionary (Fred Russell) was astonished to find eight new congregations that had sprung up during the difficult period of the Fascist occupation.

The American Presbyterian Mission had extended its outreach to Illubabor before the Italian invasion and, setting up a mission station at Goré, had started evangelistic, educational and medical work. It had also built a large hospital in the Gulele Quarter of Addis Ababa in 1923 and begun evangelistic and educational work as well. And, in course of time, it had begun to work in Kafa province including in the Ghimira and Maji districts. More recently, evangelistic work had been started in Mettu town and its neighbourhood by Qes Terfa Jarso from Dembi Dollo. Many people had heard the Gospel and believed in Christ as a result.

The Presbyterian believers of Qellem and the Lutheran believers of Ghimbi district were left without teachers and leaders on the expulsion of the missionaries from Ethiopia by the Italians. They therefore determined to get closer together and collaborate in proclaiming the Gospel to their own people. The believers in Qellem, who had secured the services of two pastors, had sent to those in the Ghimbi area Qes Gidada and Qes Mammo to baptize their children, celebrate Holy Communion and comfort them with the preaching of the Word. In like manner, when the two pastors were imprisoned, the believers in Ghimbi district had sent their evangelists to Qellem to visit the believers and give them succour. Thus the Evangelical Christians in the two districts found their faith in Christ and their unity in the Spirit to be immensely stronger than the doctrines that had for many centuries separated the Lutherans from the Presbyterians in Europe and America. It is believed that their common ethnic, linguistic and cultural heritage had further strengthened this realization.

---

3 Mammo Chorqa was ordained first in 1938 and Gidada Solen, because he was in prison, was ordained a year later.

On the expulsion of the aggressor and the restoration of the national Government, the Evangelical believers in other provinces met in council every January beginning in 1994 with the aim of giving continuity to their unity under the name of 'Ethiopian Evangelical Church.' However, the missionaries who had been expelled by the enemy were bent, on their return to Ethiopia, on insisting to underline the creeds of their respective Churches as before and had no desire to respect the feelings and to support the wishes for unity of the Ethiopians. They made use of the funds sent from their countries to cajole and harass the believers who gradually allowed themselves to weaken in the idea of unity. Consequently, the believers who used to go to the council annually from Kambata, Wolamo (now Wolaita), Sidamo and Gamo-Gofa stayed away and only those from Qellem and Ghimbi districts and from Addis Ababa met every year without interruption to consult as to how their unity could be placed on a firm basis.

The Evangelicals of Wollega Qellem were so determined to strengthen their relationship that, rejecting the divisive attempts of the Presbyterian Missionaries, they made every effort to establish closer relations with their brothers and sister, the Mekane Yesus Evangelicals.

To realize this desire, the two bodies planned to join in a federation and, meeting several times in annual consultation, prepared a draft agreement on federation and presented it to the 4th General Assembly of the EECMY on January 22, 1965. The Assembly accepted the idea of federation in principle and appointed a committee consisting of 15 persons to study the draft in detail and present a recommendation to the Executive Committee to enable it to take final action. The ad hoc committee presented the result of its study, entitled 'Constitution,' to the Executive Committee on May 31, 1965. The Executive Committee considered the draft both in Amharic and English, approved it and, in the hope that other Evangelical Churches might join the federation decided that the title of the constitution be changed to 'Council of Ethiopian Evangelical Churches.' But, with a view to holding exploratory talks prior to sending them copies of the draft constitution, three persons were instructed to consult with the Ethiopian Lutheran Church-Friends of the Bible and two with the Evangelical Church of Eritrea and report before the end of August 1965.

On January 20, 1967 a report on the relationship of the EECMY to other churches was presented to the 5th General Assembly. It was resolved that the ad hoc committee appointed by the 4th General Assembly report the result of its study to the next meeting of the Executive Committee. It was emphasized that the negotiations with the Bethel Church be finalized as soon as possible.

The negotiations with the Bethel Church lasted several years and the persons sent by the Mekane Yesus Church to tour the area and evaluate the situation of the congregations arrived at the conclusion that, since Bethel hardly received any assistance from abroad, the idea of a federation would not be in her interest.

The Bethel Church decided to join the Mekane Yesus Church on the synod level and applied to the Executive Committee for membership at its 25th meeting in December 1972. The Executive Committee received the application with pleasure and resolved to recommend, upon her acceptance of the Constitution and by-laws of the EECMY, Bethel's membership as a Synod to the 8th General Assembly in January 1973.

The General Assembly resolved that the matter be determined in accordance with the following directives: 1). That the Church Officers appoint a study committee on the Bethel Church; 2). that the committee study Bethel's present and future position and the consequences of her membership as a synod, and present its findings to the Executive Committee; 3). that the Executive Committee consider the study committee's report and, if it found it to be acceptable, admit Bethel as a synod.

The study ordered by the General Assembly was completed after several months. The Bethel Church chose to be divided into two Synods and the constitutions prepared for the Synods were presented to the Executive Committee at its 30th meeting and approved on September 22, 1974. It was resolved that the two Synods be full members of the Mekane Yesus Church as from September 1974 under the names they had chosen for themselves, viz. 'Qellem Bethel Synod' and 'Illubabor-Kafa-Shoa Bethel Synod.' The number of the Synods of the Church thus grew to seven.

It was found to be necessary to find ways and means to strengthen the work of the two Bethel Mekane Yesus Synods and the Executive Committee, at its 32nd meeting in January 1975, resolved that the Church Officers contact the United Presbyterian Church in the USA. After protracted discussion and correspondence an 'Agreement on Policy for Transfer and Cooperation' was signed between the two Churches on December 2, 1976. An agreement similar to that concluded with the Lutheran Churches and Missions detailing the basis of cooperation between the two Churches was also signed.

Even though the United Presbyterian Church would give no support for evangelistic work, it provided aid to the Bethel Synods in educational and some development activities. With respect to Evangelism, the EECMY gave the Synods a share from funds and personnel that she received from the other Cooperating Churches and Missions, thus enabling them to perform their task with renewed spirit. The Synods were also in a position to undertake a number of development projects with funds obtained from the LWF and the Donor Agencies.

After sometime, the Synods changed their names; the Qellem Bethel Synod was called 'The Western Wollega Bethel Synod' and, on the integration of the Gulele Bethel Congregation into the Addis Ababa Synod, the Illubabor-Kafa-Shoa-Bethel Synod became the 'Kafa-Illubabor-Bethel-Synod.'

In March 1978, the Administrator of Kafa Province closed down the Synod Office in Jimma and confiscated all of the Church's property. He also closed down the work of the Ghimira Presbytery and dispersed the believers, forcibly seizing the schools, the clinics and the residential houses transferred to the Church by the American Mission. The Synod was thus reduced to working only in Illubabor Province. In spite of the severe persecution and oppression, however, the believers in Ghimira remained more than ever devoted to their faith, meeting in the forest to comfort one another with the Word and to take part in Holy Communion. Reports were received from time to time indicating that the believers were continuously increasing in number. "The Word of God is not bound."

21. THE STATE OF THE SYNODS

1. The Western Wollega Synod (the Western Synod)
The Western Wollega Synod, later known as the Western Synod, belonged to the group of founding congregations when the EECMY was established as a national Church in January 1959.

I have narrated in Part 1 above that the Gospel of Christ was first proclaimed in Western Ethiopia when two Ethiopian Evangelists and their wives, sent by the SEM which was then in Eritrea, started work at Boji Karkaro in 1898.

Evangelistic outreach was begun in Lalo Aira, Western Ethiopia, in 1928 by Missionaries sent out by the GHM. The Mission had tried before the Swedish Mission arrived to send its Missionaries to Ethiopia to preach the Gospel to the Oromo people. It was unsuccessful after two or three endeavours and it was only after 75 years, in December 1927, that its Missionaries were able to arrive in Addis Ababa. They soon obtained permission from the government and travelled to Aira to initiate Evangelistic outreach. They also rendered outstanding service to the population of the Province by opening schools and a hospital. Multitudes, including 'qalicha,' heard the Gospel and believed in the Lord Jesus.

The Gospel was preached with zeal at Boji Karkaro and many persons, including the youth, believed in the Lord. Even though the first Evangelists passed away not long after their arrival, the work was continued by their wives and other Evangelists until 1926. After that, persons who were faithful to the Gospel and their families, meeting in homes by turn, continued in sharing the Word and in prayer until the Swedish Missionary, Pastor Martin Nordfelt opened a Mission Station at Nejo in 1927. As Nordfelt had opened a school and a clinic in addition to starting evangelistic work, the Evangelical Christians were happy to get a centre for their meetings. The custom of meeting for weekly worship continued until the invasion by Fascist Italy (1935).

The Evangelical Christians in the Aira area also continued to worship in the same manner so that the preaching of the Gospel sent deep roots unobtrusively in Western Wollega and many people embraced the Christian Faith. There was not a single Ethiopian pastor at Boji or at Aira when the Missionaries were expelled by the Italians. Italy and Germany being allies during the Second World War, the German Missionaries stayed on in Ethiopia until 1941 when the Swedish Missionaries were expelled from the country. When the enemy was defeated and driven out of the country, they were expelled in their turn by order of the Government. They hurriedly ordained Ato Daffa Jammo just before their departure.

Qes Daffa served the believers in Aira, Boji, Nejo and Mendi until the return of the Missionaries. Due to the tremendous increase in the number of believers which reached 5,000 during the period of occupation and later, it became an uphill task for one man to give them satisfactory service as well as to those who were being added every year. The Missionaries observed this predicament on their return and began the training of pastors at Nejo in 1949. As a result, five men were ordained after three years (1952). This process was continued and there were a fair number of pastors and evangelists by the time the Church was established in 1959 on the national level, and the number of the believers continued to rise.

After the restoration of the Ethiopian Government in 1941 and previously to that, the clergy of the Orthodox Church, with the support of the authorities and officials of the government, had made it their business at every turn to disturb, accuse and cause the imprisonment of the Evangelicals and to get their Church buildings closed and demolished. They also used craft to confuse the issue before the Emperor and obtain an order to have all the Church buildings constructed without official sanction closed, to be opened when permitted.

Qes Daffa Jammo was hard pressed, as representative of the Evangelicals, being dragged to court and often travelling back and forth to Naqamté and Addis Ababa to seek justice. The leaders of the Addis Ababa Mekane Yesus Church gave him every assistance possible on those occasions. The matter was finally submitted to the Emperor through the Ministry of Education and written order was sent to Naqamté in May 1949 that permission be given them to build when they requested for it. Thus, permission was obtained for 14 Church buildings and a good few others were constructed after that.

Nevertheless, it can be stated that until the popular movement later called 'abiot' was started, there was no time when the Wollega Evangelical Christians had respite from ill-treatment by the officials. For instance, I was compelled on January 28, 1967 to write, in my capacity as President of the Church, a hard-hitting letter to the Imperial Representative in Wollega, Dejazmach Berhane

Mesqel Desta, on the persecution and imprisonment inflicted on the Evangelical believers in Nole Kabba and its surroundings. I wrote as follows:

"I refer to the petition Qes Daffa Jammo has presented to you and to the letter addressed to you on January 27 concerning the Ethiopians imprisoned and maltreated by the governor to compel them not to preach their Christian faith and not to build their own churches in Lalo Qilé and Leqa Suchi sub-districts in Qellem district.

"I reckon that many people will find it unbelievable that Ethiopians are suffering imprisonment with shackles due to their faith and prevented from building their own Churches in Ethiopia, a land known as a Christian country and an 'Island of Christianity.' But it grieves us deeply that it is an undeniable fact that there are persons who are suffering imprisonment and ill-treatment in the Province administered by your Excellency because of this. I quote Article 40 of the Ethiopian Constitution about the freedom of religion: 'There shall be no interference with the exercise of the rites of any religion or creed by residents of the Empire, provided that such rites not be utilized for political purposes or not be prejudicial to public order or morality.'

"As I understand it, the people imprisoned at Lalo Qilé are not suffering for doing anything to prejudice public order or morality, or for a political purpose, but for their desire to preach the Gospel and build their own houses of worship. It should also be recalled that His Majesty the Emperor, speaking in Asmara a few days ago, has said that any individual is free to preach his own religion. Moreover, there is no authority or official who does not know that His Imperial Majesty has often stated that religion is the private affair of the individual and the nation the common affair of everyone.

"In these circumstances, it is contravening the law for a sub-district governor to abrogate the freedom and rights granted to his subjects by our Emperor and imprison his subjects for preaching the Gospel and building churches. I therefore respectfully invite your Excellency to consider this matter as extremely serious and, in accordance with the letter from H.E. the Minister of the Interior, to see to it that the imprisoned persons are released and that they are allowed the free exercise of the rites of their faith."

There being no let-up in the oppression inflicted on the Evangelical Christians in Wollega, the problem was placed before the Emperor and we entreated that the freedom of religion granted to every Ethiopian by the Constitution might not be denied to the people of that Province. His Majesty gave orders that the previous prohibition be lifted. The order was transmitted by the Prime Minister's Office to the Minister of the Interior and Dejach Kifle Ergetou wrote to Dejach Berhane Mesqel Desta on May 12, 1967, as follows:

"The dispute between the Orthodox Church and the Ethiopian Evangelical Church Mekane Yesus in the Nejo sub-district of the Ghimbi district has been submitted to His Majesty the Emperor. It was recalled that the Churches built without permission by the Evangelical community had been ordered to be closed to be reopened in time when permission was granted. The President of the Ethiopian Evangelical Church Mekane Yesus has presented a petition that, in view of the fact that, in conformity with the laws of Ethiopia, there is full freedom of conscience in the country, the Evangelical community has not stopped building Churches and that in consequence the provincial administration has continued to imprison and ill-treat their believers. The Prime Minister's Office of the Imperial Government has now written to us by a letter dated April 27, 1967, that it has been commanded that, with due observance of the laws in force in the Empire, they be allowed to teach and to preach to their own believers, and to build their own churches without hindrance. I am therefore respectfully to inform you that steps be taken in accordance with the command."

It is timely to state in this connection that, even though oppression and imprisonment had often been their lot, the believers had stayed firm in their faith and proclaimed the Gospel with diligence. As a result, the number of believers grew so much year after year that the Western Synod had more members than any other Synod for a number of years.

As the evangelistic and other activities of the Synod were extended to Arjo, Qellem and Asossa in Wollega and to Bunno Bedele in Illubabor, the name of the Synod was changed to 'Western Ethiopia Synod' in April 1969; and sometime later to 'Western Synod.'

In the same month and year, the Synod Office was established at Boji Karkaro (now Boji Dirmeji), the place in Wollega where in 1898 the proclamation of the Gospel was started. The President and his co-workers took up residence there and the Synod is continuing to render extended service to the population in evangelistic, educational, health care and other development activities.

2. Sidamo and Gamo-Gofa Synod (South Ethiopia Synod)

The proclamation of the Gospel in Sidamo and Gamo-Gofa Provinces was set in motion earnestly when the NLM sent out its Missionaries to Ethiopia in 1948 by permission of the Government.

The Mission had been founded by the Norwegian Evangelical Christians 90 years earlier with the aim of carrying the Gospel to the people of China. The Missionaries were compelled to leave China after 40 years' of service because Mao Zedong and his followers had overthrown Chiang Kai-shek's Nationalist government in 1948 and established a Communist regime. But, as the mission had determined to continue its policy of preaching the Gospel, it began to look around for a suitable country. The leaders of the SEM who were aware of this recommended that the NLM send its Missionaries to Ethiopia. The leaders of the Mission accepted the recommendation and came to Ethiopia to place their desire before the Emperor who gave them permission to work in South Ethiopia and to open schools and clinics as well.

It was in these circumstances that the NLM missionaries came to Ethiopia to start work as soon as they left China. A large number of the Missionaries who had worked in China were transferred to Ethiopia and laboured with great diligence in Sidamo and Gamo-Gofa. They established mission stations in a number of towns and, in addition to evangelistic work, opened schools, clinics and hospitals. They faced great difficulties with regard to transportation because there were no proper roads as now (1993) in those days. However, the Missionaries withstood with faith and patience every obstacle they encountered in transporting building materials and other supplies from Addis Ababa and built mission stations at Yirgalem, Dilla, Hagere Mariam, Mega, Hagere Selam, Negelle in Borena and Moyale; and in Gardulla, Konso and later at Arba Minch and other localities in Gamo-Gofa. In the same period, the Danish Evangelical Mission also began evangelistic work as well as educational and health care activities in Balé Province.

On arrival in Ethiopia, the missionaries recruited some Evangelical Christians from Kambata and Wolaita and from other places to help them in the preaching of the Gospel. Within five years of the beginning of mission work, 50 Missionaries were sent to Ethiopia. The number of believers was 3,000 during that period. By 1974, the number of Missionaries had reached 200. The number of the believers continued to grow year after year until it reached 200,000 in 1985, 36 years after the arrival of the Missionaries. As a result, the Sidamo and Gamo-Gofa Synod (including the work in Balé) was named the 'South Ethiopia Synod' and became the Synod with the largest number of believers in the Mekane Yesus Church. The Synod Office was built at Hawasa in 1967 with financial aid from the Mission.

Even though the work of the Gospel was proceeding in such a gratifying manner and, in addition to evangelistic work, the service rendered on a large scale by the mission and the Church in the areas of education, health care and development had been of much benefit to many hundred thousand people, the change noticed in the people due to the preaching of the Gospel gave no pleasure to the governors and 'neftegnoch' who had been sent to South Ethiopia from Shoa and imposed on the local population in the reign of the Emperor Menelik and later, and who had appropriated most of their land and reduced them to the status of 'gabbar.' The fact that the preaching of the Gospel and the spread of education had aroused the spirit of freedom in the hearts of the people – 'where the Spirit of the Lord is, there is freedom' - and that because they had felt the oppression more than ever, they had begun to complain and show unwillingness to obey orders without a murmur as previously, had awakened a sense of apprehension and hatred in the hearts of the militiamen. They were therefore set on imprisoning and harassing the subject people more and more. The people were in great distress and, having no land of their own, many were even denied a plot on which to build a chapel and worship their Creator.

The militiamen and the landed people were not content with this. In Sidamo in particular, they had threatened that they would burn down the buildings of the Mekane Yesus Church and the Mission and begun to plot the destruction of the Evangelical Christians. This was revealed in November 1971 when I happened to be in Sidamo on Church business. One morning, as I was starting from the Mission Station in Yirgalem to return to Addis Ababa, a number of young men approached me and said they had something to tell me. We went into a room and I asked them what the matter was. The young men reported that many of the propertied persons and militiamen in Sidamo were making preparations, under the guise of celebrating the traditional community feast, to brew 'tej' and procure oxen for slaughter, with a view to getting together to discuss and agree under oath as to how to massacre the Evangelical Christians and burn down the Churches and Mission stations on the occasion of 'Timqet' in January. They emphasized that, unless I did something to prevent this happening on my return to Addis Ababa, they believed that a frightful massacre would be the fate of the believers irrespective of age.

I told them that the information had deeply disturbed me and that I would do everything possible to thwart the plot, and left for Addis Ababa. As soon as I got home I obtained an appointment with the then Minister of the Interior, Ato Getahun Tesemma, and told him what I had heard. I then earnestly requested him that he take the necessary steps at once, since he was especially responsible for the security of the people. The Minister summoned and explained the matter to the Commissioner of Police of Sidamo (General Qelbessa Beka) and gave him instructions to render the plot harmless. The Commissioner investigated the matter and, after ascertaining the facts, invited the leaders of the association to see him and told them that, although it was permitted to hold a social meeting, it was illegal to make speeches at the feast. He therefore warned them to refrain from making any speeches. When the plotters were assembled for the feast, he caused policemen to mix with them in the temporary structure where they met. In the circumstances, the plot could not be continued, nor could the oath be administered. The massacre aimed at innocent people was averted and nothing more was heard of it. On the nationalization of land after 1974, the oppression of the landed people and the militiamen that had weighed so heavily on the population was lifted.

Nevertheless, the Evangelical believers in Southern Ethiopia had endured trials and persecutions, though in different forms, under the military regime like the ones in Western Ethiopia. But this only impelled thousands of people to hear and sincerely believe in the Gospel of Christ and caused them no spiritual harm. On the other hand, it was a fact that thousands in the two Synods who had professed faith in Christ earlier, had turned to be backsliders under the pressure of events and in pursuit of temporary gain.

3. The Dissolution of the North Ethiopia Synod
The North Ethiopia Synod, established by the ALM in September 1957, was one of the four Synods which founded the Evangelical Church Mekane Yesus. It was then called the 'Wollo-Tigre Synod.' (The other three Synods were the 'Western Wollega Synod,' the 'Eastern Wollega and Shoa Synod' and the 'Sidamo and Gamo-Gofa Synod'). The Director of the ALM, Dr. Herbert G. Schaefer, was one of those who laboured to draft the Constitution of the Church. The Synod consisted of the Adwa, Dessie and Addis Ababa International Lutheran Congregations.

When the American Lutheran Church sent Dr. Schaefer and the other Missionaries to Ethiopia to start mission work and the Emperor sanctioned that the Mission operate in Northern Ethiopia, especially in Wollo, it was with the stipulation that in conjunction with evangelistic outreach, development work should be undertaken for the benefit of the population of that part of the country. To be sure, the fact that the Mission appeared to have brought more resources than any other Mission was a source of hope for the provincial authorities.

Soon after their arrival, the Missionaries approached the leaders of the Addis Ababa Mekane Yesus Church and informed them of their desire to cooperate with them in the work of the Gospel. The leaders welcomed them with joy and assured them of all possible cooperation. This created a spirit of mutual confidence and the leaders joined hands with them to purchase, in the name of the Church, a large piece of freehold plot in the Mekanisa area on which to construct the offices of the Mission and the Mekane Yesus Seminary and residential houses. The work was started on an extensive scale in Wollo, Tigrai and Gonder for the construction of church buildings and institutions for development projects, schools and clinics on land granted by the Government or bought in the name of the Church with outlay from the Mission.

No sooner had the work begun than a large number of people, mainly from Wollo, flocked to the Mission stations; many of them professing to be believers, and thousands were baptized. Hoping that the baptized would grow in faith, the Missionaries worked out programmes to give them instruction in the Bible for limited periods. Seeing that the men who attended the courses were given daily allowances while the courses lasted, many Muslims came to the conclusion that accepting Christianity assured one of a lot of income and they continued to crowd the mission stations in large numbers. Not a few even got to preaching their new-found faith to others.

As soon as the courses were over, the allowances were discontinued and as a result many of those who had professed belief and baptized reverted to their old faith. Consequently, the number of the believers was so reduced that much disillusionment was caused. This so discouraged the Missionaries that their desire for work grew more and more minimal. The people the ALM employed locally in Northern Ethiopia, especially in Wollo, were persons who had migrated to Wollo from the other Provinces in search of work and who approached the Missionaries, posing as Evangelical believers, with the hope of obtaining temporary gain. They were thus not so desirous to proclaim the Gospel to the population which was the aim of the Mission.

The Missionaries, being complete strangers to the country and the people, and having no notion of the varied history of the Ethiopian people as well as the long-standing ethnic and religious conflict between Wollo and the other North Ethiopian provinces, endeavoured to discharge their mission with superficial knowledge. Many of them were young and knew hardly anything about mission work and Ethiopian history before coming to Ethiopia. They were therefore disturbed, being at a loss to know how to go about it in the complex religious and cultural situation of Wollo. Being unable to adapt themselves to the conditions, many abandoned the work within a few months and returned to America. It was obvious that hundreds of thousands of dollars, contributed by American Christian people for Mission work, were spent just for the transportation of those persons and their families, not to mention for other expenses.

Moreover, the Missionaries had no acquaintance with one another before they arrived in this country, having been gathered from the vast United States. On their part, they were people who highly valued their individual knowledge and points of view. There were few persons among them who had acquired experience by working in other countries and who could help them with counsel and the discharge of the work. They were therefore at variance in opinion and method of work, and spent a lot of time accusing one another. We used to receive reports that some of them were so disenchanted with the country and the work that they spent their time in bed pending their departure.

The persons who returned to America in this mood were apt to speak at congregational meetings and write articles expressing their disillusionment and criticizing the method of work. So much so that none could be found who would volunteer to come out to Ethiopia as a Missionary and the Mission personnel in this country was reduced to two persons (a husband and wife)! It is also felt that the Revolution in Ethiopia was a discouraging factor. Nevertheless, the ALM has never stopped transmitting its annual allocation for the work of the Gospel in Northern Ethiopia.

As has been pointed out in this Part above, the ALM had been the first to transfer the administration and leadership of the Synod to Ethiopians. Even though it was commended for setting an example to the others in passing on the leadership to the nationals, a disappointing situation ensued, the transfer of authority and large sums of money were entrusted to persons whose faith had not been confirmed, whose character left much to be desired and whose performance had not been tested. The Constitution of the Church having given no authority to Church Officers to intervene directly in the internal affairs of the synods, they had no freedom of action.

As indicated above, the persons who had taken over the administration of the Synod had come together from various areas and, being immature in the direction of affairs and in their views, they were overwhelmed with the abundance of funds that had suddenly fallen into their hands and became victims of self-interest. So much so that they became irresponsible to the people entrusted to their care. They competed with one another in the act of plunder, not to be outdone by others. As the remaining workers and the believers had no share in the spoil, there were complaints and accusations galore. The situation became critical and bickering and mutual accusations were rife whenever they met at Synod meetings. It was feared that the Synod might disintegrate. The Church Officers therefore appointed a committee to investigate the differences that had arisen. They considered the committee's report on October 8, 1972, and declared null and void the decisions made at the annual convention of the Synod because they were not in line with the Synod Constitution. They then called on the Synod President to issue invitations to the members for a special Synod Convention in Addis Ababa in the course of October.

The Church Officers attended the convention on the first day and urged the members to dispel their differences and work in harmony. They had a heated debate on November 25 but were unable to compose their differences. The Synod President (a man from Gonder) wrote me a letter on November 29 to report that, since the majority of the members of the convention failed to observe Section 5 of Article 6 of the Synod Constitution, he was unable to conduct the meeting and that the convention had risen without any decision being given on the question for which they had been invited to Addis Ababa. The Church Officers were deeply disappointed, but being responsible for the affairs of the Church, they saw that they had not alternative to declaring, in accordance with Section 2 of Article 9 of the Church Constitution, that the North Ethiopia Synod had been dissolved as from November 26, 1972, the date on which it ceased to work in conformity with its Constitution, and that they had taken over, in the name of the Church, the duties and responsibilities of the Synod, in conformity with Section 8 of Article 5 and Section 5 of Article 6 of the Constitution of the Church. They appointed a five-member committee to assist them in the discharge of their functions with respect to the congregations and institutions of the Church in Northern Ethiopia.

While the committee endeavoured to direct the work from Addis Ababa, the Church Officers, wishing to ascertain the reason for the Synod's dissolution, sent out in October 1973, with the approval of the Executive Committee, Qes Asfaw Qalbero and Ato Tewoflos Qena'a to make a study tour of the three Provinces. They obtained useful information. And to enable them to determine whether there was a possibility of reconstituting the Synod, the Church Officers sent Pastor Jurgen Wesenick to Wollo in June 1975 to make a final study of the problem in-depth. He presented a report containing valuable insights. The Church Officers considered the report and sent it to the Synods for information in November 1975. In January 1976, a policy decision was made at the 37th meeting of the Executive Committee with special reference to Wollo.

In a report to the 9th General Assembly at Nejo in April, I set out details of the policy decision as follows: "The main points of the policy decision were: 1) that the work of the Northern Area be placed under the EECMY at large as a Programme for the Church; 2) that the Programme be called the 'EECMY Evangelistic Outreach for the Northern Area'; 3) that initially, the Programme be for a period of three years; 4) that the Synods send experienced workers to the Area for a specific period of time to carry out the Programme; 5) that a special Fund be established for Evangelistic Outreach in accordance with the General Assembly's resolution at Yirgalem (1973); and 6) that the Programme be launched before the end of June, 1976." Even though the Synods failed, for various reasons, to act on the decision about workers, the policy decision is still in effect being extended from time to time.

As elicited in Pastor Jurgen Wesenick's report, the ancient Oromo culture and the Muslim religion had for several centuries pervaded the spirit of the Wollo people in a subtle manner; so much so that the people have not found it easy to open their hearts to the message of the Gospel. As a result, there could not be found more than one thousand Evangelical Christians in Wollo in 30 years, from 1958 to 1988. But there appears to be no alternative for the Church to continuing the work she had started, with faith and patience.

4. The Establishment of the Addis Ababa Synod
The Addis Ababa, Naqamté and Bako congregations were among the founding members when the Evangelical Church Mekane Yesus was constituted on the national level in 1959. They met in Naqamté in June 1961 to set up their own synod and called it 'Eastern Wollega and Shoa Synod.' They adopted their constitution and put it into effect at the same meeting. The term 'Eastern

Wollega' was applied to the area in Wollega lying between the Didessa and Gibe rivers with Naqamté as the centre. By 'Shoa' was meant that part of the Province extending from Addis Ababa to Ambo, Fiche, Debre Berhan, Adama and Woliso. It was also to include Bako. I was elected in November 1961 to be the Synod's first President. The membership of the Synod was then 1,758. The name was changed to 'Central Synod' in November 1968.

One main difficulty that became apparent in course of time was that it was not possible to plan one line of action due to the fact that the members of the Synod were partly town-dwellers and partly country-residents with differing ways of life and work. The fact that the majority of the administrators of the Synod lived in Addis Ababa and were only part-time workers, and that they were far from Naqamté and Bako made it difficult for them to adequately discharge the Synod's work. An additional difficulty came to light when the workers who were in Naqamté failed to cooperate due to rivalry and lack of respect for one another.

The population of Addis Ababa and its environs was growing year after year and, while the Evangelistic work in the countryside was proceeding at a gratifying pace, the work of the Mekane Yesus Church in the Capital was not seen to be conspicuous. The position of the congregations in Addis Ababa was the same as when they were established independently by the various missions on their arrival in Ethiopia. There was hardly anything to link them together except their faith. Some persons who strongly felt responsibility for the spread of the Gospel in the City, led by Secretary General Gudina Tumsa, were determined to unite the congregations in Addis Ababa which were under the Central, North and South Ethiopia Synods and set up one new synod. With this in view, the eight congregations in the Capital and the congregation in Debre Zeit met to make plans, beginning in 1966, to make plans. The idea grew steadily and the meeting was called 'Council of the Lutheran Congregations,' and Qes Gudina became chairman.

The activity appeared to slow down after some time, but due to Qes Gudina's efforts a draft constitution of the Synod was prepared after six years and presented to the 28th meeting of the Executive Committee in January 1974. The Executive Committee considered and amended the draft constitution, and directed that the Church Officers to call a convention of the Addis Ababa congregations to organize a synod; that the constitution and by-laws be presented to the convention for consideration and adoption and that, as soon as the synod was set up, the budget allocated to the Addis Ababa congregations as well as all movable and immovable property be transferred to the new synod.

In conformity with the Executive Committee's decision, the founding convention of the Addis Ababa Synod met in Addis Ababa on March 29, 1974, under my chairmanship. There were representatives of nine congregations on the occasion. Pastor Per Stjarne, who was one of the first leaders when the Addis Ababa Congregation was established half a century earlier, was present at the convention as a guest.

The founding convention went through the constitution and by-laws article by article and adopted them, after receiving explanations and making amendments. A nomination committee, consisting of one member from each congregation, was appointed to nominate the administrators of the Synod. It presented the candidates on March 30 and the convention, adding one candidate each, proceeded with the election. Qes Gudina Tumsa was elected to be president; Ato Fasil Nahom, vice president; Pastor Johannes Launhardt, treasurer; Fitaurari Baissa Jammo and Pastor Manfred Lundgren, members of the administrative council. The number of the Synods was thus increased to five.

5. The Strengthening of the Central Synod

It is fit to recount how Evangelistic Outreach was initiated in Naqamté before discussing the current state of the Central Synod. It is as follows:

After completing the translation of the Bible into the Oromo language and seeing it through the printing-press in Switzerland, the eminent native of Oromoland, Ato Onesimus Nesib, served for years as an elder of the Asmara Evangelical Congregation and an Evangelist. He then travelled to Addis Ababa in 1904 with his family and co-workers. He met Abba Mateos, then Archbishop of the Orthodox Church, who presented him to the Emperor Menelik. The Emperor gave him a pass to travel to Wollega and the Archbishop gave him a letter permitting him to preach provided his teaching was not at variance with the beliefs of the Orthodox Church. Onesimus arrived in Naqamté in April 1904. From there he proceeded to Nejo where the Governor, Dejazmach Kumsa Moroda (Gebre Egziabher) was residing at that time. Since his fame as translator of the Oromo Bible had preceded him, he was welcomed with great pleasure and honour by the Governor. He built him a dwelling house and a school near his own residence at Nejo. He also gave him a tract of farming land to help support him.

Onesimus and his co-workers started a school soon after and began to give formal schooling and instruction in the Gospel. In January 1905, Qes Gabre Sellassie Tesfa Gabir and his wife Woizero Sendeq Gabre Mariam were sent from Asmara to Nejo to assist Onesimus. As Onesimus preached the Gospel in Oromo and as they found certain things to criticize in his teaching, the Orthodox clergy at Nejo tried to lodge complaints against him to the Governor, but found no satisfaction from Dejach Kumsa. Since Onesimus was a man who would accept no belief outside the Gospel, the misunderstanding between him and the priests grew more and more acute. In the meantime, Dejach Kumsa had to return to Naqamté in November 1905, 18 months after the arrival of Onesimus. Not wishing to leave Onesimus behind, he took him and his companions to Naqamté. It thus became inevitable that the school at Nejo should be closed. The Naqamté Orthodox clerics, like those at Nejo, criticized Onesimus' preaching of the Gospel and accused him before Dejach Kumsa in the first instance. Obtaining no satisfactory decision, they got together with Amhara officials who were at Arjo and wrote accusations to the Archbishop against both Onesimus and the Governor. The two men were summoned to Addis Ababa and were compelled to appear before the prelate. After having him travel to the Capital two or three times, the Archbishop pronounced Onesimus guilty of offence and decided in 1906 that he should be put in shackles and his property confiscated. He then sent it to the Emperor for confirmation. He also advised His Majesty that Onesimus' followers and the Governor should undergo the same punishment. However, the Emperor put the prelate's sentence aside and commanded Aleqa Estifanos (later Chief Justice) to investigate the matter. Estifanos heard what the parties had to say and came to the conclusion that Onesimus had committed no crime. His offence was that he maintained that the Virgin Mary and the Saints did not intercede. The Emperor gave orders that Onesimus should preach no more and that he should be sent to the Ministry of Commerce to be given tests in language, accounting and handicraft to see whether a government job could be given him. But since he had no technical knowledge, he was allowed to return to Naqamté and earn his living by farming and trading. Onesimus was under strict control not to preach at any gathering of people and not to teach anyone even in his own house, except his children. He lived therefore under acute stress in Naqamté for almost 18 years.

Dr. Erik Soderstrom was the first Missionary of the SEM to arrive in Oromoland, having reached Naqamté in 1923 by permission of the Government to build a hospital and a school. For Onesimus, Dr. Soderstrom's arrival was a source of joy and the opening of a new chapter for work. The Evangelical believers in Naqamté were able to meet in the doctor's house with Onesimus without fear. Evangelistic work was started for the patients, the people who accompanied them to hospital and the employees. The number of worshippers on Sundays grew steadily and the doctor's house became inadequate for meeting. So a church was built near the hospital. It became the inception of the Naqamté Mekane Yesus Church. Onesimus preached in the Church and taught the Gospel every week until his death on June 19, 1931.

Thus, the hero of Faith who had laboured hard to translate the Holy Scriptures into the Oromo language and present them to his people and who had endured great suffering in his endeavour to proclaim the message of the Gospel to the people of Wollega, Onesimus Nesib, rested from his labours and went to meet his Lord and Saviour. The Evangelistic outreach he had initiated in the town of Naqamté has in course of time, spread out and grown into a major Synod and a means for the salvation of multitudes of human beings.

After the establishment of the Addis Ababa Synod in 1974, the Central Synod was left with the believers in Naqamté and its surroundings and those at Bako. This made it administratively weaker and difficult to obtain leaders. The president, vice president, and one council member who were residents of Addis Ababa, resigned in July 1975 and the Synod sustained more difficulty. And as the feeling of contempt and rivalry became more acute among the other workers, there could be no peace. This became an additional obstacle for Evangelistic work. Realizing that, the Church Officers appointed two committees in March and in July 1975 to make a detailed study of the situation. It became apparent that the basic problem was the disruption of the administrative structure. They therefore procured from the Western Synod for a short time the services of one person who had administrative experience and of another worker on a permanent basis. While maintaining the structure and the constitution of the Synod, the Church Officers determined to direct the Synod's work themselves and appointed a provisional administrative committee (PAC) to discharge the day to day work of the Synod. A committee consisting of seven members was designated accordingly in February 1976. They appointed Qes Gamachu Denu to be chairman of the committee and Ato Desta Buba to be vice chairman and gave them directives to initiate the work. After a few months, Qes Gamachu had to return to his work in the Western Synod and Ato Desta Buba replaced him as Chairman. An Evangelism Board and a Development Board were set up.

After some time, young men who it was hoped could be potential leaders of the Synod were selected and sent to the Mekane Yesus Seminary for Theological training. In due course, a number graduated and were ready for service. They were then made to acquire experience by working on the congregation and parish levels. As it was found to be necessary to revise and bring up-to-date the Synod constitution and by-laws, the Church Officers, in consultation with the PAC, appointed a study committee in Naqamté to go through the constitution and present an amended version.

As soon as the draft constitution was presented, the Church Officers examined it in detail, one member of the study committee being present to explain the amendments. Having made their own amendments both to the constitution and by-laws, they sent them back to Naqamté. Considering the geographical position of the Synod, it was recommended that the name should be changed to 'West Central Synod.' They gave directives to the PAC, in December 1979 that instruction and clarifications be given to all the congregations on the constitution and by-laws to enable them to understand their rights and obligations in readiness to elect their leaders.

Due to the fact that many congregations were new and the Synod was in an area where the situation was disturbed, it took two years to complete the process. Instructions were given early in December 1981 to ascertain whether all the congregations had been properly familiarized with the constitution and report to the Church Officers. They would then meet with the PAC, and the parish and institution leaders at Bako to evaluate the report and decide whether it was time to get leaders elected on the Synod level. The responsible persons met on December 10 to assess the situation and reported that it was possible to meet at Bako in the course of December to consult with the Church Officers, who decided to hold the meeting on January 1 and 2, 1982.

On December 31, four of the Church officers and one other person travelled to Bako and began to meet the following day with 19 representatives of the Synod in the Bako Mekane Yesus Church. After meditations, the Chairman of the PAC, Ato Temesgen Feisa, (Ato Desta Buba was then under detention) had presented a report and discussion had just been started when the administrator of the Bako-Tibbe sub-district arrived with the local deputy commissioner of police and a man who had come from the Ambo Security office and declared that the meeting contravened an order issued by the Government in a circular letter on December 16, 1981. He then stated that, in view of the fact that the Church was cooperating with the Bako municipality to supply piped water to the population, he had agreed that we visit the project but not to hold a meeting. The order transmitted to the government offices by circular letter was confidential and its purport was to prohibit meetings prior to authorization by the relevant government bodies. As he had officials who supported him at Ambo, the onus of the so-called contravention was passed on to us.

We contended that our meeting related to religious and development matters and that traditionally no permission was required for such a meeting; that the government order we were said to have contravened was not known to us; that it had neither been published in the press nor broadcast over the radio. We then told them that, if the meeting was not allowed, we were prepared to abandon it and depart. The administrator said we could go ahead with the meeting, and the police and security men, desirous to attend the meeting, stayed with us until 1 p.m. The administrator came in the afternoon to tell us to continue the meeting. Sometime later, he came back to tell us that he was proceeding to Ambo to report on the meeting to his superiors and requested that one of us accompany him and that we give him the loan of a vehicle. After consultation, we decided that Ato Temesgen Feisa go along with him and we placed a vehicle at his disposal.

The administrator came back from Ambo on January 2, and informed us that he had presented the case to the district administrator and that he expected to hear a decision by telephone that same day. No decision was received, so he requested again the loan of a vehicle to go back to Ambo and obtain a decision. We gave him one and he travelled to Ambo in the afternoon. (The return journey to Ambo is 250 km).

The district police commissioner who had arrived from Ambo that day and the local police commissioner came to tell us that we had to be taken into custody until an order was received from higher authority. A small bus was then brought and we were taken to the Bako Police Station. We were kept there until 6:30 p.m. and then taken to the 'qebele' meeting hall where it had been decided that we should pass the nights. They told us that we could get mattresses and blankets brought over from the Mekane Yesus compound and left. We had mattresses and blankets as well as food brought from the compound and slept there. The dust in the hall was horrible but we were compelled to lay the mattresses on it and sleep. We spent the days at the police station doing nothing from 7 a.m. to 6 p.m., had breakfast, lunch and supper brought from the Mekane Yesus compound and passed the nights in the 'qebele' meeting hall until January 6. The gesture of friendship and sympathy shown us by many residents of Bako during those four days by visiting us and bringing us food and drink is unforgettable.

On Sunday, January 3, we gave declarations to the police station that the purpose of our journey to Bako had been solely for the Church's business and for development work. The police commissioner informed us that he had been ordered to send the documents to Ambo and asked that we give him the loan of a vehicle to hasten the process. We acceded to his request and he left for Ambo on January 5. He returned in the afternoon of the following day and told us that he had been instructed to let us stay in the Mekane Yesus compound. He entreated us not to leave the compound and we returned to our place at 5 p.m. On January 7, we celebrated Christmas with the Bako Mekane Yesus Congregation.

Even though we had gone to Bako to hold consultations on the affairs of the Synod for two days, the fact that we were detained there until January 14 enabled us to go into the matters in depth. In addition to having fellowship by sharing the Word of God and uniting in prayer, we were of the opinion that it would be helpful to hold exhaustive discussions on the administrative structure of the Synod and its problems with the representatives. We therefore had separate discussions with each of the 18 persons present for two days and obtained the benefit of their views.

Although it was gratifying to note from the report of the Chairman of the PAC that the administrative process had been strengthened on the congregation level, it did not appear to us that the Synod was ready to take over responsibility. So we agreed that more time was needed for the parish leaders to continue to work at that level to acquire additional experience so as to be able to compete for leadership on the synod level. We decided and informed them that in the meantime the PAC should consist of the chairman, the secretary and the three heads of section. We enjoined that they guide the work of the Synod in accordance with the revised constitution and by-laws.

Since they knew one another well, we asked them individually to indicate their views as to who should be chairman and secretary respectively. The majority view was that Ato Temesgen Feisa should be chairman and Ato Berhanu Ofga'a, secretary. The two men were then interviewed and they agreed to serve for a limited period. Ato Faqadu Jiregna, Ato Feisa Negasa and Ato Mosisa Duressa were designated as heads of the Development and Evangelism and Treasury sections respectively and named, together with the two men, to be members of the PAC. We told them that this decision would take effect after it had been presented to and approved by the full meeting of the Church Officers.

Moreover, believing that it would help the future executive committee of the Synod to acquire experience in the discharge of its functions if a provisional executive committee were appointed to meet and consult every three months with the administrative committee, we resolved that the parish leaders and two persons to be elected by each parish council constitute an executive committee together with the administrative committee. The Central Office transmitted this decision to the Synod Office in due course.

On January 14, the Bako-Tibbe commissioner of police came to our compound to tell us that we had to go to Ambo at 5 a.m. the following day and appear before the court of justice. We started at the appointed time and arrived at Ambo at 8:30 a.m. We proceeded to the court of justice and appeared before the judge at 10:30 a.m. The prosecuting lawyer (withdrawing one person from the group who came from Naqamté), preferred a charge against 24 persons for illegally holding a prohibited meeting without permission from the relevant authorities. The judge registered our names and addresses and asked us whether we were guilty or not guilty. With one voice, we affirmed loudly that we were not guilty. As the article cited against us from the Criminal Code allowed bail, our defence lawyer requested that we be released on bail and, the lawyer for the prosecution having agreed, we gave surety. The judge ordered that we appear before the court again on February 5 and we returned to Addis Ababa. Even though our stay at Bako was longer than we had expected, we were able to look deeper into the state of the Synod and derive a better appreciation of the fact that the Gospel was being widely proclaimed and that many had been added to the Church through faith in the Lord. This gave us distinct pleasure and we praised our God for His inscrutable providence.

The court case dragged on for several months when we had to travel to Ambo from Addis Ababa and Wollega half a dozen times before the judge found us guilty of offence and imposed a fine of 100 Birr on each of us. We protested that we should not be penalized for a breach of an order of which we had no knowledge and that the article quoted against us from the Criminal Code had no relevance to the charge preferred against us. But he passed the sentence on us blindly, scoffing at the same time, that as knowledgeable persons, we should have known it. We realized that 'he was baking his own bread,' in Amharic parlance, i.e. he was trying to ingratiate himself with the high authorities so as not to endanger his livelihood.

We were of the opinion that it was an unjust sentence and appealed to the High Court. Not long after the case was taken to the High Court, the judge overruled the decision of the District Court judge and on November 22, 1982, declared us not guilty of the charge. He ordered that the sum of 2,400 Birr we had paid as fine be refunded to us. We received the amount from the District Treasury and the case was closed. The High Court judge marvelled greatly by what law the District Court judge could base his decision on a circular letter which the attorney of the District Court had not produced as evidence.

Following the appointment in January 1982 by the Church Officers of a new PAC and the decision that the Synod elect its own administrators in due course, the representatives of the congregations met in convention in Naqamté on May 7, 1983 and elected their leaders. The Synod was thus able to regain its autonomy. Having directed the work of the Synod until May 1983 by appointing a committee to guide the work from nearby and given it a revised constitution, the Church Officers reported to the Executive Committee with pleasure that the Synod had elected its leaders on May 7 in the presence of their representative, Qes Yadessa Daba, and that those elected were Ato Berhanu Ofga'a, president; Ato Gabbisa Baro, vice president; Sister Bodil Petterson, treasurer, and that they had taken over the work and started to discharge their duties.

Although it took the Central Synod over eight years to obtain trained leaders, it was obvious that its evangelistic activities were equal to those of the other Synods. When it was established in 1961, the Synod had only three congregations in Addis Ababa, Naqamté and Bako. Even though the Addis Ababa Congregation was separated from it in 1974, its work had spread not only in the Naqamté and Bako areas but also in the districts of Gudru and Arjo, Mecha and Jibat, and Limmu in Kafa. As a result, a large number of people had come to faith in the Lord Jesus and many congregations had been started. So much so, that in 1986, the number of believers had reached over 100,000. This astonishing growth was achieved through the efforts of the regular workers as well as the witness and endeavour of the voluntary preachers and evangelists. Praise be to the Most High for granting them such spiritual zeal and devotion.

22. DEVELOPMENT WORK OF THE MEKANE YESUS CHURCH

During my long tenure of office as President of the EECMY many tasks were accomplished by the Central Office, the Synods, and the Cooperating Missions and Churches for the growth of the Church, for the spiritual and physical well-being of the human person, and for nation building. As it is neither possible nor desirable to enumerate them all here, I shall record the ones I consider to be important by way of reminiscence, leaving the details for future historians of the Church.

Agricultural and Technical Institutions

1. The Bako Project

Bako is a small town built on the Nonno Gibe river and situated 250 km from Addis Ababa and 80 km from Naqamté. Formerly, the main road from Wollega to Shoa passed through the village of Billo in Wollega, crossed the Gibe and the wilderness and led to the Ghedo hill country. Travellers used to start from Billo or Ghedo towards evening and made every effort to escape the forbidding malaria and heat of the Gibe valley. Malaria was so virulent and often fatal that no traveller would lay down to sleep in the valley. I remember crossing the valley during the night when I came to school in Addis Ababa in 1925.

When the administration of the Italian invading forces began to build a vehicular road from Addis Ababa to Wollega, it aimed for Bako and not Billo, thus avoiding the wide Gibe valley and abandoning the old track. The position of Bako afforded an additional advantage as a convenient approach to Gudru. Bako being situated in the northern end of the Gibe valley near mountain slopes, the heat is not excessive. The severity of malaria has also decreased due to the growth of the population and the use of preventive medicines.

The SEM, which many years before the arrival of the aggressor had served the people by proclaiming the Gospel and running educational and health care institutions and which had been expelled by the enemy, was given permission to resume its activities after the restoration of the national government in 1941. It consolidated its work and continued to serve the people in Addis Ababa and Wollega. Observing that there was hardly any evangelistic or development work between Addis Ababa and Wollega, the Missionaries determined to start a development project at Bako and a clinic at Ijajji, and they took land on lease from the authorities. In 1952, they opened a small clinic in a rented house at the request of the population of Bako. The clinic at Bako was started by the Missionary nurse, Miss Ruth Perman.

The Government gave permission that land be leased to the Mission on the Gibe river adjacent to Bako for the planned development project and 80 hectares (two 'gasha') were leased through the Ministry of Education for a limited period. Mr. Thorsten Månson pioneered the work at Bako. Houses were built and the clinic was moved there in 1955. A school for the blind which the Mission had started earlier in Addis Ababa was moved to Bako in 1959. Since the land was wild jungle, clearing and farming was started in the course of that year. However, work on the project was properly begun in 1965 when the buildings for agricultural training were ready. The school for the blind was enlarged and began to give training in handicrafts in 1966. Training in domestic science was started in 1967 and the school for this purpose was completed in 1970. The trade school was enlarged in 1970 with the addition of an auto mechanic stream.

Thus the training programme in agriculture, mechanics, domestic science and health care to serve the population of Bako and the surrounding district, estimated to be from 80,000-100,000 persons, was gradually developed to its full extent in 1973. The full complement of the Bako Project was: 1). the agricultural school; 2). the school for domestic science; 3). the trade school; 4). the school for the blind; 5). the health programme; and 6). the demonstration programme. The outlay for the whole project was 1.231 million Birr. The funds were obtained from the LWF, the Swedish International Development Agency, and various Swedish Welfare Organizations.

The Swedish Mission had leased the land for a limited period and, as the time approached when the lease would be up, it became apprehensive lest the donors would withhold their aid and its service come to an end if the buildings were taken over with the land and used for purposes not intended for them. Its representatives, therefore, approached the Church Officers to acquaint them with their problem. After a discussion, we concluded that the only solution was to place the matter before the Emperor and plead with him to grant the land to the Mekane Yesus Church. While we were considering how to approach His Majesty, it transpired that the Emperor was proceeding to that area at the request of the Emperor's Representative in Wollega to visit a plantation he had started on the Gibe river opposite Bako. As soon as the date of the visit was known, we advised that Pastors Per Stjarne and Manfred Lundgren, who had lived in Ethiopia for many years and spoke Amharic fluently, should go to Bako and request His Majesty to visit the Mission's development project and, after he had seen what was being accomplished, tell him of their preoccupation and entreat him to grant the land to the Mekane Yesus Church to enable them to continue the development of the project with equanimity.

The Missionaries went ahead to Bako and made the necessary preparations and, on the Emperor's return from the Representative's plantation, paid their respects at Bako and requested him to visit their project. His Majesty readily acceded to their request and proceeded to the office of the project to listen to the briefing presented by Pastor Lundgren in Amharic. He then went around the project area at the end of which Pastor Stjarne told him of the Mission's predicament and that they would be reassured if the Emperor would graciously grant the land to the Mekane Yesus Church; the welfare organizations would then not hesitate to give financial aid for administrative costs as well as for the further development of the project. The Emperor told them that he had been gratified with what he had seen and that he would consider the matter.

As soon as His Majesty returned to Addis Ababa, I was summoned to the Palace. As I did obeisance and approached him, the Emperor said, "Do you want land?" Observing that I was nonplussed at the sudden and veiled question, (our Swedish friends had not yet returned from Bako to report to us), he said that he had been pleased with what he had seen of the development project on his recent visit to Bako and of his admiration of Pastor Lundgren's Amharic. He then informed me that it was his pleasure to give the land to the Mekane Yesus Church, and forthwith commanded the Secretary to write the order. I remarked that the project was giving signal service to the population of Bako and the surrounding district. I then thanked him for the grant, bowed and retired.

On taking delivery of the land from the Ministry of Education, we leased it to the SEM in January 1965. When they heard this, the Missionary Society and the international welfare organizations were so pleased that they generously gave large amounts from time to time to help in the further development of the project. The Bako Project became so well-known for its usefulness beyond Bako district in Wollega and Shoa as far as Addis Ababa that many young people resorted there to learn skills. Broken-down vehicles, especially from Wollega, were taken to Bako for repairs.

While the project was thus engaged in serving the community in various ways and just before the change of regime took place, the workers and the trainees, who were acquiring experience after the completion of training, made it their business to take every occasion to trouble the director and the instructors, causing them to be dragged to the police station and detained, charging them with one thing or another, and generally trying to obstruct the proper functioning of the project.

In April 1974, I stopped at Bako on my way to Wollega on Church business, and I called the workers to a meeting to warn them that, if the disturbances continued, the project would be closed down and that, in the event of this happening, they and the people would suffer. I then tried to admonish them to live in peace. But they were emotionally disturbed by the state of affairs in the country and unable to dispassionately assess the dire consequences that might ensue. They therefore persisted in their antagonism and we parted without reaching an understanding. From what I heard later, the workers met again that evening and debated whether to detain the President or not; but because the majority opposed the proposal, I was not placed under custody! (It would appear that, even though I was no longer in office, the fact that I had been a government minister had made them apprehensive). For my part I spent a peaceful night ignorant of what was being plotted against me and continued my journey to Naqamté on the next day.

On my return from Wollega, I was taken into custody by the military and when I was released after nine months, I learned that the disturbances by the workers had reached such a climax that the project could no longer be operated and that the instructors had resigned and returned to Sweden. The Church which had taken over the project and was therefore responsible for it was being accused before the authorities and brought to court. In the end, we made it clear to the authorities that, in view of the fact that the project had been established to serve the people and not for profit, it should neither be troubled nor accused by the workers before the courts; that, for fear for their lives, the instructors had abandoned the work and left the country, and that therefore we had no alternative but to close down the project. We then offered them to take it over if they wished. They agreed to take over parts of it and we retained the Church building, the clinic and the school for the blind, transferring in the course of 1975 the other sections and the training equipment, the farm and several residential buildings. We discharged the workers. On learning the firm decision of the Church, those persons who had given so much trouble were alarmed and some of them, expressing their remorse, entreated us to reinstate them. Even though they were remorseful and crying, proving the truth of the Oromo proverb, 'remorse and tail trail behind,' it was a tragedy they brought on themselves and no way could be found to reverse the decision. They therefore dispersed and endured much suffering.

It had been decided before all this happened to purchase more land for farming because the 80 hectares graciously granted by the Emperor had been fully developed. We discovered on inquiry that there was wasteland on the Gibe river belonging to the heirs of Prince Sahle Sellassie. I requested His Majesty in May 1967 to give orders for us to buy 800 hectares (20 'gasha'). Two-hundred and forty hectares were purchased for 40,000 Birr with the assistance of the SEM. It took a considerable time before the legal formalities of the sale could be finalized to take delivery of the land. A change of regime ensued in the meantime and we could not start any type of work on the land. It remains the preserve of wild animals as formerly.

The Gospel has been preached in Bako and the surrounding district for many years. As a result, a large number of people have believed in Christ and joined the Mekane Yesus Church. Every year, thousands have been treated at the Bako Clinic; instruction in health care has been given to mothers in homes and villages; a mobile clinic has been taken around in the district to serve in midwifery, medical treatment and instruction in hygiene. The school for the blind has been helped to be self-supporting and is carrying out its functions in cooperation with the blind in other parts of the country and with assistance from abroad.

Evangelistic work has spread widely in Chalia district of Shoa Province and its vicinity through a clinic started 35 years previously by the Swedish missionary nurse, Miss Margit Pettersson, at Ijajji and later taken over by Miss Ruth Perman who encouraged the initiation of Evangelistic outreach in the Ijajji area.

The village of Ijajji is 220 km from Addis Ababa on the Wollega highway. No less than 25,000 persons have believed in the Gospel as a result and a large Church building has been erected at Ijajji. The number of believers is increasing every year and the parish has become the largest in the Central Synod. The clinic has since been transferred to the Government and is continuing to serve the people.

2. Wondo Gennet Agricultural and Trade School

As the South Ethiopia Synod and the NLM had planned to establish an agricultural and handicraft school in the Wondo Chabicha area of the Haikochina Butajira district of Shoa, I requested the Emperor that '10 gasha' (400 hectares) of forest land belonging to the 'Haile Sellassie I Welfare Foundation' be sold to the Church. It was granted and we bought the land in 1964 for 112,000 Birr. A Norwegian agricultural expert, Mr. Trygve Haugland, was invited through the Mission to build an agricultural and trade school. He lived in a caravan with his wife in the dense forest for about one year and constructed buildings for classrooms, living quarters for students and teachers and for workshops. Instruction was given to married farmers who came with their wives and children from districts in Sidamo and Gamo-Gofa. They were given practical training for about a year in improved farming methods, and others were instructed in handicraft. The women were given lessons in health care and hygiene together with reading and writing as well as instruction in vegetable gardening. The children were given normal classroom tuition. After training was thus given to many farmers and their families in farming and other matters to improve the quality of their lives and instruction to young people in handicraft skills, we had to hand over the school to the Revolutionary Government which confiscated it in 1976.

3. Wuchale and Selekleka Agricultural Schools

Agricultural training schools were built at Wuchale Tisabalima in Wollo and at Selekleka in Tigrai with the assistance of the ALM. Married farmers went along with their families and were trained for almost one year in improved farming methods and learned reading and writing. Their women were taught to read and write as well as in hygiene and vegetable gardening. A considerable number of people had taken advantage of the training before the Revolutionary Government confiscated the school at Selekleka in 1976 and the one at Wuchale in 1977.

4. Dabena Trade School
The Western Synod, in cooperation with the GHM, purchased a piece of land in 1964 near Bedelle town in Bunno district of Illubabor for a school. Buildings costing not less than one million Birr were erected in 1966. Machinery as well as handicraft equipment and instructors were brought from Germany and vocational skills were taught for about a decade. The 'qebele' authorities forcibly took over the school in 1977 and the plan which had been intended to help in the improvement of the quality of life of the provincial population was suddenly nullified!

5. Nejo and Chalia Trade Schools
The Western Synod, with the help of the SEM, had built a trade school at Nejo in Wollega beginning in 1972 for almost one million Birr on a ten-hectare site granted by the Government. Equipment and other implements were installed and instructors brought from Sweden. The school was dedicated in April 1974. A number of young people were trained and the population of the area benefited from the various pieces of furniture it produced until the Revolutionary Government confiscated it in 1982. Similarly, a smaller trade school has been built at Chalia Eka in Wollega and is serving the district under the supervision of the Western Synod.

6. Arba Minch Hostel and Vocational School
The Emperor who had been considering how something enduring could be done for the people of Gamo-Gofa raised the matter when I was at the Palace one day in 1965 and commanded me to make inquiries as to whether Missionary Societies could establish an institution with assistance from the Government. I asked the director of the NLM which had been working in that Province for many years in cooperation with the Mekane Yesus Church to set up an institution at Arba Minch. He told me he would write to the Mission Board in Norway to consider the matter.

In January 1966, when the King of Norway came on a state visit, the leaders of the Mission accompanied His Majesty here and paid a visit to me with the Mission director. I raised the matter with them and they promised, after a discussion, to place the request before the Board on return to their country. They would inform me of its decision. They were certain that the fact that the Emperor had the matter at heart would concern the Society all the more. The director some time later informed me that after due consideration the Board had decided that it would build a hostel for 150 students from the districts who had to attend the government secondary schools at Arba Minch.

I reported this to His Majesty and, expecting that the establishment would be enlarged, in course of time, requested on June 9, 1966, to give order that from 40,000 to 50,000 sq m of plot be given and that financial assistance be granted for the project. This matter took more than six years to bring to completion in spite of the fact that it was started at the Emperor's behest and his Representative in the Province had actively supported it. As it appears to me to be a striking example of the red tape we had inherited from the West, I will present the story in some detail.

The Emperor's Representative in Gamo-Gofa Province wrote in September 1966 that the Emperor had commanded that the plot be registered in the name of an Ethiopian association. I wrote back that it be registered in the name of the Mekane Yesus Church and the title deed delivered to us. I informed the Norwegian Mission Board of the fact in November. With respect to the financial assistance to be given towards the construction of the buildings, I wrote the Board in December that the Representative had indicated he would submit the amount necessary to His Majesty as soon as the work had been started. I then stated that I was prepared to take delivery of the plot if they were ready to begin construction work in line with their promise, now that the Emperor had made a free grant of 50,000 sq m. They informed me in January 1967 that they agreed to start work on that basis, and I requested the Representative in February to hand over the plot to the President of the South Ethiopia Synod and to finalize as soon as possible the matter of financial assistance due from the Government.

The Representative wrote in April to say that he had caused the site to be handed over to the Synod President and that, in compliance with my suggestion that more land be reserved for the enlargement of the Mission's work, he was holding in reserve 25,000 sq m adjacent to the plot granted us. Soon after we took delivery of the plot, I sent a reminder to the Mission Board in June to commence construction with due speed. The General Secretary wrote in July that he was hopeful that the necessary funds would be allocated in August or September, even though it would take time to prepare the plan.

In the meantime, the Mission's representative presented an application to the Ministry of Education in September for a permit to establish a mission station at Arba Minch in accordance with the law. As the reply was delayed, he went to the Ministry to remind the official in charge of the request and to show him the plan of the buildings to be set up. The official told him that no permit could be issued unless he received a letter from me confirming the Mission's application. I wrote to the Ministry in November indicating that we had taken delivery from the Representative of 50,000 sq m of land graciously granted by His Imperial

Majesty for the construction of a hostel and a vocational school and that funds were available for construction work, and urged that a permit be issued as soon as possible. The request was granted and a hostel and residential houses were built.

After this was settled, it was found that the available plot was not adequate for the construction of the vocational school. The Director of the Mission came in August 1968 to recommend that I obtain the grant of additional land. I informed the Representative of the matter within a week and asked him that the 25,000 sq m kept in reserve be given for the purpose. After a correspondence lasting 16 months, I approached the Emperor on January 6, 1970, to grant an additional 22,000 sq m to the Church with a title deed. His Majesty readily consented to my request and I received an order from the Ministry of the Pen on the same day. I forwarded it to the Representative with a covering letter dated January 14 asking him to hand the plot over to the Synod President. He wrote back on March 13 to inform me that he had had 72,000 sq m of plot registered in the name of the Church and that the title deed had been delivered. It was now possible to start the construction of the vocational school after a delay of 18 months!

As the site had again been found to be inadequate, it was not possible to erect additional buildings for the hostel and to expand the agricultural workshop as had been planned. So the director of the school came in February 1972 to ask me to obtain a grant of more land. I presented a plan to His Majesty showing the plot and the position of the buildings and requested that another 15,000 sq m be given us. The Representative happened to be in Addis Ababa at the time and was asked if land was available. He answered in the affirmative and the Emperor ordered that a plot be given to the Mekane Yesus Church to the extent I had requested together with a title deed. I received an order from the Ministry of the Pen to the Representative on March 16 and we got delivery of the plot and construction was resumed. The Missionary Society undertook to defray all the building expenses and the work was completed in the summer of 1972. The whole amount spent for the project was well over 800,000 Birr and the annual running expenses were estimated at the time to be more than 73,000 Birr.

The construction of the 'Arba Minch Hostel and Vocational School' was thus completed and made ready for service. It was decided to hold a dedication ceremony and I went to Arba Minch with some colleagues. The Emperor's Representative, Dejazmach Aimero Sellassie Abebe, formally opened the institution on October 22, 1972, in the presence of many provincial officials, a number of Missionaries and a large number of people. I spoke in part as follows at the dedication ceremony: "I should congratulate ourselves that this day is the beginning of a new chapter in the history of development of Arba

Minch and Gamo-Gofa Province. We are exceedingly happy that the Evangelical Church Mekane Yesus and the Norwegian Lutheran Mission have together been instrumental in making available this development project which we are gathered to dedicate. Praise be to the Lord Jesus Christ who blessed our efforts to complete this project, planned and executed for the glory of His Name and the extension of His Kingdom. I tender grateful thanks to His Majesty the Emperor Haile Sellassie I for taking the initiative and giving the directive that this institution be established for the welfare of his people, and for granting this large plot of land on which the buildings are erected. I express my sincere wish that He be vouchsafed health and a long life. I also thank sincerely the Representative of Gamo-Gofa Province, H.E. Dejazmach Aimero Sellassie Abebe, for the assistance he has afforded in the execution of this project ever since he was informed of the plan six years ago. It is my firm hope and prayer that this institution, which we are dedicating today with great joy and thanksgiving and which is a special ornament for the growing town of Arba Minch, will be a source of well-being and true development for the entire Ethiopian people, and especially for our fellow-citizens who live in the Provinces of Gamo-Gofa and Sidamo, and that it will be a place where our Lord and Saviour Jesus Christ will be praised from generation to generation."

7. Henna Rural Development Pilot Project

As the Mekane Yesus Church had been greatly concerned in 1970 about rural development at the time when the LWF's 5th Assembly was held at Evian, France, a document was prepared and sent to the Assembly for consideration. The tenor of the document was to convey the Church's considered view that, rather than spend huge sums on major projects of no benefit to many people, it would greatly help to improve the living conditions of a large number of people in the rural areas if attention were given to the development of smaller projects.

Such documents were presented to the delegates and observers at open meetings in the course of the Assembly through the Commissions of the Federation. I presented the document of our Church at the open meeting conducted by the Commission of World Service. Even though the many persons who had heard it gave it no thought, the chairman of the Commission and of the meeting, my friend Dr. Paul C. Empie, took to the idea and decided that it should be tried. He pledged to try to procure funds from the American Lutheran World Relief, whose delegate he was, to launch a five-year rural development project. He informed the officials of the Federation accordingly and we were asked to present a programme for the development plan.

As soon as I returned to Addis Ababa, I reported what had taken place to the Church Officers and we set about to find an agricultural expert to prepare a plan. Mr. Eigil Sanna of the NLM who was working in the South Ethiopia Synod was indicated and the Synod and the Mission were requested to transfer him to the Western Synod on a temporary basis. This was granted and the study of the plan as well as a search for a locality where it could be executed were set afoot. Since, of the various provinces in which the Mekane Yesus Church conducted its activities, Wollega was the one in which many farmers had their own free holdings and it was believed that they would be in a better position to take part in the project, it was decided to start the pilot project in Wollega and that the station be located in Ghimbi district. The site considered to be suitable by the experts for the station was situated on the Henna river, 500 km from Addis Ababa on the Wollega highway. A 'gasha' of land I had there was indicated and I presented half of it to the Church to build the station, retaining the other half for the tenants who lived on it.

As soon as we informed the LWF Headquarters that the plan for the five-year pilot project was ready and the site for the station had been secured, Dr. Empie made the necessary funds available. It was decided that the development work be conducted in line with the directives issued by the Ministry of Agriculture, and construction work was started on the site in March 1972. The first employees were recruited in May and the agricultural expert arrived at Henna and started work in September. The development programme was intended to cover the sub-districts of Boji Dirmeji, Boji Choqorsa, Nejo and Jarso in Ghimbi district and meant to serve 25,000 families, i.e. about 225,000 individuals.

The expert took the indigenous grain seeds in the area and planted them on different plots without fertilizer and by mixing differing quantities of fertilizer with the soil. After they began to sprout, he invited the farmers from time to time to observe the differences in the growing crops, thus demonstrating to them not only by word of mouth but by making them see with their own eyes and understand the advantage that could be derived. The farmers understood the aim at once and many asked that fertilizers be given them on credit. The Church was ready to respond and sent fertilizers from Addis Ababa for distribution on credit to all who asked for them. As the crops began to be gathered in, no less than 10,000 farmers were assembled at Henna on Saturdays to receive instruction from the expert and to see for themselves the result obtained from the various grain seeds.

To save the farmers time in travelling due to the distance of the station, four sub-stations were set up to begin with, and crowds of people visited them every Saturday to take advantage of the instruction given and benefit from what they heard and observed. Many a farmer was happy to obtain four or five times the usual yield by the use of fertilizers on his field which enabled him to begin improving his life-style. Noticing this, farmers in other districts requested for the benefit to be extended to them as well. Before long, the programme had been operated for about three years when the nationalization of all land in Ethiopia was proclaimed in 1976 and the farmers' associations were formed. The Church thereupon had to hand over the Henna Rural Development stations to the farmers' associations.

8. Didessa Dimtu and Dilla Settlement Programmes

A couple of settlement programmes should be mentioned in conjunction with the development projects. The Mekane Yesus Church, through the Central Synod and the SEM, had established a settlement station at Didessa Dimtu on land granted by the Government, in the belief that several 'Shanqella' (Nilotic) clans who lead nomadic lives in the Didessa valley of Naqamté district could be given a better chance in life if they were assembled in villages on fertile land in the valley and given instruction in farming and other skills by experts. It has been indicated in this Part above that a plan had been executed with this in view and that a group of the nomadic population had been persuaded to settle in villages and allotted plots of land to cultivate under the guidance of agricultural experts.

For generations, the Shanqellas of the valley and the Oromo hill dwellers had been at enmity with one another. As a result, the Shanqellas were fearful and were rather slow in accepting the friendly invitation to settle in one place. However, by patiently endeavouring to convince them that the Church had approached them in the spirit of Christ and in love, a few consented to settle around the station, to build houses and to learn farming skills. Seeing these and observing what they were doing other nomads came along to join them. Landless Oromo farmers from the hills were also brought down to the valley to settle with them and engage in cultivation. Accordingly, the village grew and became lively. Formal classroom teaching was started and a clinic opened. The village population grew steadily and various types of instruction were given to the settlers until 1980 when the project was confiscated by the government authorities.

Many people in Ghimbi district had endured hardship for lack of arable land and the Church, through the Western Synod planned to settle farmers along the Dilla river. A settlement project was prepared and presented to the LWF for funding. Funds were granted and many families from the neighbouring districts went down and settled in the river valley. They engaged in improved cultivation under the guidance of experts and were thus able to improve the quality of their life-style. Upon completion of the period set for the programme and the farmers having become self-supporting, the settlement station was transferred to the Government in 1985.

I wish to record in this connection my tribute to the LWF and the Lutheran Welfare Agencies for continually providing funds and expertise to the EECMY over many years. My gratitude is especially due to the Directors of the LWF Department of World Service, Dr. Bruno Muetzelfeldt and Dr. Brian Neldner, and to Dr. Christa Held, Director of the Community Development Service, for their untiring efforts to procure funds for our many development projects. I had watched with admiration, Dr. Christa Held's feminine tact and persistence in inducing the Welfare Organizations around the world to grant funds for the numerous activities of our Church and of the Lutheran Churches in Africa and Asia.

23. CONFISCATION OF THE CHURCH'S CENTRAL OFFICE BUILDING

I have recounted in this Part above that the Mekane Yesus Church had constructed in 1963 her first Central Office building and a youth hostel on a plot granted by the Emperor Haile Sellassie adjacent to the Addis Ababa Mekane Yesus Church. As the Church grew very fast year after year, the administration also expanded and the office building became quite inadequate. The Church Officers therefore decided that a larger and more commodious building should be constructed. A suitable site was purchased not far from 'Mesqel Square' and our Partner Churches and Missions as well as the Donor Agencies were requested to contribute to the building fund. The Synods were also asked to contribute as much as they were able. All our friends made generous contributions.

The aim was to set up a seven-storeyed building to accommodate the increasing offices with two floors of flats at the top to help alleviate the housing problem for senior staff. Construction was started in the course of 1974 but could not be completed in the time stipulated due to the disappearance of the foreign contractor. Nevertheless, we moved into it in January 1978 before it was quite ready for fear of confiscation. It was a time when the 'Derg' was busy appropriating any solid and well-built edifice it fancied. Our new office building which cost over one million US Dollars to construct is solid and much to be desired. But, for some reason, we were allowed to retain it until November 1981.

One day in the middle of that month I looked out of my office window in the new Central Office building and saw a stout man with a couple of other men on the top of the adjoining low building which had served as the radio studio of our Church before it was confiscated in 1977 with RVOG. The man was surveying our seven-storeyed office building. I inquired who he was and was told that he was Colonel Tekka Tullu, Derg Member in charge of Public Security. I had a faint feeling that he was after our building but gave it no further thought that day.

He came to the Central Office the following day and asked to see me. The secretary came to tell me that a man in uniform desired to see me. I asked her to show him in and in a few minutes he stood before my desk and announced that he was Tekka Tullu. I greeted him and asked him to take a seat. He said he desired to see the inside of the building. I took him to the lift and we went up to the top of the seventh floor from where a good view could be obtained of that part of the City. We then walked down the stairs and I explained to him that the two upper floors were being used as flats for members of the staff. He noted that all the other floors were being used as offices. I then took him to the ground floor and the basement where we had the filing cabinets, office supplies, books, committee rooms and a chapel.

On the day after Tekka's visit, a Colonel Solomon who was in charge of the administration of rented houses appeared and told my secretary that he wished to see me. He was shown in and as soon as he sat down he announced that he had been instructed by higher authority to inform me that we had to vacate our office building in 24 hours as it was to be used for urgent government business!

I told him it was Church property and that the law had exempted Church property from confiscation. He could say nothing to that but that the building had to be vacated in 24 hours. I remarked that the order was so sudden and the time allowed so short he could not possibly expect us to remove everything out of the seven floors; could we not be given more time? I added that I had to have a signed letter from whoever gave the order for confiscation. He said he could not produce a letter but repeated that he had been instructed to tell me that the building was urgently needed and had to be vacated in 24 hours. I then asked him to give me a written order himself since I did not have a mandate to hand over just by word of mouth a building that had cost the Church over two million Birr to construct. He warned me that anything found in the building would be confiscated if not removed in the time stipulated and left my office.

I immediately called my colleagues to my office and told them of the difficulty that was suddenly facing us and asked them to inform our Church people by telephone to bring along every available vehicle to transport all movable property elsewhere. The alarm was flashed around to all our Congregations and Missions as well as to those in the districts outside the City. They came rushing with trucks from as far away as Kambata to take part in vacating the building. They all worked like a Trojan with nobody telling them what to do. It was amazing to watch some of the Missionaries carrying on their backs filing cabinets full of paper down the stairs. The Colonel who sat all day at the entrance of the compound and watched our people at work wondered how it was that everything was being done so quietly and smoothly. He inquired who was in command. The reply was that it was God's Spirit who was in command. He marvelled and exclaimed he had never seen such discipline.

In the event, everything was removed from the building by sundown and we gathered in the chapel for prayer. The members of the staff were talking to one another in agitation; some were in tears. I asked someone to read a verse from the Gospel of Luke, "Do not be afraid, little flock, for it is your Father's good pleasure to give you the kingdom" (Luke 12:32). I then exhorted them not to lose heart; our Lord had prepared a kingdom for us and the loss of a building would not make any difference to the quality of our service to Him and humankind;

it was my conviction that our office building would be restored to us some day. We would come together again the following morning to deliver the keys. I was pleased to see that they appeared comforted and departed in hopes of one day coming into our own.[4]

On November 16, we were all assembled in the forecourt of the building when Solomon appeared to demand the keys. I had to tell him that I was prepared to hand over the keys only against an official receipt. He was irritated and shouted at the women workers who stood solidly around me to leave the place. No one budged. He then said no receipt would be given; I had to give him the keys at once or else he would call for armed assistance to enforce his demand. I said he was free to do what he wished but I would not deliver the keys unless he gave me an official receipt signed by him and sealed with the seal of his office. He must understand that I could not hand over a building which had cost the Church a considerable amount of money without a receipt. He rushed off in a huff and telephoned somewhere from his office to obtain assistance. Apparently, the response was negative because he came back alone and asked me to talk to him in private. We went aside and I reiterated that I would give him the keys only against a signed and sealed official receipt. He had no alternative but to go back to his office and write out an official order and a signed and sealed receipt. I read both to my colleagues and the Church Officers countersigned the receipt. I then handed him the keys and we left the premises for good.

Not long after this incident, we noted that Col. Tekka Tullu had been favoured above his peers by being allowed to take over the building and turn it into the headquarters of his so-called Public Security. This was no doubt a reward from his 'Communist Leader' for despoiling the property of a defenceless Church.

24. APPENDICES

1. The First All-Africa Lutheran Conference

It will be remembered that I indicated in Part 9 above that the proceedings of the Conference of Lutheran Christians held at Marangu in Tanganyika from November 12 to 22, 1955 would be narrated in another Part.

On my return from Tanganyika, I submitted on December 3 a report to His Majesty the Emperor and, since I feel an additional report on the matter is not called for, I present it as follows:

"Your Majesty: Having attended, with Your Majesty's gracious consent, the

---

[4] The Central Office was returned to the EECMY on September 5, 1997 by decision of the Federal Democratic Republic of Ethiopia.

Conference of African Lutherans which was convened at the town of Marangu in Tanganyika, I humbly present a brief report on the events which took place at the Conference.

"I left Addis Ababa at 12 noon on November 10 by aircraft in the company of other Ethiopians and arrived in Nairobi after a flight of four hours. I spent the night in Your Majesty's Consulate General. I proceeded to Marangu by bus at 9:30 a.m. on November 11 and, after travelling all day, arrived at Marangu at 7 p.m. The Conference began at 8 p.m. on November 12 with public worship. On November 13, some 10,000 Christians gathered at 10:15 a.m. and an opening service was conducted with prayers and a sermon. In the afternoon, about the same number of people assembled at 3 p.m. and the Governor of Tanganyika, Sir Edward Twining, delivered a welcome address. He was followed by the Paramount Chief of the people of the district (the Chagga) who welcomed the Conference. Then, I read Your Majesty's message which the gathering received with applause.

The provisional chairman of the Conference asked me to convey their deep appreciation to Your Majesty. The message was again presented to the Conference a few days later when a draft reply was read and adopted with applause to be telegraphed to Your Majesty.

"The Conference began its formal deliberations on Monday, November 14, and five presidents were elected to conduct the Conference; of these, three were Africans, one was an American, and one a European. Your servant was one of the Africans. The number of delegates from the various African countries, including the Missionaries was about 150. Besides, there were persons from America, Germany, Sweden, Switzerland and England. The African countries which sent delegations were Ethiopia, Cameroon, Nigeria, Liberia, South Africa, South West Africa, Rhodesia, Madagascar and Tanganyika.

"From November 14 to 22, the Conference met from 8 a.m. to 10 p.m. and discussed in detail the evangelistic work performed by the followers of Luther in Africa. Generally speaking, the activities of the Missionaries are gratifying and fruitful, but it was clear from what was said and left unsaid that the Africans living in South Africa are experiencing great difficulties due to racial discrimination. The South African blacks were averse from speaking about the oppression they were enduring because of differences of race, the reason being fear of being subjected to worse treatment on returning home. In spite of the fact that it was apparent that the spirit of equality and unity prevailed in the Conference where the people believed they were genuine Christians who followed Luther's faith and example, it was painful to observe at times that differences engendered by race and colour were looming large. The reason being that, although it was a novelty for most of the Africans at the Conference to talk to the whites freely even in spiritual matters, some of the blacks had to speak candidly about the obstacles placed in the way of the extension of the Kingdom of Christ and the whites, not accustomed to hear such remarks from the blacks, showed feelings of displeasure. Even then, appreciating the truth of what was said, the whites got over it quickly. The Africans were often reluctant to repeat in the Conference what they told us plainly outside. We understood this was because they did not trust one another or were unwilling to offend the Whites who paid for them to go to the Conference. When such situations arose, the Ethiopians were able to act as their spokesmen by expressing views on matters under consideration without apprehension. And the whites appeared to accept without demur statements by Ethiopians which perhaps might have offended them had they been uttered by other Africans.

"Even though differences in race and colour created by man's malice sometimes disturbed the people who were assembled in the interest of spreading the Gospel of Christ, there were occasions when all differences were submerged and Christ alone was supremely in evidence and people were absorbed in considering how human beings, irrespective of their race and colour, could return to their Creator. All in all, it could be said that the Whites as well as the Blacks learned many useful things both for themselves and for the work of the Gospel. They were also more acquainted with one another and came to more understanding with one another before they separated.

"The Africans were so wary of expressing their views in the Conference that the leaders grew apprehensive and all gladly accepted the suggestion that the Africans meet on their own and present ideas which they thought would be indispensable for the spread of the Gospel in Africa. They met behind closed doors twice and asked me to chair the meetings. It was impressive to see those persons who were unwilling to speak before the whites in the Conference vying with one another to express their views at the two meetings. It was decided, after exhaustive discussions, that the following points which all agreed were essential be presented to the Conference:

'1. The African delegates feel that it is very desirable that an institution for advanced theological education be established as soon as possible in Southern Rhodesia, Liberia or Ethiopia.

'2. Until such an institution is established, it would help greatly the young Churches if scholarships were granted to enable deserving Africans to study in European and American universities.

'3. It is desirable that local institutions in the various countries in Africa be developed more fully so that the standard of training for teachers, pastors and evangelists may be more in line with the rising educational standards in Africa.

'4. It is strongly felt that it would strengthen the young Churches in Africa if more responsible positions were filled by Africans to enable them to realized more fully their responsibility for the work.

'5. It would greatly help the propagation of the Christian faith in Africa if Missionaries in their relations with Africans showed a better example of fighting all kinds of discrimination.'

"The Conference adopted the five points quietly even though it was observed that some of the Missionaries, especially those from South Africa, could not hide their displeasure. It was then moved by an American and decided that the unanimous views of the Africans should not be debated at Marangu but presented to the Lutheran World Federation, the convener of the Conference, for further consideration. The leaders told me outside the Conference that the points were good and that the LWF would consider them very seriously. One of them said that the statement on racial and colour discrimination should have been stronger. The draft discussed at the first meeting was stronger but it had to be toned down as set down under point 5 because some of the delegates were ill-at-ease and even suggested that it be dropped.

"Many of the African delegates expressed pleasure at seeing Ethiopian delegates at an African conference. They are hopeful that Ethiopia will meet and encourage its African neighbours from time to time. I believe it is a good beginning that Ethiopia has joined them on spiritual matters which, in the present circumstances, is the only ground on which all Africans are able to meet. Many Africans who have had no chance to meet and speak face to face to Ethiopians will have the opportunity to learn many things about Ethiopia, and Ethiopians will likewise learn about the other African peoples from their nationals. This process will generate better understanding and goodwill, and help dispel divisive reports and preconceived ideas about Ethiopia being in Africa but not of Africa.

"It appears that Tanganyika is more fortunate than the other East African territories because it is administered under the trusteeship of the United Nations. In line with the present trend, it is likely to demand independence like the Sudan. One wonders, though, whether it will achieve it so easily, seeing that the British are planning to create an East African federation by uniting Kenya, Tanganyika and Uganda."

The message from His Majesty the Emperor Haile Sellassie reads as follows:
"As Sovereign and Head of Church of one of the oldest Christian states in the world, We send Our greetings to the many Christian faithful assembled at the All-Africa Lutheran Conference which meets at Marangu, Tanganyika.

"The strength of Ethiopia's devotion to the Christian faith is attested not only by Christian traditions of great antiquity and continuity, but also by the vigour and importance of Christian education in modern Ethiopia. In addition to the thousands of Orthodox Church schools, the many Lutheran and other Missionaries whom Ethiopia has welcomed in a spirit of Christian brotherhood have served to strengthen the ever-vital force of Christian ideals. For 90 years

Lutheran Missionaries have carried on in Ethiopia their labours of selfless devotion to the ideals of Christ, and the heritage that they have left and are fostering today is rich and a goodly one. The cause of international friendship and understanding has had no more devoted servants.

"It is our hope that this epoch-making conference, the first to meet in this vast Continent, where peoples of so many different religious faiths live side by side in harmony, may serve to further this same cause of friendship and understanding. The antiquity and strength of Christian tradition in Ethiopia have been due to the preservation of these qualities by the Ethiopian leaders and people. May this Conference serve to advance the cause of Christianity in Africa through the same spirit.

"May the wisdom and inspiration of the Saviour of mankind guide you in all your deliberations and bless your labours. - Addis Ababa, November 8, 1955. Haile Sellassie I, Emperor."

When the Emperor's message was read at the open air meeting of the Conference to 10,000 Tanganyika Christians and interpreted into Kiswahili on Sunday, November 13, the assembly received it by acclamation. The American provisional chairman, recalling that Ethiopia was an ancient Christian nation, stated that the Emperor had demonstrated that he was a follower of Christ and a great leader when, on his victorious return from exile, he urged his subjects not to avenge themselves on their former enemies but to treat them kindly in the spirit of Christ. The message was again presented to the conference a few days later and it was agreed that a reply be sent by telegram as follows: "His Imperial Majesty Haile Sellassie I, Emperor of Ethiopia: We tender sincere thanks for Your Majesty's inspiring message. We pray that the Lord may use Ethiopia as an instrument for the extension of the Gospel of Christ in Africa: The Presidents of the Conference."

Having delivered the Emperor's message, I presented the keynote address of the Conference under the heading, "What do we Expect?" Believing that it reflects the thoughts and feelings of the period, I quote it here in part.

"What do we expect? We expect before long the Gospel to be preached in the whole of Africa. We expect myriads of Africans to turn to the Cross of the Lord Jesus Christ and find the fullest freedom which only faith in His Name can give. We expect this spiritual freedom in Christ for Africa to be followed by the relatively lesser but none the less essential freedoms to enable individuals and nations to live with dignity as human beings and at peace with their fellow-men. To this end, I shall place before my fellow-Christians the example of my own native land. Ethiopia is a land where the light of the Gospel of Christ has shone for the past 1,600 years, sometimes brightly, sometimes rather dimly, but without interruption, and who can deny that this fact of the supremacy of the Gospel among my people has been the greatest factor in the preservation of our national freedom and political independence? Indeed, until the turn of the last century we Ethiopians when we had to go to war never did so for mere patriotism but for our faith in Christ which we value above patriotism and life itself. To preserve this faith we struggled against the invader for over 1,000 years. I submit this as a classic example of the truth of the words of our Lord Jesus when He said: 'Seek ye first the Kingdom of God and His righteousness and all these things shall be added unto you.' All earthly blessings will be added unto us abundantly if we are members of God's Kingdom, and all Africa will surely come by her own in God's good time through faith in Christ Jesus.

"We expect that the Gospel of Christ will be preached throughout the length and breadth of Africa within half a century and that multitudes of our fellow Africans for whom Christ died will be gathered to His Heavenly Kingdom. We expect that this wonderful deliverance of the spirits of our fellow Africans from the shackles of superstition, fetishism and idol worship will go hand in hand with their deliverance from the shackles of ignorance, poverty, indignity and servitude.

"Fellow Christians from whichever part of Africa you may be coming, be of good cheer for your salvation in the fullest sense draweth nigh. The prospect for the future of our Continent, although not as smooth and as bright humanly speaking as one would wish for, is very encouraging indeed. But whatever the odds, it is incumbent upon each and every one of us as followers of Christ to tackle the task before us in the spirit of Christ. If we do so, it is my firm belief that we shall get through triumphantly to the glory of Him Who loved us and gave Himself for us and to the good of our fellowmen everywhere.

"Finally, what do we expect from this great assembly of Christians of like mind? We expect these ten days of Christian fellowship to be a time of great inspiration and blessing in things eternal to help us fulfil our respective tasks whatever and wherever they may be to the end that the Kingdom of our God and of His Christ may be further extended with greater faith and vigour so that the return of our blessed Lord may be hastened to gather His faithful to Himself and give peace, His peace, to our distracted world."

Dr. Frederik A. Schiotz, former LWF President, relates in the story of his life, 'One Man's Story,' that when I said, "Fellow Christians from whichever part of Africa you may be coming, be of good cheer for your salvation in the fullest sense draweth nigh," the British Governor of Tanganyika who was sitting on the stage with the LWF leaders, turned to him and whispered, "It will be a long time in coming." Dr. Schiotz comments in his book, "But there was more reality in the buoyant Christian response of the African delegates to Mr. Abraham's (Ato Amanuel's) confident hope than in the governor's scepticism." He then recalls that "in 1964 Tanganyika became Tanzania, an independent nation under the leadership of President Julius Nyerere." It is a fact of African history that a large number of African peoples achieved independence not long after the conference.

I mention this incident here because I see it as an apt illustration of the fact that it was hidden from the consciousness of many a member of the British ruling class, even after India had regained its independence in 1947, that Britain's imperial power which had held sway over a quarter of the globe for many years was fast drawing to its close.

2. The Second All-Africa Lutheran Conference

When I discussed in Part 10 above the Second All-Africa Lutheran Conference which was held in Antsirabé, Madagascar, in September 1960, I stated that the story would follow in another Part. As I believe that the report I presented to the Emperor on my return home will better reflect the proceedings at the meeting than I can now write, I present it here below:

"Your Majesty: Having attended the Second All-Africa Lutheran Conference with Your Majesty's consent and generosity, I humbly submit a report of the proceedings of the Conference as follows:

"The Conference was held in the Malagasy town of Antsirabé from September 8 to 18, 1960. The town is situated 170 km to the south of the Capital, Tananarive. Since it has hot springs and is situated in hilly country, it has become a health resort where many people go for rest. One large hotel and many smaller ones serve the visitors. Many of the delegates from Africa stayed at the Hotel des Thermes. Mohammed V, King of Morocco, lived at the hotel during his exile.

"The opening session of the Conference took place on September 8 when 250 delegates from Africa, Europe and America were assembled. President Tsiranana of Madagascar graced the opening of the Conference and the dinner with his wife and spoke on both occasions. He expressed pleasure that the Conference of Christians was held in his country soon after Madagascar regained its independence and thanked the Missionaries for the spiritual and material benefits they had brought. He then said that it was his hope that the Missionaries, in cooperation with the nationals, would make every effort to bring to the Church of Christ to about three million of his countrymen to whom the Gospel had not been preached. (It is reported that there are two million Christians in Madagascar, half of whom are Protestants and the other half, Catholics).

"President Tsiranana is a Catholic but, as he informed us when a few delegates and I visited him in Tananarive, he is a 'liberal' Catholic. He did not understand why Christians were divided to such an extent since in his view the aim of all Christians was to believe in Christ. It was his wish that all Christians unite to lead to the Gospel of Christ the peoples who live in darkness. It was therefore his earnest desire that all Christians go and work in Madagascar.

"Following the President's speech, I presented the keynote address. I began by saying that the Ethiopian people had been overjoyed to witness the liberation from alien rule and the attainment of political independence of many African countries since the meeting of the first All-Africa Lutheran Conference at Marangu, Tanganyika, almost five years earlier; that it was our expectation that at that rate most of Africa would be free from alien domination within a decade; that, since 'where there is the spirit of Christ there is liberty,' the Africans were able to find the ideal and the endurance in their struggle to regain their political independence due to the fact that the Gospel of Christ had been imparted to them. I then asked whether the African peoples were as eager to achieve spiritual freedom as they were to be free from alien rule and attain political freedom. Although I was aware that the Missionaries who had been labouring among the Africans in all parts of the Continent for so long were better able to answer the question, I felt it was a much harder task to convince the people of Africa of the desirability of attaining spiritual freedom. The reason I put forward for this was, as stated by the Apostle Paul, that the warfare of the person who struggled to enter into the Kingdom of God was not only against flesh and blood but against the god of this world. The task was bound to be all the more difficult because the message of the Gospel was first carried to most parts of Africa by members of the white race and since the white Western powers had dominated the Continent in the past century and often failed to show Christian love to the people, many Africans had come to consider Christianity to be the white man's religion and instrument. It would therefore take time to convince the Africans that Christianity was not specifically the religion of the peoples of the West but the oracle of God's love to humankind. Now that the African was coming back to his own with dignity, and with the spread of education which would enable African youth to see the difference between what was good and what was ill for them, it was my hope that they would realize that the Gospel of Christ was given by the Creator for the salvation of humankind irrespective of the colour of their skin.

"I then expressed apprehension that, since many Western people had for the most part abandoned the Christian faith, trusting to modern science and philosophy which were leading them to hopelessness and destruction, and since Africans were turning their backs to the old futile beliefs of their fathers and pursuing the teaching of science and technology which they admired and were eager to acquire, there was grave danger that they might be trapped by their philosophy and unbelief and lose the way to real life, thereby rendering their labour fruitless and their lives meaningless. Nevertheless, I exhorted the foreign Missionaries to persist in their most important task and to demonstrate their Christian love by the way they spoke, acted and lived and the Africans to work diligently more than ever before to lead our peoples to the knowledge and faith of Christ. It was my belief that African civilization would be of a very high order if it were based on the Gospel of Christ.

"Referring to the pretensions of the white people living in parts of Africa that one type of man was superior to another type because of the fairness of his skin and that they were therefore ordained by Providence to lord it over the black peoples of Africa, I expressed my credo that, believing the words of Holy Scripture that God made of one blood all nations of men (Acts 17:26), there could be no superior race on this earth. It was true that circumstances, geographic, climatic and other, might arouse some peoples to greater efforts and achievements than others; but that did not change the essential equality of human beings as proved by the Ethiopian people throughout history. I was glad to note that this was the view not only of scientists but also of most of the so-called white race and I hoped that that section of the white race which was obsessed by the notion of superiority would see the error of its ways and modify its policy which if persisted in might bring in its train a terrible racial holocaust in Southern Africa.

"Finally, in connection with the theme of the Conference which was based on the words of our Saviour (John 14:6), 'Jesus Christ: the Way, the Truth and the Life,' I affirmed that in my view and belief all roads followed by men without Christ led to disillusionment and death; that all other types of truth not based on Him were irrelevant travesties; and that all life not guided by Him was meaningless. The session was brought to a close with this and the Chairman departed. The delegates retired to their rooms.

"The Conference began its deliberations on the following day, September 9, by electing four presidents and four secretaries. The presidents were one Ethiopian, one Malagasy, one Tanganyikan and one South African. One of the secretaries was an Ethiopian. Your humble servant was the Ethiopian chosen as one of the presidents. After the election of the leaders of the Conference, the subjects prepared for discussion were successively presented during the following days and the delegates exchanged views on them. They were then passed on to the committees appointed to frame resolutions based on the discussions. The last two days were devoted to thorough discussion of the draft resolutions at the plenary sessions when the Conference amended and adopted them. They were then recommended to the African Lutheran Churches and to the Lutheran World Federation for follow-up and implementation. It became apparent in the course of the discussions that the problems faced by the Christians in the various countries were similar, even though more pronounced in some countries than in others. As a result the delegates had little occasion for differences of view. When they sometimes seemed to be at variance, it turned out to be due to misunderstanding or misconception, and agreement was obtained when explanations were given by those who understood the points at issue. I am glad to report to Your Majesty that both the Africans and the Western participants told us repeatedly that the Ethiopian delegates have given valuable assistance in this regard. Aware that the people of Ethiopia were more developed in political as in religious affairs, the delegates desired to know and to follow the viewpoints of the Ethiopians whenever difficulties arose at this Conference and at the previous one.

"The main points considered and decided upon at the Conference to be operative in the various countries or studied for consideration at the third conference to be held five years later were as follows:

"1. Since Christians share citizenship in the countries of this world, it is incumbent on the individual Christian to witness the love of Christ to all men by word, deed and Christian living to the end that his duties for the well-being of people in his area and for the extension of the Kingdom of Christ are evident to all. In view of the fact that he shares his citizenship with those outside the Church, the Christian has to make endeavours that the service he renders to his country in all spheres is superior in quality to that of others. It is the duty of the Churches to prepare plans and educate Christians to give the best service possible to their countries as people committed to their faith.

"A pastor should not be directly involved in politics but he and his church should react to society and civic government regardless of party lines in accordance with the Word of the Gospel and in faithfulness to the truth. The Church should discriminate between what is beneficial or detrimental to the nation and be ready to speak out boldly on what is in the people's interest. It should encourage Christians to participate in all areas of civic life insofar as the Christian conscience permits. It should point out the fact that every Christian holds dual citizenship, in God's Kingdom and in the kingdom of the nation of his birth, and impress on him that loyalty to God never contradicts the best interests of any nation.

"2. The Conference confirmed that the Lutheran Confessions recorded in the Book of Concord by the early Fathers, Martin Luther and his co-workers, taking the Holy Scriptures as the basis and rejecting the foreign elements that had crept into the Catholic Church, were still relevant and the best doctrinal foundation for the faith of the Evangelical Christian. Realizing, however, that the Confessions did not give complete answers to problems that had confronted the Church since Luther's day, especially in modern times, it expressed the view that studies should be made by the Churches, in the light of the Word of God, on various matters with which they were faced and with which the Confessions did not deal, and report their findings to the next All-Africa Lutheran Conference. The Churches in each country should appoint committees to effect the studies. Endeavours should be made by the individual Evangelical Churches in each country to achieve unity before initiating ecumenical dialogues on questions of faith in order to enable them to speak with one mind and voice.

"3. The Conference felt that the Churches could not dispense with medical work as it was an expression of Christian mercy. Up to then all institutions had been run and subsidized by the Missions, and as the Africans were now trying to form indigenous Churches with African leadership, these Churches ought to take also more responsibility for medical and welfare work; it was suggested that the Churches should spend from five to ten percent for this work.

"It was further suggested that the Churches should make better use of the possibility of evangelization in the hospitals, and the congregations should organize regular visits of the sick in hospitals and in the homes. It was also suggested that possibilities of further training overseas for able Christian medical assistants and nurses be explored and scholarships granted. Until then, it was emphasized that more medical Missionaries should be sent from overseas. In the light of the growing need for Christian physicians in Africa, the establishment of a Christian Medical College was recommended.

"4. It was recognized that a better and deeper knowledge of God's Word was necessary for Evangelical Christians both to be able to defend their faith with knowledge and to explain it to unbelievers. It was therefore recommended that all the Churches make every effort to get teachers trained for theological schools. To this end the Conference appealed to the Churches in Europe and America as well as to the Lutheran World Federation to give scholarships for the training of pastors and teachers in Theology.

"5. Since there were millions of adults in Africa who could not read and who would remain illiterate unless helped by the Church, and since they would never experience the power and joy that came from reading the Word of God for themselves, and since moreover there were not enough books available in Africa and those available were not answering to the needs of Africans, the Church in Africa should provide as an integral part of its programme adequate facilities to enable its illiterate members to cross over to the world of literacy. It should also make every effort to secure African writers to provide suitable literature for Africans.

"6. Seeing that pastors give too little time to the teaching of the Word, this often being limited to the Sunday sermon only; that some pastors devote time to other gainful pursuits because of inadequate congregational support; that some pastors hesitate to assume the responsibilities of congregational leadership; that some pastors lack confidence in the laity; that the laity often assume that it is only the pastor or other paid Church workers who should assume responsibility for the work of the Church, not believing every Christian has a personal call to be a steward; that they fail to recognize that stewardship is more than Sunday offering and that it includes time and other resources in everyday life; that they lack motivation regarding life's basic purpose and goals because they lack spiritual certainty; that they fail to see that all of one's life is sacred before God and that in consequence they fail conscientiously and with bold confidence to put the things of the Kingdom of God first in life's relationships.

"It was therefore resolved that ways be sought for a greater emphasis in Bible study using methods that would most adequately meet the needs of people in daily life and acquaint them with the teachings of Scripture regarding stewardship; that methods be adopted for an effective distribution of responsibility among the Church members that they might discover the joy of work in the Kingdom of God; that pastors not be hampered in their ministry by details of administrative work and other tasks that the congregational members could assume; that pastors be encouraged to keep aware of the implications for the Church of civil and political developments.

"7. Realizing that the task of the Church was primarily to proclaim the love of God to all humanity, and the task of the individual Christian was to proclaim this love in all his relationships with his fellowmen, and recognizing that the Church has had a strong influence on culture and economic life throughout the past centuries, it was recommended that the Church concern itself more actively with the social and economic life of the nations.

"In order to enable themselves to do so, the Churches might recommend to the congregations to establish trade schools, introduce small industries, conduct agricultural experiments and demonstration projects in order to encourage the use of improved farming methods, aid needy and unemployed individuals to establish themselves in farming, business or other self-employment projects, and encourage congregational leaders and members to increase their contributions by various methods such as tithing, larger offerings, special donations, etc.

"8. In view of the fact that the schools established by the Missions were being nationalized and that the young people, absorbed in the pursuit for secular education, were in danger of being indifferent to the Church; that Christian instruction in nationalized schools was restricted or even practically eliminated and that Christian principles were apt to give way to a secularized atmosphere which was influenced by political, social or educational ideals from sources other than the Word of God, it was recommended that the Churches be encouraged to examine their existing educational institutions in order to render a really effective Christian instruction to the future generations of Churches members; that, where the Churches operate a system of schools with government aid, special care be taken to reserve sufficient time for Christian instruction to give practical, concrete and living instruction which helps students, to relate Christian living to their everyday life; that the task of Christian education, although taken up in most Churches in Africa mainly by the schools, should be seen under its other vital aspects as well, which among others are that Christian education begins in the homes by parents, and especially mothers and preachers should be given continuous help in the educational ministry; that, in view of the critical situation of young people all over Africa, the pastors should have consultations on this important matter, funds should be collected to establish student hostels, especially in large cities, for work among young people.

"9. Whereas today division and strife among men was such that the sin of discrimination against men on the basis of race, culture, nation or tribe must be pointed out and spoken against; that the evil of discrimination divided men and, as such, was also an obstacle to the work of the Holy Spirit among men and the spread of the Gospel of love; that the will of Almighty God, as revealed in His Son, our Saviour Jesus Christ, in His Holy Word and by His Spirit of grace manifesting itself among men was to call upon all men to live as children of God in brotherly love and fellowship; and as Christians who were one body in Christ could not claim always to have been free from forms of discrimination against men and penitently in Christ confessed their guilt.

"It was resolved that the Second All-Africa Lutheran Conference accept that we were under obligation to remove from our midst all vestiges of discrimination against men on the basis of race, culture, nation or tribe; to bear witness to the world and all men that all attitudes and practices of racial discrimination were sin and evil which could not be countenanced by either our Creator or man himself, and must be replaced by an attitude and practice of love and equality among men; and to respect the right of all nations, peoples and Churches to be free and to exercise the gifts with which God had endowed them, and to request all Lutheran Churches everywhere to pray and work for the effective application in our midst of the foregoing resolution by the help of Almighty God."

"After the main points indicated above and other related matters were presented and adopted, Dr. Sigurd Aske who is negotiating with Your Majesty's Ministers on the establishment in Addis Ababa of a radio station, called 'Voice of the Gospel,' by gracious permission of Your Majesty's Government, presented a report. He stated that according to a professional survey Ethiopia was found to be the most ideal country in Africa for radio transmission and that, since the purpose of the station was radio evangelism for Africa and Asia, the 'Voice of the Gospel' would serve not only Africa but also the peoples of the Arab world, Iran and South Asia. He expressed great gratitude to Your Majesty for granting a franchise to build the radio station in Addis Ababa. He further reported that he was hopeful that a contract under which the station was to operate would be signed this month and that the work would soon be started in earnest. (Dr. Aske has arrived in Addis Ababa with us to sign the contract).

"The Conference was gratified to note that the radio station would soon be established and gave praise to Almighty God that many millions of the peoples of Africa and the other continents who have no other means of hearing the Message of the Gospel would before long be able to hear the Word of God in their own homes.

"We informed the Conference that it was Your Majesty's good pleasure that the Third All-Africa Lutheran Conference be held in Addis Ababa in 1965 and extended an invitation in the name of the Evangelical Church. The Conference accepted the invitation with pleasure and expressed its thanks to Your Majesty and to the Evangelical Church Mekane Yesus.

"Sunday, September 18, was the last day of the Conference and the Christians living in Antsirabé and its neighbourhood attended an open air meeting at 2 p.m. and heard addresses. The speakers to the crowd of believers estimated to be over 7,000 were Ato Emmanuel Gabre Sellassie and Dr. Birkeli, General Secretary of the Norwegian Missionary Society. (It was Dr. Birkeli who five years ago came here to request Your Majesty to send a message to the First All-Africa Lutheran Conference). Dr. Birkeli preached in Malagasy since he was born and grew up in Madagascar when his Missionary parents worked in that country and spoke the language like one of the people. This marked the end of the Second All-Africa Lutheran Conference and the delegates returned to their respective countries.

"Your Majesty: my observation at this Conference has given me the impression that the leaders of the African Evangelical Churches have in the past five years acquired maturity both in outlook and action, and are striving to liberate their peoples spiritually in the same way as the political leaders have tried and are still trying to free their countries in the political sphere. And the Missions have realized that the Africans are determined to assert their freedom in all spheres and that consequently the best thing for them to do in the interest of the extension of the Gospel is to relax their former predominance and work with them as helpers. Nevertheless, in the same way as the political leaders are convinced that their political freedom does not mean much unless they obtain economic assistance from foreign governments, the African Church leaders realize that their work will not be much developed if the financial assistance and expertise of the Missions are decreased. It therefore appears certain that the two sides will understand each other and cooperate more than ever to exert their efforts to extend the Kingdom of Christ among the African peoples.

"Even though Ethiopia is a self-sufficient country, Your Majesty had the foresight many years ago to realize that the task was immense and decided that the Missions should be invited to Ethiopia to preach the Gospel and at the same time take part in Your programmes of education and health care as a result of which thousands of Ethiopians have passed from unbelief to belief and from ignorance to enlightenment. They are now an asset to their people and in process of acquiring a better quality of life in all respects. In view of the fact that even Ethiopia, where the Gospel has had the predominance for centuries, is benefiting by the aid provided by other Christians, it may be said that, had they had no assistance from the Missions, countries like Madagascar and Tanganyika would still be living in darkness and without adequate education, deprived of leaders of the calibre of Nyerere in consequence.

"With this in mind, the young African Churches are asking the Missions not to discontinue their assistance. It is evident that the Churches in America and Europe, which had sent out Missions originally and are still doing so, have set their mind on continuing assistance lest the work of the Kingdom of God for which they had laboured so hard goes to ruin.

"I hazard the view that there is promise of the light of the Gospel shining all the brighter among the Africans if both sides continue periodically to meet in conferences and consult with each other as it will lead to better mutual acquaintance, understanding and goodwill which in turn will develop Christian love. - Addis Ababa, September 24, 1960."

When I went to the Palace the next day, His Majesty told me that he had read the report and commented, "You should have been a bishop!"

3. The Third All-Africa Lutheran Conference

I have recounted in Parts 9 and 10 above that, at the initiative and with the LWF leadership, the All-Africa Lutheran Christians had been assembled for the first time in African history in November 1955 in the town of Marangu in Tanganyika (now Tanzania) and that the Second All-Africa Lutheran Conference had been convened in September 1960 in Antsirabé, Madagascar, for the Christians to get more acquainted with one another and deliberate over questions of mutual interest. I have also indicated that the Mekane Yesus Church had, with the Emperor's consent, extended an invitation for the Third Conference to meet in Addis Ababa.

Ato Emmanuel Gabre Sellassie, President of the Mekane Yesus Church, reported to the 2nd General Assembly of the Church which met in January 1961, that the Conference had accepted the invitation. It was decided that contributions be collected from the Synods and the Missions annually to meet expenses in connection with the Conference and an ad hoc committee was appointed to start preparations.

Another preparatory committee was set up by the LWF Commission on World Mission which consisted of members from Ethiopia, Tanganyika, and the Federation to prepare a programme for the conference. This committee met in Addis Ababa in May and October, 1964, and elaborated the programme. It was determined that the theme of the conference be 'A living Church in a changing Society.' Qualified persons were requested to present papers to the Conference on various questions.

The Conference met in Africa Hall from October 12 to 21, 1965, and was attended by about 250 delegates and observers. The Emperor was present in Africa Hall on October 13 and addressed the delegates as follows:

"We welcome to Our Capital the delegates of the All-Africa Lutheran Churches and also those members of the same Church who have come from the United

States of America, Europe and Asia. It is Our duty to be among you at this moment and to open the Conference.

"It is gratifying to recall that after nearly 1,500 years of division in the Christian Church, venerable Heads of the Oriental Orthodox Churches assembled together in this very Hall in January of this year for deliberations on Christian Unity, the spread of the Teachings of the Gospel and World Peace. World Church leaders have also been frequently assembling in other countries to discuss the responsibilities of the Church of Christ and how to execute them efficiently in order to promote closer relations and cooperation among themselves. It has given a sense of satisfaction to see that Christians and their leaders, realizing the need for closer relations and aware of their great spiritual responsibilities, have in our time come closer in the promotion of their noble cause.

"Peace, universally heralded by the Angels at the Birth of Our Saviour, has become even more necessary to mankind than ever before. The alternatives confronting the governments of today are no longer peace or war, but peace or the annihilation and complete doom of mankind. Therefore, it has now become the noble responsibility of Christians and peoples of other faiths and their leaders throughout the world to pray and to work hard for the preservation of world peace.

"It is not an exaggeration to say that the spread of the teachings of the Gospel in Africa and Asia by various Christian Missionaries in the past centuries has served as a guiding factor and instrument for the freedom and independence enjoyed by many Africans and Asians today. St. Paul has said, 'where the Spirit of the Lord is, there is liberty.' Many of the present day distinguished leaders of the newly independent African States are men who received their education in Church schools and who, inspired by the teachings of the Gospel on human freedom, succeeded in liberating their peoples after patient and great struggle. When we look at this unchallengeable fact, we can clearly see that all their tireless efforts and sacrifices in this glorious struggle were not in vain.

"Although the Ethiopian people were among the first to receive Christianity and have, with great sacrifices, protected and sustained their faith and human rights, including their independence up to the present day, it is an established fact that in the past hundred years foreign Evangelical Missionaries have greatly assisted many thousands of Ethiopians. Moreover, it is also a fact that they have brought up and educated many Ethiopians among whom, We are happy to see, many are placed in responsible posts and are serving their country with diligence and devotion. Along with the Missionaries' assistance towards the spread of modern education and the betterment of the health of the people, their contributions towards the building of hospitals and the running of clinics is not a matter to be overlooked. Besides teaching the Gospel, they have also given all types of disinterested aid throughout the world. In the social field, in morality, education, food and clothing, these Missionaries have stretched their helping hand to Africans, Asians and to other peoples of the world.

"Motivated by the teaching of Christ as recorded by St. Mark, 'Go ye into all the World and preach the Gospel to every creature,' We are happy to see that the Lutheran World Federation has succeeded in building and establishing a radio station in the Capital of Ethiopia, the ancient island of Christianity, to spread the teachings of the Gospel to the peoples of Africa and to those of other countries.

"We thank the Almighty for the great services that the Station has been rendering to Ethiopians and other Africans in particular. Our own Missionaries, spread out within our country, are making use of this medium to preach the Gospel which has been the tradition in the past. It is Our hope and wish that it will continue to be the light of the Gospel to many people for many years to come. In its great task, Our support and that of Our Government has never been and will never be withheld.

"We do not believe that the religious and social problems that you members of this Conference are going to discuss are less significant than the political and economic problems confronting the governments of Africa. However, since the Holy Scriptures have taught us that every thing can be accomplished by those who have faith, We hope that your few days of deliberations here in Addis Ababa on spiritual and social problems will be successful through the guidance and the power of Our Saviour. We wish you a pleasant time with your Ethiopian brothers and sisters during Your stay among them. May God Almighty bless Your deliberations."

The Conference divided the delegates into three sections and directed them to study in detail the main presentations, and prepare draft resolutions for its consideration and adoption. The draft resolutions were then discussed, amended, and recommended to the Churches and the LWF for implementation. The salient points of the recommendations were as follows:

1. Independence and Partnership
The independence of a church is a gift given to it by God as it grows into a fuller realization of its calling and a more mature sense of responsibility to its mission. The term independence, however, must be understood within the interdependence of all Churches in the one Church of Christ and the dependence of all members of the Body of Christ on Him who is the Head of the Body. Such independence does not assume that the Church does not need the brotherly help of other Churches in fellowship, advice, personnel and finances.

Any help or assistance given by an older Church directly or through a Mission agency to a younger Church is to be seen as an act of communion and cooperation of two Churches as fellow members in the Body of Christ. Partnership is an understanding between the Churches (young and old) to pray and work together in the unfinished task of bringing the Gospel to the whole world. This means being partners in the mission of the Church to the world.

It was recommended that the older and younger Churches be urged to foster such partnership and be encouraged to utilize the services of the LWF in working out the practical aspects of the partnership in any given area.

2. Institutionalism and the Preaching of the Gospel

1. There is no easy answer to the question, "What is an institution?" An institution could be defined as a pattern of behaviour or a line of action that is perpetuated from one time to another. A building is something of an institution but it is not an institution unless it serves some purpose. What goes inside the building may be the institution rather than the building itself.

The subject of "institutionalism," however, is much bigger than what is commonly known as institutions associated with buildings. It does not appear that Jesus and His intimate Twelve wore any special robe to distinguish them from common people; yet, some Christians do. The robe, therefore, is a kind of institution. Holy Communion is not a man-made institution, but once-a-month communion is man-made.

2. The fact that God has worked through our man-made institutions does indicate what God can and does do through earthen vessels, but we must be on our guard lest we equate our institutions with God's;

3. The Church ought to be continually scrutinizing her institutions, re-examining their purposes, their potentiality, and their accomplishments. "The Church is subject unto Christ," and as such must continually remain in subjection to Christ. It can thus be concluded that institutions need not be a hindrance to the proclamation of the Word.

It was therefore recommended:

1. that each Church, synod and congregation ought to re-examine every institution which forms a part of their Church life, including the very organizational structures of the Churches themselves;

2. that they should seek to determine whether, in the Gospel proclamation, present institutions are best used as they are, or whether they need to be modified so as to cope with new challenges, or whether they should be discarded in order that new institutions might take shape;

3. that they make a continuing effort to keep every institution in subjection to Christ and His Word, as through these institutions they proclaim His Gospel and manifest His love with their lips and their lives.

3. The Lutheran Church, Other Churches and "the Christian Church"

1. The unity of the Church is found in Jesus Christ our Lord, through whom all believers are children of the Father. Our unity is the gift of the Holy Spirit, a unity in which we as Christians live with all other Christians. Our unity in Christ is no to be equated with the organizational union of Churches.

2. The call to Christian unity is expressed most clearly in Jesus' high priestly

prayer, in which He prays for the unity of His people so that the world may know Him as the One sent from God (John 17:21). God's mission in the world requires the unity of His Church.

3. We are guilty of causing disunity in the Church in several ways:

a) where we misunderstand and misinterpret, where we add to or reduce the message of Scripture, there we set obstacles to unity;

b) pride in whatever form, be it confessional, national, class, personal or ecclesiastical keeps us apart;

c) the fear of losing our traditions, which is lack of faith, prevents us from receiving greater blessings.

4. We do not believe that the unity of the Church is dependent on unity in organization or in ceremonies. We do believe that a faithful Christian Church must submit itself to the Scriptures as the only source and norm of Christian teaching and practice, and that Church union therefore must be based on agreement in the essentials of the Gospel as the way of Salvation and in the Sacraments.

5. We are agreed that we can help to heal the disunity of the Church in several ways:

a) by careful and prayerful study of the Scriptures and criticism of our Church life in their light;

b) by a friendly and understanding attitude toward other Churches and a willingness to learn from them;

c) by serious dialogue and a common search for Theological agreement with other Churches;

d) by cooperation with other Churches in all matters in which we together can serve God's mission among men.

It was resolved that the above statement be called to the attention of the Churches here represented, and further, specifically that it be recommended:

1. That since we have nothing that we have not received by grace alone, the Lutheran Churches in Africa seek to enter into dialogue with other Churches that we may share this faith with them;

2. That the Churches examine themselves and the Confessions to find whether it is really the essentials of our faith that hinders union with other Churches, or simply our outward customs and organizational problems.

4. The Ministry of Word and Sacrament

The Church lives by her communion with Christ, realized by the means of grace given by Him through the Church's ministry. Unfortunately, there were many congregations in Africa which were cut off from the sustaining principles of spiritual life because they lack the full ministry in their midst. Often Western patterns of ecclesiastical offices not applicable in the African situation have been followed uncritically and have therefore delayed the evaluation of a properly functioning Church.

It was recommended:

1. that the Churches be urged to reconsider their traditional policy with regard to the prerequisites for ordination and to the institution of the ministry in the ecclesiastical structure;

2. that the Churches pay attention to the possibility of creating a variety of offices, to each one of which a specific task is assigned under a clear commission, and that everything is done to prepare and nurture such people for their ministry;

3. that the Churches pay serious attention to the possibility of a "tent-making ministry," that is to select, in view to ordination, Church members in secular occupations who are faithful, apt to teach and well thought of by outsiders (1 Timothy 3). They should be trained on a part-time basis over a long period.

5. Congregation and Family Life

As the theme indicates, our immediate concern is related to the congregation's role in the building up of a Christian family life. Many Christians in Africa can testify that the Gospel has brought a completely new spirit in family relationships, both between man and wife and between parents and children. On the other hand, there is ample evidence that factors such as urbanization, industrialization, migratory labour, excessive drinking and our own failure as congregations have created the complex problems that exist today in many families in our midst.

In order that our congregations may be increasingly instrumental in fostering Christian family life, we make the following recommendations:

1. that in the preaching and teaching strong emphasis be laid on the fact that the home is the local point of Christian nurture, and that the daily example of both father and mother is basic in all such nurture;

2. that strong efforts be made in each congregation to interest the parents in having their children active in Sunday School;

3. that pastors and members of congregations be made aware of the fact that one of the greatest contributions the local youth groups can make to family life is to provide a place where young Christians can become acquainted;

4. that one of the basic aims of the women's organizations should be to provide training for Christian motherhood and family nurture;

5. that each congregation be constantly reminded of its deaconal responsibility to help the families in its midst, i.e. the poor, the sick, widows, orphans, strangers and refugees to the best of its ability.

6. Education for Christian Living and Stewardship

In recognizing the Church's responsibility to provide Christian nurture to her members and to proclaim the Gospel message to the world, we see this to be a continuous and continuing educational process going on throughout lifetime, from the cradle to the grave.

It was therefore recommended to the Churches:

1. that they consider it as an urgent need to expand their present training programmes for pastors and to include Christian education, in the broadest sense of the word, as an integral part of their training;

2. that they also consider it an urgent need to expand the present training programmes for laity so as to make them more aware of their responsibilities in the teaching ministry of the Church;

3. that in order for the Churches to accomplish this, Theological Colleges, Bible Schools, spiritual retreats, vacation and refresher courses, women's and men's organizations, literacy programmes, etc., be used to their utmost;

4. that each congregation should seek to involve all its members, the laity as well as the clergy, in this continuous programme of Christian nourishment from the cradle to the grave; and this means the full giving of one's total life and talents, and proportionate giving of one's income.

7. Word and Sacrament in Church Discipline

1. It is acknowledged that the Word of God is the proper, spiritual instrument for discipline and that this discipline is exercised every time the truth of the word is proclaimed. It is further acknowledged that the New Testament never mentions exclusion from the Lord's Supper as a means of Discipline. Resort to such a severe measure as excommunication is made only when a sinner, inspite of adequate soul-care and numerous admonitions to repent, remains adamantly unrepentant (see Matthew 18).

2. The purpose of Church discipline is instruction which should lead to true repentance and a revitalized faith. This purpose has been very much misunderstood and has too frequently become a vehicle of punishment rather than instruction.

3. It is imperative that the congregation's care of its members through a correct interpretation of Church discipline be inaugurated where lacking and encouraged or improved where already present. Basically, this would emphasize private confession and pastoral counselling.

It is therefore recommended:

1. that instruction with respect to hearing private confession be made available to all pastors, and that congregational members be instructed in regard to private confession;

2. that Churches take necessary steps to guard and secure the confidential nature of private confession;

3. that the relationship between the Lord's Supper and Church discipline be re-evaluated by the Churches;

4. that, if an individual falls into sin and is under conviction, there should be opportunity for him to confess his sin privately and receive assurance of forgiveness and aid in overcoming temptation. If his sin is known to members

of the congregation, they should admonish him in love so that he may repent and be retained in the fellowship of the congregation (Galatians 6:1-2); and

5. that the Churches replace legalistic practices in Church discipline with pastoral and spiritual care (1 Corinthians 5).

8. Sexual Ethics, Marriage, Divorce and Polygamy

Since polygamy is still a continuing problem in many areas, and since many Churches are still uncertain as to how to deal with the problem, it is recommended that Churches restudy the resolutions of the Antsirabé Conference and apply them to their situations. These resolutions say:

1. that we affirm that monogamy is God's plan for marriage, that it is the teaching of the New Testament, that it is the ideal relationship for the expression of love between a man and a woman and is the proper atmosphere within which to develop a Christian family. The entering into a polygamous marriage by a Christian, whether through the normal channels of giving a dowry, or through inheritance, or gift, is an offence against the laws of the Church;

2. that it is the responsibility of each Church, being guided by the Word of God through the Holy Spirit, and being cognizant of the particular time, circumstances, and conditions in which it finds itself, to seek that way which on the one hand will not weaken her standards of faith and practice in the eyes of the world, and on the other hand, will not arbitrarily place upon some who desire its blessings a burden, the consequences of which may be in opposition to the very message of the Gospel.

Furthermore, to counteract the temptation to enter into polygamy and to better enable Christian families better to show forth to their neighbours a godly example in marriage, it is recommended that a new emphasis be placed upon the task of congregational and pastoral counselling:

1. that young people be counselled as to the choice of marriage partners and the responsibilities of marriage;

2. that husbands and wives be counselled as to the partnership responsibilities involved in marriage, including planned parenthood;

3. that fathers and mothers be counselled as to their joint responsibilities in nurturing their children in the way of life;

4. that special efforts be made patiently, lovingly and forgivingly to counsel and help those who have fallen into immorality and sexual sin; and

5. that concerned and patient efforts be made to counsel people with special marriage problems such as separated couples, divorced persons, and polygamist households that they come to know the will of God for them.

9. Individual Freedom and Christian Obligation

The Third All-Africa Lutheran Conference,

1. Recalling the teachings of our Lord Jesus Christ and the heritage of the

Lutheran Church from the Reformation which obliges the Lutheran Churches to social responsibility;

2. Facing far-reaching changes and historical transition in the societies in which Lutheran Churches live;

3. Recognizing the manifold human problems caused by the emerging of new and unfamiliar political, economic, social and cultural structures which are often breaking down traditional African patterns, as well as traditional values and norms, recommends:

That each Church appoint Social Action Committees with the following goals:

a) to evaluate relevant social studies;

b) to develop adequate methods for social action on the part of the Churches, congregations and their institutions;

c) to establish, sponsor, and arrange courses for pastors and laymen such as teachers, medical personnel, etc., to enrich and broaden their knowledge and insights in the fundamentals of Christian social responsibility, and equip them for action, enabling the Church thereby to fulfil its obligation in proclamation, counselling, diaconia, education and stewardship in a broad sense.

10. Nation, Politics and the Church

The political situations in Africa present a widely divergent picture. The situation of the Churches in Africa differs just as much. There are countries where the Churches enjoy full liberty to preach, to act to and to find opportunities far beyond their resources, to contribute to the life, culture and destiny of their people. In some areas religious liberty is limited. Members of several Churches are denied basic human and political rights. In some parts of Africa, governments violently suppress justice and prevent fundamental principles of Christian love and brotherhood.

But whatever the situation may be, all Christians are under an obligation to make a constructive contribution to their own country and to the whole world by upholding justice and seeking the good of all men, irrespective of race, tribe or creed. This they do while building their nation and shaping its religious, social, economic and political life.

The State and the Church are both of divine origin. The function of the State is to govern and to regulate the life of the nation. The function of the Church is to serve all men and declare the will of God for man's life. The most important and unique contribution of the Christian Church to nation and politics is, however, her proclamation of the Gospel of the forgiveness of sins in Jesus Christ.

It is therefore recommended that through its leadership and clergy each Church should:

1. deliberately seek answers to the problems of justice in the nation;

2. inform its members of its findings;

3. in cooperation with all other Christian bodies, openly and fearlessly criticize

all violation of justice, suppression of human rights, corruption in its manifold shapes, and excessive nationalism which idolizes the nation or its leader;

4. teach its members to fulfil their obligations to the State faithfully and to honour the laws of the country in all matters not contrary to the Word of God;

5. fight ignorance, poverty and disease by promoting literacy, social security, opportunities for work, public health, etc.;

6. encourage its members to take an active part in political life in order to promote the welfare of the people while seeking God's constant guidance on how to act wisely, justly, charitably and in love to all men.

11. The Church in Village and City

In view of the trend of the people to move from rural into urban areas, it is recommended:

(A). that the Churches in Rural Areas exercise a total concern for the whole person, which could be expressed in:

1. Intensification of literacy efforts so that rural people might also benefit from the advances of the modern world, in agriculture, in health and in other fields;

2. Encouraging where possible, government and industry to decentralize their projects in such a way that rural people might benefit from opportunities offered by them, yet remain rural;

3. Encouraging the establishment of reading rooms and meeting places where people might meet for casual fellowship in a Christian environment;

(B). that in Urban Areas they consider again the following proposal from the Antsirabé Conference:

1. "The Lutheran Churches are most seriously asked to provide funds for youth work, especially in the big cities, for the establishment of Christian youth centres, and for an effective ministry to students in higher education institutions, and to the rising intellectual class."

2. "Do this work in cooperation with other Christian youth groups and clubs working in the cities."

12. The Conflict of Generations

Whereas the Conference realizes that owing to the rapid social changes, there is a widening gap between the old and the young generations, and

Whereas the Conference maintains that the conflict of generations arises from the impact of modern education which clashes with African traditions and culture, religiously, socially and economically, and

Whereas the Church still feels it an incumbent duty upon her to reconcile these two factions,

Be it recommended to all the Lutheran Churches in Africa:

1. that every Christian home should not lose the first opportunity of teaching young children the fear of the Lord and respect to all, even at the very tender age;

2. that the youth and the aged should be recognized as co-responsible officers in our Churches, thus giving the young generation the opportunity to utilize their modern educational concepts, and also giving the older generation the opportunity to utilize their experience and insight;

3. that all efforts be made to arrest the exodus of our youth from villages to cities by reviving our almost-lost African traditional fine arts and culture through the establishment of handicraft centres to create occupations for their livelihood;

4. that where possible, and in areas where electricity is available, our Churches in such areas should endeavour to own a projector and, with this visual aid, present pictures that reflect the Christian background, and

5. that the conflict of generations be made subject for discussion at the theological training institutions, pastoral meetings, Church elders' courses, etc.

4. On Caring for Creation
EMMANUEL ABRAHAM

Presented to the LWF Seventh Assembly
Budapest, July 24, 1984

It is with diffidence that I stand before this Assembly of Lutheran Christians from all over the globe to address you on the theme, 'Caring for Creation.' I do not claim to be a trained theologian or an erudite intellectual. My remarks are therefore based on my reading of the Holy Scriptures and on observation and experience during my progress in this life for the past three score and eleven years. In the tradition of the East, they come from the heart, rather than from the head.

Creation presupposes a creator and that leads me to the first chapter of Genesis: "In the beginning God created the heavens and the earth." As I presume God's creation of the heavens to be outside the scope of this Assembly, I shall confine my remarks to the planet earth. The Lord God created the earth and other living creatures. To crown his creative act he made humankind in his own image and likeness, "and God saw everything that he had made, and behold, it was very good" (Genesis 1:31).

Having created humankind in his own image, and having made them male and female, God blessed them and said to them: "Be fruitful and multiply, and fill the earth and subdue it; and have dominion over the fish of the sea and over the birds of the air and over every living thing that moves upon the earth" (Genesis 1:28). The Psalmist, contemplating the Lord's wonderful creation of the universe and considering the deplorable state into which humankind had fallen, asked the rhetorical question: "What is man that thou art mindful of him, and the son of man that thou dost care for him?" Then in great wonderment the Psalmist exclaimed: "Yet thou hast made him little less than God, and dost crown him with glory and honour. Thou hast given him dominion over the works of thy hands; thou hast put all things under his feet" (Psalm 8:4-6). Had the Psalmist lived in this dispensation of grace, there would no doubt have been an addition: "Thou hast given thine only Son that humankind should not perish but have eternal life through faith in his name."

The Lord God, in placing humankind in a perfect environment, subjected them to a simple test and warned of the consequence of disobedience. But they chose deliberately to disobey the Creator and brought untold suffering and death on themselves and their progeny. The ground was cursed for their sake and they were condemned to eat of it in toil all the days of their lives (Genesis 3:17). All the generations of the children of Adam and Eve have endured the effects of this curse, and it would appear that it is getting worse for every succeeding generation. But it is a matter for unceasing praise to our God that this is not the end of the story. With this judgment, God, in his infinite love and mercy, promised humankind a Redeemer who would restore them to the first estate.

Pending the fulfilment of this most precious promise, the human race multiplied. It occupied fertile areas of the earth and built civilizations. But wittingly or unwittingly, it neglected to care for creation; it systematically destroyed animal and plant life in the most callous manner. In some regions of the earth, which the human race has occupied for several thousand years, the destruction of plant life has been such that areas that were most fertile and thickly forested have virtually been turned into deserts. Through centuries of carelessness, the top soil has been washed away, as is the case in the northern districts of Ethiopia, where one hardly sees any woods except the groves around the churches. As a result, the land has ceased to yield enough crops to feed the population, and there have been frequent droughts. The floods that have for generations destroyed millions of people and animals in India and China are, to a large extent, the result of humankind's betrayal of the trust given them to care for creation. The destruction of primeval forests in other regions of the earth has meant a dwindling of the wild animals that were appointed to live in them - quite apart from their slaughter by the thousand every year. As a consequence, it is feared that many of them will be extinct before long. There is moreover the problem of pollution of a number of rivers in the industrial countries and of dumping nuclear waste in the seas, with the attendant danger to human and marine life. The testing of nuclear weapons by some states is causing deep concern to the nations of the South Pacific and elsewhere for fear that nuclear radiation may endanger human and animal life. The whole creation is truly groaning in travail together until now.

Not only that: Throughout recorded history, strong groups of people, whether they are called clans, tribes, or nations, have preyed upon weaker groups and exploited their resources, both human and material. World empires from the

Egyptian and the Assyrian down to the British have risen in succession and, after a period of domination and ruthless exploitation of weaker peoples, have decayed and disappeared from the face of the earth. It is impossible to imagine the degree of suffering of the unnumbered millions of men and women throughout the centuries who toiled as slaves and subject peoples for the benefit of their relatively few oppressors. Consider the toil and misery of the masses of humanity who were forced to build the great pyramids and temples of Egypt, the great buildings and the "hanging gardens" of Babylon, the canals that crisscrossed the valley of the Euphrates and the Tigris, the Roman highways and public buildings, and the great cities of the ancient and modern world empires! Unregenerate humankind has been so cruel to fellow human beings as to lose almost completely the image and likeness of his Creator.

I cannot do better here than quote the words of President Abraham Lincoln (in March 1865) with reference to the great American Civil War, one of whose main causes was the evil of slavery. Lincoln said:

"Fondly do we hope, fervently do we pray, that this mighty scourge of war may speedily pass away. Yet, if God wills that it continue until all the wealth piled by the bondman's two hundred and fifty years of unrequited toil shall be sunk, and until every drop of blood drawn with the lash shall be paid by another drawn with the sword, as was said 3,000 years ago, so still it must be said, "the judgments of the Lord are true and righteous altogether."

I am persuaded that, had he lived in this generation, the wise statesman would have applied these words to the two unprecedented scourges of war that took place during the first half of this century. The two world wars consumed untold wealth piled by four centuries of the toil and sweat of the weak and subject peoples of the Americas, Africa, Asia and other areas of the globe. Moreover, imagine the rivers of blood that flowed and the millions of lives that were sacrificed in the Holocaust! Indeed, the judgments of the Lord are true and righteous altogether!

It is over two decades now since the colonial peoples of Africa and Asia recovered their political freedom, but what is political freedom worth without economic freedom? The industrial nations have developed their economies and amassed vast riches, mainly at the expense of the undeveloped nations. They have for generations acquired raw materials produced by these peoples at minimal prices and sold them finished goods made for the most part from these very materials at many times their original prices. This process is still continuing and has produced imbalance and resentment that threaten to explode into open hostility. In my view, this form of exploitation will have no better chance of success in the long run. The nations that are piling wealth at the expense of the less developed nations will surely pay up sooner or later, for it is impossible that people should live on the same planet for long, half rich and half poor, half overfed and half starving.

Parallel with this deeply somber and seemingly hopeless picture of the human race is the provision the Lord God has made for its redemption. When the time had fully come, the grace of God appeared for the salvation of all men (Galatians 4:4; Titus 2:11). God sent forth his Son to redeem humankind and to give them the adoption of sons and daughters. The promise given to our first parents when they had to leave paradise was fulfilled. The Son of God became the Son of Man; he humbled himself and became obedient unto death, and by his resurrection opened the way for humankind to return to their former estate through faith in his name. On his ascension, the Lord Jesus commissioned his followers to go out into the world and proclaim the gospel, the good news of salvation. The Gospel was spread far and wide until the Roman world was turned upside down and within three centuries Christianity became the state religion with all the advantages and disadvantages that ensued.

In later centuries, the gospel spread to all Europe and eventually to the Americas. The influence of the gospel upon those nations was such that European civilization was given the epithet "Christian." But we learn from history that, for the most part, the nations concerned used the gospel of the grace of God to serve their selfish purposes, and their treatment of their fellow humans was far from Christian. The church of Christ, which had to live and work in these historical developments, kept the light of the gospel shining - at times brightly, and at other times, rather dimly. After the Reformation, however, millions of men and women in Europe rediscovered the true meaning of the Christian message and from the 18th century onward many were fired with the vision of going out into the world and proclaiming the gospel to peoples who were without Christ. As a result, millions in Africa, Asia, and the other continents accepted the Lord Jesus as their Lord and Saviour. In our time, multitudes in these continents are crowding into the church every year, and it is expected that before long the gospel will have been preached to all the tribes and nations of this world, and that all will be able to read the Holy Scriptures in their own native tongue.

In addition to this activity, especially since the end of the Second World War, many Christian denominations and specifically the Lutheran family of churches, through the Lutheran World Federation, have considered it their binding duty to give massive aid to distressed humanity through relief and rehabilitation, first in war-ravaged Europe and later in Africa, Asia, and Latin America. We in Ethiopia consider this type of Christian service as proclaiming the gospel with deeds that speak louder than words. Even then, hundreds of millions of our fellow human beings today cannot get one square meal a day. They are perpetually hungry and are dying a slow and painful death while in the affluent section of humanity many people are said to suffer and even die from the effects of overfeeding. It is also said that food sufficient for millions is thrown away every day. The affluent nations have amassed vast riches beyond the imagination of the unlettered and hungry peoples of the poverty-stricken nations. Billions of dollars are being spent for the exploration and conquest of outer space, by which a segment of the human race, "neglecting justice and the love of God," is striving to immortalize its scientific achievements and fame in the tradition of the people long ago who tried to build the tower of Babel and brought the Lord's judgment not only on themselves but upon all succeeding generations of men and women with the confusion and multiplicity of tongues. To paraphrase the words of Scripture, they ought to have done this without neglecting the other (Luke 11:42).

Many people appear to be so apprehensive about the state of the world as to believe that the race in nuclear and other armaments - at the cost of billions of dollars - is certain to lead to war and the annihilation of the human race. In my view, this belief can only be based on the assumption that the Creator of the universe has either ceased to exist for them or has completely withdrawn from the affairs of this world. But we learn from the Scriptures that the Lord Jesus wondered not at the lack of people but at the lack of faith on earth when he comes (Matthew 25:31,32; Luke 18:8). Whatever men and women may think or do, the Lord God has worked and is working to bring about his eternal purpose for his creation. Although untold misery and destitution for the underprivileged will continue for a time through man's inhumanity to man, it is my belief that the light of the gospel of Christ will continue to shine on this earth and that his Church will strive to hold him up as the only hope for this world while endeavouring to care for his creation with love that reflects his unspeakable love.

As an illustration of this, allow me to report briefly the endeavour of the Ethiopian Evangelical Church Mekane Yesus in the field of "integrated human development." In the situation in which it lives and works, this church determined to serve the "whole human person" - spirit, soul, and body - and embarked upon development work as a facet of its witness to the love of God in Christ. To help achieve this aim, the church in May 1972 addressed a document, entitled "On the Interrelationship between Proclamation of the Gospel and Human Development," to all the member churches of the Federation and to the Donor Agencies through the General Secretariat of the LWF. The document attracted attention on the international level and was the subject of a number of consultations and theological discussions for several years. It may be affirmed that it received general acceptance in the Lutheran family of churches and beyond and helped to advance the notion of a "holistic" approach in Christian service. With the active support of the Lutheran World Federation and our cooperating partners, the overseas churches and missions that have been labouring in Ethiopia for many years, we are striving to help people improve the quality of their lives through proclamation and development, viz. evangelistic outreach and nurture, basic literacy, general education, health care, agricultural and water development, vocational training, resettlement, reforestation, improvement of the means of communication, and construction of bridges and roads in the country districts where they do not exist. The Mekane Yesus Church sees its task of proclamation and development as an effort whereby the spiritual and material needs of the human person are seen and met together and as caring for God's creation, albeit on a modest scale. Both aspects of this task are regarded as essential, and to try to separate them would be as dangerous as an operation on Siamese twins and an ill-service to creation.

I have referred to the fact that in recent years Christians of the Lutheran confession and others have made considerable efforts toward the relief and rehabilitation of distressed humanity. Let me now take the liberty to address some questions to the Assembly: How adequate is this relief and rehabilitation work when seen in the light of the suffering and starvation of nearly a quarter of the human race? Could one affirm with confidence that the followers of Christ are doing all they can to care for his creation? Could Christian people who live in affluent societies be educated to give more from the abundant resources with which the Lord has blessed them? In other words, could they be challenged to reduce their lifestyles somewhat for the sake of Christ so as to enable their less fortunate fellow humans to experience something of the life which they themselves take for granted? Could this crucial problem of caring for creation be lifted up to the ecumenical level and placed on the agenda of the ongoing consultations between the Lutheran World Federation, the Lutheran churches, and the other Christian churches for discussion as to how to evolve an agreed plan for all Christians to act as one body in the name of Christ to rescue his creation?

I am convinced that the concerted and practical action of all the followers of Christ will transform the lot of the millions of human beings who live in wretched poverty. By this act of Christian love and service, the followers of Christ will become the salt of the earth and thus come up to the expectation of their Lord. In this connection, I should express fear that, although necessary in cases of emergency, relief aid alone will tend to take something away from the dignity of the human person and reduce him/her to the status of a beggar. The ideal thing, it seems to me, would be to help people help themselves to stand squarely on their own feet. Rehabilitation and Development should be the goal of the Christians in the task of caring for God's creation. May I then make bold to appeal to all the churches that constitute this Lutheran World Federation and to all the followers of Christ everywhere to take seriously to heart this matter of caring for creation and to make a united effort to pool their resources and know-how for the rehabilitation and development of the underprivileged, wherever they may be, and of their natural resources. It is my firm conviction that such an act of love and concern in the name of Christ will be a shining example worthy of emulation by the affluent peoples and their leaders, and a sacrifice acceptable and well-pleasing to God our Father.

INDEX

Abraham Tato 3, 241
Abye Abebe 40, 49, 175, 206, 228, 229, 231, 232, 263
Abyssinia Association 32
Accra Conference 148-150, *See also* Conference of Independent African States
Addis Ababa Evangelical Church Mekane Yesus 244, *See also* Addis Ababa Mekane Yesus Church
Addis Ababa Mekane Yesus Church 58, 255, 256, 258, 270, 271, 302, 307, 330
Addis Ababa University 219, *See also* Haile Sellassie I University
Adere Crest (Benti Adere) 3, 4
Agreement on Integration Policy 276, 281-283, *See also* Church-Mission integration
Agreement on Policy for Transfer and Cooperation 300
Aklilou Habte Wold 40
Aksum monument, 98, 110, 112, 113, 115, 117, 363, *See also* Aksum obelisk
Aksum obelisk 98
All-Africa Conference of Churches 296
Amare Mamo 269
Amenti (Abraham) 58, 75, 151, 152, 246, 249
American Community School 209
American Lutheran Church 307, *See also* Lutheran Church in America
American Lutheran Mission (ALM) XII, 262, 276

American Presbyterian Mission 298
Arén, Gustav 263, 295, 296
Asbe Tafari VII, 16-20, 23, 25, 26, 32, 50, 259
Asbe Tafari School 19, 20, 50, 259
Aseffa Haile Sellassie 13, 14
Aseffa Lemma 219, 222
Asfaw Qalbero 310
Aske, Sigurd 264, 266, 344
Asmara Evangelical Congregation 312
Asrate Kassa 40, 225, 234

Badima Yalew 50, 244, 262
Baissa Jammo 266, 312
Benti Mosisa 6
Berhanu Ofga'a 317, 318
Berhe Beyene 266
Betre-Tsidk Kassa 18
Bible Churchmen's Missionary Society 50
Birkeli, Fridtjov 122
Board of Telecommunications (IBTE) XII, 190, 245, 265
Boji Choqorsa 6, 8, 49, 328
Boji Dirmeji 304, 328
Boji Karkaro 3, 5, 14, 241, 301, 304
Bulti Aleku 269

Cederquist, Karl 8
Chief of Political Affairs II, VII, 167, 187, 265
Christofel Blindenmission 282
Church-Mission integration 278
Church of Sweden Mission 282

Clarendon School 152
Clewer, Selby 56
Committee of Mutual Christian Responsibility (CMCR) XII, 255, 284
Concordia College 219
Conference of Independent African States 148
Congo Crisis 178
Council of Ethiopian Evangelical Churches 299
Council of Ministers 53, 97, 168, 170, 194, 196, 200, 202, 204, 213, 218
Council of the Lutheran Congregations 311

Daffa Jammo 302, 303
Daniel Assefa 252
Daniel Lulu 4, 14, 49
Danish Evangelical Mission 284, 305
Danki Tufa 4
Dawit (Abraham) 58, 80, 91, 151, 152, 246, 249
Deressa Amenti 13
Derg XIII, 228, 230, 233, 235-237, 330
Desta Buba 314, 315
Dibaba Bakare 3
Douglas O'Hanlon 32

Efrem Tewolde Medhen 26
Egypt General Mission 142
Eknor, Ingvar 271
Elleni Alemayehu II, V, XV, 58, 150, 238, 246
Emmanuel Gabre Sellassie 50, 123, 244, 255, 262, 266, 267, 270, 289, 345, 346
Empie, Paul 218
Empress Menen School 57, 58
Endalkachew Makonnen 211, 226, 227, 232
English School 152
Eritrea 4, 5, 21, 71, 72, 76, 77, 84-86, 89, 90, 101, 103, 122, 123, 142, 175, 216, 218, 299, 301
Ethiopian Airlines 62, 101, 117, 205
Ethiopian Building and Road Construction Company (ETBURC) XII, 195, 196
Ethiopian Evangelical Church Mekane Yesus (EECMY) II, XII, XV, 186, 229, 239, 254-256, 260, 262, 264, 266, 267, 269, 272, 273, 275, 283-285, 289, 290, 293, 294, 299-301, 303, 304, 310, 319, 329, 332, 360
Ethiopian Evangelical College 263, 264
Ethiopian Lutheran Church-Friends of the Bible 299
Ethiopian Orthodox Church 56, 261, 275
Ethiopian Shipping Lines 205
Evangelical Church Mekane Yesus in Ethiopia 274, 281
Evangelical Church of Eritrea 299
Ezra Gebremedhin XI, 269, 289

Faqadu Jiregna 317
Feisa Negasa 317
Finnish Lutheran Mission 290
Finnish Missionary Society 290
First All-Africa Lutheran Conference IX, 261, 332, 339, 345
Fourth Army Camp 175, 230, 232-234, 236, 237
Francis Stephanos 266, 267
Franco-Ethiopian Railway Company 113, 205
Fry, Franklin Clark 270

Gabbisa Baro 318
Gabre Sellassie Tesfa Gabir 312
Galata Woltaji 289
Gebre-Ab Biadigilign 269
Gebre Egziabher (Kumsa Moroda) 4, 6, 8, 10, 312, *See also* Kumsa Moroda
Gebre Statios Zemikael 4
Gebre Yesus Tesfai 5, 50
Germame Neway 174
German Hermannsburg Mission XII, 262
Gidada Solen 297, 298
Gudina Tumsa 219, 229, 269, 280, 286, 289, 311, 312
Gumesh Wolde Mikael 4, 241

Habte Mariam (Gebre Egziabher) 7-11
Hagos Legesse 262, 269
Haile Sellassie I, *Emperor* II, 11, 17, 29, 34, 36-38, 121, 122, 157, 165, 176, 226, 233, 243, 245, 265, 327, 330, 335, 336

Haile Sellassie I University 216
Haile Sellassie I Welfare Foundation 323
Hailu Kabtih-Yimer 23
Hailu Wolde Semaiat 266
Haugland, Trygve 323
Held, Christa 329, 330
Herouy (Wolde Sellassie) 11, 34, 35

Imru (Haile Sellassie) 174
International Committee of the Red Cross 236
International Lutheran Congregations 307

Jalata Jafaro 289

Kibre-Ab Gabre Sellassie 14, 18
Kovacevic and Straus 195
Kumsa Moroda (Gebre Egziabher) 4, 312

Lambie, Thomas 296
Launhardt, Johannes 312
Lilje, Hans 260
Lindtjorn, Omund 266
Lundgren, Manfred 262, 276, 280, 287, 312, 320
Luther, Martin 267, 296, 341
Lutheran Church in America 282
Lutheran Confessions 341
Lutheran World Federation (LWF) VIII, XII, 122, 218, 239, 255, 260-265, 270-273, 276, 282, 285, 288, 290, 291, 294, 296, 300, 320, 327-329, 335, 340, 342, 346, 348, 349, 356, 359-361
Lutheran World Relief 327
Lutherhjälpen 272

Mageroy, Magnar 266
Makonnen Endalkachew 54
Mammo Chorqa 297, 298
Månson, Thorsten 320
Mau, Carl 239
Medferiash Worq Abebe, *Crown Princess* 166
Mekane Yesus Church VIII, IX, XVII, 58, 186, 219, 225, 227, 230, 231, 239, 246, 255, 256, 258, 260, 261, 263-266, 269-273, 275, 285, 288, 290, 295, 296, 299, 300, 302, 305-307, 311, 313, 315, 319-321, 323-330, 346, 361,
See also Ethiopian Evangelical Church Mekane Yesus
Mekane Yesus-Ethiopian Evangelical Church 122
Mekane Yesus Seminary 254, 262, 288, 307, 314
Menen, *Empress* 10, 40, 57, 58
Mengistu Haile Mariam 237
Mengistu Neway 174, 187
Merdazmach Asfa Wossen, *Crown Prince* 166, 227, 233
Michael Imru 232
Miller, Robert J. 269
Ministry of Communications 196, 198, 199-201, 204, 205, 211, 212, 222
Ministry of Education 15, 19, 20, 53-57, 59-61, 80, 120, 142, 261, 263, 302, 320, 321, 325
Ministry of Foreign Affairs 51, 142, 177
Ministry of Mines 152, 212, 213, 215, 216, 218, 219, 221, 222, 224, 225
Ministry of Posts 188-196, 198, 200, 211, 266
Mosisa Duressa 317
Muetzelfeldt, Bruno 255, 329
Muhlenberg College 218
Mussolini, Benito 21

Naomi Desta XI, 252
Neldner, Brian 329
Norwegian Free Church 282
Norwegian Lutheran Mission (NLM) XII, 262, 266, 269, 276, 280, 283, 284, 286, 288, 304, 305, 323, 324, 327
Norwegian Missionary Society (NMS) VIII, XII, 285-287, 345

Onesimus Nesib 297, 312, 313
Organization of African Unity (OAU) 149
Oseng, Gunnar 266

Pankhurst, E. Sylvia 43
Petterson, Bodil 318
Presbyterian Church, (United Presbyterian Church) 296, 300

Qanatu Malimo 3, 241
Qena'a Borcha 8

Radio Voice of the Gospel (RVOG) VIII,
    XII, 212, 261, 264-266, 272, 330
Road Transport Board 204, 205
Ruth (E. Abraham) XI, 58, 59, 62, 151, 152,
    165, 228, 229, 246, 249, 251, 254

Saeveraas, Olav 266, 269
Salah Hinit 196, 237
Samuel Danki 6
San Francisco Conference 77
Sanna, Eigil 327
Sarah (E. Abraham) 58, 62, 151, 152, 165,
    205-209, 246, 249, 251
Schaefer, Herbert G. 262, 266, 307
Schiotz, Frederik A. 337
Second All-Africa Lutheran Conference IX,
    186, 338, 344-346
Sendeq Gabre Mariam 312
Shorro Ambel 297
Society of International Missionaries 288
Staalsett, (Gunnar) 286
Stjarne, Per 123, 312, 320
Sudan Interior Mission (SIM) 288
Swedish Evangelical Mission (SEM) XI, XII,
    4-6, 49, 122, 262, 276, 281, 285, 295,
    301, 304, 313, 319, 321, 322, 324,
    329
Tafari Makonnen, *Ras* 9, 34, 168
Tafari Makonnen School 9-13, 15, 16, 19,
    20, 26, 34, 50, 53, 242, 259

Tarekegn Adebo 269
Temesgen Feisa 315, 317
Terfa Danki 8, 242
Terfa Jarso 298
Third All-Africa Lutheran Conference IX,
    345, 346, 353
Thomas Assefa 252
Tiru Gebre 4, 14

United Nations (UN) XII, 44, 55, 58, 59,
    63, 71-73, 75-78, 125, 132, 134, 136,
    138-141, 147, 150, 162, 178, 180-185,
    198, 216, 335
Universal Postal Union 192, 194

War reparations 89-94, 97-101, 105, 108,
    109, 111, 113, 115, 116, 118
Wolde Giorgis Wolde Yohannes 31, 38
World Council of Churches (WCC) 296
Worqneh C. Martin 10, 242, *See also*
    Worqneh Ishetu
Worqneh Ishetu 12, 15, 22, 24

Yemisrach Dimts 272
Yilma Deressa 89, 93, 98, 191

Zauditu, *Empress* 11, 80, 168
Zaudé Gebre Heywot 82, 190, 208
Zekewos Edemo 288